week

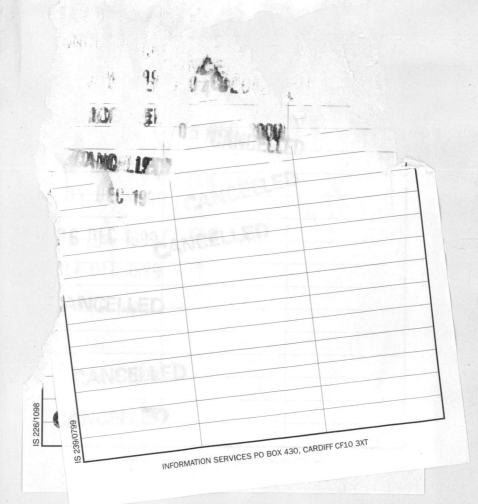

NUFFIELD EUROPEAN STUDIES

Series Editors: Joachim Jens Hesse and Vincent Wright

CONSTITUTIONAL POLICY AND CHANGE IN EUROPE

NUFFIELD EUROPEAN STUDIES

The purpose of the Nuffield European Studies Series is to provide, for students and teachers in the social sciences and related disciplines, works of an interdisciplinary and comparative nature dealing with significant political, economic, legal, and social problems confronting European nation-states and the European Community. It will comprise research monographs as well as the edited proceedings of conferences organized by the Centre for European Studies at Nuffield College, Oxford. The general editors of the series are Joachim Jens Hesse, Ford-Monnet Professor of European Politics and Comparative Government in the University of Oxford and Vincent Wright, Official Fellow of Nuffield College and Director of the Centre for European Studies.

CONSTITUTIONAL POLICY AND CHANGE IN EUROPE

Edited by
JOACHIM JENS HESSE
and
NEVIL JOHNSON

OXFORD UNIVERSITY PRESS

1995

Oxford University Press, Walton Street, Oxford OX2 6DP
Oxford New York
Athens Auckland Bangkok Bombay
Calcutta Cape Town Dar es Salaam Delhi
Florence Hong Kong Istanbul Karachi
Kuala Lumpur Madras Madrid Melbourne
Mexico City Nairobi Paris Singapore
Taipei Tokyo Toronto
and associated companies in
Berlin Ibadan

Oxford is a trade mark of Oxford University Press

Published in the United States
by Oxford University Press Inc., New York

British Library Cataloguing in Publication Data
Data available

Library of Congress Cataloging in Publication Data
Constitutional policy and change in Europe / edited by Joachim Jens
Hesse and Nevil Johnson.
—(Nuffield European studies)
Includes index.
1. Europe—Constitutional law.   I. Hesse, Joachim Jens.
II. Johnson, Nevil.   III. Series.
KJC4445.C667   1995 342.4—dc20 [344.02] 94-47644
ISBN 0-19-827991-4

1 3 5 7 9 10 8 6 4 2

Typeset by Best-set Typesetter Ltd., Hong Kong
Printed in Great Britain
on acid-free paper by
Bookcraft (Bath) Ltd.
Midsomer Norton, Avon

Preface

The papers assembled in this volume have their origins in a conference held at the Centre for European Studies in Nuffield College.
The purpose of the meeting was to enable a number of specialists in
constitutional matters to come together to examine and discuss
from various perspectives the needs and claims of constitutional
adaptation and reconstruction in contemporary Europe.

It goes without saying that the range and complexity of the
constitutional challenge in Europe differs markedly from one country to another, and in particular as between the Eastern and Western parts of the Continent. In the latter, the need generally is for
adaptation and further development of existing practices and principles; in the former, far-reaching constitutional reconstruction has
been an imperative, a task which has had to be tackled in the
difficult and uncertain conditions of radical social and economic
transformation.

The chapters which follow do not claim to provide a comprehensive survey of contemporary constitutional change and the policies
applied in the process. Instead, they are illustrative of certain aspects of the constitutional challenge as it is perceived in various
European countries, and of the different responses to it. In some
cases the contributors approach the problems discussed as constitutional lawyers, in others more as political scientists. And there
are, too, contributions which address some of the underlying issues
of political theory presented by the notion of liberal constitutionalism itself. The process of constitutional adaptation is continuous,
and the present phase of it in Europe is by no means yet concluded.
It is hoped that these essays succeed in throwing some light on the
direction of such change.

J.J.H.
N.J.

Nuffield College, Oxford
July 1994

Contents

IV CONSTITUTIONAL REVIEW AND CHANGE I: THE WESTERN EUROPEAN EXPERIENCE

V CONSTITUTIONAL REVIEW AND CHANGE II: THE CENTRAL AND EASTERN EUROPEAN EXPERIENCE

Contributors

ATTILA ÁGH, Professor of Political Science, University of Economic Sciences, Budapest

GUY CARCASSONNE, Conseiller d'État, Paris

DIETER GRIMM, Judge, Federal German Constitutional Court, Karlsruhe

DUSAN HENDRYCH, Professor of Law, Charles University, Prague

JOACHIM JENS HESSE, Professor of European Institutions and Politics, Nuffield College, Oxford

NEVIL JOHNSON, Professorial Fellow, Nuffield College, Oxford

DONALD KOMMERS, Professor of Law, University of Notre Dame, Indiana

GEOFFREY MARSHALL, Provost, The Queen's College, Oxford

ASCENSIÓN ELVIRA PERALES, Professor of Law, Carlos III University, Madrid

ULRICH PREUSS, Professor of Law, University of Bremen

CHERYL SAUNDERS, Professor of Law, University of Melbourne

MICHIEL SCHELTEMA, Professor of Administrative Law, University of Groningen

GUNNAR FOLKE SCHUPPERT, Professor of Law, Humboldt University, Berlin

WOJCIECH SOKOLEWICZ, Professor of Law, Academy of Sciences, Warsaw

WALTER J. THOMPSON, Teaching Fellow, Department of Government and International Studies, University of Notre Dame, Indiana

PART I
INTRODUCTION

1

Constitutional Policy and Change in Europe: The Nature and Extent of the Challenges

JOACHIM JENS HESSE

During recent years constitutional issues have claimed increasing attention in many European countries. In Central and Eastern Europe there can be no doubt about what has thrust constitutional debates into the foreground of public life: the social and political transformations which have occurred there present a constitutional challenge of the most urgent kind. These societies, caught up in the simultaneous process of democratization and economic reform, need to establish as soon as possible institutions which will be accepted as legitimate and offer promise of stability. In Western Europe constitutional debate has occurred in the past decade in several countries with varying degrees of intensity and range. It is now assuming greater prominence generally, both on account of the commitment to closer economic and political integration within the European Community and as a result of changes within particular countries, such as the achievement of unification in Germany, the breakdown of the domestic political order in Italy, and the need to react to profoundly changed environments in quite a number of countries.

There are perhaps two special features of the contemporary situation in Europe which make it particularly appropriate and, indeed, urgent to engage in the comparative study of constitutional change and policy. One is the fact that the scale and complexity of Europe has been immensely extended as a result of the changes in the East. The countries there are in search of viable models for constitutional reconstruction and, not surprisingly, it is to Western Europe that they first look for guidance and inspiration. This presents a challenge in the West just as much as in the East, though of a different character. For the West the need to consider carefully how best to advise and assist the process of constitutional reconstruction in the East imposes an obligation to examine closely the West's own institutions. How are they functioning? Do they meet contemporary demands? On what values do they rest and how effectively do they sustain them? This kind of critical approach to democratic constitutionalism in the West must surely be an integral part of any consideration of the models which it may be practicable and desirable to recommend to the East. The other crucial feature of the situation is that the member states of the European Community find themselves caught up in processes of change which present for them serious and novel constitutional problems. The dynamic process of economic integration is seen by many as requiring major steps along the path of political union, including sensitive issues such as the loss of national sovereignty, the creation of a common defence and security policy, and the merger of national policies and institutions. Whereas in the East there are many societies engaged in rediscovering themselves as nation-states and in giving constitutional shape to that new identity, a process accompanied by the risk of serious conflict in some of them, in the West it is more a question whether the nation-states will remain politically and constitutionally distinctive one from another, or commit themselves decisively to a merging of sovereignties and thus, in some degree, to a fusion of constitutional forms in a new political entity.

1. IN SEARCH OF A CONSTITUTION: CENTRAL AND EASTERN EUROPE

It is not surprising that the process of constitutional reconstruction in Central and Eastern Europe has been marked by the search for viable constitutional models which might satisfactorily be adapted to domestic conditions and requirements. There is effectively no scope for going back to pre-war constitutional arrangements in these countries, even though certain elements in earlier political experience, e.g. of parliamentary institutions and practices, continue to exert some influence. On the whole, however, the work of constitutional reconstruction starts from *tabula rasa*: there has to be a complete redefinition of the terms of political life and of the conditions under which the societies are governed. This is one of the principal reasons why there is a strong impulse to look towards the constitutions of the Western European democracies for guidance on workable practices. It follows that what is of most immediate interest in the democratizing countries is the political and constitutional reality in Western democracies—the success of systems of law and political institutions in ensuring democratic stability and effective government, and thereby maintaining the framework for economic prosperity. In the main, attention focuses on several familiar features of constitutional development and forms in Western Europe: the Westminster model of parliamentary government as practised in Britain; what might loosely be called the Napoleonic or French model of a unified administrative state, linked today with a popularly elected political executive; and the *Rechtsstaat*, social, democratic, and federal, as exemplified in Germany under the *Grundgesetz* or Basic Law. There are, of course, other patterns of government and variations on these models in Western Europe: a federal structure in Switzerland, a multi-party parliamentary republic with French administrative forms in Italy, a deeply rooted parliamentary monarchy in the Netherlands, and the well-established consensual parliamentary democracies of Scandinavia, to mention only some. Doubtless some features of these will attract attention and require examination. But it is likely to be the larger countries of Western Europe that will be most closely scrutinized for guidance and examples to follow. In contrast, the constitution of the United States of America seems to command less attention as a possible model for constitutional design, no matter how generally influential the American approach is to the rule of law, the protection of constitutional rights, and the maintenance of a highly developed form of political pluralism.

Considering the immediacy of the political, social, and economic problems with which the nascent Eastern democracies are confronted, it can occasion no surprise that the constitutional discussion centres first of all on relatively straightforward substantive concerns. These include the political role and formal structure of the core state institutions, i.e. Parliament, the executive, the head of state, the judiciary; the status of local and regional politico-administrative organs; and the definition of the political and civil rights of citizens. The experience of many decades of totalitarian rule explains why the precise definition and the 'taming' of the state's

power are at the heart of the attempts at constitutional modernization in the East. In essence, the constitutional debate is dominated
by the desire to signal a radical break with the Communist past:
hence the emphasis on the protection of civil rights and liberties and
the limitation of state power, in particular as it is exercised by the
agencies of central executive authorities.

However, there are signs that the discussion is beginning to move
on to wider issues still. What emerge, albeit in still rather rough
outlines, are efforts aimed at a redefinition or, perhaps more accurately, reconceptualization of what is involved in being a state and
in membership of it. This includes attempts to formulate basic
social rights, entitlements, and provisions to be guaranteed by the
state; arguments concerning the nature of the triangular relationship between the individual citizen, society, and the state; a reconsideration of state tasks, responsibilities, and activities which aims
at much more than the mere dismantling of the totalitarian state;
institutional issues; and the discussion of the guiding ends and
purposes of the constitutional organization of the body politic. In
this way, it becomes evident that the central concern of the renewed
constitutional discourse is nothing less than the definition of a new
conception of statehood.

In parallel, there is a growing realization of the importance of
establishing conditions favourable to the consolidation of a genuine
pluralism both at the level of political parties and in society at large.
Although both the extent of the transformation processes that have
thus far taken place and the pace differ considerably from country
to country, it is undoubtedly possible to detect a number of shared
characteristics which suggest a common pattern of political and
societal change. The distinguishing features include the transition
from what were effectively, if not in name, systems of one-party
rule, in which the leading role of the Communist party in all sectors
of society was firmly entrenched, to pluralist, multi-party parliamentary systems with democratically elected and accountable
governments; the abandoning of the principle of 'democratic
centralism' in favour of a far-reaching deconcentration and decentralization of political power to be exercised under the rule of law;
the rejection of the principle of unity between politics and economy
which involves the emergence of distinct spheres of political and
economic life; and far-reaching economic reforms whose principal
aims are the strengthening of private enterprise, the denationaliz-

ation (or rather privatization) of a large share of the previously state-controlled productive capital, and a substantial deregulation and liberalization of the national economy. The underlying ideas spurring the ambitious reform attempts at replacing a nationalized, centralized, and planned economic system with a market economy are, in principle, also being applied to the task of reorganizing or perhaps re-establishing the public sector. Thus, there are moves to strengthen democratic controls over state administration and to increase its accountability to democratically elected bodies; efforts are under way which aim at the deconcentration and decentralization of the bureaucratic apparatus; the need to bring public institutions strictly under the rule of law and to guarantee the legality of administrative acts is stressed; and it is universally accepted that administrative efficiency, effectiveness, and flexibility must be increased. All this implies that the organization of governance is subject to the same pressures for change which have already led to radical political reforms, which show signs of transforming the economy and, partly by extension, revolutionizing the fabric of society. Without a congruent structure of political interests in the widest sense, there can be little prospect of effective stabilization of democratic constitutional procedures.

But the picture that emerges today is still one of transition and volatility: whereas the old political framework has irrevocably broken down, the new framework has yet to be consolidated. In particular, key aspects of the triangular relationship between president, government, and Parliament remain contentious. It is unlikely that this will change until their respective powers and privileges are authoritatively redefined in new constitutional agreements. However, a decisive breakthrough in the constitutional debate has not yet been achieved. Contrary to the high hopes of 1989, when many expected a swift new constitutional settlement, the preparation and adoption of completely new constitutions have not yet progressed significantly. As time has passed, the process of constitutionalization has, perhaps inevitably, become more and more subject to the same political pressures affecting other areas of reform. No longer is there a common spirit of opposition against a hostile regime that could hold the contending forces together.

It cannot be denied, therefore, that the failure to resolve fundamental constitutional questions introduced a critical element of fluidity into the reform process at large. However, it should also be recognized that, as Jon Elster has pointed out, 'for countries undergoing rapid social and economic change, commitment to standing rules may not be desirable. The future of many Eastern European countries may prove to be a succession of emergencies, in which constitutional self-binding might be disastrous.' It would, potentially, make more sense to talk of an open rather than an unstable constitutional situation at the present time. Yet, as Elster also notes, the potentially tragic element is that the future without a constitution to regulate expectations and behaviour might be equally bleak.

2. ADAPTING TOWARDS A CHANGED ENVIRONMENT: CONSTITUTIONAL POLICIES IN WESTERN EUROPE

In the constitutional preoccupations of the Central and East European countries and those of the Western nations there are more points of contact and signs of congruence than might at first be expected. For quite different reasons, in the West too there is a concern with practical and theoretical efforts to redefine the relationships between state and society, and more particularly between national states themselves in the European Community. It is this element of common interest and concern in relation to some of the fundamental constitutional issues in both Western and Eastern countries which justifies a comparative analysis of constitutional policies in Europe. On both sides, constitutional models are being sought which will be adequate to confront the problems of the future.

Looking at the Western constitutional discourse we seem, at first glance, to be faced with a paradox. The 1980s, which saw determined political efforts in a number of Western countries 'to roll back the frontiers of the state', were also a decade in which some social scientists showed a growing interest in 'bringing the state back in' as a useful, some would say indispensable, analytical category in the study of political, social, and economic developments. Admittedly, both the practical concern with reducing state intervention in the economy and society and the rediscovery of the state as a central analytical category in the characterization of modern industrialized societies can partly be explained by reference to political and academic issue-cycles or, less euphemistically, fashions. Beyond this there are, however, a number of substantial practical issues which have contributed to the renewed political and academic interest in the state, its nature, and its functions.

What are these practical concerns which have highlighted the need to rethink the constitutional role of the state? They include, first, new *economic* challenges which require new forms of economic policy-making and governmental involvement in the economy; second, the emergence of new types of *social* problems and conflicts which cannot be dealt with successfully by relying on the traditional instruments of the classic welfare state; and, third, new *political* and even *cultural* claims and demands on the state and its major institutions. What makes it difficult to devise political and constitutional answers to these new challenges is that they cannot be reduced to a simple choice between 'more' or 'less' state. Rather, many of the issues at stake are of a qualitative nature which largely defy conventional constitutional formulations.

It is in this connection that the question of how a constitution can be rendered flexible whilst at the same time maintaining its quality as a reliable, permanent basis for the regulation of political, social, and economic life has received growing attention. The acceleration of political, social, economic, cultural and, not least, technological change seems to necessitate forms of constitutionalization that allow for swift adaptation if the constitution is not to be rendered obsolete and lose its centrality for a nation's public life. Whether constitutional evolution should largely be effected through legal interpretation (propelled perhaps by extensive judicial review) or through changes to the corpus of positive constitutional law is the object of much dispute. What has received insufficient attention so far is the possibility of gradual constitutionalization, for example through a succession of individual constitutional laws, or the possibility of adding to the 'bloc of constitutionality' through quasi-constitutional institutional norms, a method which can be studied in the case of the basic statutes of the Spanish autonomous communities.

All this is not to deny that constitutional policy is, for the most part, concerned with relatively specific constitutional arrangements; but a growing number of more fundamental topics find their way on to the agenda of constitutional discussion. In most European countries, and at the supranational level, one sees a growing interest in questions of (i) constitutional *teleology* (i.e. what are the principal ends of constitutionalization?); (ii) constitutional *extension* (i.e. what further new issues need to be and should be addressed in constitutional charters?); (iii) constitutional *substance* (i.e. what form should constitutional arrangements take?); and (iv) constitutional *praxeology* (i.e. under what conditions and how can constitutions be made to work?).

A brief look at the more recent experience of constitutional policy and change in some Western European countries may help to illustrate this point. The following short sketches focus on the evolution of the Westminster constitution under Conservative governments since 1979, and the consequences of a policy of reducing the sphere of the state; constitutional reform in countries under the influence of the Napoleonic state tradition, notably France and Italy; a constitution for a united Germany; and the future constitutional evolution of the European Community. As was noted above, it is also the British, the French, and the German constitutional traditions which are studied particularly closely in the Central and Eastern European countries as potential models for constitution-building. It makes sense, therefore, to highlight some of the topics raised in constitutional discourse in Western Europe, since this points to important empirical and analytical issues to be pursued in a comparative study of constitutional change and policy in Europe.

In *Britain*, the 1980s were marked by determined and sustained efforts to redefine the economic and social role of the state. To this end, the Conservative administration sought to effect fundamental changes in the relations between the government and the economy on the one hand and in the responsibilities of the state for the well-being of citizens on the other. As regards government–economy relationships, the most extensive and widely discussed development was the privatization of large parts of the nationalized industry sector. Whilst privatization meant that the state relinquished ownership rights, it did not imply complete disengagement of the government from the economy, since the process of selling off public enterprises was accompanied by the introduction of a range of new regulatory instruments. Certainly, however, these measures, along with a decisive break with the post-1945 commitment to full employment and a return to balanced budgets, brought about a qualitative change in the approach to state–economy relations.

There was also a very marked shift in the principles which had hitherto been held to justify the welfare state. Much emphasis was placed on individual responsibility and self-help, though in the event social transfer payments continued to rise under the Thatcher administration, so that it would seem mistaken to argue that the past decade witnessed anything like the disappearance of the British welfare state. None the less, there was a fundamental change in the terms of public debate relating to the welfare state and some very important changes in the practice of public welfare and service provision. All this was accompanied by far-reaching alterations in the organization and structure of government. Examples include the highly politicized field of intergovernmental relations, where there were strong signs of a progressive centralization of powers in order to achieve changes, and a new approach to the administration of public services which found its most visible manifestation in the setting up by the central government of largely self-managing administrative agencies.

It is in reaction to such changes, which involved a practical redefinition of the state's responsibilities, that there was a revival of the call for a written constitution and for the enactment of some kind of constitutional charter. Without going into the details of these proposals, it should be noted that, typically, they advocate a decentralization of political power through the strengthening of local and intermediate levels of government, administrative devolution, electoral reform, and the entrenchment of a code of civil rights. As protagonists of 'a new constitution' furthermore indicated, the overwhelming emphasis in British modern constitutional history on the sovereignty of Parliament has had an unintended corollary. Parliamentary government has become party government, and party government, because of the salient features of the British electoral system, has become two-party or, more accurately, alternating-party government. Though it would seem odd to deny the merits of such a system, critics refer to one doleful effect on the political debate: it forces protagonists to be with someone, or against them; it sets people apart from each other; it presupposes a dialectic without allowing the possibility of synthesis. It militates against compromise. That would make sense if only the most crass of two-class analyses of British society is correct.

In contrast to the Conservative government in Britain, the socialist administration in *France* in the first half of the 1980s was committed to extending the role of the state in the economy. In addition, it came to office with an agenda of institutional change related chiefly to decentralization. Thus the policies pursued in the two countries could, initially, scarcely have differed more. Whereas the British government intended first to restore monetary and fiscal discipline, and then to reduce state involvement in the economy through its increasingly ambitious policy of privatization, the Mitterrand administration after 1981 embarked on a massive nationalization programme. The boundaries of the state were to be extended in an attempt to increase the effectiveness of economic policy-making. To be sure, these nationalizations did not introduce a new element into the constitutional structure of the French state, since large parts of French industry were already state-owned none the less. These policies, still held to be 'socialist', signified a further extension of direct state influence over the economy, and thus a political development quite contrary to what was happening in Britain. However, as is well known, most of this experiment in wider public ownership was put into reverse, first in the period 1986–8 when the parties of the Right had a majority, and second after 1988 by Mitterrand himself. In short, the French came to adopt much of the British approach to direct state ownership in the economy.

In terms of their long-term effects and constitutional implications, the Socialists' initiatives for the reorganization of government have probably been more important than the policy of nationalization. Amongst the measures announced by the Mitterrand administration after 1981, its decentralization proposals resulted in the most decisive and radical institutional change. The establishment of a regional level of popularly elected councils and the loosening of central controls over the activities of local authorities, combined with a substantial transfer of resources to the sub-central levels, marked a notable departure from French constitutional traditions. Whilst there was certainly no commitment to dismembering the 'one and indivisible' Republic, the extent of the reforms pointed towards a break with France's customary pattern of highly centralized government.

But regional issues have certainly been only part of the constitutional agenda in France. As highlighted by the work of the consultative constitutional committee created by President Mitterrand in November 1992, three broad issues came recently to the forefront of the debate: to define better the power of the executive, to create a more active parliament, and to allow citizens to play a greater role within the political system. The resulting report, presented in February 1993, extended those issues to questions of the length of the presidential term of office, tried to clarify the competences of the president and of the government, and added a number of largely technical recommendations concerning the activities of parliament. As regards the role of citizens in public life, the committee envisaged a procedure of minority-initiated referendums, organized by the constitutional council. The citizens should furthermore be allowed to appeal directly to the council. Although the new conservative government, led by Prime Minister Balladur, approved a number of the proposals brought forward by the committee, the power of initiative to amend the constitution still lies with the president and the members of parliament, not the government; even if a parliamentary majority takes the initiative and votes in favour of a constitutional bill, which should be easily achieved when the same tendency controls both chambers, the amendment still requires a referendum; if the government wishes to avoid a referendum, it has either to agree with the president on a new initiative or to alter in parliament the substance of the current presidential initiative. The first option remains, therefore, a tentative possibility, while the second is likely to prove politically difficult to achieve.

Measures of decentralization in France had been preceded more or less a decade earlier by a far-reaching reorganization of territorial government in *Italy*. The creation of an effective layer of regional government in the whole of Italy, and not just in the 'special regions', did not require a constitutional amendment. The establishment of governmental institutions at the regional level represented in fact the fulfilment of commitments made in the constitution of the Italian Republic, which had always provided for regional government. Whilst there appear to exist wide variations in the performance of regional government across Italy, the overall pattern of state organization and relations between institutional levels were undoubtedly substantially affected by the regionalization thus achieved.

With the basic structure of regional government in place, the last few years have seen attention shifting once again to the future of Italy's central political institutions. Many observers have argued that constitutional reforms were inevitable if the central government and its administrative services are to perform more effectively. Thus there have been calls for a simplification of constitutional amendment procedures, for a far-reaching parliamentary reform (which might improve the representation of regional interests—possibly through the transformation of the senate into a body resembling in some ways the German *Bundesrat*), and a strengthening of the position of the prime minister, to name but three examples. The dramatic breakdown of basic elements of the Italian political system during the first half of 1993 indicated that reforms are indeed inevitable. They might amount to nothing less than a new political order, brought about by an overhaul of the party system, profound electoral reform, and a consequent drive towards responsive and accountable political institutions. The degree of inefficiency and mistrust has obviously reached a level where broad-scale constitutional reforms seem to be the only way left to overcome a discredited political system and to re-establish basic elements of a domestic political order accepted by the broader population. The outcome of the referendum on constitutional reform in April 1993 gave the transitional administration a mandate to introduce electoral reform. The overwhelming vote ending public funding of political parties and introducing a reform of the proportional representation system was a profound message of protest from the electorate. Italy could now adopt, following the outcome of the referendum, a first-past-the-post system for two-thirds of the deputies and senators, the remainder still being elected by proportional representation to safeguard minority interests.

Turning to the German case, it should first be noted that there was some revival of the constitutional debate in the *Federal Republic* during the later 1980s, i.e. before unification refashioned the German political landscape. It is difficult to identify a single unifying theme in this discussion, which often focused on very specific substantive amendments. Only a few participants explicitly addressed the question of how constitutional law could be made to respond to qualitatively new demands on the state and long-term political, social, economic, and cultural trends. But a concern with modernizing the constitution in a way which would ensure its continued relevance was apparent in much of the more reflective writing on constitutional issues. This was particularly clear in the discussion relating to a specification of the essential purposes or 'ends' of the state (*Staatszwecke* and *Staatszielbestimmungen*) and to proposals for adding to them. In addition, the topic of constitutional flexibility also surfaced in connection with proposals for wide-ranging reforms in the area of intergovernmental relations and in what has sometimes been referred to as the rediscovery of *Länder* constitutional law. With unification the constitutional debate then acquired a different quality and degree of urgency, as new issues and concerns were introduced into the argument. Initially, much turned on the question whether the unification of the two Germanys should be followed by a comprehensive revision of the Basic Law which might subsequently be put to a popular vote, or whether changes to the federal constitution should be kept to a minimum and be effected in the usual manner, i.e. through approval by two-thirds majorities in both the *Bundestag* and the *Bundesrat*. Whilst the procedural question has not yet been resolved, constitutional changes do, however, seem likely. A *Verfassungskommission*, composed of Federal and *Länder* politicians, is expected to propose not only the inclusion of *Staatsziele* ('state objectives'), such as the protection of the environment, but also to advocate a reform of intergovernmental arrangements, adapting the overstretched federal system to the demands posed by unification and Europeanization. The still contentious issue of allowing the federal army to take part in UN missions, as in Somalia or the former Yugoslavia, has to be added to this agenda.

The tasks of the constitutional commission remain, therefore, extensive. In the context of shaping the democratic principle, it has to deal with the strengthening of parliamentary rights and with the introduction of elements of direct democracy into what had been a Basic Law with an obviously representative orientation. Within the scope of the federal principle, the demand of the *Länder* for a strengthening of their position *vis-à-vis* the federal authorities is under discussion. Above all, they demand the return of legislative powers, increased autonomy over administrative competences, a greater say in the attitude taken by the federal government in the Council of the European Community and, finally, an improved distribution of finances in the federal state. Attributable to the principle of a welfare state are those changes which are concerned with the new *Staatsziele* mentioned above, with new social guarantees (relating to employment, housing, and childcare), and with the extension of the principle of equality (relating to the position of women) as well as with the strengthening of the family.

Critics argue, though, that a number of urgent issues are not the subject of the Commission's work. This refers to a number of problems arising from reunification, necessitating a reassessment of the economic, social, and even cultural means available. Since appropriate solutions require legal backing, and since they invariably affect property rights and standards of the old Federal Republic, they become constitutional questions. A second problem is linked to the ongoing debate on the role of the political parties in Germany. It cannot be denied here that some constitutional guarantees are indeed threatened by political parties, a situation that is compounded by the fact that the parties have taken the issue of constitutional reform completely into their own hands, with the consequence that the readiness to call their own position into question can be expected to be minimal. The constitution, which is concerned with the separation of powers and the preservation of open access to the political process, is often at a disadvantage in this context. It can distribute decision-making powers among different governmental levels and, horizontally, among different institutions. It furthermore protects political institutions against direct influence of the state; yet it does not succeed in preventing political parties from making their influence felt in all those institutions. In their capacity as a mediator between state and society, parties have always managed to complete their task before the constitutional legislation relating to the state has become applicable. Public institutions which have become mutually dependent are thereby being held in check. Instead, political parties co-operate with each other in different roles.

3. THE CONSTITUTIONALIZATION OF THE EUROPEAN COMMUNITY

During the second half of the 1980s the future constitutional evolution of the *European Community* began to be discussed with renewed emphasis. To a large extent, the growing interest in the political aspects of European union can be interpreted as the result of the new momentum of economic integration which can be traced back to the adoption of the Single European Act through which the member states committed themselves to the completion of the internal market by the beginning of 1993. Discussion of the possible constitutional implications of further economic integration brings into the open the existing political disagreements about how far political union should go, what form it should take, and how best it can be achieved. It also illustrates the diversity of the national constitutional traditions in the member states of the Community: there are profound differences still, and these are reflected in political statements on the revision of the Community treaties and—though perhaps to a lesser extent—in the draft charters drawn up by academic working parties.

The conflicts among member states, the European Commission, and the European Parliament on the constitutional future of the Community are presently highlighted in the debates about the future of the Maastricht Treaty. The discussion on the most sensitive issues, such as the powers and responsibilities of the Commission, the role of the Council of Ministers, and the status of the European Parliament, remains yet unresolved. The disputes over the allocation of policy-making powers between Community institutions, member state governments, and regional and local administrations, which are crystallized in the concept of subsidiarity, underline the lack of political agreement on the guiding aim of creating a European political union: the struggle between the federal European conception and a solidly intergovernmental constitutional framework is as unresolved today as it was at the inception of the Communities.

Both 'deepening' and 'widening' of the Community will be of significant influence on the constitutional reality of both the EC and its member states. Questions of institutional change rank, therefore, high on the present agenda. Among the contentious issues are: more responsibilities to the European Parliament, including voting on the membership of the Commission and new, limited revenue-raising powers; stronger powers for the Commission president, possibly by creating a troika of vice-presidents responsible for the internal market, trade, and political co-operation; limited membership to the Council of Ministers; and limits on the number of languages used in the bureaucracy. As critical observers rightly put it, before the latest enlargement some 10,000 EC meetings were interpreted in 9 official languages, requiring 72 combinations for interpreting purposes; the use of 16 languages would result in 240 combinations, requiring then 55 interpreters for one meeting of a single committee. But nobody really wants to open up the debate on institutional change. It might alienate the broader European population, which has already sent ripple effects through the Community via the Danish and French referendums, and it could furthermore enrage Eurosceptics in all member states. So at times there existed a certain constitutional vacuum, rightly described by some critics as surreal: the accession negotiations with new members were conducted on the basis of a non-existent treaty, a non-existent consensus among the applicants, by an EC presidency (Denmark) whose country had not even ratified the treaty. Sooner or later all member states of the Community will, therefore, have to make tough choices on how to pursue deepening integration whilst continuing to offer wider membership in the Community. On this very fundamental question, the debate over the Maastricht Treaty had little or nothing to say.

4. AN AGENDA FOR RESEARCH

This brief overview about important trends and issues in current European constitutional development might indicate that it is possible to discern a number of crucial and worthwhile topics justifying sustained study and analysis in a comparative perspective. The following articles try to do so by engaging in an exploration and characterization of the principal factors propelling constitutional change in different parts of Europe; by developing methods of achieving constitutional change, including procedures for securing approval for such change; by highlighting the remarkable varieties of constitutional law and the ways in which constitutional law reflects prevailing social values; by shedding light on different methods of constitutional interpretation, including judicial review; by discussing constitutional principles and their contentious application in the sphere of the economy, including property ownership; by examining processes of constitutional cross-fertilization, especially in the West, and variations in the conception of the state; and, eventually, by looking at processes of constitution-building in Central and Eastern Europe and the relevance or otherwise of

Western models and experience. The ideology of liberal constitutionalism, with particular reference to the rule of law and political pluralism, obviously plays a crucial role here.

These topics embrace a very wide spectrum of issues. Contributors have been invited, therefore, to concentrate on only some of them. Which topics were selected for detailed exploration and analysis depended on their relevance and applicability in the particular national contexts. For example, in some cases it proved that constitutional debates related principally to the organization of government, whereas in others the determination and protection of the civil rights of individual citizens were of prime importance; limits of state action in relation to the economy or social aspects of citizenship were further issues that claimed attention. Though specific national circumstances were, of course, of crucial importance, it is hoped that this publication succeeds in placing their evidence within a wider comparative framework.

PART II
CONSTITUTIONALISM:
IDEAS AND CONCEPTS

2

Fundamentals in the
Liberal Constitutional Tradition

DONALD P. KOMMERS AND W. J. THOMPSON

1

In recapitulating the essentials of the liberal constitutional tradition, we are faced at the outset with severe problems of definition.
We could, for example, spend much of our time clarifying the
concept of a 'tradition'. What constitutes a tradition? How and
when do ideas or practices evolve into a tradition? Is a tradition the
same as an ideology? We shall pass on these questions, because for
present purposes it is more important to focus on the meaning of
liberal constitutionalism. Yet here too we face problems of definition. The focus of this volume is constitutionalism, and the assumption seems to be that we all adequately grasp what this term
means. But Walter Murphy has suggested, and we agree, that
'without a clear definition, the term "constitutionalism" is an invitation to debate about ghosts or, to shift the metaphor, to enter a
trackless verbal swamp'.[1] The fog thickens when we add the specification 'liberal', in so far as the adjective suggests that there may be
different kinds of constitutionalism. One of the questions we
should ask ourselves is whether the term constitutionalism contains
its own *essential* core of meaning, distinguishing it conceptually
from notions such as democracy and liberalism with which it has
often been identified.

As a first step toward clarification of these issues, we shall begin
by specifying what we intend by liberal constitutionalism. Constitutionalism in general has most often been conceived of negatively,
as a system of legal limitations on governmental power. Its opposite
in this sense would be arbitrary or despotic government.[2] Emphasis
on the negativity of constitutionalism arises whenever reflection is

focused on abuses of political power, as in the typical account of modern English constitutionalism, which tells the story of the progressive wresting of political power from the hands of an absolute—in principle if not in fact—monarch by a more or less representative institution. In the face of these precedents, it is important for us to emphasize that the concept of constitutionalism is two-edged, that it has a positive as well as a negative aspect. A constitution both empowers and delimits power, both grants authority and specifies its scope and purpose. Recognition of this duality is especially important in the case of the United States, where an essential part of the argument for the Constitution of 1787 was an account of its superiority as an effective instrument of government.[3]

When we speak of liberal constitutionalism we refer to that species of constitutionalism which has its origins in, or takes its inspiration from, the political philosophy of such thinkers as Hobbes, Montesquieu, and especially Locke. These modern theorists sought to restrict the scope of politics in favour of individual liberty, as against what they took to be the teaching of the earlier classical and Christian tradition. No longer would government tend to the lofty end of promoting the virtue or salvation of its citizens, but rather to the low but necessary end of preserving peace and order in a society of diverse individuals. The scope of legitimate political power was specified by pre-political natural rights—rights which belong to an individual *qua* human being and not *qua* member of any political society—and its purpose was limited to the protection and, so far as possible, promotion of such rights. Such political theories were liberal in carving out for the individual a sphere of freedom within which to pursue his own conception of happiness, without governmental interference, within the necessary limits of the preservation of mutual peace and order. In sum, the essence of liberal constitutionalism is government grounded in, limited by, and devoted to the protection of individual rights.

2

Liberal constitutionalism so conceived is the offspring of the new political science of the Enlightenment. The Constitution of the

United States was the first, and remains the longest-lived, of liberal constitutions. Yet the American Constitution is in many ways exceptional among liberal constitutions, not least in its durability. Perhaps this is so because in the American context the leitmotivs of the Enlightenment were tempered by a pragmatic cast of mind, and informed by extensive experience in colonial self-government and deep reflection on the lessons of political history. The Enlightenment is perhaps notorious for celebrating three things: popular sovereignty, the rights of man, and the autonomy of human reason. In the American context these three themes were to take on a meaning quite different from that common in Europe.

Regarding the first, in America the notion of popular sovereignty was understood as the ultimate foundation of legitimate government in the consent of the governed. Because all men were by nature free and independent, naturally sovereign unto themselves, no man could be subject to the rule of another except by his consent. The 'pure original fountain of all legitimate authority', argued Alexander Hamilton in *The Federalist*, is 'the CONSENT OF THE PEOPLE'.[4] It is from this ultimate sovereignty of the people that the powers of government are derived, and it is the sovereign people who determine the particular form and the limits of that power. As the preamble to the US Constitution reminds us, 'we the people' are the authority that ordains and establishes the frame of government that is the Constitution.

In the American system, however, the sovereign people are limited—indeed, in ordaining the Constitution they consent to limit themselves—in two important ways. First, their sovereignty remains something ultimate: they are the original fountain of authority, but they do not exercise authority in the day-to-day working of government.[5] The administration of government is delegated to a body of representatives ultimately responsible to the people, but who are allowed the breathing-room necessary to choose responsible over merely responsive action should the two conflict. In this way the regular operation of government is insulated from immediate and possibly irresponsible influxes of the popular will. Second, in ordaining a Constitution, the sovereign people commit themselves to be bound by a fundamental law which limits what any popular majority may legitimately do or the way in which it may legitimately do it.[6] The people, that is, authoritatively bind themselves to respect for the forms of the Constitution.[7]

The concept of popular sovereignty, then, meant something quite different in America from what it meant in Europe. In Great Britain, for example, the constitutionalism of consent was equated with parliamentary sovereignty, a principle based on the theory—advocated by Jefferson in America—that the rights of the people are best protected when lodged in the hands of the people themselves. Government by consent would be assured as long as the people controlled parliament and parliament controlled the executive. This was—and to a certain extent still is—the essence of English constitutionalism. But is English constitutionalism, if identified with parliamentary sovereignty, an example of liberal constitutionalism? Following James Madison, we would say no.[8] If the essence of liberal constitutionalism is limited government devoted to the protection of individual rights, then liberal constitutionalism cannot admit the *de jure* unlimited power of parliament.[9]

What gives English constitutionalism its liberal hue, we would argue, is less the supremacy of Parliament than the deep-rootedness of the common-law tradition which holds that majorities cannot—or at least should not—trample on rights established in the common law. It is this tradition of respect for common-law rights that differentiates English from French—and perhaps from European—constitutionalism. In the absence of such a tradition, there is little to prevent popular sovereignty from descending into majority tyranny, as it did after the French Revolution and as it threatens to do today in some Eastern European states. What the English case shows, then, is the possibility of constitutionalism without a written constitution. Indeed, it is arguable that, for the past two centuries, basic liberties have been as well protected in Britain under an unwritten constitution as in the United States with its written Constitution, and certainly better than in Europe with its tradition of written constitutions. This fact would hardly surprise the framers of the American Constitution, in so far as they too recognized that the security of rights 'must altogether depend on public opinion, and on the general spirit of the people and of the government'.[10] However, because they admitted the decisive importance of formalities in the development of informal traditions, they were bound to quarrel with the absence of express constitutional limitation on parliamentary power.[11]

Liberal constitutionalism may be further clarified by contrasting it with a constitutionalism of a different kind, which we shall call 'authoritarian'. Much has been written about the influence of American constitutionalism on the development of European constitutionalism, but the political theory which undergirds the latter departs in decisive respects from that of the former. This is particularly so regarding the doctrine of popular sovereignty. The history of modern European constitutionalism is the history of the progressive transfer of sovereignty from princes or kings, under whom state power had been centralized and consolidated, to the people or their representatives. This relocation of sovereign power, however, did not limit the power of the sovereign. State power continued to exist in all its plenitude, but simply changed hands, residing now in the people rather than in kings. In the liberal constitutional tradition, on the other hand, sovereignty itself was limited, and the state was consigned to play a limited role in the organization of social life.[12] In the United States the ultimate foundation of the government in the consent of the governed did not entail direct or plebiscitary democracy. The US Constitution created a representative government in which popular majorities were bound by the limits of a fundamental law. Fear of majority tyranny led the framers to insulate the normal operation of government from the immediate influence of the popular will.

Let us turn now from popular sovereignty to the second of our Enlightenment themes, the rights of man. In the American context, the celebration of individual liberty—the recognition that the natural rights of individuals come before government and set powerful limits to the legitimate powers of government—was tempered by a sober recognition that individual rights could only be secured by effective government. 'The vigour of government', argued Hamilton, 'is essential to the security of liberty . . . In the contemplation of a sound and well-informed judgment, their interest can never be separated.'[13] If human beings by nature possess certain inalienable rights, still it is to render the possession and exercise of these rights secure that they institute governments. There is little advantage in a government powerless to encroach on individual liberty if it is powerless to secure it as well. In a similar vein, the framers recognized that the security of liberty required moderation in the zeal for liberty, that, in Madison's words, 'liberty may be endangered by the abuses of liberty, as well as by the abuses of power . . . and that the former rather than the latter is apparently most to be apprehended by the United States'.[14] If rights are to be secured, unlimited but unprotected natural rights must become limited but protected civil rights.[15] In this respect, then, the framers put their hope for the security of liberty less in lofty statements of principle than in a well-constructed system of limited government.[16]

Our final Enlightenment theme concerns confidence in the powers of autonomous human reason. If at first sight the attitude of the American framers seems to echo that of Continental *philosophes*, in the end profound differences emerge. In *Federalist* No. 9, Hamilton admitted the indebtedness of the American constitutional system to certain improvements in the science of politics, improvements developed by the great modern liberal thinkers.[17] And in *Federalist* No. 1 he identified the universal significance of the American experiment in these terms:

It seems to have been reserved to the people of this country, by their conduct and example, to decide the important question, whether societies of men are really capable or not, of establishing good government from reflection and choice, or whether they are forever destined to depend, for their political constitutions, on accident and force.[18]

America was to be the first regime of reason, a *novus ordo seclorum*. Still, Hamilton's proud formulation does recognize the importance of that fortunate concatenation of circumstances which made possible the work of reflection and choice that was the drafting and ratification of the Constitution. The founding moment, the framers all admitted, was peculiarly auspicious and would not come again.[19] The framers were guided in their work, moreover, by the insight that the security of government by reflection and choice depends largely on constitutionalized limits to choice, limits which encourage reasonable choices. In the American context, celebration of the human power to fashion reasonable solutions to political problems was tempered by a recognition of the limited hold of reasonableness on human behaviour. 'Is it not time', asked Hamilton rhetorically, 'to awake from the deceitful dream of a golden age, and to adopt as a practical maxim for the direction of our political conduct, that we . . . are yet remote from the happy empire of perfect wisdom and perfect virtue?'[20] The Constitution as an instrument of government was designed for the rule of those imperfect in virtue and wisdom by those also imperfect in virtue and wisdom. The institutional structure it established was designed to impede, so far as possible, the political expression of human vice and folly, so as to encourage, so far as possible, good and reasonable choices. How it was to accomplish this task we shall examine next.

3

We turn, then, from the broad principles of liberal constitutionalism to their institutional implications. Once again we will take as our point of reference the American case, not because we wish to elevate American institutions to the status of timeless models—this would be imprudent, not least because the institutions themselves have changed markedly in the course of their 200-year history—but because we have in the American example clear evidence of the connection between institutional means and the ends for which they were designed. The evidence is contained in *The Federalist*, admitted by all proponents of the Constitution to be the best exposition and defence of the principles inherent in it.[21] A brief consideration of the theory of society, politics, and human nature underlying American constitutionalism will serve as a convenient bridge from principle to practice.

We have already seen that for the American framers society was no mysterious organic entity, but a union of individuals, each by nature free and independent, and possessed of certain rights. We have seen as well that the origin of government lay in the consent of the governed and its purpose in securing individual rights. From this priority of individual liberty followed a limited politics. The Constitution, argued Hamilton, 'is merely intended to regulate the general political interests of the nation . . . [and not] every species of personal and private concerns'.[22] These general political interests were broadly specified in the preamble as the administration of justice, the preservation of social peace, the common defence, the promotion of prosperity, and the protection of liberty.

The vision of human nature which underlies the American scheme of limited government is a realistic one, characterized by a distrust of common human motivations. Human beings are partial in their desires and fallible in their reasoning, susceptible to the sway of immediate passions, and so typically self-interested and short-sighted in their action. The system is designed, as we have said, for the governance of such persons by such persons. Unlike pre-liberal regimes, it seeks to combat unruly passions less by transforming them—which would require obtrusive intervention—than by obstructing or channelling them, curbing their public expression or, if possible, turning it to public advantage.[23] Because human partiality and fallibility are ineradicable, a frame of government must be devised which incorporates them, if only to turn them to contrary purposes.[24]

Such a portrait of human nature, if sceptical, is not utterly bleak or cynical. 'As there is a degree of depravity in mankind which requires a certain degree of circumspection and distrust,' Madison argued, 'so there are other qualities in human nature, which justify a certain portion of esteem and confidence. Republican government presupposes the existence of these qualities in a higher degree than any other form.'[25] Partisans of popular government—and the framers understood themselves to be designing a system that was 'wholly popular'[26]—must suppose that the people possess sufficient wisdom and public-spiritedness to select and reward competent rulers,[27] sufficient docility to recognize their mistakes and be corrected should their impulses conflict with their interests,[28] and sufficient self-knowledge and patience to abide by the forms of a constitution designed to meliorate the effects of their own partiality and fallibility.[29]

The framers' understanding of human nature and its political implications is well illustrated in this passage from Madison:

What is government itself but the greatest of all reflections on human nature? If men were angels, no government would be necessary. If angels were to govern men, neither external nor internal controls on government would be necessary. In framing a government which is to be administered by men over men, the great difficulty lies in this: You must first enable the government to control the governed; and in the next place, oblige it to control itself.[30]

Let us turn then to a consideration of political institutions under these two headings: controlling the governed and controlling the government.

The broad task the framers set themselves in designing the constitutional system was to reconcile popular government with limited but effective government.[31] They sought to create a republican government sufficiently vigorous to promote the general welfare but sufficiently restrained to render individual rights secure. In their own experience, the national government under the Articles of Confederation had failed in respect of the former, many of the state governments in respect of the latter.[32] To remedy the former, the framers ensured that the national government would operate directly on individuals rather than on sovereign states,[33] invested that government with the broad powers necessary to promote the general ends of the preamble,[34] as well as with whatever particular powers might be found necessary to execute those broad powers in diverse situations,[35] and guaranteed the supremacy of the national over the state governments in all matters pertaining to the exercise of the broad powers of the former.[36] Still, we must remember that however vigorous the national government was to be in its proper sphere, that sphere itself was limited, comprising only the 'general political interests of the nation'.[37]

In popular government, the framers argued, the principal threat to both the public interest and private rights is posed by the problem of faction, and to solving this problem they devoted much of their attention. Indeed, the great virtue of their scheme, they maintained, lay in providing a 'Republican remedy' for this disease 'most incident to Republican government'.[38] In The Federalist No. 10, Madison defined a faction as 'a number of citizens, whether amounting to a majority or minority of the whole, who are united and actuated by some common impulse of passion, or of interest, adverse to the rights of other citizens, or to the permanent and aggregate interests of the community'.[39] It was this spirit of faction, of oppressive partisanship, that introduced into the administration of government that 'instability, injustice and confusion' from which popular governments of the past had perished.[40]

In seeking to combat faction, the framers rejected the ancient strategy of removing its causes, for this would require either an excessive deprivation of personal liberty or an impossible homogenization of individual options, passions, and interests. Because the causes of faction are ineradicable, being rooted in the natural partiality, fallibility, and inequality of men, the framers looked instead to controlling its effects. The means they devised to this end were principally two: representation and an extended republic. Let us examine each in turn.

The new American republic differed from popular governments of the past in being founded on the principle of representation. In the American system, the ultimately sovereign people are removed from the daily operation of government, which is delegated to a chosen body of representatives. This delegation brings two advantages. First, the representatives act as a filter to 'refine and enlarge the public views'.[41] They bring to bear on public problems whatever qualities of character and intelligence have commended them to the esteem of their fellow-citizens. Second, the principle of representation insulates the working of government from immediate and overwhelming influxes of the popular will. It opens up space and provides time for deliberation, so that the choices of the people's representatives might be reflective choices.

The principle of representation also carries a further advantage: it makes possible an extended republic, one which takes in a greater number of citizens and extent of territory than would be possible in a direct democracy. Such an expansion of the sphere provides the principal remedy for the problem of faction. In an extended republic, interests and the parties which form around them are multiplied and dispersed. The greater the variety of interests and parties, the less likely it becomes that any one will form a majority of the whole; the greater their dispersion, the more difficult it becomes for a possibly factious majority to combine to execute its designs. Thus, as Madison concluded,

In the extended republic of the United States, and among the great variety of interests, parties and sects which it embraces, a coalition of a majority of the whole society could seldom take place on any other principles than those of justice and the general good.[42]

The very form of an extended republic provides a remedy for the problem of faction by curbing its public expression. In extending the sphere to take in a greater variety of interests, then, the framers did not intend—as some have claimed—to encourage a politics of log-rolling among interest groups, nor to frustrate majority rule simply, but rather to facilitate the emergence of non-factious majorities, of coalitions characterized by respect for the public interest and private rights.[43]

Such were the means by which government was empowered to control the governed; but what of those by which government was to be obliged to control itself? It is important to recognize here that, in a popular government, means designed to control the government also have the effect of controlling the people, by limiting what popular majorities may do through the government. The framers certainly recognized this. They saw two dangers to be guarded against: that of oppression of the whole society by ambitious rulers, and that of oppression of one part of the society by another.[44] They sought as much to prevent any part of society from using the government to trample on the rights of others as to prevent the aggrandizement of ambitious governmental officials. The means which they devised to combat both dangers was a complex system of separated and checked governmental powers.

The framers attempted, in Madison's words, to give to 'those who administer each department, the necessary constitutional means, and personal motives, to resist encroachments of the others'.[45] Security would derive not only from an institutionalized separation of legislative, executive, and judicial functions, but also from the jealous competition among ambitious individuals in the different branches. The 'private interest' of the rulers in maintaining their own authority would become 'a sentinel over the public rights', preventing the usurpation by one department of the powers of another.[46] Because in a popular government the legislative branch necessarily predominates, encroachments from this quarter were most to be checked. To this end the framers divided the legislature into two independent branches, differing in their mode of selection, length of tenure, and constituency. The small districts, short terms, and direct election of the House of Representatives would ensure its closeness to the people, binding each representative to the particular concerns of a particular locality. The expanded constituency, longer terms, and indirect election of the Senate would provide a certain distance from merely parochial concerns, allowing Senators to take a longer and broader view of the public interest. The necessity of co-operation among two such branches different in character would promote deliberate, reflective legislation, legislation reflecting the people's interests and not their immediate impulses alone.[47] Again, the framers' intent here was not simply to obstruct majority rule, but to provide the institutional means by which 'the cool and deliberate sense of the community' could prevail.[48] The limits they placed on popular government were in the service of responsible self-government.

Further protection was to be had from an independent executive and judiciary. The independence of each was secured by its mode of selection and tenure, the former indirectly elected by a national constituency and of median tenure, the latter appointed by the executive with senatorial confirmation and serving on good behaviour. Each was then empowered to serve as a check on legislative encroachments. The executive was invested with a limited veto on congressional legislation, the judiciary with the power of judicial review.[49] Once again, the intention behind these institutional means was not simply to frustrate majority rule, but to ensure responsible majority rule. The executive veto was seen as a means by which a nationally minded president could obstruct perfidious legislation, or at least force its deliberate reconsideration;[50] judicial review as a means by which the supremacy of the deep and abiding intentions of the people, expressed in their fundamental law, could be upheld over the temporary caprices of their representatives.[51] In both cases, the framers' intent was to reconcile majority rule with respect for the public good and private rights.

A last institutional safeguard was derived from the federal system. In the compound republic of America, power was divided not only between branches of the national government but between the national and the state governments as well. While the precise boundaries of this division were never specified, the very existence of dual authorities was deemed sufficient to prevent grossly unconstitutional usurpations of power from either quarter.[52]

Let us summarize our survey of the institutional implications of American liberal constitutionalism. Representation, an extended republic, separation of powers, checks and balances, federalism— these were the means by which the framers of the American Constitution attempted to institutionalize their liberal constitutionalism. Their guiding concern in devising such a scheme was, we have seen, to reconcile popular government with responsible government, to create a republican government structurally disposed to foster the promotion of the public interest and the protection of private rights. Constitutionalism in the American context is inseparable from this dual commitment.

4

The essence of liberal constitutionalism, we have said, is the notion of government grounded in, limited by, and devoted to the protection of individual rights. Before moving on to contemporary liberal constitutionalism, let us briefly consider the distinctive character of liberal rights.

In the liberal tradition, rights belong to individuals and are negative in form. Rights, that is, are primarily individual-liberty rights: they reserve to some person the right to do this or that, or, conversely, the right not to have this or that done to him. They differ in this respect both from communal rights—rights which belong to an individual only by virtue of membership in some group—and from positive rights—rights which entitle an individual to have this or that done for him.[53]

The individualism and negativity of rights at the basis of American constitutional practice was recently dramatically illustrated in the case of *Deshaney* v. *Winnebago County* (1989). The facts of this case are the following. A father over a two-year period mercilessly beat his young son into a condition of profound retardation. State officials, aware of the danger to the child, had chosen only to arrange counselling sessions for the father. The child's mother, having divorced the father, sued the state under federal law for not intervening more forcefully to rescue the child from the father's abuse. In failing to come to the boy's aid, she claimed, the state had deprived him of the liberty protected by the Fourteenth Amendment.[54] The Supreme Court rejected her claim. Chief Justice Rehnquist, speaking for the majority, said in part:

[There is] nothing in the language of the Due Process Clause [that] requires the State to protect the life, liberty and property of its citizens against invasion by private actors. The Clause is phrased as a limitation on the State's power to act, not as a guarantee of certain minimal levels of safety and security . . . [Its] language cannot fairly be extended to impose an obligation on the State to ensure that those interests do not come to harm through other means.[55]

Our Constitution, continued Justice Rehnquist, was designed 'to protect the people from the state, not to ensure that the state protected them from each other'. While this view may be controversial even in America—not to mention how it must shock, for example, members of Germany's Federal Constitutional Court—it does rather baldly illustrate the logic of liberal rights. Liberal rights are predominantly individual-liberty rights.[56]

In the twentieth century, liberal constitutionalism has been torn from its roots in earlier natural rights teachings. Today it is Kant more than Locke or Montesquieu who shapes liberal thought—but a Kant who has been decisively modernized, a Kant situated in a contemporary context characterized by interminable disagreement on questions of political morality. In such a context, the appeal of Kant is his formality, his derivation of political morality not from any contestable account of the human good but from the very form of human rationality. It is Kant the defender of autonomy as the core of human dignity who is the champion of much contemporary liberalism. In our contemporary pluralistic context, the realist liberalism of the framers has given way to a sceptical liberalism which finds it necessary to deny the possibility of knowledge of the good in order to affirm the value of liberty. The framers' defence of liberty had proceeded from an argument about human nature and its requirements: because all human beings are created free and independent, no one can be deprived of his liberty without his consent. The contemporary defence, on the other hand, rests on an argument from the impossibility of knowledge of human nature and its requirements: because no one can know what human nature requires, no one can tell another how to live. Liberty emerges as the consequence of moral scepticism in a pluralistic society. Its value lies primarily in its being the necessary condition for the pursuit of any value.

It is this conception of liberty that lies at the heart of contemporary liberal constitutionalism. Because each person is an autonomous individual, the argument runs, each is entitled to equal concern and respect. And because the principal expression of human autonomy is the capacity to formulate and pursue a life-plan, each of these too must receive equal concern and respect. No one vision of the good life can be publicly privileged over another. Government must be founded on neutral principles of justice designed to be acceptable to all, independent of any particular conception of the good. Its purpose is to provide a neutral framework that can peaceably accommodate an unspecified multiplicity of ways of life.[57] Only those minimal goods acceptable to all as instrumental to the pursuit of any conception of the good can receive governmental promotion.

To the extent that they thus radically privatize the good,[58] contemporary liberals are even more individualistic than their predecessors. They expand the sphere of liberty protected against governmental interference far beyond the limits envisioned by the framers. Unlike the framers, contemporary liberals are inveterately suspicious of talk of civic virtue or the public good, fearing it as merely a pretext for an authoritarian politics.[59] Liberal constitutionalism so conceived has implications for what should go into a modern constitution. Such a liberal would, for example, exclude the stipulation of broad social goals that cannot be vindicated through the rule of law. He would also insist on an active constitutional judiciary, one prepared to strike down legislation that conflicts with the basic right of individuals.

Contemporary liberal constitutionalism is characterized as well by an acute tension between constitutionalism and democracy, between responsible and responsive government. The inherent tension between these two values has been exacerbated by the erosion among sceptical liberals of belief in any rationally accessible criteria of responsibility. This sceptical position has been developed in two contrary directions: one libertarian, the other majoritarian. On the one hand are those who argue that the absence of shared criteria of the good deprives the government of good reasons for substantive limitations on private liberty. Liberty can be limited only in the interest of further liberty and never in the interest of some contestable conception of the good, whether public or private. On the other hand are those who argue that the absence of common rational criteria leaves us with the will of the majority as the only source for standards of public morality.

There is, of course, a great debate going on in the United States at present between constitutionalists and democrats—not only in the academic legal community but in the Supreme Court as well. The constitutionalists would maximize judicial power to secure individual rights against encroachments from the political branches, the democrats would minimize it.[60] Chief Justice Rehnquist and the new conservatives are the democrats. They hold to both a positivistic conception of law and a majoritarian theory of democracy. The authority of law, they argue, derives not from its moral content but only from its proper enactment. Because enactment alone can confer authority on principles of public morality, it is the chief right of citizens in a democracy to form majorities to enact their preferences into law. Consent or consensus is the only reliable source of moral principle in a democratic society. In the absence of clear violations of constitutional provisions, then, questions of public morality should be left to the political process to

resolve as it will. The democrats, therefore, preach judicial restraint. At the root of their view of judicial power is a deep moral
scepticism which rejects the possibility of any objective criteria by
which to adjudicate questions of justice and the common good. For
judges to decide cases by appeal to moral criteria, they argue,
would be to violate the democratic principle by elevating judicial
preferences over those of a majority.[61]

In addition to conservative democrats, there are those on the Left
whose impatience with the limits which constitutional forms
impose on popular rule has led them to call for the radical
democratization of the American constitutional order. Unlike the
framers, who candidly argued that popular government is in need
of institutional restraint which fosters responsible government,
these critics admit few public ills and so see little need for remedies
which frustrate the popular will.[62] There are those in Germany as
well, particularly would-be constitutional reformers in the new
Bundesländer, who speak of amending the Basic Law so as to
render it radically democratic. But, we would submit, to render
the Basic Law—or any constitution—radically democratic would
be to undermine the very notion of constitutionalism, if by
constitutionalism we mean a scheme which puts substantive limits
not only on the power of the state but on the power of the people
as well.

5

In conclusion, let us return to our opening remarks on the relationship between constitutionalism, liberalism, and democracy. We
would argue that constitutionalism, as the legal delimitation of
political power, is possible both without liberalism—as in the
Athenian democracy of the fourth century BC—and without democracy—as in the nineteenth-century German Rechtsstaat—but
liberal democracy is not possible without constitutionalism.[63] Liberal democracy, that is, requires for its institutionalization constitutional forms that limit what both the state and popular majorities
may do vis-à-vis the individual. Such institutional mechanisms are
a necessary bulwark against illiberal encroachments on the rights
and liberties of individuals. In the United States, the judicial en-

forcement of negative rights has become the principal component in the practice of liberal constitutionalism.

But what relevance does the American variant of liberal constitutionalism have for the new states of Central and Eastern Europe? Earlier in this essay we referred to Hamilton's observation that in 1787 Americans found themselves in the unique position 'of establishing good government from reflection and choice' and not merely on the basis of 'accident and force'. With the collapse of communism, a constitutional moment of great significance has arrived in Eastern Europe, for the states there are now in a position self-consciously and freely to determine their own futures. The Marxist belief that political systems are predetermined by objective material conditions has crumbled along with communism as a way of life. As they transform themselves into constitutional democracies, the new states emerging from communism might be guided by the American constitutional experience. Several points invite re-emphasis.

First, the American framers were political realists. They accepted human nature as they found it and organized a system of government that acknowledges the inevitability of the fallible, self-regarding behaviour of individuals. According to Madison, as we have observed, the purpose of *constitutional* government is to control the factious passions, not to abolish them. It was his view that all governmental efforts to reshape human persons in accordance with some abstract plan of human existence result in arbitrary or tyrannical control, increasing rather than decreasing the torments of political life. In short, the goal of liberal constitutionalism is to provide scope for the creative energies of individuals and groups without endangering domestic tranquillity or ordered liberty.

Second, in the interest of both liberty and tranquillity, the American framers also favoured a representative form of government overlaid by separated powers and a system of checks and balances. Their constitutional design was intended not only to confine each department to its specified functions, but also to prevent the legislature from enacting oppressive or ill-considered measures, a constraint on popular government additionally reinforced by a stringent constitutional amendment procedure. We do not suggest that the American design will of necessity meet the needs of post-communist states. We are, however, concerned with

the insurgent populism reflected in practices such as the direct
election of national presidents and various forms of direct democracy appearing in some Eastern European constitutions, not to
mention provisions making constitutional amendment relatively
easy. From the liberal constitutionalist perspective—a perspective
in which the constitution should be a limit not only on the power
of the government but on the power of the people as well—such
practices expose the law-making process to unstable passions and
sudden impulses, and pose a threat to the kind of balanced government the American framers sought to achieve.

Limited government, separation of powers, and the rule of law
are bedrock principles of American constitutionalism. Central
and Eastern European constitution-makers are also committed to
these principles, but some of the mechanisms and institutions
meant to embody them seem deficient in comparison to their
American counterparts. An example of one such deficiency is the
decree-making power of the president under the draft constitution
of the Russian Federation, effectively sanctioning the creation of a
constitutional dictatorship. On the other hand, the granting of
excessive parliamentary control over the impeachment of the
Russian president and the right of the constitutional court to initiate legislation blurs the distinction and disturbs the balance of
power among the branches of government. If constitutionalism
denotes limits on the exercise of political power—which is the
American understanding of the term—then post-communist constitution-makers would be well advised, in the interest of limited
government and the rule of law, to prevent one branch from encroaching on the others.

Finally, one of the purposes of the American Constitution was to
secure the blessings of personal liberty. What the framers had in
mind was the protection of natural rights, together with certain
civil and political liberties, capable of judicial enforcement against
the state. Developments in the post-communist nations raise
questions about the degree to which they are prepared to protect
these rights. One is the threat, especially to the rights of privacy and
association, arising from the tendency to impose retributive justice
upon persons implicated in the abuse of power under communism.
Another is the emphasis upon the values of duty and solidarity.

Both developments could lead to the suppression of legitimate
dissent. We do not for a moment question the importance of the

solidarity rights that have loomed so important in some of Eastern Europe's draft constitutions. Many of these values trace their origins to pre-communist religious and cultural traditions, others to the legacy of state socialism; and many may be worth preserving. The liberal constitutionalist would simply suggest, without presuming to know what is best for the new states of Central and Eastern Europe, that freedom, order, and prosperity—central goals of any constitutional democracy—can only be achieved under a constitution that requires the vigorous defence and impartial enforcement of basic liberties.

Notes

1. W. Murphy, 'Constitutions, Constitutionalism, and Democracy', in D. Greenberg et al. (eds.). *Constitutionalism and Democracy* (Oxford: OUP, 1993), 3–25.
2. See C. H. McIlwain, *Constitutionalism Ancient and Modern* (Ithaca, NY: Cornell University Press, 1947), 21–2; N. B. Reynolds, 'Constitutionalism and the Rule of Law', in G. C. Bryner and N. B. Reynolds (eds.), *Constitutionalism and Rights* (Provo, Ut.: Brigham Young University, 1987), 91–2.
3. See H. Belz, 'Constitutionalism and the American Founding', in L. Levy et al. (eds.), *Encyclopedia of the American Constitution* (New York: Macmillan, 1986), ii. 480–1.
4. *The Federalist*, ed. J. E. Cooke (Middletown: Wesleyan University Press, 1961), no. 22, p. 146. (Subsequent references to the *Federalist* will be to the number and page of this edition.) See too no. 39, p. 251, and no. 49, p. 339. All such formulations, of course, echo Jefferson in para. 2 of the *Declaration of Independence*.
5. James Madison took this to be the decisive difference between ancient direct democracies and the American republic, and an essential factor in the superiority of the latter to the former.
6. See *Federalist*, no. 78, pp. 527–8.
7. On the Constitution as an act of sovereign self-restraint, see H. C. Mansfield, Jr., *America's Constitutional Soul* (Baltimore: Johns Hopkins University Press, 1991), 210–11; and S. A. Barber, *On What the Constitution Means* (Baltimore: Johns Hopkins University Press, 1984), 113–14.
8. See *Federalist*, no. 53, pp. 360–1.
9. On American reactions to the unlimited sovereignty of the legislative

power in Great Britain, see J. Agresto, *The Supreme Court and Constitutional Democracy* (Ithaca, NY: Cornell University Press, 1984), 40–5; and G. Stourzh, 'The American Revolution, Modern Constitutionalism, and the Protection of Human Rights', in *Truth and Tragedy: A Tribute to Hans J. Morgenthau* (New Brunswick, NJ: Transaction Books, 1984), 166–9.

10. *Federalist*, no. 84, p. 580.
11. Recall as well that from the American colonists' perspective the informal tradition of respect for common-law rights proved insufficient protection against the encroachments of Parliament. See Stourzh, 'The American Revolution, Modern Constitutionalism, and the Protection of Human Rights', 167–8.
12. See again Madison's analysis in *Federalist*, no. 53, pp. 360–2.
13. Ibid., no. 1, pp. 5–6.
14. Ibid., no. 63, pp. 428–9.
15. See Mansfield, *America's Constitutional Soul*, 82–3.
16. See *Federalist*, no. 84, pp. 578–80; and H. J. Storing, 'The Constitution and the Bill of Rights', in R. A. Goldwin and W. A. Schambra (eds.), *How Does the Constitution Secure Rights?* (Washington, DC: American Enterprise Institute for Public Policy Research, 1985), 15–35.
17. *Federalist*, no. 9, p. 51.
18. Ibid., no. 1, p. 3.
19. Ibid., no. 2, pp. 9–11, and no. 85, p. 591.
20. Ibid., no. 6, p. 35.
21. Ibid.
22. Ibid., no. 84, p. 579.
23. Ibid., no. 51, p. 349. Desires of the former sort are factious, i.e. tend to the violation of private rights or the public interest. These are malignant, and cannot be allowed public expression. Desires of the latter sort—e.g. personal ambition—though dangerous in themselves, can be politically useful if properly directed. Cf. *Federalist*, no. 10, pp. 56–65, and no. 72, p. 488.
24. See ibid., no. 10, pp. 58–9; and M. Diamond, 'Ethics and Politics: The American Way', in R. H. Horwitz (ed.), *The Moral Foundations of the American Republic*, 3rd edn. (Charlottesville: University Press of Virginia, 1986), 82–3.
25. *Federalist*, no. 55, p. 378.
26. See ibid., no. 14, p. 84, and no. 10, p. 61; and M. Diamond, 'Democracy and *The Federalist*: A Reconsideration of the Framers' Intent', *American Political Science Review*, 53/1 (1959), 53–61.
27. See *Federalist*, no. 57, pp. 384–8.
28. Ibid., no. 71, pp. 482, and no. 63, p. 425.
29. Ibid., no. 78, pp. 527–8.

THE LIBERAL CONSTITUTIONAL TRADITION

30. Ibid., no. 51, p. 349.
31. See ibid., no. 9, pp. 50–2; and S. A. Barber, 'Judicial Review and *The Federalist*', in *University of Chicago Law Review*, 55 (1988), 841–5.
32. See J. Madison, 'Vices of the Political System of the United States', in R. A. Rutland and W. M. E. Rachal (eds.), *The Papers of James Madison* (Chicago: University of Chicago Press, 1975), ix. 345–58.
33. See *Federalist*, no. 39, pp. 255–6.
34. Art. I, sect. 8, Art. II, sects. 2 and 3; Art. III, sect. 2.
35. Art. I, sect. 8, para. 18.
36. Art. VI, para. 2.
37. *Federalist*, no. 84, p. 579.
38. Ibid., no. 10, p. 65.
39. Ibid., p. 57. What follows in the text is a summary of the argument of this most famous number of *The Federalist*.
40. Ibid., pp. 56–7.
41. Ibid., p. 62.
42. Ibid., no. 51, pp. 352–3.
43. Against 'pluralist' readings of the extended sphere argument that see it as an endorsement of interest group politics, see G. Carey, *The Federalist: Design for a Constitutional Republic* (Urbana: University of Illinois Press, 1989), 9–44; N. Tarcov, 'The Social Theory of the Founders', in A. Bloom (ed.), *Confronting the Constitution* (Washington, DC: AEI Press, 1990), 178–80; and H. C. Mansfield, Jr., 'Social Science and the Constitution', in Bloom (ed.), *Confronting the Constitution*, 424–30.
44. *Federalist*, no. 51, p. 351.
45. Ibid., p. 349.
46. Ibid.
47. Ibid., no. 62, pp. 417–20, and no. 61, pp. 424–5.
48. Ibid., no. 63, p. 425.
49. Though judicial review is nowhere mentioned in the Constitution, Hamilton in *Federalist*, no. 78, saw it as inherent in the very notion of a constitution as fundamental law. See too Chief Justice Marshall's opinion in *Marbury* v. *Madison*, 5 US (1 Cranch) 137 (1803).
50. *Federalist*, no. 73, p. 495.
51. Ibid., no. 78, pp. 524–6.
52. The authors of *The Federalist* were themselves more apprehensive about state than national government abuses. They seemed to think it likely that 'the General Government [would] be better administered than the particular governments', because composed of more fit characters, and especially because further insulated by its structure from the spirit of faction. See *Federalist*, no. 27, p. 172, and no. 46, pp. 316–20. On the inherent ambiguity of the framers' federalism and the ways in which it has been overcome in practice, see G. Carey, 'Feder-

alism: Historic Questions and Contemporary Meanings', in Valerie Earle (ed.), *Federalism: Infinite Variety in Theory and Practice* (Ithaca, Ill.: Peacock, 1968), 42–51.

53. See N. Tarcov, 'American Constitutionalism and Individual Rights', in Goldwin and Schambra (eds.), *How Does the Constitution Secure Rights?* 103–5, 118; and G. Casper, 'Changing Concepts of Constitutionalism: 18th to 20th Century', in G. Casper and D. Hutchinson (eds.), *The Supreme Court Review 1989* (Chicago: University of Chicago Press, 1990), 312–16.

54. 42 USC see 1983, under which the suit was brought, holds that 'Every person who, under color of any statute, ordinance, regulation, custom, or usage, of any State or Territory or the District of Columbia, subjects, or causes to be subjected, any citizen of the United States or other person within the jurisdiction thereof to the deprivation of any rights, privileges, or immunities secured by the Constitution and laws, shall be liable to the party injured in an action at law, suit in equity, or other proper proceeding for redress.'

55. *Deshaney* v. *Winnebago County Department of Social Services*, 489 US 189, at 195 (1989).

56. For a survey of cases in which the Supreme Court has managed to derive positive state duties from negative individual rights, see D. Currie, 'Positive and Negative Constitutional Rights', *University of Chicago Law Review*, 53 (1986), 864–90. For an analysis which illuminates the strengths and weaknesses of the American conception by casting it into comparative perspective, see M. A. Glendon, 'Rights in Twentieth-Century Constitutions', *University of Chicago Law Review*, 59 (1992), 519–38.

57. The classic statement of this view is J. Rawls, *A Theory of Justice* (Cambridge, Mass.: Harvard University Press, 1971). Its transmission into constitutional theory was effected by R. Dworkin, *Taking Rights Seriously* (Cambridge, Mass.: Harvard University Press, 1978).

58. See A. MacIntyre, 'The Privatization of Good: An Inaugural Lecture', *Review of Politics*, 52 (Summer 1990), 344–61.

59. The exceptions here are those liberal theorists who abandon liberalism's aspiration to neutrality and argue instead that, far from being neutral on the question of the good, liberalism in fact fosters a particular, and rationally defensible, answer to that question. See W. Galston, 'Defending Liberalism', *American Political Science Review*, 76 (1982), 621–9; S. Macedo, 'Liberal Virtues, Constitutional Community', *Review of Politics*, 50 (1988), 215–40; and S. Salkever, 'Lopp'd and Bound: How Liberal Theory Obscures the Goods of Liberal Practices', in R. B. Douglass, G. M. Mara, and H. S. Richardson (eds.), *Liberalism and the Good* (New York: Routledge, 1990).

60. For an overview of the contemporary debate, see G. Walker, *Moral*

Foundations of Constitutional Thought (Princeton, NJ: Princeton University Press, 1990), 23–64.

61. For examples of this view see R. H. Bork, 'Neutral Principles and Some First Amendment Problems', *Indiana Law Journal*, 47 (1971), 1–31; R. H. Bork, *Tradition and Morality in Constitutional Law*, Francis Boyer Lecture on Public Policy (Washington, DC: American Enterprise Institute for Public Policy Research, 1984); and W. H. Rehnquist, 'The Notion of a Living Constitution', *Texas Law Review*, 54 (1976), 693–706. For a trenchant critique of these views, see S. A. Barber, 'The New Right Assault on Moral Inquiry in Constitutional Law', *George Washington Law Review*, 54 (1986), 256–66.

62. See the instructive exchange between Robert Dahl and James Caesar in Horwitz (ed.), *The Moral Foundations of the American Republic*, 230–81.

63. On the development of constitutionalism in ancient Athens, see M. Ostwald, *From Popular Sovereignty to the Sovereignty of Law* (Berkeley: University of California Press, 1986); and M. H. Hansen, *The Athenian Democracy in the Age of Demosthenes*, trans. J. A. Crook (Oxford: Blackwell, 1991), ch. 7. On the medieval roots of modern constitutionalism, see H. J. Berman, *Law and Revolution: The Formation of the Western Legal Tradition* (Cambridge, Mass.: Harvard University Press, 1983), 205–24 and *passim*.

3

Constitutionalism: Procedural Limits and Political Ends

NEVIL JOHNSON

1. THE FOUNDATIONS OF LIBERAL CONSTITUTIONALISM

Constitutional design and change never occur in a vacuum or in what might be called laboratory conditions. Such efforts are bound to reflect the impact of all kinds of practical problems and political demands. At the same time they will express a range of normative assumptions or more explicit commitments about social life and relationships which are to be found in whatever society it is that we are considering. It follows, of course, that constitutional arrangements and the formal documents in which they may be expressed reveal great variation and diversity: constitutions come in all shapes and sizes. Despite that there are, however, certain continuing themes and recurrent patterns to be found in constitutionalism as it has been exemplified in the Western world, and it is with these that I shall be principally concerned here. Furthermore, it has to be remembered that there is today far more pressure than in the past for the harmonization of at least certain features of constitutional government, at any rate in respect of basic human rights and the requirement of something like democratic consent. In Western Europe there is the added dimension of harmonization both in pursuance of economic integration within the European Community and its Single Market and, more recently, under the broadly stated objectives of the European Union.

This essay is concerned with the traditions and practices of liberal constitutionalism and seeks to make explicit some of its underpinning values. This tradition, which has been concerned essentially with the freedom of the individual and his protection against the abuse of power, has a lineage that can be traced back over at least three centuries. It has been expressed in different ways in the practices of the United States on the one hand and of Europe on the other, something of which we are reminded in Donald P. Kommers and W. J. Thompson's contribution to this volume. For practical purposes the liberal constitutional tradition in something like its modern shape owes much to the arguments raised by the Civil War in England in the mid-seventeenth century, and to the subsequent efforts of political thinkers, notably John Locke, to provide a reasoned case for government by consent.[1] The contributions to this line of argument become richer and more numerous in the course of the eighteenth century, and the idea of a separation of powers emerges as an important element in the liberal constitutional tradition.[2] The identification of the protection of individual rights as one of the principal commitments of the liberal constitutional state only becomes fully explicit, however, with the establishment of the United States and the Declaration of the Rights of Man and the Citizen of 1789 in France. Previously rights had been seen, at any rate in England, as best protected within the wider framework of a body of common law. But these momentous political changes encouraged a belief in the desirability of giving special status to at least some basic human rights. This has now become a familiar element in the liberal constitutional tradition, attested to by the many and varied catalogues of individual rights to be found in so many European constitutions, and in international conventions such as the European Convention on Human Rights.[3]

What these introductory comments suggest is that at the core of liberal constitutionalism there is a commitment to individual freedom, often expressed in the form of statements of rights intended to protect individuals in the use and enjoyment of their freedoms. The deduction made in relation to the design of institutions has been generally that they should distribute or disperse power—the capacity to act under the claim of public authority—in such a way that there is effective protection against abuses of such power. All this is well known. What is sometimes neglected, and more so now than it was thirty or more years ago, is that this commitment to the protection of individual freedoms has in actual historical experience been closely associated with rules and institutional practices that have been seen as providing essentially no more than a framework for both individual and collective choices.

In other words, the constitutional conclusion drawn from the postulate of individual freedom and protection against the abuse of power has been procedural in character. The state, if that term may be used for a moment in relation to a liberal constitutional order, is conceived as primarily procedural in form and negative in its effects on citizens.

It is obvious, of course, that there is bound to be a tension between the liberal constitution so understood and the contemporary belief in the need for and desirability of extensive public provision of many services which support the individual in all sorts of ways. The negative state comes into conflict with the positive state, to express this tension in a simplifying formula. The feature of this tension which it is desired to stress here is, however, political rather than social or distributive, and arises from the very nature of contemporary democratic politics in many societies. In some degree tension and conflict between particular objectives and interests on the one hand and the respect for the limits imposed by any serious procedural framework on the other is always likely to occur. People, individuals or groups, want to pursue specific objectives, often for self-interested reasons, and this may be possible only at the cost of weakening some of the procedural values and methods designed for the preservation of individual freedom, and of extending the powers and demands of 'the state'. This problem and the risks inherent in common responses to it have become much more serious and persistent under the imperatives of democratic politics. For, paradoxically, the universalization of equal political rights (more or less) and the assumption that all authority depends on the constantly renewed consent of the governed has tended in many countries to generate pressures working against a strictly procedural understanding of a liberal constitution.

As a rule, political democracy entails the competition of parties for voter support. This means that there is always a strong inducement for political parties to commit themselves to the pursuit of all kinds of policies calculated to increase the support they enjoy by holding out the prospect of more benefits for those to whom the appeal is made. The past thirty or forty years in European political history reveal many examples of such competitive bidding by parties. And what is promised is generally the realization of substantive objectives, not the maintenance of a liberal state and its procedural conditions. Working in the same direction is the pressure in Europe and beyond for greater equality of living conditions, a demand which is clearly closely related to the universalization of political rights.[4] The outcome has been numerous commitments to policies held to be favourable to economic growth and to the extension of social benefits, for example in health and education.

This evolution presents a continuing challenge to the underlying commitments of liberal constitutionalism. For the danger is that the procedural values embodied in this view of an acceptable constitution will be chipped away or distorted for the sake of an enhanced ability to pursue objectives which are popular and intended often to serve the short-term needs of politicians competing for public office. So there arises a real prospect that the rule of law understood from a liberal standpoint becomes radically instrumentalized for the sake of substantive interests and objectives which both politicians and voters wish to pursue. What follows is directed to identification of some of the manifestations of this in recent European experience.

2. THE GROWTH OF CONSTITUTIONALISM IN EUROPE

The rule of law in its modern form—which is pre-eminently the liberal constitutional mode—was then, by genesis and conceptual definition, procedural. A crucial feature of the negative, procedural view of a constitution exemplified in such early examples as the English Bill of Rights of 1689 and the American Constitution of 1787 is that liberal constitutionalism hardly had a teleology at all: what with hindsight we often designate 'the liberal state' was justified not by reference to social or collective 'objectives' or ends but principally by its claim to establish and sustain conditions in which citizens are as free as possible to pursue their own chosen ends with whatever means are available to them. It is precisely in the strengthening of the tendency to move away from this non-teleological view of a constitution, towards a taste for using the constitution to specify all kinds of 'objectives' to which the society, and a fortiori its citizens, are supposedly committed, that constitutionalism in modern Europe and elsewhere has moved away from the earlier liberal traditions.

This is not the place to trace the often chequered history of efforts in many parts of Europe in the course of the past two centuries or so to establish systems of government based on the ideas of liberal constitutionalism. It is enough to say that liberal constitutionalism encountered other traditions in which a paternalistic view of the role of government and a notion of the state as the political expression of a solidaristic society were powerful factors. Both have left residues which continue to influence contemporary Continental constitutional thinking and practice. Nevertheless, in the course of the nineteenth century and on into the twentieth it was the ideals of liberal constitutionalism which became established in Continental Europe as the dominant 'progressive' tradition. They inspired the revolutionaries and reformers of 1848, and gradually found expression in the extension to many European states of parliamentary government and a rule of law based on liberal principles. In this process the British model was highly influential, though its impact did not displace the older Roman-law way of thinking nor supersede the widespread effects of Napoleonic state rebuilding in France and beyond at the beginning of the nineteenth century. After the shattering experiences of the 1930s and then of the Second World War, it was not surprising that the liberal heritage—individual rights and limited government—should once again play an important, though not exclusive, role in much of the constitutional reconstruction which had to be undertaken.[5]

The process of rebuilding which took place in 1945 and in the years immediately following involved in some cases a straightforward restoration of methods of parliamentary government and the rule of law that had been suspended as a result of German occupation. This was, for example, what happened in Norway and the Netherlands, where the constitutions reached back into the nineteenth century.[6] In both France and Italy there was a return to traditional republican forms of government which treated parliament as the central institution, though in practice it came to be dominated by parties which used its procedures largely to their own advantage. In the French Constitution of 1946 (for the Fourth Republic) there was explicit confirmation of rights as affirmed in the famous founding declaration of 1789, together with a preamble supplementing and widening them. The French Constitution of 1958 (for the Fifth Republic) repeated this commitment, but did not go as far as to confer a special and superior legal status on the rights referred to, though subsequently the jurisdiction of the Constitutional Council established under the Constitution was to develop in that direction.[7] In the Italian case, rights were elaborately stated,[8] though in the subsequent evolution of the country's constitutional system it is questionable whether this turned out to be a factor of critical importance. Germany was for obvious reasons in a different situation. The supposedly provisional constitution drawn up for the western part of the country in 1949 established the Federal Republic of Germany as a federal and parliamentary state. In all essentials it is this constitutional settlement which holds good today in the reunified Germany established in 1990. What needs a special mention in the present context is that the German Basic Law made at the outset a very explicit commitment to the classical liberal view of a constitution: it envisaged rights as essentially protective of individual freedom, it gave them pre-eminence in the legal order, and it contained several provisions clearly intended to restrict the scope of public powers and to guard against the re-emergence of an over-mighty state.[9] Formally, all this remains unchanged today. Nevertheless, the German Constitution also contains other political and ethical components which express to some extent the traditions of social solidarity familiar in earlier German development and endorsed in particular by the Catholic Church.[10] A similar concern with the support of individuals in society and with the distribution of benefits was expressed in the 1946 Italian Constitution, and was certainly present in French political life in the early post-war years.

In the decades since 1945, legal argument and philosophy in the Anglo-American tradition has continued to be faithful on the whole to a 'negative' account of the rule of law. In Britain the commitment to and establishment of what came to be known as the 'welfare state' did not in radical ways change this approach, in part perhaps because legal thinking continued to be shaped chiefly by judges and practising lawyers rather than by theorists. H. L. A. Hart's well-known and influential analysis of the foundations and form of a legal system remained true to many features of Hobbes's legal positivism, and certainly offered no great comfort to those who sought some objective foundation for basic or 'natural' rights.[11] The same was also true of a more explicitly political theorist like Michael Oakeshott, whose account of the rule of law was openly contemptuous of efforts to give human rights some kind of superordinate status. And one of the most notable protagonists of the market economy and individual freedom, F. A. Hayek, presented analyses of a rule-of-law state in which public powers are most austerely limited and the liberty of the individual secured far more by something like a common-law jurisdiction than by appeal to grand statements of rights.[12]

In the United States the evolution has been somewhat different, but has none the less proceeded in a way that still puts great emphasis on the limits of state action and interference with the individual. Beginning in the early 1950s with the epoch-making decision of the Supreme Court on equal rights in education, judicial interpretation of the Constitution shifted towards a very strong emphasis on what might be called 'equal freedoms'. Gradually this approach has been applied to many different claims advanced by individuals belonging to what have been seen as disadvantaged minorities, in particular those of Negro descent. Whilst this evolution has certainly resulted in the extension of various forms of social provision for the poorer sections of the society, and to that extent has pointed towards greater material equality (or social justice, as some might want to call it), it has in general remained faithful to the individualist bias in the interpretation of rights in the American Constitution. The Constitution (again as Professor Kommers reminds us) remains a formidable obstacle in the way of public decision-makers, for not only does it limit their powers, it also offers virtually unrivalled opportunities for the pursuance of individual claims through the courts. In this way liberal constitutionalism in the United States does remain strongly committed to a rule of law envisaged in procedural terms: its conditions limit governments and legislators, but are there to be used also by individuals for the protection of their rights and the advancement of the claims they make as citizens enjoying the protection of the Constitution.

3. QUALIFYING LIBERAL CONSTITUTIONALISM IN POST-WAR EUROPE

Reference has already been made to the fact that, in the constitutional reconstructions which followed the Second World War in

Western Europe, there was in several countries a desire to give extensive recognition to the component of social solidarity and support alongside the commitment to individual freedom and limited government. In Italy, the 1946 Constitution went into some detail in specifying what 'social-ethical relations' were to be protected and in providing a basis for state intervention in the economy.[13] The West German Basic Law pointed to some extent, though less decisively, in similar directions. Alongside the strong commitment to separation of powers and a classical liberal view of rights as essentially claims to protection against external interference with enjoyment of them by individuals, there was in the Basic Law the commitment to what later became known as the *Sozialstaat*.[14] Moreover, although the West German economy was to be rebuilt on market principles, much of the writing propagating this course of development referred to a social market economy rather than to a market economy as such. This in turn was to provide a normative foundation for the steady extension of social claims under the Constitution itself.

What happened generally in most of Western Europe during the 1950s and later was that successful economic reconstruction made it possible to realize to a substantial extent policies designed to provide for a high level of social benefits and services—health, welfare at work, education, pensions for old age and disability, a wide range of social and environmental amenities, and so on. Gradually such benefits came to be regarded as 'rights' even in those countries in which it was hard to find any explicit constitutional warrant for such a conclusion.[15] Individuals came to be enclosed within networks of state provision of welfare services and of state-regulated activity for many other purposes, so that inevitably the older liberal account of a rule-of-law state retreated into the background. The notion of limited government was watered down to accommodate extended government, provided the public authorities acted within the law and with some respect for popular feelings. The earlier stress in liberal constitutionalism on the constitution as essentially a framework for individual responsibility became muted: rights, or the claims justified by appeal to such rights, began to take precedence over notions of obligation and responsibility. The growth of the 'social state' and all that it has meant had a further consequence in relation to thinking about constitutionalism. More and more it encouraged people to regard legislation and even a constitution as means for the pursuit of specific objectives:

the procedural conception of the constitution began in some places to give way to something much more teleological. The constitution was supposed to serve the end of advancing human welfare, happiness, and prosperity. Or, even more narrowly, it might be used to legitimize the pursuit of very specific purposes agreed upon by the dominant political forces.

4. LIBERAL CONSTITUTIONALISM IN HARNESS WITH THE WELFARE STATE

For well over two decades after about 1960, the prospects for extending welfare and satisfying more and more material claims advanced by individuals appeared to be highly favourable. Much of Western Europe began to believe in the possibility of more or less continuous economic growth, a happy state of affairs which appeared to offer a prospect of combining a strengthening of the 'social component' in constitutionalism with continued respect for the individual freedom and responsibility components. Nevertheless, there were countries like Britain where the rate of growth was hesitant and where doubts were expressed more often and earlier about many aspects of the welfare state and its social service commitments.[16] In the early 1980s, and again at the end of the decade and on into the 1990s, there has been far more experience of what can be termed 'the limits to growth'. This has resulted already in a slowdown in the quantitative expansion of the social benefits available to citizens in most Western European countries.

Despite an economic context which is now far less favourable to growth than it used to be (and for reasons with worldwide ramifications), the general European commitment to the social component in the constitutional order remains strong. This is illustrated clearly both in the overall development of the European Community and in the continuing effort within the Community to secure an extension of Community competence in relation to social policy.[17] This became a matter of serious dissent in the negotiations leading up to the Maastricht Treaty, and, as is well known, the British government secured an opt-out clause exempting it from the 'social' component eventually embodied in the Treaty. There is no need in the present context to express a view on the merits or otherwise of the Community's 'social charter' or on the motives and interests of its supporters and opponents. What is significant is that, as written into the Maastricht Treaty on European Union, it does constitute an attempt to commit the member states of the Community to the pursuit of substantive policies. It opens the way to future regulation in the direction laid down in very loose terms in the Treaty itself, and assumes that member states will regard themselves as bound to uphold the policy commitments and objectives laid down in the relevant social clauses of the Treaty.

The example just quoted is drawn from the level of the European Community where further examples of the same method and tendency can be found. But the same trend is observable in constitutional discussion and change in some of the member states. This appears very clearly in Germany where, following reunification, some adaptation of the Basic Law has become necessary, a matter referred to in some detail in Dieter Grimm's chapter.[18] As a result, a special 'commission' of members of both chambers of the legislature was established to consider what constitutional amendments might be deemed necessary and desirable. What is striking in such public argument as has followed is the tendency when discussing constitutional change to introduce the idea of 'state aims' (*Staatsziele*), and to see amendment as an opportunity to write into the Constitution such new or revised aims. Typically, they are expressed in terms such as the promise to maintain a good-quality environment, to ensure adequate housing for all, to provide the maximum range of opportunities for all to enjoy satisfying work, or to increase the range of social benefits available for particular persons and circumstances. Yet it is widely recognized, even by the protagonists of such commitments, that, strictly speaking, they can mean little unless there are concomitant obligations to pursue these objectives and to secure the resources for so doing. To follow the logic inherent in the constitutional recognition of policy objectives this far would, however, plainly entail conflict with the underlying procedural values of a liberal constitution. Consequently, we rarely if ever find such accompanying obligations laid down. Instead, there is faith in the purely persuasive political effect of such commitments: it is believed that their formal embodiment in the Constitution will induce political parties and others in the future to continue to pursue whatever are the policy objectives given such elaborate recognition.

One further feature of the tendencies so far noted deserves comment. This is the temptation to define constitutional commitments in ever greater detail. This is particularly true of recent German efforts to amend the Constitution, notably in the case of the right to asylum.[19] But it is also a tendency exemplified by the Federal German Constitutional Court, whose judgments are in many instances presented with considerable elaboration of detail and numerous injunctions directed at future legislative or executive action.[20] A similar concern with detailed provision is sometimes manifested in constitutional arguments and provisions enacted in Central and Eastern Europe. Here there is both an understandable impulse to provide multiple safeguards against the abuse of powers and the destruction of individual rights familiar under the communist regimes which have been replaced, and a desire on the part of many to protect a wide range of interests and benefits enjoyed by different sections of the population under these regimes. This trend towards exact specification of what may or should be done in the future clearly suggests a very different understanding of a constitution from that expressed in liberal constitutionalism. It means that the constitution is no longer viewed in the main as a statement of procedural values and methods, but at least as much as a means of determining the character and ends of future policies. In this way the constitution becomes strongly programmatic, the expression of a claim to decide in some detail what future generations shall do.

The developments and tendencies referred to all point to a wider collective action, and the pursuit of substantive policies legitimized by reference to the constitution. In the new democracies of Central and Eastern Europe there has in general been a strong desire to reconstruct on the basis of liberal principles in respect both of human rights and of limited government. But at the same time, as noted above, there are strong pressures working in different directions. There is the objective need for economic and social reconstruction on a comprehensive scale, involving the introduction of a market economy in difficult conditions. How is this to be achieved except initially through extensive legislative action which also involves a strong and effective arm of executive government? In contrast, a strong version of liberal constitutionalism has severely restrictive implications for the acceptable range of state powers and public regulation, and this seems often to be unrealistic. Similarly, there are powerful pressures to retain or take account of what are still seen by many as the 'social' achievements of the collectivist systems which have collapsed. In such conditions it is hardly surprising that so few of the newly democratized states have actually succeeded so far in giving themselves a definitive constitutional settlement. Instead, as is explained in the contributions of Wojciech Sokolewicz and Attila Ágh, it has been necessary in many cases to rely on heavily amended constitutional documents dating back to communist rule, or to make use of other provisional constitutional enactments. All this means that the process of constitutional adaptation is likely to continue for several years to come, and it would be unwise at the present time to make predictions about the character of the final results.

In the West there are also examples of enhanced public powers, even in countries like Britain in which the procedural notion of a liberal constitution has strong roots. There, in the years since 1979, the effort to restore effectiveness to market principles and in theory to diminish the role of the state led paradoxically to a strengthening and extension of the powers of the central government in many fields and *pari passu* to a substantial weakening of locally elected authorities. Naturally, it can be argued that all this has been but a means to an end, and that the aim is eventually to see the ambit of state action in whatever guise reduced. The case is, however, not entirely convincing in the face of efforts, for example in the field of education, to impose centrally agreed standards and requirements on what were previously strongly autonomous service-providing agencies.[21] In Germany, the demands imposed by economic reconstruction in the new eastern provinces have combined with the need to achieve social integration of the two parts of the country to require a strengthening of the role of the central political authorities. And in several other countries the strains imposed by economic recession now point towards demands for state action which in turn are likely to work against the commitment to market methods and solutions as well as to liberal constitutionalism in its more traditional sense. All in all, whilst the preoccupation with constitutional adaptation or design is now fairly widely diffused in Europe, the outlook for constitution-making of the liberal, individualist sort is hardly promising.

5. LIBERAL CONSTITUTIONALISM ON THE DEFENSIVE

The arguments put forward here are not directed against redistributive policies generally, nor against pleas which may be put forward in the name of social justice for the reduction of inequalities in any particular society. Such 'social' objectives could be pursued even within the limits imposed by a strictly negative and procedural rule of law. The problem that is presented by the attenuation of the practices and values of liberal constitutionalism in favour of what we might call 'social constitutionalism' is that the scope for individual liberty, and its effective use by individuals to help shape their own lives, is steadily reduced. Underpinning a procedural account of the rule of law is the belief that it is individuals who are best capable of making use of the liberty and civil rights which the rule of law allows them. It prescribes the conditions under which freedom may be enjoyed and rights exercised. In general, the limits set to such an exercise of individual freedoms are justified by reference to the harm that might be done to other individuals in the absence of such limits to impose restraint or prohibition. But for the rest individuals are expected to set and seek their own ends, free from external interference and direction. Even in matters for which compulsory requirements are usually prescribed—for example the education of children or the payment of pension contributions—the liberal constitutionalist would prefer to express such requirements in terms of an obligation on parents that can be met in a variety of ways, for example by allowing them to send their children to schools of their choice rather than being confronted only with a state monopoly. The consistent application of such principles imposes considerable restrictions on the acceptable scope of law, and on the powers which public authorities can properly claim to exercise. What is more, a rule-of-law state of this kind is likely to be characterized both by the readiness of citizens to challenge public decisions restrictive of their freedoms and by restraint in the imposition of binding conditions on the part of legislative and executive authorities.

Constitutional reality in most parts of Europe no longer corresponds closely to the model just outlined. Widespread acceptance of extensive measures of social regulation and provision, along with the readiness to practise public interventions of all kinds in the sphere of the economy, have over many years increased greatly the powers of governments and diminished severely the range of individual responsibility and action. So long as policies of the kind just referred to are regarded as open to modification or revision, there must remain some prospect of maintaining at least the core elements of the procedural, negative rule-of-law state: pendulums can swing and societies can experience shifts of opinion and perception which make it possible to move the boundaries between public powers and individual responsibilities, between state intervention and market forces. But this possibility is diminished or made more difficult of realization when an ever wider and more heterogeneous range of 'objectives' are written into a constitution and the state is said to be committed to them. When this happens, it means that governments and legislatures in the future, as well as the active political forces and interests in the society, are expected and in some degree constrained to follow policies for which there may in fact turn out to be little support and no practical need. In short, the constitutionalization of substantive policy objectives represents an attempt, short-sighted though it often may be, to bind the future to what are in reality just current demands and preoccupations. This is something that liberal constitutionalists have usually tried to avoid. The constitutionalization of certain policy aims also offers additional leverage to those who may wish to use the constitution to advance whatever sectional interests may be associated with such objectives. Examples of this can easily be found in the field of environmental protection, where there are numerous and often vocal pressure groups, all ready to invoke whatever special status may be given to the protection of the environment. In short, commitments of this nature tend to result in measures to satisfy particular claims and interests rather than in the maintenance of a framework of law within which individuals, groups, and organizations can then decide how best to proceed.

The modern European state, as it is exemplified chiefly in the Western part of the Continent, shows many signs of being a curious hybrid. The commitment to the preservation of individual freedom and to the maintenance of limited government under the rule of law remains in most cases politically firm. But what this means and what it might entail has been interpreted ever more flexibly. There has for many years now been a strong tendency to conclude that constitutions are there to be stretched to accommodate a remarkably wide range of social and economic objectives, justified often enough by appeal to notions of social equality. These developments threaten to undermine liberal constitutionalism by imposing on it a teleology incompatible with the values embodied in it. For the limited and liberal constitution does not serve the purpose of advancing particular policy objectives or of realizing defined end states and conditions. Instead, it has the purpose of defining and sustaining a framework within which innumerable different ends and interests can be pursued by citizens, singly or in groups. If the procedural view of the rule of law has a teleology at all, then it is something like this: it represents a society's commitment to procedural conditions intended to constrain both citizens and public authorities in the manner in which they pursue their various and often conflicting purposes. The danger in contemporary Western Europe is that this core element in liberal constitutionalism is steadily being eroded. Instead of justifying this tradition by reference to the value it attaches to individual freedoms and responsibilities, there is a tendency to let the preservation of a liberal constitutional order rest on little more than a broad commitment to the collective provision of social benefits for all and the exercise of public powers according to law.[22] All this facilitates acceptance of a strongly instrumental view of law, whether constitutional or ordinary law, and of the institutions of public life and service provision.

In Eastern Europe the position is plainly different in that there is no recent experience of liberal constitutionalism. It is, therefore, inappropriate to talk in terms of its erosion through the acceptance of policy commitments which may weaken its original rationale. The problem is instead set by the tensions inherent in trying to establish in unfavourable conditions of social turbulence and economic crisis at least some of the basic elements of a liberal constitutional system. Often there is bound to be a trade-off between getting something urgently needed for economic reconstruction done, even at the cost of high-handed action by political leaders or public bodies, and support for procedural conditions affecting law or institutions which might well render the necessary action difficult or impossible to achieve. Indeed, in some circumstances there will even be dispute about what is law and what is not: the familiar assumptions of societies in the liberal rule-of-law tradition may be remote from reality. The hope must remain that, through the links which have already been established between organizations like the

Council of Europe committed to the cause of limited government and respect for individual freedoms in the Western half of Europe, the newly democratized states of Eastern Europe will be assisted in the difficult process of reconstruction on which they are launched. On this account alone it is important that the values of liberal constitutionalism should not be further eroded in those parts of Europe where hitherto they have been strong, and that such countries in Western Europe should remain open towards their neighbours to the East who at the present time face such a daunting challenge.

Notes

1. John Locke, *Second Treatise on Government* (1690). Locke's case for a contractarian theory of government is but one of the most notable contributions to the effort in the 17th century to elaborate a new foundation for political obligation following upon the erosion of its grounding in religious faith.
2. A notion of separated powers is presented by Locke, but receives its classic formulation in Montesquieu's *Spirit of the Laws* (*De l'Esprit des Lois*, 1748). All this was well known to those who 40 years later drafted the American Constitution.
3. The European Convention on Human Rights and Fundamental Freedoms is an agreement binding members of the Council of Europe which came into force in 1953. The UK has not embodied its terms in its domestic law, but does allow the right of individual petition to the European Court of Human Rights in Strasbourg.
4. The commitment to equality of living conditions is echoed in, for example, art. 72 of the German Basic Law, where it figures in para. 3 as one of the reasons for the conferment of concurrent legislative powers on the Federation, thereby allowing it to regulate matters otherwise falling to the *Länder*.
5. For comments on post-1945 constitution-making in Europe see N. Johnson, 'Constitutionalism in Europe since 1945: Reconstruction and Reappraisal', in D. Greenberg, S. N. Katz, M. B. Oliviero, and S. C. Wheatley (eds.), *Constitutionalism and Democracy: Transitions in the Contemporary World* (Oxford: OUP, 1993).
6. The modern Dutch Constitution dates back to 1814, having been revised in 1848, 1887, 1917, and most recently 1983; the Norwegian Constitution (which persisted throughout the union with Sweden dur-

ing the last century) also dates back to 1814 and has been revised several times since.

7. For analysis of the legal protection given to basic rights in France see J. Bell, *French Constitutional Law* (Oxford: OUP, 1992), ch. 5.

8. The Italian Constitution, pt. i, contains a statement of individual rights, but they are not given the special status which in Germany has facilitated direct appeal to the Federal Constitutional Court in cases of alleged infringement of them.

9. Basic rights are set out in arts. 1–19 of the Basic Law, and are by art. 19 made binding on all ordinary law and enforceable in legal proceedings.

10. Notable examples are the protection of marriage and the family provided for in art. 6 of the Basic Law and the duties of the state in relation to education laid down in art. 7. There was in the years after 1945 a revival of Catholic social theorizing, to which German theologians such as O. v. Nell-Breuning made substantial contributions.

11. H. L. A. Hart, *The Concept of Law* (Oxford: OUP, 1961).

12. M. J. Oakeshott, 'The Rule of Law', in *On History and Other Essays* (Oxford: Blackwell, 1983); F. A. Hayek, *The Constitution of Liberty* (London: Routledge & Kegan Paul, 1960), and *Law, Legislation and Liberty* (3 vols., London: Routledge & Kegan Paul, 1973).

13. The Italian Constitution 1946, pt. i, titles ii and iii.

14. The *Sozialstaat* is to a large extent an elaborate political and juridical deduction from the simple terms of art. 20, Basic Law, in which the Federal Republic is described as a 'democratic and social federal state'. See for detailed exposition of the matter H. H. Hartwich, *Sozialstaatspostulat und gesellschaftlicher Status quo* (Cologne: Westdeutscher Verlag, 1970).

15. It became common in Britain too, despite the absence of a formal constitutional basis for such conclusions, to argue that social benefits were to be treated as rights by virtue of the part they play in defining citizenship. As an example of this approach see T. H. Marshall, *Citizenship and Social Class, and Other Essays* (Cambridge: CUP, 1950).

16. It is perhaps a reflection of the strength of the traditions of liberal constitutionalism in Britain that criticism of the development of the welfare state and the managed economy from 1945 onwards was always voiced by some: the Keynesian or social democratic consensus was never universal, even before 1979.

17. The protocol on social policy and the agreement attached to it in the Maastricht Treaty embody the terms of a wide-ranging 'Social Charter' agreed in 1989. See *Treaty on European Union*, Cm. 1934 (London: HMSO, May 1992), 117–20.

18. The Basic Law contained two articles intended to meet the contingency of reunification of the two German states. One of these (art. 146) foresaw its replacement by a new Constitution, freely accepted by the people; the other (art. 23) simply provided for the accession of new territories to the existing constitution. In the event, art. 23 was invoked and consideration of constitutional adaptation was promised in the treaty providing for reunification. The parliamentary commission which deliberated in 1992–3 was the outcome of this compromise.

19. The right to asylum was formerly dealt with in art. 16 of the German Basic Law in four words. The recent amendment (art. 16a) supplements this by four paragraphs running to about 300 words.

20. A striking recent example of careful instruction and guidance to the legislators is provided by the decision of the Federal Constitutional Court on the constitutional status of revisions to the law on abortion. Reported in the *Frankfurter Allgemeine Zeitung*, 29 May 1993, and commented on later in the same newspaper by a former judge of the court, who remarked that the court's instructions on the guidelines to be laid down for the counselling of mothers contemplating abortion were 'unusually comprehensive and detailed'. Prof. Dr Hans Faller, in 'Beratung und Hilfe statt Strafe', ibid. 8 June 1993.

21. Much of the writing on the Thatcher era (1979–90) notes the paradox referred to here, often with critical comments on the extension of central government powers and the diminishing role of elected authorities. Radical changes in the organization of school education have been in train since 1988; similar changes are being introduced into the structure and operating terms of the National Health Service.

22. The transition referred to here might be characterized as a move away from the liberal *Rechtsstaat* (i.e. a state embodying a liberal and individualist theory of justice) to a *Gesetzesstaat* (i.e. simply a state ruled by laws).

PART III
CONSTITUTIONAL SYSTEMS: EVOLUTION AND CHANGE

4

Evolution and Adaptation of the British Constitutional System

CHERYL SAUNDERS

1. INTRODUCTION

The British Constitution is the distinctive product of centuries of constitutional evolution in conditions necessarily unique to Britain itself. Partly through colonization, but partly also because of its apparent success, the model has spread to countries throughout the world. In each of them, inevitably, it operates differently from the original. Whatever the impact of deliberate modification or local context, however, some distinguishing features or characteristics can still be discerned. Chief amongst them are the principles, institutions, and procedures of the common law.

The first part of this essay deals with the British Constitution now, with some reference to the process by which it assumed its present form. The discussion is organized around the three principal objectives of most twentieth-century systems of government descended from the Western tradition: to derive legitimacy from democracy; to govern effectively; and to operate within constitutional limits, whether procedural or substantive in kind. The second part uses these same objectives to examine the adaptation of the British model to the United States, Canada, New Zealand, and Australia. These countries are chosen from the many common-law systems in the New World because their constitutional expectations are roughly comparable to those of Britain and to each other, although the end-products are very different. The essay concludes by considering likely future directions, in the light of existing tensions and emerging pressures, at least some of which, whatever their source, apply to all constitutional systems.

2. THE BRITISH CONSTITUTION

Two underlying influences have had a significant effect on the form
and substance of the British Constitution. The first is the relatively
peaceful and gradual transition of Britain from autocracy to democracy and limited government. Important staging-points along
the way were the conceptual distinctions of legislative and judicial
from executive power and their actual separation, at least in the
sense that neither could be exercised by the executive branch of
government acting alone.[1] Another was the acceptance, in 1689, of
the supremacy or sovereignty of the Crown in Parliament, exercising legislative power.[2] Leaving aside the Civil War and the ensuing
republican Commonwealth, the entire process took place without
major disjunction or the aid of an overriding constitutional instrument.[3] Such formal changes to constitutional law and practice as
occurred tended to be understated, to the point of invoking tradition to justify the new regime.[4] Unwritten practice, or convention,
played a major role.

The second, connected influence is the common law, which accepts judicial decisions as a source of law, subject to statute. This
characteristic leads inexorably to the doctrine of precedent to guide
decisions of inferior courts, and influences decisions of all courts in
the same hierarchy, in the interests of consistency, certainty, and
fairness. It has resulted in the establishment of the judiciary as the
third arm of government, co-equal in status with the other two, its
vulnerability balanced by conventions and some statute law[5] protecting judicial independence. Through positive action or negative
forbearance, the judges have shaped key constitutional principles,
including the doctrine of parliamentary sovereignty itself,[6] and are
both the authors and the ultimate enforcers of the rule of law. The
creative role of the courts under the British constitutional model
and the ambiguity of its limits adds to the paradox that the system
which insists most strongly on the absolute power of the legislature
has done little to design procedures to give the legislature a distinctive and effective role in practice.

The contrast traditionally drawn is with the formative influences
on constitutional systems elsewhere in Europe. Most existing Western European constitutional orders can be traced to major and
sometimes repeated upheavals since the later eighteenth century,
forcing transition from autocracy to more popular rule. In each

case one result has been a formal, written constitution with the status of fundamental law, usually expressed to derive its authority from the popular will and regulating relations between the state and its citizens. Consistently with the civil-law tradition, itself built on mistrust of the courts, the primary source of law is the legislative code. Historically, the general courts have ranked below the other branches of government. Actions involving the public sector still tend to be dealt with by specialist bodies, whether in the administrative or judicial sphere.[7]

The key features of the British constitutional system are familiar. Not all are unique to the British model, although most take a characteristic form. They include a constitutional monarchy under which the Crown, possessing formal power, acts on the advice of a government drawn from an elected Parliament in all but the most exceptional circumstances; the principles and practices of responsible government, regulating relations between Parliament, ministers, and public officials; subject to the effects of membership of the European Community, the acceptance of the sovereignty, or absolute supremacy, of Parliament; within these constraints, a separation of legislative, executive, and judicial power; court structures, procedures, and powers in the common-law tradition; subject again to the European connection, reliance on common law and the political process to preserve individual rights and freedoms *vis-à-vis* the state.

The evolution of each of these features is a study in itself. Collectively, however, a simple catalogue provides an uninspiring basis for comparison, either with later derivations or with different systems. What follows, therefore, examines the British constitutional system as a whole by reference to objectives which are common to all Western constitutional systems: the achievement of democratic, effective, and limited government.

2.1. Democratic Government

Democratic government for this purpose is defined narrowly, to mean government by the people or, more usually, their elected representatives. More complex notions of democracy, which qualify majority power, are considered below in the context of limited government.

Democracy in this sense is achieved in Britain through the election of the lower house of a bicameral legislature, the Parliament, from which the government is drawn. The franchise is broad. The first-past-the-post, constituency-based voting system sometimes returns a parliamentary majority with minority electoral support, and is a frequent target of criticism for this and other reasons, but the problem is within the bounds of democratic tolerance. Coalitions are rare, in what essentially is a highly adversarial two-party system. The upper house, the House of Lords, is hereditary or appointed but now has only limited powers to delay money[8] and ordinary bills.[9] Elections for the House of Commons must be held at least every five years. In normal circumstances an election takes place at the instance of the prime minister, who is likely to choose a date which is perceived to maximize his or her electoral advantage.

The government is chosen because it possesses the confidence of the House of Commons. It holds office as long as it continues to do so. In this sense it is indirectly elected. All ministers are Members of Parliament; and most of them Members of the House of Commons. Precisely what amounts to a confidence issue which will bring down a government is not always clear and depends partly on the government itself, as the recent vacillation over the significance of an adverse vote on the Maastricht Treaty showed.[10] Adoption of a specific no-confidence motion, of course, will suffice, however; as will rejection of Supply. In practice, party cohesion and a sense of self-preservation makes a deliberate expression of lack of confidence in a government unlikely.

Under common-law principles or statute, legislation is required for certain purposes: to impose taxation,[11] appropriate funds,[12] create or alter legal rights or duties, change existing law.[13] Equally, the common law accepts that other functions can be carried out by executive government, without parliamentary authority.[14] Some of these are significant, and increasingly so: the powers to contract and to enter into international arrangements are examples. Whatever problems this division of function creates for government accountability, however, it has no necessary implications for democracy in the limited sense in which the term is used here. It follows from the principles of parliamentary supremacy, in any event, that the exercise of the prerogative or inherent executive power can be legislatively controlled; and historically this has occurred.[15]

The democratic character of the British Constitution is partly obscured by the outward form. The Crown nominally is involved in all branches of government. Most obviously, it is the formal repository of executive power, but the courts also are the Queen's courts, the legislature comprises the Queen in Parliament, and legislation requires the Royal Assent. The reality is different, of course: with the small, if important, and disputed exceptions of the reserve powers, all royal functions of a public nature are exercised on the advice of elected ministers or, in the case of judicial powers, members of the judiciary itself. Nevertheless, the retention of the fiction of royal authority has prevented the occasion arising for reconsideration of the British Constitution in the light of democratic principle, which might have led to formal articulation of the democratic premiss that authority to govern in fact derives from the people.

Democracy under the British Constitution is firmly, even fiercely, representative in character. While there is continuing ambiguity about the nature of the relationship between the representatives and the represented,[16] once elected, MPs collectively become all-powerful, in legal theory. Parliament can override the actions of either of the other two branches of government. It is supreme, in the sense that there is, again in theory, no limit to the legislative power. Government is responsible to the Parliament and may be held to account, if the Parliament has the will to do so. One corollary is that direct popular participation in government through referendum is rare, permitted only in the most extreme circumstances and always accompanied by controversy about whether it is appropriate at all.

2.2. *Effective Government*

One of the principal acknowledged strengths of the British Constitution is its effectiveness, in the sense of producing strong government which in normal circumstances can achieve implementation of its decisions with little hindrance or delay.

The explanation for this achievement lies largely in the institutional structures of the system and the way in which the relationships between them have developed over time. In so far as a particular function lies with the executive alone, it will be exercised by the Crown on the advice of the government, or within the executive branch itself. Foreign policy is a significant and increasingly important example, although municipal implementation of international obligations involves parliamentary approval. Initiatives which require legislation do not normally encounter much greater difficulty, however. The cohesiveness of the political party system in most circumstances can be relied upon to ensure that MPs retain their party allegiance between elections, support government measures, and refrain from public criticism of government action including, in particular, criticism in the all-important forum of the House of Commons itself. Since 1911 the House of Lords has lacked power to do more than delay proposed legislation, and even this power is exercised sparingly.[17] The relative secrecy in which British government is conducted, particularly at the stage of policy formulation and cabinet decision, minimizes impediments to the implementation of decisions from groups outside the public sector.

It is possible to overstate the position. The traditional authority of the Crown to 'be consulted . . . to encourage to warn'[18] inhibits government action to a degree, and in some circumstances may have a substantive effect on the outcome. All governments necessarily have an eye to the electoral impact of their policies and actions, in the interests of their own re-election. Government members on the back bench of the House of Commons may be even more attuned to the likely reaction of the electorate, particularly if they hold marginal seats: their relative quiescence on the floor of the House of Commons, therefore, is not necessarily a feature of deliberations in the privacy of the party room. Backbench MPs have a tendency to take a more independent stance when the government has either a very small parliamentary majority, making individual MPs correspondingly more important, or a very large one. The activities of an independent judiciary and the media further inhibit the freedom of government decision-making.

There are at least two other perspectives, however, from which the effectiveness of British constitutional arrangements are less clear-cut. The first concerns the calibre of government. Adversarial decision-making of the kind found in most common-law political systems is not necessarily conducive to the best decisions in the long term and may tend to produce unnecessarily large policy swings, and hence disruption, with changes in administration. Equally important, the selection of ministers under the parliamentary system as it operates in Britain is confined to parliamentarians. It offers limited, if any, opportunity to introduce into the government people with particular talent or expertise in the wider community who may not be prepared to subject themselves to the time-consuming and occasionally demeaning process of party politics at the constituency level.

Secondly, inefficiency and probable lack of effectiveness results from uncertainty about the rules governing the relationship of bodies within the executive branch itself. The system assumes a neat chain of authority connecting the Crown, the Parliament, and the public service, with the ministers of state the common, pivotal link. In fact, at least at the margin, the rules are unclear about when the Crown will act without or contrary to advice,[19] a circumstance which has caused greater practical disruption in derivatives of the UK system of government than in the country of origin itself.

Even greater uncertainty attends the powers and responsibilities of ministers in relation to public-service agencies. The traditional position, which had the minister as the principal, responsible to Parliament for the activities of agencies, has long since broken down.[20] Ministers may be answerable to Parliament for the acts of agencies within their portfolios, but the ultimate sanction of dismissal or resignation of a minister for agency failings is rare, in consequence of a combination of the *Realpolitik* of the party system and recognition that the complexity of modern government often makes a ministerial sacrifice unfair and, probably, unproductive. The emergence of different forms of public-sector agencies has increasingly complicated the picture further.[21] The traditional relationship is feasible, at least in theory, in application to the departments of state. It may run directly counter to the objectives of other agencies, deliberately designed to operate at arm's length from government to encourage commercial performance or to preserve independence for some other reasons. A lack of clarity over precisely what powers and responsibilities, if any, are possessed by ministers in relation to bodies of these kinds, and doubt about the

adequacy of alternative mechanisms of accountability, has repercussions for the effectiveness of government as well as for the
integrity of the political process.

2.3. Limited Government

The objectives of effective and limited government do not coexist
happily. Any constitutional system seeks to strike an appropriate
balance between the two. Opinions inevitably will differ on the
success of the results. Not surprisingly, then, the British system,
which is noted for its ability to achieve strong government, is also
notorious for the absence of formal checks on government power.
The very features which contribute to the effectiveness of government under the British Constitution also represent a concentration
of final authority beyond that found in many other systems. The
centrepiece is the combination of parliamentary sovereignty with
institutional arrangements under which the executive government
almost invariably controls the decision-making processes of Parliament, in the absence of an overriding constitutional instrument
stipulating limits to which public power is subject and the manner
in which it must be exercised.

The principal limit on the power of government under the British
constitutional system, therefore, comes from the discipline of regular elections, on the basis of a broad franchise, in a polity with
well-established understanding of the consequences of electoral loss
and traditions of a quick and peaceful transition to a new administration. It is a limit which should not be underestimated. Nevertheless, on its own it may be regarded as inadequate, judged by
constitutional standards elsewhere, in at least three respects. First,
it offers no protection of the rights or interests of long-term minorities in the electorate, and even less to those who have no right to
vote. Secondly, it leaves majoritarian democracy itself protected
only by convention and the self-restraint of the majority of the day.
Subject to the extreme possibility of intervention by the Crown,
even such fundamental features of the democratic process as the
length of parliamentary term, the distribution of electorates, and
the franchise are exposed to alteration by a simple Act of Parliament. And, finally, the influence of elections on the exercise of
public power is naturally at its height as an election approaches,

and may have relatively little influence in early or mid-term especially where, as in Britain, the parliamentary term is a long one.

As always, the apparent position is tempered by tradition, convention, and widely accepted but unstated informal constraints, making the export of the British Constitution to other communities more difficult and complex than has often been assumed. It is affected also by other features of the British constitutional system itself. Chief amongst them are the separation of the powers of government and its implications for the rule of law.

There is no formal constitutional separation of powers under the British Constitution. On the contrary, deliberate overlap and interconnection exists between institutions exercising legislative, executive, and judicial powers. Examples include the multiple functions of the lord chancellor, the dual character of the House of Lords, and the need for ministers to become MPs. Nevertheless, under well-established principles which in some cases have the backing of law, core legislative and judicial functions must be exercised by their corresponding institutions, with all the procedural safeguards which that entails. Thus measures which require the authority of Parliament normally secure public exposure before they are implemented, with opportunity for public dissent. Similarly, the adjudication of disputes through the authority of the state is the province of the courts, members of which hold office on conditions designed to secure their independence from the other branches of government.

The independence of the judiciary in turn assists to secure the rule of law, representing another important limitation on the operations of government. As a minimum, the rule of law involves the proposition that government is subject to law, which in Britain includes not only legislation, where construed to bind the Crown, but the principles of the common law. In the hands of the judiciary, the need for executive government to act within the limits of power conferred by statute has been elaborated to place tangible constraints on power, albeit of a largely procedural kind.[22] Subject to statute, the common law also recognizes certain substantive standards to which the exercise of public power prima facie will be assumed to comply.[23] While both the common law and an unpalatable judicial interpretation of statute can be overridden by legislation which is sufficiently clearly expressed, this is not always a practicable political option.

2.4. *Conclusion*

Representative democracy in Britain was achieved through a process of historical evolution which left the outward forms of the Constitution largely untouched, but fundamentally altered their actual operation. In the absence of a formal written instrument, the British Constitution is superficially flexible, even as far as its most basic rules are concerned. One effect of its operation in practice is to concentrate significant power in the hands of executive government, which exercises extensive authority over, and usually controls, the legally sovereign legislature. Aside from convention and political constraints, or the extreme circumstances of the exercise of the reserve power of the Crown, the principal limitations on government in Britain derive from the rule of law, implemented through the courts, and based on the substantive and procedural principles of the common law, to the extent that they have not been superseded by statute.

While in many respects the British Constitution offers a contrast with those of the other countries of Western Europe, their differences can be exaggerated. Statutes are increasingly pervasive as a source of British law, although typically their style is more detailed than in Continental systems. The latter, for their part, now rely more extensively on judicial decision than has been the case in the past. Any tendency of the two systems to assimilate may be hastened by the homogenizing effect of the European Community and the closer integration of Europe as a whole. Already, these have diminished the absolute sovereignty of the British Parliament,[24] introduced a form of superior protection of rights,[25] and complicated the authority of the Parliament to demand an account of administrators acting in relation to British affairs.

Nevertheless, for the moment the continued British emphasis on parliamentary sovereignty and the status and function of the courts remain points of major distinction between the British Constitution and those of most countries of Continental Western Europe. Ironically, they represent inherent contradictions in both systems, which have become more pronounced as dissatisfaction with the practical operation of representative democracy has provided an impetus for a more significant constitutional role for the courts. In Britain, this development has profound implications for the relationship between courts and Parliament. This same tension has long since been evident in most of the constitutional systems derived from the British original, some of which are considered below.

3. DERIVATIONS

The British constitutional model, or particular features of it, have been adopted and adapted for countries throughout the world. While the genealogy may be obvious, each derivative system differs significantly from the original and from the others. In part this is the consequence of the point of time at which the constitution was created and the stage of evolution which the British system had then reached. In part also it is the result of deliberate variation. But in any event, the context in which any constitution operates—including the geographical and demographic size of the polity, its history and tradition, or lack thereof, and the internal and external pressures which it faces—ensures the distinctiveness of that constitution from others, even where they are identical in form.

The process of decolonization left countries with new constitutions derived in some degree from the British model at widely spaced points in time from the eighteenth to the twentieth centuries. Those whose separation occurred in the same period tend to have more characteristics in common: compare, for example, the continued reliance of the nineteenth-century Constitutions of Canada and Australia on conventions to support the operation of responsible government with the attempts at a detailed articulation of the relevant principles in the constitutional systems of the twentieth century.[26] Whatever the date of creation, all share at least two features, however. The first comprises the principles, approach, and institutional structure of the common law. The second is the incipient tension between legislatures and courts, which emerged in most of the derivative systems earlier than in Britain, through the constraints imposed by written constitutions.

This essay traces the evolution of the British Constitution through four later systems: those of the United States, Canada, New Zealand, and Australia. The Constitution of the United States took its basic form at the end of the eighteenth century, and those of the other countries at various times over the ensuing century and a quarter.[27] They have been chosen for this purpose because the circumstances of the countries concerned have greater similarity with those of Britain than is the case with others whose constitutions also are based on the Britain model. Initially, at least, the bulk of the population of each of these countries was of British descent. This, and the economic and social conditions which they came quickly to enjoy, endowed them with comparable expectations of a constitutional system, narrowing the range of variations which might have affected their constitutional evolution and increasing the likelihood that any conclusions may be more widely applicable.

The four constitutions are nevertheless very different in a variety of ways. All except New Zealand are federations, necessitating written constitutions beyond the power of a single level of government, and hence a single parliament, to amend. The USA and Canada provide protection for civil and political rights in those same constitutions;[28] and New Zealand does so through a statute which is rapidly becoming quasi-constitutional in character.[29] A further feature of the Constitution of the USA, which is unique in this company, is the separation of legislative from executive power in the sense that the chief executive, the president, is directly elected and does not owe office to the majority in the legislature, leading to other consequential differences of a constitutional kind.[30] All four countries have indigenous populations with traditions of governance which do not accord with many of the assumptions of Western systems, and which pose some problems of reconciliation as these communities assert their right to self-government.[31]

3.1. Democratic Government

Each of the countries chosen is a representative democracy, in the sense that the legislature and, directly or indirectly, the executive branch of government is elected by the people. In the three federations of the USA, Canada, and Australia, however, the democracy is of a more complex kind.

Provision for the election of both national and sub-national governments, each with absolute authority within constitutionally assigned spheres, on one view enhances and on another view detracts from representative democracy in the sense of majority rule. It also contributes, although not exclusively, to variations in the constitutional system which makes departure from the British paradigm inevitable. Among them are reliance on a written constitution with the status of fundamental law, judicial review of the constitutional validity of legislation, a correspondingly limited conception of parliamentary sovereignty, and a bicameral legislature in which power is more evenly distributed between the two houses. In both the USA and Australia, the upper house or Senate is elected and designed to represent the sub-national units equally.[32] Whatever doubts may be raised about their actual federal role, these features give both these chambers a degree of legitimacy in government which is denied to the Canadian Senate: a position which presumably will continue, following the failure of proposals for an elected, equal, and effective Senate in the form embodied in the Charlottetown Accord in 1992.[33] As one consequence of their status, the US and Australian Senates have significant powers in relation to all forms of legislation, and can frustrate the will of a lower house elected on a population basis.[34] The extent to which this has implications for democracy again depends on the conception of democracy that is accepted, particularly within a federal structure. The phenomenon is not confined to constitutional systems in the common-law tradition, as the examples of Germany and Switzerland show.

In Canada, Australia, and New Zealand, the particular form of representative democracy adopted is responsible government, superficially along Westminster lines. In these countries, in other words, the government is appointed from and responsible to the legislature: in that sense, it is indirectly elected. By contrast, the president of the USA is directly elected for a fixed term, and holds office independently of the House of Representatives and the Senate, members of which also are elected for a specified period.[35] The interconnection between the legislative and executive branches, which contributes to the checks and balances which characterize the exercise of government power in the USA, may hinder action, but does not detract from the fundamentally democratic nature of the system.

Partly in response to concerns about the implications for national majoritarian democracy of the constraints imposed by federalism and constitutional guarantees of rights, the concept of democracy has been the subject of reflection, amplification, and qualification in the jurisprudence of each of these countries. Ironically, at the same time, the central characteristics of majoritarian democracy have been given protection by the very features of the constitutional system which might be alleged to erode the basic principle. The entrenched Constitutions of the USA, Canada, and Australia limit the length of term of elected office, thus securing the requirement for regular elections from intrusion by a current but insecure majority in the legislature.[36] Despite broad adherence to the institutions of parliamentary government, some Australian jurisdictions also have moved to limit the discretion of the leader of the government to choose the timing of an election, through constitutional restrictions on dissolution before the final year of the parliamentary term except in rare, specified circumstances.[37] Guarantees of political rights in the USA, Canada, and New Zealand also give protection to the right to vote and to the popularly representative basis of electoral districts.[38] In Australia, the latter has been implied from a constitutional provision requiring the House of Representatives to be 'directly chosen by the people'.[39] By a parallel process of reasoning, the Australian High Court recently recognized also the existence of constitutional limits on the power of the Commonwealth Parliament to restrict political speech as an attribute of representative democracy.[40] The potentially far-reaching debate to which this has given rise, about those elements of a democratic system which should be designed to transcend the will of a current majority, has particular importance in a political tradition which so far has assumed that individual and collective rights can best be protected through the democratic process.[41]

Canada, Australia, and New Zealand have retained the principle of parliamentary sovereignty and the attitudes which it engenders. In the case of Canada and Australia, with their entrenched, overriding constitutions, parliamentary sovereignty necessarily takes a modified form, creating conflicts which surface from time to time in both political pronouncements and judicial doctrine. The principle could not survive the separation of powers in the USA, which assumes that the powers of Congress are subject to constitutional restrictions, including those which assign functions to the executive which cannot be usurped by the legislative branch.[42] Even so, there is a familiar tension between Congress and the courts exercising the function of judicial review of the constitutionality of legislation, flowing rather from the deference that is expected or due from the unelected to decisions of the elected branches of government, than from any legal notion of legislative supremacy. The separation of legislative and executive power in the USA also provided an opportunity to reconsider the content of each, which was taken at least to the extent that the US Senate has a role in the ratification of international treaties and of major public appointments.[43]

Canada, New Zealand, and Australia retain the Crown as the head of state, represented in each country and in sub-national jurisdictions by a personal representative of the Queen. Superficially, the arrangements are the same as in Britain: namely, formal authority is vested in and flows from the Crown, but is exercised in a manner consistent with democratic principle, on the advice of elected representatives. While the link with Britain was initially colonial in nature, each of these countries has gradually acquired complete independence, with consequential adjustment to the principles of constitutional monarchy and, incidentally, some erosion of the sovereignty of the British Parliament.[44] Thus the Queen is now specifically designated Queen of Canada, New Zealand, and Australia. The personal representatives of the Crown in each country are appointed by the Queen on the advice of the leader of the government concerned.[45] Both the Queen and her personal representatives act on the advice of local ministers in matters affecting that jurisdiction, with no involvement of the British government.[46] And the circumstances in which the Queen will act personally at all have become limited by law or convention, leaving the personal representative of the Crown the effective head of state in each case.[47]

As in Britain, one effect of this process of constitutional evolution has been to leave nominal power in the head of state, obscuring the fact that legitimacy, and hence ultimate authority, flows from the people. By contrast, the Constitution of the United States formally recognizes popular sovereignty, with consequences which may reverberate throughout the system.[48] The implications of the monarchy for democratic government may in fact be greater in the newer constitutional systems than in Britain, through differences in the way in which it works in practice. For whatever reason, the possibility of intervention of the Crown in political affairs may be more real in these countries. The chief evidence comes from Australia, where two notorious examples can be cited[49] and several lesser ones suggest that uncertainty about the scope of the reserve powers is an element in political strategy employed by government and opposition alike.[50]

One explanation may be that the head of state representing the Crown is appointed for a term of years and therefore does not risk the entire institution of the monarchy by precipitate action. Another may be that advisers in these countries are less affected by the constraints which traditionally have influenced their counterparts in Britain in dealing with the Queen. In consequence, some advice which is tendered may be questionable, posing a dilemma for the Crown which cannot satisfactorily be resolved.[51] Articulation of the powers of the Crown in written constitutions, however general in their terms, also may encourage closer, legalistic scrutiny of their precise scope, with results that broaden, rather than limit, their operation. No such difficulties arise in the USA, where the Constitution confers substantive power on the president, deliberately created as both effective and ceremonial head of state.

The traditions of representative democracy as they have evolved in Britain have been modified in these constitutional systems in one other respect as well: a more ready acceptance of the direct participation of the electorate in fundamental public decisions. In the USA, this phenomenon is confined to the state and local levels of government, where election of judges and other public officials, the constitutional and legislative referendum, the popular initiative, and popular recall are familiar instruments. In Australia, consistently with the approval of the initial federal Constitution by a popular vote in all federating colonies,[52] constitutional amendment also requires a popular referendum, which has become part of the Australian political culture.[53] Similarly in Canada and New Zealand, greater resistance to the use of the referendum, on grounds comparable to those often advanced in Britain, seems to be breaking down. In Canada, the sweeping proposals for constitutional amendment in the Charlottetown Accord were put to a popular vote in 1992 as a result of a political decision that it was necessary to do so before the formal amending procedure, involving the federal and provincial legislatures, was attempted. Despite rejection of the proposals, those events prompted speculation that the referendum had now effectively been entrenched as a prerequisite for constitutional change.[54] A recent referendum on the electoral system in New Zealand, followed by another on the same subject in 1993, provides evidence of an emerging acceptance in that country as well that, whatever the traditional assumptions and internal coherence of representative government modelled along British lines, there are some fundamental issues on which either community pressure or political comfort requires the support of a popular vote.

3.2. Effective Government

The deliberate separation of legislative and executive power in the US Constitution affects the manner in which the goal of effectiveness is pursued in that country. To the extent that decision-making is stymied by deadlocks between the president and the Congress, it also affects its achievement. Contemporary evidence nevertheless supports the view that the framers of the Constitution had the effectiveness of the system in mind, and sought to achieve it through the direct election of a president on whom executive powers were constitutionally conferred.[55] As experience has shown, the result from time to time in fact depends on a range of factors, including the personality of the president and the circumstances with which the US government is called upon to deal, in addition, more obviously, to the inclinations of the majority in each house of the Congress. The question whether British or US-style government is more conducive to strong decision-making and more at risk of transformation to authoritarianism is a pressing one for new democracies throughout the world—in Eastern Europe, the former Soviet Union, and Africa. The lesson of comparative constitutionalism so far is that it cannot be answered in the abstract, but depends on the political, economic, and cultural context in which the constitution will be required to work.

The adoption of the institutions of responsible government in Canada, New Zealand, and Australia, in political conditions roughly comparable to those of Britain itself, suggests that a similar measure of effectiveness in government might be expected in those countries as well, in the sense of the speedy implementation of executive decisions, through the Crown or legislative enactment. In many respects, this is so. Typically, in all three countries the government enjoys a secure majority in the popular chamber of the legislature. Typically also, the party system is strong and cohesive and does not tolerate public dissent from its members. If anything, the discipline wielded over back-bench members is greater, in part because of their relatively smaller numbers and their correspondingly more rational expectations of ministerial preferment. Further, whatever unanswered questions there may be in these systems about the scope of the reserve powers of the Crown, where day-to-day executive government is concerned it is clear that no hindrance can be expected in practice from the Crown, and little from the legislature. The tendency for executive power to become more rather than less significant as the medium for the implementation of public policy has further streamlined the process in this regard.[56]

On the other hand, there are features of the constitutional systems of all these countries which modify the British model and affect its operation. Most obvious is the federal division of power in the USA, Canada, and Australia, ensuring that no single level of government can act in relation to all matters. One reaction in Canada and Australia has been the proliferation of intergovernmental co-operation, made possible to a degree that could not be achieved in the USA by executive domination of the legislatures, ultimately having profound implications for the accountability of governments to parliaments.[57] In the USA, much of the practical inconvenience of divided power has been dealt with through a broad judicial interpretation of the powers of Congress, justified by a majority of the Supreme Court on the basis that federal institutions were themselves designed to preserve the federal system, obviating the intervention of the court.[58]

Another inhibition on action by some governments lies in the power of upper houses of bicameral legislatures to prevent passage of legislation, scrutinize government and administration more rigorously than can usually be expected from the popular chamber, and, in extreme circumstances, force an election and the removal of a government. Upper houses currently exist in Canada and Australia and in most Australian states, but not in New Zealand, where the upper house was abolished in 1949. There is wide variation both between the powers of all these chambers and between their willingness to use them. The Australian Senate is undoubtedly the most active, although by no means as vigorous and self-confident as the US Senate, on which it was roughly modelled. Constitutional or legislative guarantees of rights in Canada and New Zealand, judicial review of legislation as well as executive action in Canada and Australia, and far greater insistence on openness in government are further modifications of the British model in all these countries which affect the speed and ease of the implementation of government decisions, although not necessarily their quality.

The earlier discussion of the British Constitution mentioned aspects of its operation which detracted from effectiveness in a broader sense. They included the consequences of adversarial decision-making, the calibre of those attracted to and able to obtain prominent positions in government, and the uncertainty of lines of responsibility and accountability in an increasingly diverse public sector. These points apply with at least equal force to the responsible-government model elsewhere in the world. If anything, in the systems here under consideration, uncertainty about public-sector accountability and appropriate structures is even more pronounced: in Canada, because of the influence of the US model on the evolution of its public agencies; in Australia, because of the tradition of reliance on agencies ostensibly at arm's length from the normal political processes;[59] and in New Zealand, through experimentation with models of commercialized public enterprise, often in transition to private enterprise which, however controversial, is already having an impact on comparable movements elsewhere.[60]

In the USA the picture is different in most respects. A positive attribute of that Constitution, admired but probably beyond emulation in practice by parliamentary models, is its ability to draw into government, by appointment rather than by election, for the term of the current administration, people with a high degree of experience and skill in key areas. Nor is the USA plagued by uncertainties about the rules of collective and ministerial responsibility and their implications for the structure of the public service, although constitutional distinctions between the powers of the president and Congress create conflicts and uncertainties of their own.[61] The US model, in its own way, nevertheless is as adversarial in its politics as its common-law parliamentary counterparts, despite the relatively less cohesive discipline to which the elected representatives of the two main parties are subject. If anything, the established tradition of sweeping change in the upper echelons of all government agencies with each new administration accentuates the winner-take-all nature of the system to a degree not yet achieved by the parliamentary models, inexorably but without clear design drifting in that direction.

3.3. Limited Government

A hallmark of the British constitutional system is the absence of constraints on government with the status of fundamental law. From the standpoint of law, the result is to concentrate power in the executive branch, through a combination of the principles of parliamentary sovereignty and the institutions of responsible government, under the influence of a small number of tightly disciplined political parties. This rather simplistic picture, however, is qualified to a degree by institutional and behavioural checks which may lack legal force but which have the sanctions of tradition and long-standing practice. They include the separation of the functions of government, at least in broad outline; the independence of the judiciary; its role in review of the lawfulness of executive action; the central, if formal, role of the parliament in public decision-making; the influence of an unaligned and professional public service; the authority and latent powers of the Crown; even, in extreme circumstances, opposition from the House of Lords within the very limited ambit of the functions remaining to it.

Leaving aside the American Constitution, which for this purpose again is in a category of its own, the constitutional systems of Canada, New Zealand, and Australia have the same basic features which in Britain lay the ground for executive domination of government: the need for the ministry to have and retain the confidence of the legislature, coupled with assumptions about the supremacy of executive action. Nevertheless, examination of the scope of the constraints on government yields significantly different results.

In some respects, the constraints are even less. While more detailed work is needed, actual practice in all countries suggests that the influence of tradition is less, with implications for the status of the parliaments, relations between the judiciary and other branches of government, expectations of the public service, and the extent of the involvement of the Crown in political affairs. At the same time, however, although in different ways, the constitutional systems of each of these countries incorporate a range of formal legal and institutional checks on power of a kind notoriously absent in Britain. Most represent a deliberate modification of the British system: federalism in Canada and Australia; guarantees of rights in Canada and New Zealand; upper houses of Australian legislatures; reformed mechanisms for independent review of administrative action in Australia and New Zealand;[62] and the acceptance of the need for greater openness in government in all three countries. Others are the inadvertent consequence of the prescription of the institutional framework for government in a written, entrenched constitution. The effect is most obvious in Australia, where, for example, the constitutional separation of federal judicial power[63] precludes parliamentary interference with both the tenure of judges[64] and the jurisdiction of the High Court to hear administrative law cases involving an 'officer of the Commonwealth'.[65]

The limitations on government under the US Constitution are consistent with the philosophy of its framers. Elsewhere, however, the limitations were less deliberate, with varying implications for the integrity of the system. Federalism was the result of circumstance in Canada and Australia. Other constraints followed inexorably in its wake. The most obvious were the entrenched constitutions and judicial review of the constitutionality of legislation. In Australia, a powerful Senate and the constitutional separation of judicial power[66] on one view are consequences of federalism as well. Some of the other constraints are reactions against the concentration of power which a common-law parliamentary system in the Western tradition represents, but without fundamental reassessment of the system itself. The Canadian Charter of Rights and Freedoms and, to a lesser degree, the New Zealand Bill of Rights Act 1990 fall into this category.

Whether the product of circumstance or design, each of these features contradicts to a degree fundamental assumptions of the British Constitution about the prerogatives of elected governments and the supremacy of the Crown in Parliament. The tension manifests itself in both judicial doctrine and political disputation. It is not solely attributable to British-style parliamentary government but stems also from the underlying conflict between the status of representative institutions and courts in a common-law system.

Even in the USA, where limited government is a deliberate choice, the boundaries of power between Congress and the courts is a controversial question.

The point may be illustrated by reference to different categories of constraints, in each of the countries concerned. The clash with federal principle is most evident in Australia, where the reluctance of the High Court to impose limits on Commonwealth power can be traced, at least in part, to deference to the decisions of the national Parliament under conditions of responsible government.[67] Whatever its natural predilections may have been, there has been no comparable course of development in Canada, where the method of the allocation of power, in lists exclusive to the dominion and the provinces respectively, placed constitutional limits on the expansion of each through judicial interpretation.[68]

Consistently with this, and perhaps also in response to the influence of the USA, the Canadian constitutional system has adapted more readily than its heritage may have suggested to the 1982 constitutional entrenchment of rights and freedoms. Debate about the propriety of judicial decisions, individually and collectively, is vigorous in Canada, but appears to have more to do with democratic principle generally than with a specific concern for parliamentary sovereignty and the rights of elected governments. By contrast, Australia so far has resisted the notion of judicially enforced rights, ostensibly preferring to rely on highly traditional assumptions about parliamentary government. Under similar influences, New Zealand represents a half-way house, with a Bill of Rights with legislative status, constraining executive action and imposing moral if not legal restraints on inconsistent action by the New Zealand Parliament.

Internal conflict between inherited principles and more recent constitutional innovations is evidenced in political discourse as well. Such conflict appears regularly in connection with the function and powers of upper houses in bicameral legislatures, although it could be illustrated also in relation to administrative law reforms and the creation of rights of access to government information. The Australian Senate provides a case in point. The Senate has not played the federal role for which it was designed, largely because Senators, almost from the outset, displayed greater allegiance to the parties of which they were members and on which their preselection depended. The Senate has, however, proved a moderately effective house of review, as an unexpected by-product of the introduction of proportional representation in 1949, making it difficult except in rare circumstances for either major party to hold a majority of Senate places. To the extent that systematic parliamentary scrutiny of proposed legislation and government action occurs at all, it is confined to the Senate. Nevertheless, neither the theory nor the practice of Australian politics has adequately adapted to the presence of the Senate, which continues to be treated as an excrescence on responsible government. Similar vacillation between adherence to traditional forms of responsible government and recognition of the contribution that an upper house may make to the effectiveness of the institution of parliament is evident in the current debate in Canada and New Zealand as well, so far without producing change in the *status quo* in this regard. From the standpoint of the criterion of limited government, each of the parliamentary models under examination in this part is in a state of some indecision and flux. The conceptual difficulties are less in the USA, where limited government was an overt goal. They appear to have less effect in Canada as well, possibly because the influence of the USA in that country is greater than generally acknowledged. But in Australia and New Zealand, the characteristic concentration of power produced by the Westminster model has been the object of concern which, once met, raises further questions for the integrity of the system. The debate is far from over. In New Zealand, mechanisms to improve the effectiveness of the institution of Parliament are actively under examination, including radical changes to the electoral system and, perhaps, reintroduction of an upper house. And in Australia, reconsideration of the role of Parliament and of mechanisms for the protection of fundamental values is attracting increasing attention in the approach to the centenary of federation.[69]

4. CONCLUSION

On the threshold of the twenty-first century, the influence of the British constitutional system is evident in countries around the world. For common-law countries it is, and has been, one of the great constitutional models, with the US Constitution its only obvious rival. Nevertheless, it is under stress. It is almost inevitable that major adaptation will be required to meet the conditions of the future.

The uncertainties and tensions in the British-style constitutional model tend to be more obvious in the derivative systems than in Britain itself. They include disagreement about the outer limits of the powers of the Crown; lack of clarity concerning the lines of accountability between ministers, public-sector agencies, and parliaments, in the complex circumstances of modern government; a tendency to politicization of the public service; differing and irreconcilable views about such fundamental aspects of representative democracy as the role of parliament, the responsibility of elected members of it, and the propriety of direct popular involvement; and mounting conflict between the elected branches of governments and increasingly creative courts.

Most of these problems are latent in the system and have been evident, albeit in a lesser form, for some time. They cannot continue indefinitely, however, without affecting the performance of governments and their credibility in the eyes of the communities which they represent. Attempts to devise remedies so far have been *ad hoc* and have not resolved underlying problems. Other pressures likely to emerge in the future may create the opportunity to do so.

One would be transition from a monarchical to a republican form of government, forcing attention to the powers of the head of state and, more importantly, requiring replacement of the Crown as the formal source of authority to govern. Another may be the rapidly developing internationalization of public decision-making and basic norms for the constitution and actions of governments. At the level of Western Europe, this process has already caused significant modification to fundamental tenets of the British Constitution. Similar consequences can be expected in the other countries considered here. In all except the USA, reconsideration is already overdue of the assumption that entry into international arrangements is an executive prerogative, postponing the role of the legislature to the process of implementation. In a country such as Australia which, following Britain, hitherto has eschewed constitutional protection of individual rights, these developments may produce more profound consequences still. Already, Australian ratification of the first optional protocol to the International Covenant on Civil and Political Rights has affected the decisions of

Australian courts[70] and may cause a re-examination of mechanisms for the domestic protection of basic rights. Whether that should be achieved through judicialization, or improvements in the political process, or both, are questions which are likely to be at the forefront of the public debate in the immediate future.

The role of the courts in a common-law system gives constitutional issues a distinctive character in those countries. But at another, more general level, the pressures that have become catalysts for change under common-law constitutions exist elsewhere as well. The novel challenges of internationalization are not confined to common-law countries. Dissatisfaction with the performance of representative government is widespread in Western democracies. One reaction is an enhanced constitutional role for the courts, even in civil-law countries with very different judicial traditions. The tendency of these two seminal legal systems to borrow from and to drift towards each other, given impetus by their proximity in the European community, increasingly may be evidenced in the constitutional context as well.

Notes

1. *Prohibitions del Roy* (1607) 12 Co. Rep. 63; *Case of Proclamations* (1611) 12 Co. Rep. 74.
2. Bill of Rights 1689.
3. An Instrument of Government was produced during the Commonwealth, in 1653.
4. e.g. the preamble to the Bill of Rights 1689: '. . . the said lords spiritual and temporal and commons . . . do in the first place (as their ancestors in like case have usually done) for the indicating and asserting their ancient rights and liberties, declare . . .'.
5. e.g. the protection of judicial tenure originally achieved in the Act of Settlement 1701.
6. S. de Smith and R. Brazier, *Constitutional and Administrative Law*, 6th edn. (Harmondsworth: Penguin, 1989), 70–3.
7. M. Cappelletti, P. J. Kollmer, and J. M. Olson, *The Judicial Process in Comparative Perspective* (Oxford: Clarendon Press, 1989).
8. Parliament Act 1911.
9. Parliament Act 1911; Parliament Act 1949. The limitations do not apply to bills extending the duration of the House of Commons beyond 5 years.

10. In particular, the speculation and negotiations leading to the debate in the House of Commons on 4 Nov. 1992.
11. Bill of Rights 1689.
12. Erskine May, *Parliamentary Practice*, 18th edn. (1971), 683.
13. *Case of Proclamations* (1611) 12 Co. Rep. 74.
14. A. V. Dicey, *Introduction to the Study of the Law of the Constitution*, 10th edn. (London: Macmillan, 1959), 424.
15. de Smith and Brazier, *Constitutional and Administrative Law*, 132–3.
16. Cf. the concept of the MP as trustee and as delegate: Hugh Berrington, 'MPs and their Constituents in Britain: The History of the Relationship', in Vernon Bogdanor (ed.), *Representatives of the People* (Aldershot: Gower, 1985), 15.
17. de Smith and Brazier, *Constitutional and Administrative Law*, 305–6.
18. W. Bagehot, *The English Constitution* (1915; London: Fontana, 1963), 111.
19. G. Marshall, *Constitutional Conventions* (Oxford: Clarendon Press, 1984), ch. 2.
20. C. Turpin, 'Ministerial Responsibility: Myth or Reality?' in J. Jowell and D. Oliver (eds.), *The Changing Constitution*, 2nd edn. (1989), 53–86.
21. N. Lewis, 'Regulating Non-Government Bodies: Privatisation, Accountability and the Public–Private Divide', in Jowell and Oliver, *The Changing Constitution*, 219–45.
22. *Padfield* v. *Minister of Agriculture* [1968] AC 997.
23. D. Pearce, *Statutory Interpretation in Australia*, 3rd edn. (1988), 104, citing the presumption that legislation does not alter common-law doctrines.
24. European Communities Act 1972.
25. In accordance with the provisions of the European Convention on Human Rights.
26. S. de Smith, *The New Commonwealth and Its Constitutions* (London: Stevens, 1964).
27. British North America Act 1867, New Zealand Constitution Act 1852, Commonwealth of Australia Constitution Act 1901.
28. Constitution of the United States, Amendments i–x; Canadian Charter of Rights and Freedoms 1982.
29. New Zealand Bill of Rights Act 1990.
30. Art. 2, sect. 1.
31. For an overview of the constitutional framework, see Senate Standing Committee on Constitutional and Legal Affairs of the Commonwealth Parliament, *Two Hundred Years Later . . .*, Parliamentary Paper 107 (1983), 50–8.
32. Constitution of the United States, art. 1, sect. 3; Commonwealth Constitution, sect. 7.
33. *Consensus Report on the Constitution* (Charlottetown, Aug. 1992).

34. Constitution of the United States, art. 1, sect. 7; Commonwealth Constitution, sect. 53.
35. Constitution of the United States, art. 2, sect. 1.
36. Ibid., art. 1, sects. 2, 3; art. 2, sect. 1; Canadian Charter of Rights and Freedoms, sect. 4; Commonwealth Constitution, sect. 28.
37. Constitution Act 1975 (Vic), sect. 8; Constitution Act 1934 (SA), sect. 28a.
38. Constitution of the United States, art. 1, sect. 2; Canadian Charter of Rights and Freedoms, sect. 3; New Zealand Bill of Rights Act 1990, sect. 11.
39. *Attorney-General (Cth); ex rel. McKinley* v. *Commonwealth* (1975) 135 CLR 1.
40. *Australian Capital Television Pty Ltd* v. *Commonwealth* (No. 2), 55 of 1992 (unreported).
41. e.g. Justice John Toohey, 'A Government of Laws, and Not of Men?', paper presented to the conference on Constitutional Change in the 1990s, Darwin, 4–6 Oct. 1992.
42. L. Fisher, *Constitutional Conflicts between Congress and the President* (Princeton, NJ: Princeton University Press, 1985).
43. Constitution of the United States, art. 2, sect. 2.
44. Statute of Westminster 1931; Canada Act 1982; Australia Act 1986.
45. *Proceedings of the Imperial Conference 1930*, Cmd. 3717 (London, HMSO).
46. *Summary of the Proceedings of the Imperial Conference 1926*, extracted in C. Howard and C. Saunders, *Cases and Materials in Constitutional Law* (1976), 30–2.
47. A rule which is made explicit in relation to the Australian States in the Australia Act 1986, sect. 7.
48. Thus the preamble: 'We the People of the United States . . . do ordain and establish this Constitution . . .'.
49. The dismissal of Premier Lang by Sir Phillip Game in 1926 and of Prime Minister Whitlam by Sir John Kerr in 1975.
50. I. Killey, 'Tasmania: A New Convention', (1991) 2 *Public Law Review* 221.
51. The Australian Constitutional Convention sought to deal with this in its articulation of constitutional practices by placing a duty on the relevant minister to give proper advice: 'Report of the Structure of Government Sub-Committee to the Standing Committee', Aug. 1984, in *Proceedings of the Australian Constitutional Convention 1985* (Brisbane: Govt. Printers), ii.
52. As required by the Enabling Acts, passed in all colonies.
53. Commonwealth Constitution, sect. 128.
54. T. Courchene, 'After the No: A Search for a New Order', *Toronto Globe and Mail*, 27 Oct. 1992.
55. Fisher, *Constitutional Conflicts*, 11.

56. T. Daintith, 'The Executive Power Today: Bargaining and Economic Control', in Jowell and Oliver, *The Changing Constitution*, 193–218.
57. C. Saunders, 'Accountability and Access in Intergovernmental Affairs: A Legal Perspective', in *Papers on Federalism*, 2 (University of Melbourne Press, 1982).
58. *Garcia* v. *San Antonio Metropolitan Transit Authority* 469 US 528 (1985).
59. D. P. Gracey, *Report on Ministerial Responsibility and Public Bodies in Australia* (Public Bodies Review Committee, 1981).
60. M. Taggart, 'Corporation, Privatisation and Public Law', (1991) 2 *Public Law Review* 77.
61. Fisher, *Constitutional Conflicts*, chs. 2, 3, 8, 9.
62. In Australia, the interpreted administrative review system introduced from 1975, comprising the Administrative Appeals Tribunal Act 1975; the Ombudsman Act 1976; and the Administrative Decisions (Judicial Review) Act 1977. In New Zealand, the Ombudsman Act 1975.
63. *R* v. *Kirby; ex parte Boilermakers' Society of Australia* (1956) 94 CLR 254.
64. Commonwealth Constitution, sect. 72.
65. Ibid., sect. 75(v).
66. *R* v. *Kirby; ex parte Boilermakers' Society of Australia* (1956) 94 CLR 254.
67. *Amalgamated Society of Engineers* v. *Adelaide Steamship* Co. (1920) 28 CLR 129.
68. Constitution Act 1867, sects. 91, 92.
69. 'Final Statement of the Constitutional Centenary Conference 1991', (1991) 2 *Public Law Review* 151.
70. *Mabo* v. *Queensland* (1992) 66 *Australian Law Journal Reports* 408.

5

Patterns of Constitutional Evolution and Change in Eastern Europe

ULRICH K. PREUSS

1. CONSTITUTIONALISM

1.1. Its Uncertain Meaning

Constitutions are not all alike. They differ according to the tradition, physical, economic, and social conditions, world-view, culture, and historical experience of a people which gives itself a constitution. Despite this diversity of constitutions, it is justifiable to claim a universally valid concept of constitutio*nalism*: a set of ideas and principles which form the common basis of the rich variety of constitutions. According to probably the most commonplace understanding, constitutionalism embraces essentially the idea of limited government.[1] Although this meaning is undoubtedly an indispensable ingredient of constitutionalism, it does not fully grasp its principle. It would suggest that the constitution plays a purely negative and defensive role in the polity. In fact, if we are not willing to conceive of political power as an existential, unrationalized, and unfathomable fact of life which originates and persists prior to any kind of cultural rationalization, we must realize the constituent and constitutive role of the constitution for political power. In this sense Holmes rightly claims that liberal constitutionalism, the prototype of the power-restricting function of constitutionalism, 'aims not only at obstructing sovereign power, but also at organizing and even creating sovereign power'.[2] He views the separation of powers or the guarantee of individual rights—the main institutional devices for the realization of the limiting force of constitutions—as creative devices because they

increase the functional specialization and the sensitivity of the political system to social problems.

In a somewhat pointed manner we may say that the idea of constitutionalism is neutral *vis-à-vis* the amount of power, whereas it is very much concerned about the mediation, civilization, and rationalization of political power—which does not necessarily mean to minimize it. The criterion by which to distinguish constitutional from absolutist, authoritarian, or totalitarian states is not the amount of power but its quality. The property of a constitutional state consists in the subjection of its political power to rules which claim validity as legal norms, and which are implemented by specialized law-enforcement agencies (particularly courts, including constitutional courts). Essentially, therefore, constitutionalism embraces the idea of the normative penetration of the polity to the effect that its institutions continue and operate irrespective of changing majorities and of the vacillations of politics in general— it is the idea of normative supremacy and continuity. This bears the implication that political decision-making and the processing of social conflicts, including the conflicts between the individual and the government, are subject to a class of legal rules which claim supreme legal validity and which we call a constitution. Constitutionalism means that the authority of a government is not wielded according to the will and the arbitrariness of men but according to legal rules—rule of law rather than of men. Thus a constitution is not just a manifesto or a political programme, nor a merely factual description of the state of a polity, nor the pure political will of the sovereign or of the ruling élite(s), but the embodiment of a legally enforceable normative programme which generates legal obligations both for the rulers and for the ruled. The character of this normative programme varies considerably according to the specific historical experience, tradition, and hopes of a country: it may have a rather limited scope, in that it contains no more than an organizational device for the operation of the machinery of government, or it may (as is typical of constitutions of liberal democracies) set out both a bill of rights and the major principles of government, or it may (as I shall demonstrate below) in addition to that include elements of policy programmes such as positive individual rights to labour, shelter, health, etc.

Some other properties are frequently associated with the concept of constitutionalism: that constitutions are laid down in written documents and hence embody the unequivocal certainty of the supreme legal principles in one single and coherent text; that they are the supreme law of the land and hence obligate not only the executive branch of government but the legislature as well; that they contain a bill of rights; and, finally, that they define the scope of admissible ends, means, and strategies of individuals and groups pursuing their interests and realizing their values. However, none of these characteristics is an indispensable element of the idea of constitutionalism, at least not of what we conventionally would be ready to accept as constitutionalism. For instance, the British political system, which was the first to be shaped according to the concept of constitutionalism and which is rightly regarded as the source of modern constitutionalism, has no written constitution, no bill of rights, does not accept the supremacy of the constitution over the Parliament, and does not define the scope of political ends and means.[3] This latter property applies to the US Constitution and a great number of other modern constitutions as well. And whereas the French Declaration of Rights of Men and Citizens of 26 August 1789 preceded the first post-revolutionary French Constitution by about two years, the reverse order, as is generally known, took place in the USA; there, the Constitution was enacted without a bill of rights, which was supplemented only two years later with the first ten amendments (which were ratified in 1791). The German Imperial Constitution of 1871 had no bill of rights whatsoever because its authors and framers, the princely sovereigns of Germany and Bismarck, aspired to no more than a mere legal framework for the operation of the state organization and for the smooth co-operation between the Reich and the states (*Länder*). This constitution was not even based on the principle of popular sovereignty which today is rightly regarded as an essential premiss of any kind of constitution.

These examples clearly show that there is as yet no clear indication of the likely course of the East European countries' quest for constitutionalism. There are simply too many alternatives. In order to understand their options and to develop criteria according to which they can make reasonable choices, it seems appropriate to add some considerations about the functions which constitutions may exercise. To elucidate their variety and their latent tensions may help us to understand the serious conditions under which the main actors in the post-communist countries have to make their choices.

1.2. Its Various Functions

The idea of constitutionalism encompasses such a wide range of varieties that one may doubt whether this term can be used in a meaningful manner. If we want to compare different patterns of constitutionalism and the underlying ideas of constitutions in different parts of the world, it is probably not very fruitful—for the understanding either of the single constitutions or of the prevailing meaning of constitutionalism—to enumerate the manifold properties and divergences in the respective legal texts. It seems more appropriate to inquire into the functions which constitutions perform in their respective countries. This is not easy to achieve, however, because in the developmental history of constitutionalism its social functions have become ever more complex.

Its basic and original function has been the *limitation of power*, be it the feudal power of the king *vis-à-vis* his noble vassals or be it the sovereign power of the absolutist state over its subjects.[4] As Stephen Holmes has suggested, this function of a constitution has a Janus face. Besides its purely negative and defensive dimension, it also plays a positive role. We may call this the *authorizing function* of the constitution. This function is clearly predominant in constitutions which are very much concerned with the maintenance of the integrity of a homogeneous state power—such as the aforementioned German Imperial Constitution. But the framers of the US Constitution were also very much worried about the construction of a superior power of the Union.[5]

Under certain conditions, the purely negative function of a constitution can extend into a device of *power-sharing* between social forces none of which has the strength to assert a monopoly of authority. In the Middle Ages, contracts between princes, feudal rulers, and cities were the predominant form of institutionalizing domination—here constitutions were social compacts of the ruling élites. But in modern times also it has happened that constitutions were contracted (and negotiated). Most prominent is the so-called 'Stinnes–Legien Agreement', negotiated in 1918–19 between the presidents of the German industrial association and the unions, which laid the groundwork for the transition of revolutionary Germany to the constitutional state of the Weimar Republic. The essential content of this compact—the acknowledgement of independent workers' unions and the right to strike (in exchange for the renunciation of the unions' ambitions for a socialist economy)—was later included in the Weimar Constitution.[6] Another more recent example of a power-sharing constitution is the Round Table agreement which the then communist government of Poland concluded with the Solidarity movement.[7] Also the negotiations in South Africa between the white government and the representatives of the black majority finally engendered a constitutional device of some kind of power-sharing.

Social contracts over power-sharing point to another function of constitutions—to their capacity to *legitimize political authority*. A constitution such as the Magna Charta Libertatum, which restricts the ruler's power, neither challenged nor legitimized his rule—its legitimacy was presupposed and entrenched in the structures of the feudal-Catholic pre-modern world. The power of the modern state, however, requires a secular justification. And while, in the perspective of political theology, the people and its sovereign power have replaced an almighty God, it is the constitution which supplants the Holy Scripture.[8] It has become constitutive for the exercise of legitimate authority. Nowadays almost the only legitimizing principle which nearly all modern constitutions solemnly declare is the principle of popular sovereignty. As I shall elaborate below, this principle is in itself so powerful that it is prone to endanger the legitimation which is conveyed by the constitution—in the political culture of some countries there is a certain tension, if not hostility, between constitutionalism and democracy.

Closely related to this legitimizing function is the *integrative function* of many modern constitutions. Constitutions contribute to the integration of a society if they embody the goals, aspirations, values, and basic beliefs which that society's members commonly hold and which bind them together. In this case a constitution may serve as a kind of secular catechism.[9] The most apparent property of constitutions which are very much attentive to their integrative function is their more or less detailed catalogue of state goals, and the concomitant guarantee of so-called social rights. I speak of the teleological character of a constitution when I refer to these policy-oriented components.

It may be said, therefore, that the limiting and the authorizing functions of a constitution relate to its contradictory role in erecting a strong political power and at the same time limiting and domesticating that power. Under conditions of radical political change, such a combination of limiting and authorizing elements may entail a power-sharing constitution. However, for contemporary societies the legitimizing and the integrative functions become ever more significant, in that the legitimizing function contains the reasons which justify the citizens' duty to obey their government, whereas the integrative function contains the reasons why the citizens fulfil duties of solidarity towards each other.

Not all constitutions perform simultaneously all of these functions, nor do they always harmonize. They may even collide, to the point where a constitution breaks down if the relation of the different functions is not balanced. For instance, one of the reasons for the unremitting stress and the final collapse of the Weimar Constitution was the unbalanced relation between its legitimizing and its integrative functions: whereas the democratic principle was the essential and strongly emphasized legitimizing foundation of the Constitution, its integrative function was rather weak because it did not provide institutional devices which would encourage social and political co-operation of dissenting political forces. On the contrary, the distribution of powers between the parliament, the government, and the president (who was elected by popular vote) proved to be highly disintegrative. Another tension between the legitimizing and the integrative function may arise if the constitution stipulates many policy goals in great detail, to the extent that the democratic legislature has almost no political discretion and dwindles to a mere executor of fixed constitutional goals. In such a case, the constitution-giving generation would deprive all succeeding generations of their right to democratic self-determination[10] and hence undermine the legitimizing function of a constitution.

Others claim, for instance, that the integrative function of a teleological constitution—one which contains social rights and policy goals—is incompatible with the limiting function of the constitution, because the fulfilment of the constitutional promises requires permanent interventions into the economic and social sphere, and hence entails permanent interferences with citizens' liberty.[11] Indeed, liberal constitutions which are predominantly concerned with the protection of liberty through the restraint of state power shun the promulgation of social and economic benefits, or of social rights which would commit the state to interventionist policies. Moreover, constitutions which accentuate the teleological dimension have to cope with problems of an unbalanced power distribution between the legislature, the executive, and the judiciary. Both social rights and state goals increase the power of the executive—which has the resources to design and to implement particular policies—and that of the courts—which make the final decision about the constitutional duties of the government—at the expense of the democratic authority of the parliament. This shift of power may result in a preference of teleological constitutions for an executive president over a parliamentary government.[12] However, the question—if indeed there is such a structural affinity—needs further analysis. The following overview of features of newly enacted or drafted constitutions in post-communist countries of East Europe gives some hints to this effect.

2. 'TELEOLOGICAL' CONSTITUTIONS AS *ERSATZ* FOR CIVIL SOCIETY?

Generally speaking, we may hypothesize that constitutions which are very much concerned with the problem of social integration tend to weaken their legitimizing function, in that they rely more on the integrating and beneficial effects of constitutional pledges and the ensuing policies which they envision than on the purely procedural rights of citizens to participate in the democratic process of will-formation. In a country with a long history of constitutionalism which is deeply rooted in its political culture—such as Britain or the USA—the tensions between the different functions of a constitution are of minor importance. There is a gradual progression of consecutive steps which include the formation of the modern state, the emergence of a civil society, the privatization/ marketization of the economy, the establishment of a constitution which safeguards rights to freedom (later also rights to political participation), and, finally, the generation of the welfare state, with its bundle of legal rights to social benefits. The last step, the creation of the welfare state, largely happened within the framework of the constitutional state: it was not itself a constitutional change, nor was it commanded by the respective constitution.

In contrast to these ingrained constitutional democracies, both the Weimar Constitution contained and the Basic Law contains welfare state pledges and guarantees. Whereas the Weimar Constitution was fairly specific, the Basic Law contented itself with the general clause of the 'social state'. But this state goal has a prominent place in the constitution, in that it is associated with the fundamental principles of rule of law, democracy, and federalism (Article 20). Hence it takes part in the so-called 'eternity guarantee' of Article 79, paragraph 3, which declares as inadmissible amendments to the Basic Law affecting, among others, the basic principles of Article 20. Interestingly enough, Germany has a somewhat shady record with respect to its constitutional history. There are good reasons for Germany to be less certain of the compatibility of its political culture with the principles of constitutionalism and of the robustness of its political institutions than, for example, Britain or the USA. As a 'belated nation'[13] the processes of nation-building, of constitution-building (including institution-building), and of the marketization of the economy not only did not always harmonize, but were opposed to each other for long periods. Many students of the German Basic Law claim that the constitutional stipulation of the 'social state' goal has a very restricted relevance, if any, for the real development of the welfare state in Germany.[14] This assertion may be true, but it misses the point. It overlooks the significance that such an integrating constitutional formula may have in terms of compensating for the lack of a continual and consecutive— though not always peaceful—formation of a nation-state and of a democratic constitution.

In this respect the situation of many of the post-communist countries of Eastern and Central Europe is even worse. Given the fact that many of them are either internally or externally heterogeneous—i.e., according to Jon Elster's definition,[15] they contain either non-negligible numbers of members of several peoples, or they have one dominant people, and non-negligible numbers of that people who live outside their borders—their existence as a nation-state is all but undisputed. As a consequence, they have to accomplish the separate processes of marketization of the economy, nation-building, and establishing constitutional democracy, for which other countries needed centuries or at least decades, at the same time.[16]

An inquiry into their constitutions or the drafts[17] shows a strong inclination to determine particular constitutional pledges, such as the right to safe and healthy working conditions, to annual paid leave, to social security in case of sickness, invalidity, old age, and unemployment, the right to the 'enjoyment of the highest attainable standard of physical and mental health' (Poland),[18] the right to education, and the 'right to a healthy and favourable environment corresponding to the established standards and norms' (Bulgaria).[19] There seems to be a significant correlation between the dearth of a long-standing and firm constitutional tradition and the preference for teleological constitutions. Thus we can point to three categories of constitutional states: those with a long and continuous tradition like Britain and the USA; a country with an erratic constitutional development like Germany; and finally the post-communist countries of East and Central Europe which have to achieve the nation-state, a civil society with a private economy, and democratic structures at the same time. If a rough comparison of them is made, it is striking that the number of pledges—be they state goals or social rights—increases in inverse proportion to the extent that these countries are able and prepared to establish a welfare state and a standard of environmental protection which could compare even with the least developed West European member states of the EEC.

This hypothesis is supported by the draft of the constitution of the Republic of Kazakhstan, a country which has become an independent state for the first time in its history. This draft[20] not only contains the familiar social rights and state goals, adding the right to a home (which is not included in the constitutions quoted above), but further stipulates, in a separate chapter about 'fundamental objectives' of the state, its obligation *inter alia* to 'enact policies aimed at protecting property rights, at the development of free entrepreneurial activity and at securing social support for citizens', to 'assist the rebirth and development of the culture, traditions and language of the Kazakh nation', and to 'create conditions which accord high prestige to government service' (Article 62). Evidently, here the constitution is an essential part of the simultaneous processes of nation-building, of generating a market sphere, of establishing legality and the rule of law, and of creating the main features of democratic rule.

None of these indispensable elements of a modern society can be taken for granted in these countries, and hence the constitution cannot simply refer to a given set of rules, institutions, social practices, and cultural patterns; they must be devised and antici-pated in a written text which tends to acquire the status of a secular catechism. This character of a constitution, where the authorizing, the legitimizing, and the integrative functions almost coincide—that is, where the extremely critical and unstable steps to economic freedom and to democratic self-rule are supposed to become the founding elements of a polity, rather than evolving from the secure base of a nation-state—is arguably pivotal for the evolution of a nation. On the other hand, a constitution which is burdened with too many legal claims is exposed to the danger of collapse. The concentration of all political, economic, social, and cultural aspir-ations in a document which claims unconditional and unqualified legal force may well entail a normative devaluation, just as any inflation is only a particular expression of depreciation. This, then, would render the constitution a political manifesto and hence fail to meet the requirements of constitutionalism.

However, it is not at all clear whether constitutions—like most of those which have been or will be enacted in the post-communist countries of East and Central Europe—which serve as a kind of surrogate for the non-availability of a steady development as a nation-state are doomed to fail, and to degenerate to mere political manifestos. At first glance, the two main prototypes of modern constitutionalism—the US Constitution of 1787–9 and the French Constitution of 1791—were created in similar situations. In par-ticular, the creation of the US Constitution was at the same time the creation of the United States;[21] and the birth of the modern French nation cannot be conceived of without the process of constitution-making which began in June 1789. But there is one important difference between these traditional constitutional states and the new states which aspire to constitutionalism: while the former could restrict their endeavours to organizing or reorganizing re-spectively the state power and to setting limits to the sphere of influence of individuals and of civil society, the latter have simulta-neously to create both the constitutional structure of state power—

including, among other things, the separation of power and the efficiency and integrity of a civil service—and the basic institutions of the very civil society which in a constitutional state is not only protected and shielded against state power but is supposed to actively interact with it.[22] In a way, this is only another aspect of the great demands which are made on the constitutions of countries which have simultaneously to create the constitution itself and its most important prerequisites.

3. THE ROLE OF 'INSTITUTIONAL GUARANTEES'

Paradoxically, the poorer the conditions for the thriving of a constitution appear, the higher such demands become. If we consider a scale which reaches from the most traditional and stable constitutional states—Great Britain and the USA—through France and Germany to the post-communist countries of Eastern Europe, and inquire about their constitutions with special consideration of their respective social and economic models, we find that constitutions are more explicit and even eloquent about this point the less entrenched they are. British constitutional law is predominantly concerned with the problems of sovereignty, legitimacy, and accountability and lacks, as is generally known, a bill of rights.[23] This does not, of course, mean that the British Constitution is not based on an underlying model of society, or that it can be understood properly without a particular concept of society;[24] rather, the model is tacitly implied in the functioning of the institutions, which is one of the reasons for their often-remarked flexibility. In contrast, the US Constitution encompasses a bill of rights and thus contains, as a bill of rights is supposed to do, individual liberties. Neither the bill of rights nor the other parts of the constitution draw the picture of a particular social structure, although the history of American legal concepts and of interpretations of the American Constitution clearly reflects distinct 'social models' and their changes in the course of development.[25]

In a liberal-capitalist society private property, the family, and the right of inheritance are the basic social institutions which pre-date the constitution. None of these three institutions is the subject of a particular constitutional guarantee in the American Bill of Rights (not to mention the unwritten British Constitution). True, private property is mentioned in the Fifth Amendment of the US Constitution, but, interestingly enough, it is not guaranteed as a *social institution*. Rather, the constitutional protection of property is restricted to the protection of individuals against taking of property without due process and without just compensation.[26] This was the meaning of the right to property in all bourgeois-liberal constitutions of the eighteenth and nineteenth centuries.[27] Traditional constitutionalism does not deal with social institutions, but with individuals and their rights. It was the Weimar Constitution and the constitutional doctrine of the Weimar era which generated a new category of constitutional concepts, namely the concept of 'institutional guarantees', as opposed to subjective rights of individuals.[28] Private property, marriage and family, the right to inheritance, but also the civil service and the autonomy of the municipalities and of the universities were considered to be guaranteed as objective social institutions. Although institutional guarantees were not subjective (or individual) rights, it was possible to derive such rights. In fact, institutional guarantees had expressly been devised in order to corroborate the rights of the individuals in the respective spheres. For instance, the institutional guarantee of private property enlarged the protection of private owners, in that it inhibited the nationalization of particular categories of property like land or industrial means of production.[29]

Not quite accidentally, this doctrine, whose theoretical groundwork had been laid by French and Italian theorists,[30] flourished in Germany at a time when the very foundations of the liberal-capitalist society were in a critical condition. The political, social, and cultural shocks of the Nazi era and of the war even entailed an extension of the scope of 'institutional guarantees'. Deeply felt economic, social, cultural, and political insecurities, in addition to changes in the role of the modern state, generated the yearning for state guarantees which surpassed the traditional protection of individual liberties and tended increasingly to include the economic and social conditions which made it possible for individuals to make use of these rights in the first place. Beyond the aforementioned institutions of private property, marriage, family, self-government of the municipalities, the universities, and the like, the Basic Law established the political institution of party competition and pluralism[31] (i.e. it embedded the freedom to establish parties into an institutional framework). Elsewhere it established, although less explicitly, the basic institutions of a system of collective bargaining.[32] There was even the attempt to interpret the Basic Law as guaranteeing a system of a 'social market economy'. Although the Constitutional Court rejected this interpretation,[33] the idea that the Constitution constitutes and protects not just individual rights but establishes particular social fields of action which enjoy the protection and, eventually, also promotion by the state, has become an unquestioned part of German constitutional doctrine and practice.[34]

Profound analysis would be necessary in order to explicate why the new constitutional category of institutional guarantees has gained an ever-increasing relevance in some of the most recent constitutions. I suggest the hypothesis (which is, of course, not meant to be exhaustive) that the weakness or even complete absence of cohesive forces in the social texture—in other words, the underdevelopment of a differentiated non-statist economic, social, and cultural infrastructure—is offset by the state's guarantee either to create and organize functional equivalents or to support the existing weak dispositions. Institutional guarantees would then represent a distinctive model of state–civil society co-operation in which the state takes the responsibility for the accomplishment of social functions of institutions which, with a few exceptions, are genuinely societal in character.[35] The German case of the Weimar Constitution and of the Basic Law may serve as an illustration, although this is, of course, not conclusive evidence. Similarly, in the case of Spain a constitutional state was established on the foundations of the dried-out societal soil left by a forty-year dictatorial regime. The Spanish Constitution, which was widely influenced by the German Basic Law, went even further with regard to institutional guarantees. It did not content itself with establishing the state's protection of private property, the family, the right to inheritance, and the right to create political parties. It extended this guarantee to the concomitant framework in which these institutions are supposed to operate: sections 1 and 6 expressly declare 'political pluralism' as one of the basic constitutional values, and thus political parties are guaranteed as 'the expression of political pluralism'. Pluralism is not the effect of the exercise of the citizens' rights to political freedom, but rather something which has to be encouraged, promoted, perhaps even created by the state. As a consequence the citizens' rights follow from pluralism, not vice versa. Elsewhere, 'free enterprise' is recognized 'within the framework of a market economy' (section 38), and, in contrast to the German Basic Law, the system of collective bargaining as a basic institution of economic and social policy is explicitly determined in section 37.

Not surprisingly, similar elements can be traced in the constitutions or draft constitutions of post-communist countries in East and Central Europe. The first draft of the treaty between the Federal Republic of Germany and the German Democratic Republic about a currency union, devised in the early summer of 1990, departed from the constitutional doctrine of West Germany in so far as it established the 'social market economy' as a legally binding economic system for the GDR (which at that time was expected to last for a few years). This tendency is thoroughly elaborated in the constitutions of Hungary and Bulgaria, the two countries which were the first among the post-communist countries in East and Central Europe to enact new constitutions after the collapse of the old regime, whether in a piecemeal manner through a great number of successive amendments to the communist constitution, as in Hungary,[36] or by drafting and enacting a completely new constitution.[37] Thus the Constitution of Hungary declares in Article 15 that the 'Republic of Hungary shall protect the institutions of marriage and family', a wording which is very close to that used by the Bulgarian Constitution (Article 14). In both constitutions the rights to property and inheritance are explicitly guaranteed (Articles 13, 14, Hungary; Article 17, Bulgaria). Significantly, in neither of the two constitutions are these provisions placed where one would expect them according to the traditional structure of constitutions, namely in the chapter about the fundamental rights and duties; rather, they are laid down in the first chapter, concerning 'General Provisions' (Hungary) or 'Fundamental Principles' (Bulgaria), which specify the basic goals and structural elements of the polity. Thus, in both constitutions the right to property is framed by provisions which determine that 'the economy . . . is a market economy where public and private ownership shall be equally respected and enjoy equal protection', and that the state recognizes and supports 'the right of undertaking and free economic competition' (Article 9, Hungary). The analogous provision in the Bulgarian Constitution reads as follows: 'the economy of the Republic ... shall be based on free economic initiative' (Article 19).

There are further institutional guarantees, such as those of trade unions and other associations which represent and protect the interests of employees, members of co-operatives, and entrepreneurs (Article 4, Hungary), or provisions about political parties. As in the case of the German Basic Law, in neither constitution is the acknowledgement of political parties limited to the individual right to establish organizations and associations for any purpose not prohibited by law—this right is guaranteed separately in the respective chapters about individual rights (Article 63, Hungary; Article 44, Bulgaria)—but has the additional meaning to determine the functional capacity which political parties have to accomplish in a democratic society, namely to take part in and to facilitate the formation and expression of the will of the people (Article 3, paragraph 2, Hungary; Article 11, paragraph 3, Bulgaria).[38] The Bulgarian Constitution explicitly states that 'politics in the Republic ... shall be founded on the principle of political plurality' (Article 11, paragraph 1). Similarly, the Romanian Constitution declares that 'pluralism is a condition and a guarantee of constitutional democracy' (Article 8, paragraph 1). This is, of course, not meant to be an empirical statement, but a normative pledge of the state to guarantee the manifold prerequisites of a pluralist political system. In view of our conventional wisdom this is clearly a paradox: the state guarantees the conditions of a civil society in order to check the penetrating power of the state.

It is worth mentioning here that some Hungarian constitutional scholars dismissed the idea of regulating political parties through the constitution, arguing 'that the power of the party cannot be regulated by public legal means, but only through the functioning of the political system'.[39] This alternative clearly points to the inherent reason for this kind of institutional guarantees: since, after forty years of communist party dictatorship in these societies, one cannot rely on a normal 'functioning of the political system', this very functioning must be, so to speak, 'artificially' established and guaranteed by means of state power.

With regard to the institutional guarantee of a pluralist party system, two provisions of the Bulgarian Constitution are worth mentioning. The first is the unique rule of Article 12, paragraph 2, according to which 'citizens' associations, including trade unions, shall not pursue political objectives, nor shall they engage in any political activity which is in the domain of the political parties'. The second, which is a clear reference to the problem of the Turkish minority, prohibits the formation of political parties on ethnic, racial, or religious lines (Article 11, paragraph 4). In both cases it is clear that the attempt to devise a complete system of political pluralism and competition has meant that individual and collective rights have been transformed into dependent variables of the functional imperatives of this very system. Paradoxically, the guarantee of a system of political pluralism is considered to be incompatible with fully fledged freedom of association for all citizens. This is an indication that the constitutional guarantee of social institutions or of functional relations may be able to offset, to a certain degree, the lack of a basic texture of an autonomous civil society, but a considerable price has to be paid, namely the price of a strong state control over the democratic life.

4. THE CONCEPT OF CITIZENSHIP

So far I have mentioned only those institutional guarantees which pertain either to the socio-economic elements of society or to the organization of public authority, regarding property, the right to inheritance, the family, local self-government, the civil service, and so forth. But some constitutional rules point in another direction. In Article 13, paragraph 3 of the Bulgarian Constitution, Eastern Orthodox Christianity is considered 'the traditional religion in the Republic of Bulgaria', a somewhat surprising rule in view of the freedom of religion determined in paragraph 1 and the separation of state and church established in paragraph 2 of the same article. It is an institutional guarantee which voices the importance of the Orthodox Church for the architecture of the newly founded polity. It can be assumed that the constitutional recognition of Orthodox Christianity as the traditional religion in (not of) Bulgaria pursues the aim to use this religion as an integrative means for the formation of the Bulgarian polity. Hence it is a primary concern of the new political élites to overcome the political alienation of the citizens and to conciliate them with the new political order (and with politics altogether).

Indeed, the new constitutions in Eastern and Central Europe are very attentive to the problem of how to determine the constitutive elements of citizenship. Historical experience teaches that the incorporation of rules about acquiring, keeping, and losing citizenship in the constitution is normally due to extraordinary conditions, where the need to emphasize the integrative forces of the polity is strongly felt. In 'normal' times these rules are established by statutory law. Only the Hungarian Constitution contents itself with the determination that the regulation of citizenship is a matter of the law. However, even in this country the importance of this law is highlighted by the requirement of two-thirds of the vote of the attending National Assembly representatives (Article 69, paragraph 4). The Romanian Constitution refers to the pertinent organic law when addressing the problem of how to acquire, preserve, and lose Romanian citizenship. By speaking of Romanians outside the country's borders who are also citizens of another country, the Constitution itself clearly opts for the principle of origin and descent as the primary reason for acquiring Romanian citizenship (see Articles 5, 7). The most explicit rules can be found in the Sejm draft of the Polish Constitution and in the Bulgarian Constitution. Both determine the *ius sanguinis* as the basic (albeit not necessarily exclusive) origin of citizenship (Article 23, Poland;[40] Article 25, Bulgaria). Finally, a particular rule is laid down in the draft Constitution of Kazakhstan which determines that the principles and procedure for acquiring, keeping, and losing citizenship of the Republic have to be set down in constitutional law. To be sure, the rules mentioned so far pertain to the more formal dimension of citizenship, namely to nationality in the sense of belonging to or being member of a particular sovereign state. There are other rules which have a deeper meaning, in that they circumscribe the elements of membership in a national community. In the framework of this concept of membership nationality (in the formal sense mentioned above) is a necessary but by no means sufficient condition.

4.1. Criteria of Membership

Article 3 of the Bulgarian Constitution determines that 'Bulgarian shall be the official language of the Republic'. This rule is corroborated by Article 36, paragraph 1, which stipulates that 'the study and use of the Bulgarian language shall be a right and an obligation of every Bulgarian citizen'. Not only does the Constitution contain an institutional guarantee of the Bulgarian language; at the same time it defines the Bulgarian language as a constitutive element of Bulgarian citizenship. Evidently these rules refer to the multi-ethnic character of the Bulgarian population. The same applies to Romania, a country in which a relatively strong Hungarian and a small German minority have settled, not to speak of the Gypsies. Not surprisingly, the Romanian Constitution expressly orders Romanian to be the official language of the country (Article 13). A similar rule applies, for instance, to Estonia.[41] The Estonian election law, adopted by referendum, mandates that only those who were citizens of Estonia in 1940 or who are their direct descendants are entitled to vote. As a consequence, 42 per cent of Estonia's population were excluded from suffrage in the national elections of 20 September 1992: mostly Russians, Ukrainians, and Belorussians who settled in Estonia during the Soviet occupation and want to remain there. The Estonians have offered the Russians the opportunity to acquire Estonian citizenship by fulfilling residency requirements and passing an Estonian language test.[42] These are two examples of a constitutional pattern which is fairly widespread in Eastern and Central Europe, and whose underlying conceptual presuppositions have far-reaching consequences.

As is generally known and as was referred to above, almost all post-communist countries of East and Central Europe are, to use Elster's terminology, either internally or externally heterogeneous. The territorial boundaries of their respective polities do not coincide with the geographical place of settlement of the peoples. There is no coincidence of the nation (as a pre-political category) and the nation-state. Individuals subject to the laws of a particular nation-state may not feel that they are part of the dominant people of this country. In this case citizenship and belonging to or membership of a nation are separated. Conflicts of loyalty between state laws and affiliation to one's people can easily arise, in particular if the minority in one country is the dominant people of another nation-state. This is why the establishment of rules which determine the rights and duties of the individuals *vis-à-vis* the state and demarcate their obligations or loyalties towards their nation is of paramount significance. While a state which encompasses two or

more peoples is possible (and not infrequent), it is extremely difficult to realize multinational citizenship.[43] However, it would be
wrong to assume that the definition of citizenship is a particular
problem of multinational states. Citizenship is a basic institution of
any modern state, and it is all the more important as the modern
nation-state has been assigning rights and duties largely (though
not exclusively) along the line of citizen/non-citizen (the non-citizen
being the foreigner). True, in the territorial states which in Europe
emerged in the seventeenth and eighteenth centuries,[44] relations of
membership existed before the emergence of the nation-state, but
they were of minor significance.[45] Citizenship became the key to
access to rights which the nation-state had solemnly bestowed on
its citizens. Hence, the definition of the status of citizenship is an
indispensable part of any constitution.

As I said above, not all constitutions contain a definition of
citizenship; however, the underlying concept is always implicitly
referred to and presupposed. These concepts vary to a considerable
degree. A radically universalist notion of citizenship which is rooted
in the tenets of the French Revolution claims that all individuals
who are commonly subject to the same government and the same
laws form a nation.[46] According to this meaning, citizenship is a
more or less physical relation of the individual to the nation in that,
ideally, permanent residence in the respective country would constitute belonging to this country—the nation would then be the entirety of the people living continuously in the country. The
acquisition of citizenship *iure soli* would be the only legitimate
generation of citizenship. Needless to say, this ideal type of citizenship nowhere applies.[47] Its realization would be the most extreme
version of a concept of citizenship which tends towards self-
dissolution, in that it aspires to treat all individuals equally—as
human beings rather than as members of a particular nation.

There is an antithetical tradition whose proponents claim that
the nation is a community which exists prior to the nation-state, i.e.
prior to the national community which rests on the fact that individuals are equally subject to a common government and common
laws. This is the perspective that presently is being discussed under
the label of 'communitarianism'.[48] In this view the nation is a
community whose members share common beliefs, language, history, etc.—it is, so to speak, a community of fate. Consequently,
citizenship is a very demanding kind of membership: it is imbued

with the collective identity of the community which is based on specific and particular norms and values. Neither the individualistic concept of mutual advantage nor the universalist idea of the brotherhood of man applies; rather, citizenship encompasses special obligations to one's compatriots[49] and to the community as well. The predominant rule of acquiring citizenship according to this concept is the *ius sanguinis*.

Universalist claims are part of moral discourses which aim at justice and whose results must be universally applicable. Their question is: what is 'good for all'? In contrast, questions which pertain to the identity of a particular group are part of ethical discourses in which a common understanding is sought about what is 'good for us'. They seek an answer to the question of 'who we are and who we seriously want to be'.[50] Depending on the character of the predominant question in a society, the concept of citizenship will oscillate between being more universalist or more communitarian. This can be demonstrated with regard to the relevance of civic duties. In the framework of the universalist concept of citizenship, civic duties have no independent conceptual and political status. They are the reverse side of the equal right to freedom, and demand no more than respect for the equal freedom of others which is preserved by laws; hence compliance with the law which regulates the compatibility of individual liberties is the principal, perhaps even the only, civic duty within a universalist concept of citizenship.[51] No additional loyalties are required. In contrast, the concept of civic duties which include particular obligations to a particular class of people or to the community as such can only arise in the framework of a communitarian understanding of nation and citizenship. An answer to the question of 'who we are and who we seriously want to be' presupposes a high degree of responsibility for the thriving of the community and its capacity to preserve its collective identity. This is the proper soil for the generation of duties of mutual solidarity.

4.2. The Predominance of 'Communitarian' Concepts of Citizenship in East and Central Europe

To be sure, both the universalist and the communitarian notion of citizenship are based on the concept of the nation-state. The Declaration of the Rights of Man and Citizen was proclaimed by a revolutionary people that had constituted itself as a nation-state. Hence this universalist concept of citizenship is no less exclusive than that of the communitarians.[52] But while, ideally, the former excludes according to the criterion of who is physically part of a society, the latter makes a distinction between the physical and the social, in particular the ethnic belonging of an individual to the community. According to the former, the territorial boundaries are more or less the social boundaries of membership. This is the very essence of the *ius soli*. In contrast, the *ius sanguinis* draws boundaries which refer to a variety of non-physical individual properties which converge in the idea of descent.[53]

However, even countries which distribute citizenship according to the *ius soli* do not fully disregard the criterion of descent. The US immigration law extends the right to acquire US citizenship beyond the boundaries drawn by the Fourteenth Amendment.[54] But ultimately the criterion for acquiring American citizenship is permanent residence in the USA, so that the distinction between US citizens and ethnic Americans who have the right to American citizenship does not emerge. The relevance of this distinction increases the more one looks in the direction of Eastern Europe. In Germany, where the principle of *ius sanguinis* is followed, it is the Basic Law itself which makes the distinction between German citizens and ethnic Germans. According to Article 116 and the pertinent laws, ethnic Germans who do not possess German citizenship have the right to acquire it, whereas it is a matter of broad governmental discretion to grant German citizenship to foreigners. This is more or less the international standard in a world of nation-states: it is generally regarded as a matter of national sovereignty whether or not to grant citizenship to aliens, whereas the scope of political discretion and of acting according to criteria of expediency is considerably restricted with regard to individuals who have a closer relation to a state's people on the ground of descent. This principle is expressly stipulated in Article 25, paragraph 2, of the Bulgarian Constitution, whose rule can be regarded as paradigmatic for most of the states in the world: 'A person of Bulgarian origin shall acquire Bulgarian citizenship through a facilitated procedure.'

While, as I stated, the substance of this rule is not uncommon, its incorporation in Western constitutions is rather unusual. Whenever the criterion of descent is included in the constitution as a distinctive element of citizenship, this is an indication that an ethnic understanding of the nation prevails. But while ethnicity is then obviously regarded as an integrative element of the nation-state, it is at the same time also a divisive force. To cope with this ambiguity of ethnicity is one of the most difficult tasks of the polity. This may explain why many East European constitutions are significantly attentive to the problem of multi-ethnicity. Constitutional rules about the official language of the state nurture the impression that the co-existence of different languages—and eventually of different nations—is a serious problem. Whenever universalist rights and liberties, i.e. rights and liberties which are granted irrespective of ethnic affiliation, are supplemented by rules which grant rights by virtue of ethnic affiliation, i.e. by virtue of particularistic and exclusive criteria, the constitution contains tension which eventually may create major obstacles to the political and social coherence of the country. On the other hand, it could be even more divisive not to mention and to recognize ethnic affiliations and not to grant rights which protect and promote them. This is particularly true with respect to ethnic minorities.

Indeed, the new East and Central European constitutions deal with the widespread occurrence of individuals and groups defining themselves in terms of their origin. Thus, the Sejm draft of the Polish Constitution establishes the right of everyone 'to preserve his/her national and ethnic identity' (Article 15, paragraph 1).[55] Similar rules are included in the Bulgarian and the Romanian Constitutions, namely everybody's right to develop his or her culture in accordance with his or her 'ethnic self-identification' (Article 54, Bulgaria), or the right for members of the national minorities to 'preserve, develop, and express their ethnic, cultural, linguistic, and religious identity' (Article 6, Romania). In all three cases the protection of ethnic or national minorities is a purely individual right. But whereas the Polish draft recognizes the right of national or ethnic minorities to 'preserve their distinctive character' (Article 15, paragraph 2), both the Bulgarian and the Romanian Constitutions avoid pledging any group rights. On the contrary, the Bulgarian rule quoted above about the right and duty to use the Bulgarian language and about the prohibition on forming political parties along ethnic lines displays the concern of ethnic Bulgarians to maintain their hegemony over the Turkish minority. Moreover, the

Romanian Constitution expressly cautions the government not to take protective measures in favour of members of national minorities which violate the 'principle of equality and non-discrimination in relation to the other Romanian citizens' (Article 6, paragraph 2). The concern for national identity in both the Bulgarian and the Romanian Constitutions is also displayed in provisions according to which foreigners cannot acquire ownership over land (Bulgaria, Article 22, paragraph 1; Romania, Article 41, paragraph 2. ii).

With regard to national or ethnic minorities, Hungary's constitution is different from both Bulgaria's and Romania's. Articles 68 and 69 of the Hungarian Constitution declare national and ethnic minorities as 'constituent factors of the state'. They grant members of such groups the right to foster their culture, to use their mother tongue, and to receive school instruction in their language. But there is no individual right to ethnic or national self-identification (whatever this may mean). On the other hand, the Republic of Hungary recognizes its responsibility toward Hungarians outside the borders of the country (Article 6, paragraph 3). A similar reference to the compatriots abroad is made in the Romanian Constitution (Article 7).

It is far from clear whether the post-communist countries of East and Central Europe will succeed in reconciling the universalist principles of the nation-state with the simultaneously cohesive and divisive forces of ethnic self-definition and self-identification in their multi-ethnic countries. In order to fully understand their constitutions we must first of all understand that there *is* this tension, and that this tension is likely to determine the understanding of the constitution. For instance, a communitarian concept of citizenship is very much more concerned with civic duties than a universalist notion. The duties to defend the country, to pay taxes proportionately to one's income and property, or to assist the state and society in cases of disaster can be found in all constitutions or draft constitutions of East European countries (which are presently available to me). It is noteworthy that the Romanian Constitution furthermore declares 'loyalty to the country . . . a sacred duty' (Article 50, paragraph 1). Although communist constitutions also contained a long list of social duties of individuals, the stipulation of civic duties in the new constitutions must not be misunderstood as a relic of the communist past. Communist duties were political duties, i.e. they were owed to the state, which was dominated by the party monopoly. Moreover, they made an appeal to an abstract ideal of solidarity in that they invoked the universality of mankind as the ultimate obligating rationale. In contrast, the concept of communitarian duties embodies an idea of mutuality and social solidarity which creates obligations to 'one's own people', i.e. to a community which exists prior to any kind of political organization. To put it another way, communitarian duties have an obligating force only because they can refer to pre-political bonds. A political community which is based on universalist principles cannot create duties other than those which follow from the principle of equal freedom—the duty not to interfere with the like freedom of one's fellow-citizen. This is why the constitutions of the traditional constitutional states do not stipulate civic duties. The fact that most of the new constitutions of the countries of East and Central Europe do establish civic duties is a clear indication of their communitarian concept of citizenship.

Two additional remarks seem appropriate. First, the duties mentioned above by no means exist only in the countries of Eastern and Central Europe; in varying forms they exist in all modern states. What is particular to duties in the countries of Eastern and Central Europe is their status as constitutional duties, i.e. their character as separate and independent obligations. They cannot be conceived as mere after-effects of the universalist principle of equal liberty. In the traditional constitutional states these duties are established by law because the law is the appropriate instrument to safeguard the compatibility of the equal liberties of the individuals. These duties are rooted in an individualistic notion of liberty. In contrast, the obligatory force of communitarian duties as established in the constitution is rooted in an ideal of social solidarity.

Second, the communitarian concept of citizenship is by no means restricted to Eastern Europe. We can find it wherever tension between the universalist claims of a nation-state (and its homogenizing force) and the self-identification of individuals and groups in particularistic terms of ethnicity enters the sphere of politics. For instance, the Spanish Constitution of 1978 establishes rules about the 'official language' and the protection of national minorities, and it is also committed to the idea of including the duties of the citizens in the Constitution. In this respect it is very similar to the constitutions of Eastern Europe mentioned so far.

5. SOME PRELIMINARY CONCLUSIONS

Social and economic state goals, social rights, institutional guarantees, and a communitarian concept of citizenship are the main properties of the constitutional development in Eastern and Central Europe which have been investigated in this chapter. Although the analysis is by no means exhaustive, it is possible to draw some conclusions about the character of East and Central European constitutions which may deepen our general understanding of constitutionalism. As a matter of fact, none of the said constitutions limits itself merely to establishing more or less neutral institutions, leaving the pursuit of goals and values to the individuals and to non-statist collectivities.[56] Despite discernible differences among the available constitutions or draft constitutions respectively, there is a significant preference for a communitarian concept of constitutionalism, as opposed to a rights-based concept. Or, to phrase it in the framework of contemporary debates in the field of political philosophy, in the alternative between a political concept of the 'right' or of the 'good',[57] or between justice and community, they opt in both cases for the latter rather than for the former. To be sure, neither rights nor justice are dismissed in these concepts. The extensive bills of rights, including social rights, and the numerous state goals mentioned above bear sufficient evidence of the Eastern European constitution-makers' concern for both rights and social justice. The differences between rights-based and a communitarian concept lie in their divergent assumptions about the relations between the individuals and the society in which they live.[58] In the former concept, individuals are valued in their capacity as human beings who deserve support and assistance according to universal principles, i.e. according to rules which apply to anyone. In contrast, the latter conceives of the individual as a member of a particular community whose values and goals are shaped by this very community. The community is constitutive of the individual's identity, and therefore it cannot be dismissed should the question arise as to which kind of justice is appropriate. In this case, individuals have particular obligations to each other (as opposed to universally valid ones), namely those which affirm and support the individual's membership in and duties to the community.

The preference for economic and social state goals and individual social rights is not limited to communitarians. Egalitarian liberals concur; but they derive their commitment to the principle of social equality from universalist criteria of justice (such as those proposed by Rawls) and reject the idea of a particular justice for the members of particular communities. Both egalitarian liberals and communitarians know, of course, that the accomplishment of a welfare state's goals is a matter of economic and social policies rather than of constitutional rights. To include them in the constitution can even have negative consequences, in that it overstates the role of the judiciary at the expense of the democratic process. Therefore, many liberals who are clearly in favour of a welfare state pattern of social justice rely more on the effectiveness of economic and social policies than on what, in their view, is a more or less symbolic juridification of social rights and policy goals in the constitution. However, the incorporation in the constitution of social rights and pledges to policies dedicated to the principle of social justice can have a meaning which is not so much concerned with efficacy and the balance of the constitutional architecture as with the integrative force of a broad notion of citizenship. T. H. Marshall's concept of citizenship which includes civil, political, and social rights[59] is probably the most influential elaboration of a concept in which the individual's share in the wealth of a country is constitutive of his or her status as a citizen.[60]

The importance which membership in particular communities has for the self-identification of individuals may be one reason for the upgrading of citizenship which we observe in the new constitutions in East and Central Europe. Yet another reason which can be traced back to a quite different tradition of political philosophy may also apply. It is the Rousseauist tradition of the French Revolution, according to which citizenship is the only or, for that matter, the only morally justified status in the democratic polity. As George H. Sabine has convincingly shown in his analysis of the French and the Anglo-American concepts of democracy, the celebration of national citizenship was paralleled by a distrust of the individual's membership of any kind of association other than the nation-state.[61] The underlying radically individualistic notion of democracy not only discredited any intermediate groups and the membership in them but at the same time concentrated all social aspirations of the individual in the paramount institution of citizenship.

In a nation with a strong tendency towards a unitary and centralized structure, citizenship had the unequivocal meaning of equal citizenship. The exclusion of the whole differentiated texture of the society's associational infrastructure as a defining element of the polity entails a concept of democracy in which the power of the state is an important means for the accomplishment of national collective goals. Democratic state power can also be used as an instrument for the realization of economic and social equality. Where the associational structures of a civil society are thoroughly underdeveloped, as in the post-communist countries of East and Central Europe, the idea of equal national citizenship may well turn out to be the only viable political concept. In a still very much atomized society, the inherent tendency of this concept to instigate economic and social equality easily translates into a broad notion of citizenship which has to offset the lack of a rich texture of a pluralist civil society. This compensatory function of constitutional pledges may also explain the invocation of economic and political pluralism which, as we have seen, is characteristic of the East and Central European constitutions (but which we found in the Spanish Constitution too). The function of the state is not so much the protection of a pluralist structure of the economic and political sphere but the creation of this very structure. Citizenship becomes the homeland of the individual's political and social aspirations in a society which has still to create the conditions which support the demanding concept of citizenship, namely economic, political, and cultural pluralism.

Paradoxically, the state which is burdened with this task and which therefore needs extensive powers is at the same time the major obstacle to the realization of this goal. Its predominance is likely to undercut the emergence of an autonomous sphere of civil society. This, then, may be another reason for the emphasis of the specific constitution on national or ethnic identity. It may help to shape individual identities which do not yet have sufficient opportunities to develop and to flourish in communities which exist outside and independently of the state. If one were to characterize the kind of constitutionalism which predominates in the post-communist countries of Eastern and Central Europe, one could perhaps say that it is a rather statist variant which betrays an inclination to a somewhat authoritarian type of democracy. Or, to make a reference to the different functions sketched above, they are predominantly attentive to the authorizing, the legitimizing, and the integrative function of the constitution, whereas its limiting role is of minor importance. In view of the strong ambition of these countries to reconstitute their polity, this result cannot come as a big surprise.

Notes

1. See e.g. C. J. Friedrich, *Limited Government: A Comparison* (Englewood Cliffs, NJ, 1974); J. Nedelsky, *Private Property and the Limits of American Constitutionalism: The Madisonian Framework and Its Legacy* (Chicago, 1990), 3–9; N. B. Reynolds, 'Constitutionalism and the Rule of Law', in G. C. Bryner and N. B. Reynolds (eds.), *Constitutionalism and Rights* (Provo, Ut.: Brigham Young University Press, 1987), 79–104.
2. S. Holmes, 'Constitutional Design' (unpublished paper, Chicago), 1; and 'Precommitment and the Paradox of Democracy', in J. Elster and R. Slagstad (eds.), *Constitutionalism and Democracy* (Cambridge, 1988), 195–240, 225–30.
3. A critical examination of some of these issues is undertaken by R. Brazier, *Constitutional Reform: Re-shaping the British Political System* (Oxford, 1991).
4. For the historical development of the idea of constitutionalism see E.-W. Boeckenfoerde, 'Geschichtliche Entwicklung und Bedeutungswandel der Verfassung', in *Staat, Verfassung, Demokratie* (Frankfurt, 1991), 29–52.
5. See e.g. *The Federalist Papers*, ed. C. Rossiter (New York: New American Library, 1961), no. 15.
6. See O. Kirchheimer, 'Weimar—and What Then? An Analysis of a Constitution', in F. S. Burin and K. L. Shell (eds.), *Politics, Law and Social Change: Selected Essays of Otto Kirchheimer* (New York, 1969), 36–8.
7. See V. Osiatynski, *The Round Table Negotiations in Poland* (working paper, Center for the Study of Constitutionalism in Eastern Europe, University of Chicago, Law School, 1991).

8. See e.g. T. Paine, *The Rights of Man* (Harmondsworth, 1979), 209.
9. See U. K. Preuss, *Revolution, Fortschritt und Verfassung* (Berlin, 1990), 16–21.
10. See Holmes, 'Precommitment and the Paradox of Democracy', 200–10.
11. e.g. F. Hayek, *The Constitution of Liberty* (Chicago, 1960), 258–62.
12. For the debate about the advantages and disadvantages of parliamentary and presidential systems respectively see A. Lijphart (ed.), *Parliamentary versus Presidential Government* (Oxford, 1992).
13. H. Plessner, *Die verspätete Nation* (Frankfurt, 1982).
14. For the intense debate about the meaning of the constitutional promulgation of the welfare state see E. Forsthoff (ed.), *Rechtsstaatlichkeit und Sozialstaatlichkeit* (Darmstadt, 1968).
15. See J. Elster, 'Constitutionalism in Eastern Europe: An Introduction', *University of Chicago Law Review*, 58 (1991), 450.
16. See C. Offe, 'Capitalism by Democratic Design? Democratic Theory Facing the Triple Transition in East Central Europe', *Social Research*, 58 (1991), 872–4.
17. The process of constitution-making in East and Central Europe has been reported in the *East European Constitutional Review* since its first issue, Spring 1992; see the latest Constitutional Watch in vol. 2, no. 4, and vol. 3, no. 1 (Fall 1993 and Spring 1994), 2–22; see also the book by Sergio Bertole, *Riforme costituzionali nell'Europa Centro-Orientale* (Bologna, 1993), and its review by András Sajó in the aforementioned issue of the *East European Constitutional Review*, 126–30.
18. This is a quotation from art. 42 of the draft of the new Constitution as presented by the Constitutional Committee of the Sejm in 1992. By summer 1994 it had still not entered into force. Instead, the so-called Little Constitution of 8 Dec. 1992 has ordained in its art. 77 that the bill of rights of the communist constitution shall continue to be in force. For an accurate impression of the new constitutional spirit in Poland, the draft of the Sejm seems to be more informative than the not-yet-repealed stipulations of the old constitution. This is why in this paper reference is made to the former rather than to the latter. For the time before 1992 see W. Osiatynski, 'The Constitution-Making Process in Poland', *Law and Policy*, 13 (1991), 125–33.
19. Art. 70/B–70/F, Constitution of Hungary; arts. 15, 48, 51–3, 55, Constitution of the Republic of Bulgaria, effective 12 July 1991.
20. The latest version available to me is of Mar. 1992.
21. Leonhard W. Levy, 'Introduction: The Making of the Constitution, 1776–1789', in Levy (ed.), *Essays on the Making of the Constitution*, 2nd edn. (Oxford, 1987); G. S. Wood, *The Creation of the American Republic* (New York, 1972), 127–61.

22. Holmes, 'Precommitment and the Paradox of Democracy', 238–40; the different concepts of civil society are elaborated by J. L. Cohen and A. Arato, *Civil Society and Political Theory* (Cambridge, Mass., 1992), esp. 463–91.

23. See e.g. V. Bogdanor, 'Britain: The Political Constitution', in Bogdanor (ed.), *Constitutions in Democratic Politics* (London, 1988), 53–72; P. P. Craig, *Public Law and Democracy in the United Kingdom and the United States of America* (Oxford, 1990), 12–55, 208–44.

24. This is the theoretical claim of the work of P. P. Craig (ibid. 3–9).

25. See M. Horwitz, *The Transformation of American Law 1780–1860* (Cambridge, Mass., 1977) and *The Transformation of American Law 1870–1960* (New York, 1992).

26. On the role of private property in American constitutional law see J. Nedelsky, 'American Constitutionalism and the Paradox of Private Property', in Elster and Slagstad, *Constitutionalism and Democracy*, 241–73, and the more elaborate version in Nedelsky, *Private Property and the Limits of American Constitutionalism*.

27. A comprehensive account of the constitutional history of the right to property in Anglo-American and German law is given by H. Rittstieg, *Eigentum als Verfassungsproblem. Zur Geschichte und Gegenwart des Bürgerlichen Verfassungsstaates* (Darmstadt, 1975); see also O. Kirchheimer, 'Die Grenzen der Enteignung. Ein Beitrag zur Entwicklungsgeschichte des Enteignungsinstituts und zur Auslegung des Art. 153 der Weimarer Verfassung', in *Funktionen des Staats und der Verfassung. Zehn Analysen* (Frankfurt, 1972), 223–95; see also Horwitz, *The Transformation of American Law 1780–1860*, 31–62, and Nedelsky, *Private Property and the Limits of American Constitutionalism*, 67–95.

28. The concept was first elaborated by C. Schmitt; see his 'Freiheitsrechte und institutionelle Garantien der Reichsverfassung' (1931) and 'Grundrechte und Grundpflichten' (1932), in *Verfassungsrechtliche Aufsätze aus den Jahren 1924–1954. Materialien zu einer Verfassungslehre* (Berlin, 1958), 140–73 and 181–231 respectively.

29. For the constitutional debate about the political implications of the institutional guarantee of private property under the Weimar Constitution see A. v. Brünneck, *Die Eigentumsgarantie des Grundgesetzes* (Baden-Baden, 1984), 27–47.

30. Maurice Hauriou, Georges Renard, and Santi Romano; see e.g. Albert Broderick (ed.), *The French Institutionalists: Maurice Hauriou, Georges Renard, Joseph T. Delos* (Cambridge, Mass., 1970).

31. Art. 21, para. 1 of the Basic Law reads as follows: 'The political parties shall participate in the forming of the political will of the people. They may be freely established. Their internal organization shall conform to democratic principles. They shall publicly account for the sources and use of their funds and for their assets.'

32. Art. 9, para 3.
33. See its opinions as published in the Official Publication, vols. iv. 7–27, 17–19; l. 290–381, 336.
34. B. Rüthers, 'Institutionelles Rechtsdenken' im Wandel der Verfassungsepochen (Bad Homburg, 1970).
35. This comes close to what Schmitter has termed 'state corporatism', as distinct from 'societal corporatism'; see P. C. Schmitter, 'Modes of Interest Intermediation and Models of Societal Change in Western Europe', Comparative Political Studies, 10 (1979), 61–90; and 'Still the Century of Corporatism?', Review of Political Studies, 36 (1974), 85–131.
36. For the constitution-making process in Hungary see G. Brunner, 'Die neue Verfassung der Republik Ungarn: Entstehungsgeschichte und Grundprobleme', Jahrbuch für Politik, 1 (1991), 297–318.
37. For the Bulgarian Constitution see K. Schrameyer, 'Die neue bulgarische Verfassung', Osteuropa-Recht, 38 (1992), 159–80.
38. See also G. Halmai, 'Regeneration of Civil Society in Hungary: The Recodification of the Right of Assembly and Association', Law and Policy, 13 (1991), 135–47.
39. Ibid. 143.
40. See n. 18 above.
41. A brief report about the constitutional stituation of Estonia up to the autumn of 1992 is provided in East European Constitutional Review, 1 (1992), 3–4.
42. Moreover, it is worth mentioning that the Estonian Constitution grants non-citizens the right to vote in the municipal and local elections. As a consequence, in the local elections of Oct. 1993 two Russian parties together captured nearly 50% of the seats in Tallinn; for more detailed information see the Constitutional Watch in the East European Constitutional Review, 2/4 and 3/1 (Fall 1993/Spring 1994), 9–10.
43. R. Aron, 'Is Multinational Citizenship Possible?', Social Research, 41 (1974), 638–56.
44. See C. Tilly (ed.), The Formation of National States in Western Europe (Princeton, NJ, 1975).
45. See e.g. for Germany M. Stolleis, 'Untertan—Bürger—Staatsbürger. Bemerkungen zur juristischen Terminologie im späten 18. Jahrhundert', in R. Vierhaus (ed.), Bürger und Bürgerlichkeit im Zeitalter der Aufklärung (Heidelberg, 1981), 65–99.
46. See W. Safran, 'State, Nation, National Identity, and Citizenship: France as a Test Case', International Political Science Review, 12 (1991), 219–38.
47. An account of the legal rules about the acquisition of citizenship and about the legal status of aliens in different countries, including Britain, France, and the USA, is given in J. A. Frowein and T. Stein (eds.), The

Legal Position of Aliens in National and International Law, 2 vols. (Berlin, 1987).

48. The debate about communitarianism and justice is put together in the reader edited by S. Avineri and A. de-Shalit, *Communitarianism and Individualism* (Oxford, 1992).

49. D. Miller, 'Community and Citizenship', in Avineri and de-Shalit, *Communitarianism and Individualism*, 85–100.

50. J. Habermas, *Facticity and Validity: Contributions to a Democratic Theory of Law and the Constitutional State* (Cambridge, Mass., 1993), English Ms ch. 4, pp. 38–40, 64 (*Faktizität und Geltung. Beiträge zu einer demokratischen Theorie des Rechts und des Verfassungsstaates* (Frankfurt, 1992), 192–5).

51. For the German discussion of the constitutional concept of duties see H. Hofmann, 'Grundpflichten als verfassungsrechtliche Dimension', in *Veröffentlichungen der Vereinigung der Deutschen Staatsrechtslehrer*, xii (Berlin: de Gruyter, 1983), 42–86.

52. The interrelations between citizenship and nation-state are thoroughly discussed by R. Dahrendorf, *Der moderne soziale Konflikt* (Stuttgart, 1992), 52–79. This book is a revised and enlarged version of *The Modern Social Conflict* (London, 1988).

53. M. Weber, *Economy and Society*, ed. Günther Roth and Claus Wittich (Berkeley, Calif., 1978), 395.

54. L. Tribe, *American Constitutional Law*, 2nd edn. (Mineola, 1988), 353–61, 356–7.

55. See n. 18 above.

56. For the relevance of this distinction see N. B. Reynolds, 'Constitutionalism and the Rule of Law', in Bryner and Reynolds, *Constitutionalism and Rights*, 79–104.

57. See M. J. Sandel, 'The Political Theory of the Procedural Republic', in Bryner and Reynolds, *Constitutionalism and Rights*, 141–55; for the different positions in this debate see Avineri and de-Shalit, *Communitarianism and Individualism*.

58. This point is elaborated in M. Sandel, 'The Procedural Republic and the Unencumbered Self', in Avineri and de-Shalit, *Communitarianism and Individualism*, 12–28.

59. T. H. Marshall, *Class, Citizenship, and Social Movement* (Garden City, 1965).

60. See also R. E. Goodin, *Reasons for Welfare: The Political Theory of the Welfare State* (Princeton, NJ, 1988).

61. G. H. Sabine, 'The Two Democratic Traditions', *Philosophical Review*, 61 (1952), 451–74, 460–5.

PART IV

CONSTITUTIONAL REVIEW AND CHANGE I: THE WESTERN EUROPEAN EXPERIENCE

6

Constitutional Reform in Germany after the Revolution of 1989

DIETER GRIMM

1

Unlike the situation in other socialist Eastern European states, the revolution of 1989 did not lead to an internal rejuvenation or to a new constitution in the German Democratic Republic (GDR). Instead, the GDR acceded to the Federal Republic of Germany and the West German Constitution was adopted. At the end of the post-war era, therefore, the particular position which the GDR had occupied from the start once again becomes apparent. After the Second World War, only the smaller part of Germany had come under the control of the Soviet Union. What had been intended as an administrative division into occupation zones led to the emergence of two states with antagonistic constitutions, an outcome representing not the wish of the Germans but the will of the Allied Powers. Both German states, however, stressed in their respective constitutions reunification as a goal, albeit under different assumptions about the political order. The GDR finally abolished these constitutional provisions in 1974, and in 1976 replaced them with provisions on GDR citizenship, while the Federal Republic main-

This chapter was completed in January 1993 and updated in the spring of that year. Some time later the Joint Committee referred to below presented its report on constitutional reform. By October 1994 a process of amending the Basic Law was concluded, the effect of which was that 47 of its provisions were subject to change. Some, but by no means all, of these amendments were intended to take account of German unification and its consequences. These subsequent developments provide no grounds for changing the views expressed in this chapter.

tained reunification and an all-German citizenship as a political goal even after officially recognizing the GDR in 1972.

The division of the country into two states with different political and social orders had the consequence that a rejection of the conditions found in the GDR usually led to escape to West Germany rather than to the formation of an internal opposition within the GDR itself. Up to the erection of the Berlin Wall in 1961, some 3 million people had left East Germany. Even after the wall had been built, this form of escape remained a possibility, in particular for political dissidents. The leadership of the SED (Sozialistische Einheitspartei Deutschlands) preferred to expel rather than oppress these dissidents, not least because of the foreign currency it could earn through West Germany's readiness to pay for the release of political prisoners. The political change in 1989 was likewise the consequence of the possibility of escape without emigration. The mass exodus of young GDR citizens, made possible by the opening of the western borders of other socialist countries, and the consequent internal mass protest, initiated not only the overthrow of Honecker by reform-minded members of the politburo of the SED, but also the opening of the Berlin Wall, the appointment of the Modrow government, and the creation of the central Round Table.

While these steps were intended to instigate an internal reform of the socialist state, however imprecise in its shape and however ineffective in halting the mass exodus, the population was articulating its wish for reunification with West Germany at mass rallies even before West German politicians dared to make such a suggestion. The widespread desire for a quick accession of the GDR to the Federal Republic also had the consequence that the civil protest movements which had developed under the cover of the Protestant Church, as well as the newly founded or reformed political parties, for the most part developed close links with West German parties from whom they received ideological, organizational, and financial help as well as staff. The new set of political attitudes which had just begun to develop in the GDR was thereby brought under West German influence from the very start. This process complicated the development of a specifically East German concept or attitude about future arrangements, whether in a reformed GDR or in a unified German state. Only the former ruling SED party, which had been renamed the Party of Democratic

Socialism (PDS), remained immune to such influences, while the mass organization which had depended on the SED quickly disintegrated.

These conditions also shaped the work of the Round Table, whose most important tasks included the preparation of a new constitution.[1] Although the old and new parties as well as the social groupings were represented by GDR citizens only, the majority of the participating organizations received advice from West German politicians and academics as to the conception and formulation of the draft constitution. The draft constitution, which was completed by the Round Table immediately before the election for the Chamber of People's Deputies on 18 March 1990, therefore bore a close resemblance to the Basic Law of the Federal Republic of Germany. Yet, even where it differed from the Basic Law, one recognizes either the influence of rulings of the Federal Constitutional Court or of those constitutional policies of the West German Left, which had not found the majority required for constitutional amendments in the Federal Republic itself. Though this provides an interesting subject for debate, one cannot conclude that the draft constitution represented the specific experience or conception of the majority of the GDR population, given the history of its formulation.

The election for the Chamber of People's Deputies of 18 March 1990 irreversibly put an end to the efforts to reform the GDR in advance of the *rapprochement* with the Federal Republic. Those groups which were close to the West German governing parties and advocated a quick route to reunification received an overwhelming majority of the vote. The newly elected Chamber did not even discuss the draft constitution prepared by the Round Table (although the latter was later to have a certain influence on the constitutions of the *Länder* in the former GDR[2]). The de Maizière government regarded the preparation of the reunification with West Germany as its main task. The spring and summer of 1990 were filled with negotiations: first about the economic, monetary, and social union, which was agreed upon on 18 May 1990; second, about the election agreement of 3 August 1990 for the first all-German parliament; and, finally, about the reunification treaty, which was completed on 31 August 1990.[3] The changes made by the Chamber of People's Deputies to the GDR Constitution were likewise designed to create the conditions necessary for the ratification of the reunification treaty and for other preparatory legislation, rather than being intended to lead to an internal reform of the GDR itself.[4] On 23 August 1990 the Chamber of People's Deputies passed the resolution for the GDR to accede to the Federal Republic of Germany. On 3 October 1990 this took effect.

2

The end of the constitutional debate in the GDR coincided with the beginning of such a debate in the Federal Republic of Germany.[5] Central to this was the question whether the Basic Law should in future form the constitution for a unified Germany, or whether reunification required the formulation of a new constitution. As laid down in its preamble, the Basic Law had been conceived as an interim constitution for the period of the division only, and it prescribed in the closing paragraph of Article 146 that it was to expire as soon as the unified nation had democratically decided on a new constitution. In the mean time Article 23 allowed for the accession of other parts of Germany. Yet, over time, a broad consensus in favour of the Basic Law had developed, despite its provisional character and the absence of a referendum. Just before the revolutionary events in the socialist world it had celebrated its fortieth anniversary, and had been widely praised as a successful constitution. Although around this time, and after thirty-five amendments, there were some reform initiatives which above all argued for a clause for the protection of the environment and for the introduction of elements of direct democracy, there was no disagreement in principle about the satisfactory nature of the Basic Law.

The argument for a new constitution was therefore less concerned with a need to change the substance of the Basic Law than with rectifying mistakes made during its formulation, and with giving the population of the GDR the possibility of introducing their expectations and experiences into the constitutional debate so as to make the future constitution a basis for a political and social order acceptable to both constituent parts. Included in this conception was the idea of a constitutional assembly whose draft would be put to a referendum. While this plan received support mainly from the Left, it was fiercely opposed by the Right, which refused to risk the constitutional achievements of the post-war period in comprehensive renegotiations. The latter interpreted the revolution in the GDR and the accession to the Federal Republic as a vote in favour of the existing constitutional arrangement. According to this view, amendments to the Basic Law were to be kept to a minimum, and should be agreed upon by parliament rather than by the people.

The course of the debate can only be explained if it is viewed in the context of the central question of reunification: whether the Federal Republic was merely enlarged through reunification, or whether it had also to transform itself as a consequence thereof. Implicitly, this question also characterizes the constitutional debate. The argument about the best way to achieve unity, which had been the dominant issue in the period between the election for the Chamber of People's Deputies in March 1990 and the signing of the reunification treaty in August 1990, was already being conducted as a debate about the advantages and disadvantages of the Basic Law. Those who were in favour of the accession of the GDR according to Article 23 thereby also advocated the preservation of the Basic Law itself. Those who preferred the unification to be based on Article 146 thereby indicated their preference for a new constitution. This was, of course, an exaggeration even then.[6] In reality, there were two quite distinct questions: the procedural one of the creation of national unity, and the material one of the political order of the unified state. While the provisions of Article 146 did not rule out an agreement on the Basic Law, the path of accession by means of Article 23 equally did not preclude a subsequent formulation of a new constitution.

The subsequent course of events has confirmed this view. The decision in favour of the accession of the GDR according to Article 23, which was taken because it quickly and smoothly achieved its objective, did not resolve the constitutional question. Even after Article 23 had become irrelevant through its application and was, therefore, removed from the Basic Law, the promise in Article 146 of a constitution democratically decided upon by the whole nation remained unfulfilled. So this provision remained in force, and was merely furnished with the clarifying addition that the Basic Law from then on was to serve as the constitution for the whole German nation. Even after the achievement of unity, the Basic Law is in force only on the proviso that the people will provide themselves with a new constitution. The reunification treaty refers to this in its Article 5, which recommends that the legislative institutions of a unified Germany should deal with the constitutional questions arising from reunification within two years, and should include in this examination the application of Article 146 of the Basic Law as well as the question of a referendum.

The old lines of division reappeared in the debate about the realization of this recommendation. Those who advocated the use of a specially convened constitutional council were suspected of being prepared to abandon the Basic Law. Those who argued for a parliamentary procedure to change the constitution, as laid down in Article 79 of the Basic Law, thereby indicated that the latter should be kept. As had been the case in the unification debate, these alternatives did not in fact exist. At no time in either the West or the East had the question of a completely different constitutional order been considered. Even the Round Table, which had worked on the premiss of reforming the GDR rather than that of reunification, had closely followed the Basic Law in its constitutional recommendations. Conversely, no one could have any doubt that the constitutional changes made with the unification treaty were insufficient. Under these circumstances the intensity of the argument can, once again, be explained only by reference to the underlying central question of reunification: whether the burden of change should be carried by the former GDR alone, or whether the old Federal Republic should share in it too.

The compromise with which the procedural argument ended leaves this question open, though to a large extent it also determines the answer. Although a constitutional commission was established, it consisted of members of the *Bundestag* and *Bundesrat* only. The decision in favour of a body exclusively made up of active party politicians left the revision of the constitution up to Bonn's routine operations, a course of action which could not be without consequences for the end result. In the first place, it meant that the participants and concerns of the old Federal Republic dominated the discussion. Second, it ignored the distinction between day-to-day politics, with all its attendant concern for organization and policy content, and the permanent framework for politics. Not only were current concerns and election dates in the foreground, but issues without such immediate effects, problems with long-term consequences, and even fundamental structural weaknesses were likely to be neglected.

So far, the work of the constitutional commission has not shown these concerns to be without foundation. The commission was formed in the beginning of 1992, and is due to submit its recommendations for changes in the Basic Law, as well as for the procedural question of a referendum, in the spring of 1993. Its sessions take place at regular intervals in Bonn, usually in the late afternoon or evening, following sessions of the *Bundestag* and *Bundesrat* or of one of their respective committees. Its work sometimes involves listening to expert evidence. Since its third meeting its proceedings have been opened to the public. None of these circumstances is conducive to a thorough discussion free from the pressure of daily business. Moreover, some changes which are deemed particularly urgent are being discussed by bodies other than the commission, and they will be agreed upon before the conclusion of the commission's work. In particular, these issues include the question of asylum legislation and that of deployment of German troops outside NATO territory. The adaptation of the Basic Law to the Maastricht Treaty, the necessity for which had soon been recognized, was ratified as early as December 1992.

Nevertheless, the agenda of the constitutional commission remains extensive.[7] In the context of shaping the democratic principle, it has to deal with the strengthening of parliamentary rights and the introduction of elements of direct democracy into what had been a Basic Law with a strongly representative orientation. Within the limits of the federal principle, the demand of the *Länder* for a strengthening of their position *vis-à-vis* the federal authorities is under discussion. Above all, they demand the return of legislative powers, increased autonomy over administrative competences, a greater say in the attitude taken by the federal government in the Council of the European Community, and, finally, an improved distribution of finances in the federal state. Attributable to the principle of a welfare state are those changes which are concerned with new objectives of the state (namely those relating to the protection of the environment), with new social guarantees (relating to employment, housing, and child care), and with the extension of the principle of equality (relating to the position of women), as well as with the strengthening of the family.

However, the remainder of this chapter will not be concerned with the topics under discussion by the commission, but with those which, in spite of warranting attention, are being left out of it. The yardstick used here is the consensual capacity of a constitution. Constitutions are meant to subject political power to legal constraints, but they can only do so in so far as they represent society's consensus as to the foundations of political and social order and as to the form of conflict resolution. Constitutions do not of themselves produce this consensus, but rather confer on such consensus a binding character, continuance, and determination, and thereby form the foundation of legitimacy and the criteria for judging the exercise of political power. Whatever becomes part of this consensus is no longer an issue but a premiss of political argument. The consensus frees the political decision-making process from the search for procedure and principle, and it makes majority decisions palatable for the minority. For these reasons constitutional reform has to be orientated towards this factor of consensual capacity. Changes become necessary if the consensus has begun to falter because of changes in expectations; if novel problems require its extension; or if changed circumstances lead the regulations agreed by consent to have no—or undesired—effects.[8]

3

3.1. Reunification

Above all, this perspective raises the question whether there is a need to change or supplement the consensus contained in the Basic Law arising from reunification. Yet the cause of the constitutional debate does not play a direct role in the deliberation. It is only with the problem of the equalization of burdens among the *Länder* that it re-emerges occasionally. An explanation for this lies not only in the old Federal Republic's determination not to be distracted from its consensus by the accession of the GDR but also in an attitude which does not expect the Constitution to contribute to the solution of the problems arising from reunification. These problems are, indeed, predominantly of an economic, social, and cultural nature; they therefore have to be solved with economic, social, and cultural means. However, the solutions require legal backing, and since they invariably affect property rights and standards of the old Federal Republic, they become constitutional questions. Yet they are essentially transitional problems, and therefore have their place in legislation rather than in the Constitution. There are, however, transitional problems of such magnitude and importance that the fundamentals of their solution should be taken out of party politics and should be made the premiss of future policies. This appears especially necessary in two areas: in the distribution of the financial burden between East and West and in dealing with the legacy of GDR history.

Reunification has made the integration of the two parts of society the principal objective of domestic policy until 'East' and 'West' once again have a purely geographical connotation. Realizing this objective is protracted, difficult, and expensive, and for some time to come the bulk of the costs involved will have to be met by the Western side. However, it is not merely about money. Standards which have been formed in the old Federal Republic under conditions of considerable affluence and high productivity will have to be temporarily sacrificed. Those standards may include those of infrastructure, of social security, or even of legal cover. Cumulatively, this amounts to an equalization of burdens between East and West which, if not in detail, then at least in magnitude corresponds to the equalization of burdens in the post-war period. Since it is both inevitable and conflict-ridden, it should at least in principle be universally accepted and thereby be freed from continuous doubt. Yet this means nothing but that it should be anchored in a constitution, just as the Basic Law has anchored the equalization of burdens of the post-war period in the temporary provisions of Article 119 and those following.

An integration problem of a special nature lies in the labour productivity differentials between East and West. Knowledge and skills which were acquired in the socialist state, as well as modes of communication and orientation which were functioning therein, are mostly inapplicable in the West. In most spheres of society the West is, therefore, being put in the position of leadership, while the East is relegated to having to relearn those skills. The integration of the two parts of society can hardly be successful under such circumstances. The constitutional recognition of the quota system which is currently being fought over should perhaps not apply to women only. The problem is confounded by the political incrimination of so many East Germans. Often, it receives attention only in the shape of accusations levelled against individuals like Minister-President Stolpe and former University Rector Fink; very rarely is it recognized as a task for integration. For a long time to come one can expect every rise of an East German into a leading position to be accompanied by investigations and revelations by adversaries or the media. This is a heavy burden for a society which is dependent on the integration of both parts of the country. The damage caused by some insufficiently qualified East Germans in leading positions will be less than that caused by the perpetuation of West–East suspicion. Here, too, a constitutional precaution should be taken, as was the case after the war with Article 139 of the Basic Law.

3.2. Political Parties

Nowhere is the predetermining power of procedural regulations over substantive results more obvious than in the sphere of political parties. Since the political parties have taken constitutional reform completely into their own hands, the readiness to call their own position into question can be expected to be minimal. It cannot be denied, however, that some constitutional guarantees are indeed threatened by political parties. Of course, this should not be taken to suggest that one could do without parties. They are an essential part of parliamentary democracy, and will be formed irrespective of whether the Constitution will take note of them or not. By reducing the immeasurable variety of opinions and interests to a manageable number of political programmes, and by training political personnel to realize these programmes, parties enable the people to exercise their right to vote and to confer the political mandate. At the same time, the competition between parties for votes compels them to pay attention to the needs and attitudes of the population and to incorporate these in the political decision-making process, even between election dates. There is, therefore, no functional equivalent to political parties.

The influence of a party on the public decision-making process is, of course, dependent on its share of the vote and the extent to which it can therewith penetrate the legislative institutions. The objective of each and every party is, therefore, to achieve an election victory which allows it to form a government. Since participation in government is the essential precondition for the realization of one's own programme, increasing the share of the vote becomes the overriding motive for action. Often this leads to a reversal of means and ends: one does not strive to gain votes for a particular programme, but one formulates a programme which promises to gain votes. Because of the necessary connection between election victory and the realization of a programme, all those choices appear rational from the point of view of political parties which increase their election chances or help secure their electoral base. Therein lies the explanation for their efforts to hinder the advance of rivals and to seek a foothold wherever the outcome of elections can be influenced and where positions of decision-making power are to be filled. They are greatly helped in their task by the fact that, as parliamentary parties, they can exercise legislative and budgetary rights, and that as governmental parties they have control over personnel decisions, both of which enable them to satisfy their self-interest very easily.

The Constitution, which is concerned with the separation of powers and the preservation of open access to the political process in the interest of personal liberty and autonomy of the different social functions, is often at a disadvantage in this context. It can distribute decision-making power among different levels—Federal, *Länder*, and local authorities—and within the same level among different institutions—parliament, government, and judiciary. Furthermore, it protects those institutions which control radio and television broadcasting from direct influence by the state. Yet it does not succeed in preventing political parties from making their influence felt in all those institutions. In their capacity as the mediator between state and society, political parties have always managed to complete their task before the constitutional legislation relating to the state has become applicable. Thus it is no longer true that independent institutions of the state are held in check. Instead, political parties co-operate with each other in different roles. A controlling effect originates merely in party political competition, and it fails whenever there is identity of interests among the parties.[9]

There is much to be said for the view that the root cause of the aversion against political parties, which has become more pronounced lately, lies in this claim to oligopoly, which is detrimental to their role as mediators between state and society and which transforms them into omnipresent institutions of power. All the same, appeals to the parties to show consideration are ineffectual, for their behaviour is perfectly rational from the point of view of self-interest and can, therefore, be constrained only externally. The constitutional court has frequently proved successful in interpreting and developing the Basic Law, namely with regard to election legislation, and most recently in an effort to correct earlier concessions, in the case of party finance. However, the measures offered in the Basic Law are no longer sufficient to contain the expanding party state. Instead, the access of political parties should be reduced in all spheres in which independent and non-political decisions are made which either follow legal requirements or which are constitutionally protected. In the public domain this applies in particular to the administration and the judiciary, as well as to institutions under public law, such as broadcasting and the university system. In the private sector it applies to all those enterprises which are owned by the state or are to a large extent under its control.

The introduction of elements of direct democracy into the Basic Law, which is commonly discussed from the perspective of activating the people and increasing the legitimacy of decisions, could also serve to limit the influence of political parties. It cannot be assumed that plebiscite decisions, merely because they are taken by the people, are therefore superior to those taken by parliament. Neither can it be expected that the minority will be more willing to accept defeat simply because it has participated in the decision, especially in cases which are deemed existential, such as abortion or the use of atomic energy. It is even possible that plebiscites lead to a deeper division of society than parliamentary decision-making procedures. However, the mere possibility of plebiscites may well increase the pressure on political parties not to avoid questions which deeply move society and which require a political answer. To this end, it would be sufficient to allow for referenda to be used to force legislative initiatives onto the political agenda in order for them to be dealt with by state institutions.

3.3. European Integration

In contrast to reunification, the question of European integration could not be avoided in the constitutional debate, since it was impossible to ratify the Maastricht Treaty under the Basic Law in its previous form. Article 24 of the Basic Law does not allow for the degree of integration envisaged in the Treaty. On the one hand it involves more than just a transference of specific elements of sovereignty and, on the other, the European Community itself can no longer be regarded as just an arrangement between states. Already the EC is exercising authority with direct and binding consequences for member states, and with the Maastricht Treaty it sets out on the road to a European federal state. It had become clear that this could not be achieved without explicit constitutional approval. Furthermore, certain regulations were necessary to allow for the right of foreigners to vote, and to allow for the redefinition of the role of the *Bundesbank*. Furthermore, the *Länder* and the *Bundestag* attempted to gain more influence over the government's policy towards Europe. This led to the ratification of a co-determination arrangement which is not only complicated but also remarkably vague in definition, considering its purpose as a procedural regulation. The government only reluctantly agreed to this, for it feared the weakening of its negotiating position *vis-à-vis* the more centralized member states of the EC.

However, the constitutional commission wrongly assumes that this issue is exhausted with the agreement. This is connected with a widespread misconception about the fate of the constitutional nation-state after Maastricht. It is already regarded as indisputable among experts on European law that even the lowest rank of Community law overrides national constitutional law. So far, the Federal constitutional court has not adhered to this demand, but has only withdrawn its control over the application of Community law by German state institutions, on the proviso that the European Court of Justice guarantees appropriate constitutional protection. There can be no doubt, however, that national constitutions will become of peripheral importance with the creation of a federal European state.[10] Just as the member states will be relegated to a status equivalent to the *Länder*, and their institutions thereby to *Länder*-parliaments, *Länder*-governments, and *Länder*-courts, so will the Basic Law, as well as the constitutions of other member states, be equivalent to a *Länder*-constitution which is only applicable within the scope defined by Community law.

By itself, of course, this is no reason to oppose progressive European integration, since one cannot overestimate the importance of a unified Europe, given the history of wars and rivalries as well as the nationalistic excesses of the former socialist states of Eastern Europe. It has to be realized that this goal will not be attained without sacrificing national sovereignty. However, a constitutional state is in itself a considerable achievement, and to give up the constitution would be a high price to pay for European unity. The Maastricht Treaty is a decisive step towards a federal European state, but it does not provide the latter with a constitution which would safeguard the standards achieved on a national level. One might argue that the requirements of a constitutional state are met, since EC integration proceeds mainly in the field of providing common legislation and because the Luxemburg Court effectively controls the application of these laws. However, there is not even a catalogue of basic human rights, and the Court fills this gap rather inadequately by referring to basic human rights enshrined in the constitutions of member states.

Above all, the Community lacks real democratic substance. Although the EC Treaty mentions the European Parliament, which has been elected directly by the citizens of member states since 1979, prior to all the other institutions of the Community, it thereby attributes an importance to the latter which does not exist in reality. On the contrary, decision-making power is concentrated in other institutions such as the Council, the Commission, and the Court. The Parliament itself lacks the competences common to its equivalents on the national level, i.e. legislative power, and the right to determine the budget and to form and control governments. The decisions taken by the EC still receive legitimacy mainly from national governments, while parliamentary control is restricted to that of national parliaments over the European policies of their respective governments. The fewer decisions taken by the Council of Ministers without insistence on unanimity, and the more competences transferred to the Commission, the more noticeable will the democratic deficit become at the European level.

Therefore, it appears only logical that a demand for a European Constitution adopting the principles of national constitutions was voiced in the debate on Maastricht in the *Bundestag*.[11] This demand, though obvious, is of course more easily raised than realized. It is indeed arguable that providing the EC with a constitution may even present an insurmountable problem. One cannot hope to have made good the European democratic deficit, even if the European

Parliament were to be provided with the competences of national parliaments. Although the existence of a parliament is a necessary condition for democracy, it is not a sufficient one. First and foremost, democracy means that sovereignty lies with the people and that it is their will which is merely exercised by the institutions of the state, which themselves are again accountable to the people. In this context, parliaments fulfil an important mediating role. The democratic substance of a political regime is dependent on how reliable parliaments are in performing this mediating service. Therein, parliaments are themselves dependent on the mediation of others, namely parties, unions and associations, civic action groups, and the media. Only if a European public can be created with the help of these groups will there be a European democracy.

However, there can only be limited optimism about the creation of these conditions for democracy.[12] It can at least be assumed that a transformation of the European Parliament from a consultative to a decision-making body will lead to a Europeanization of political parties. The Strasburg Parliament is already divided not into national but into programmatic factions. The formation of parties would follow from an increase of power of the Parliament. The same can be assumed with regard to interest groups. None the less, one can also confidently predict that this Europeanization would take place among leaders and functionaries rather than at the membership level, which would tend then to increase the gap between the élites and their base. The reason is an obvious one: information and participation, which represent the basic conditions for democracy, are bound up with language. At present there are nine different languages spoken within the EC. Even if two languages dominate in EC institutions, the majority of EC nationals are still excluded from direct understanding and communication. Europeanization of the media can also be ruled out as a possibility for reasons of language. Hence the European public remains fragmented along national lines. Under these conditions one cannot expect a European public on which sovereignty can rest to emerge for a long time to come.

These prospects lead to the conclusion that the achievements of the democratic, constitutional nation-state cannot at present be sufficiently reproduced at the European level. This realization limits the extent of European integration. National constitutions which authorize integration should also be used to define the latter. Despite the necessary extension of Community competences in areas of foreign and defence policy, integration should stop wherever the EC transforms itself into a federal state. It is still only the member countries which show the attributes of constitutional states. One cannot seek comfort in the principle of subsidiarity which has been included in the Maastricht Treaty.[13] The formulation that the Community should take decisions only in areas where it can do so more effectively than the member states allows for numerous interpretations, and no obligation to specify the principle has been included in the Treaty. There is not even a consensus among the member states that the powers of the Community should be restricted at all. On the contrary, many hope to be able to offload controversial problems onto Brussels. This calls for a rethink of the Maastricht Treaty in the forthcoming intergovernmental negotiations.

3.4. *Devaluation of the Constitution*

In addition to the external weakening of the Constitution arising from European integration, there is also a need to raise the problem of internal weakening which has so far been ignored in the deliberations about the Constitution. This internal weakening is the result of secular changes in the activities of the state, and it threatens to render some important constitutional guarantees partly ineffectual.[14] The constitutional state is a relatively recent historical phenomenon. It emerged with the bourgeois conviction that prosperity and justice could best be achieved through the self-regulating power of market forces. The function of the state was thereby reduced to guaranteeing the rules of the market: the free play of social forces. To the extent to which this conviction prevailed by revolutionary or evolutionary means, it led to the different social processes being taken out of political control and left them to their own criteria of rationality. In this context the constitution had the task of legally affirming the separation of prosperity and justice from political power, as well as of regulating the relationship between state and society in a manner which permitted the state to fulfil its role as the guarantor of law, while at the same time preventing it from realizing its ambition to control.

The first of these tasks was fulfilled by the guarantee of basic rights, which defined an area in which the will of the individual was given priority over state power. Thereby, the autonomy of the different social processes was also secured. The second of these tasks was taken up in the organizational part of the Constitution, which arranged the power of the state so that it remained obliged to conform to social interests and to reduce its capacity to misuse its means of power for other purposes. The principal means of this precaution was the law. By empowering elected representatives to pass laws, society determined the limits to its own freedom and also defined the state's radius of action. For the executive power of the state, the law was at the same time an authorization for and a restraint on action. It served the independent judiciary as a standard of control, by which it could determine whether or not the executive had adhered to the restrictions on its power in individual cases. This led directly to the separation of powers as the most important element in the protection against misuse. Though limited to the two tasks of restricting and organizing state power, the Constitution developed its own rationality and achieved a high level of authority.

The conditions which led to the formation of such constitutional traditions have since changed considerably. The bourgeois expectation that society could by itself produce prosperity and justice, and that the state was needed merely as a guarantor of liberty, has not been fulfilled. Since then, prosperity and justice have once again become matters of active state involvement, though without having abandoned the principles of freedom and equality. The consequence was the expansion of state affairs, which began in the nineteenth century and has continued to this day. In the mean time, the state has assumed extensive responsibilities with regard to the social, economic, scientific, technical, and cultural stability and development of society. This cannot be viewed merely as a quantitative extension of responsibilities; it also has a qualitative character. The latter consists of the fact that the state has moved away from the concept of a social order which is not only given but also just, and which it merely has to protect and restore in case of disruptions. Instead, the state now regards itself as being responsible for shaping this social order as well as for safeguarding the future.

This carries with it two consequences for the constitutional containment of political power. The first of these results from the fact that the public good can no longer be attained only through the restriction of state power: it now equally requires an activation of the state. However, the activities of a welfare state are a far more difficult subject for legal definition than those of the state as a guarantor of social order, which weakens not only basic rights but also the law. In contrast to the protection of social order, the shaping of the welfare state occurs prospectively instead of retro-spectively, in a generalized rather than a particular way, and it has diffused rather than individual applications. With regard to per-forming the function of shaping the social order, the state appar-atus not only has to rely on its will to enforce it but is also dependent on numerous social resources outside its control. Since the Constitution subjects the performance of this function to legal foundations as well, this has given rise to a new type of legislation, what is commonly termed a *Finalprogramm* and is distinguished from the classical *Konditionalprogramm* by reason of the fact that it does not provide a conclusive definition of the work of public administration in terms of legal conditions and consequences. In-stead, a *Finalprogramm* specifies goals and lists aspects which have to be considered in its attainment. The remainder is left up to public administration itself, which then, of course, does not pronounce the application of predetermined, general, and abstract law to indi-vidual cases, but which has to arrive at original decisions on the basis of vaguely defined principles.

The second problem arises from the fact that the extension of state responsibilities has not been matched by a corresponding extension of its right to take decisions. This is partly due to the fact that the goals which are aspired to cannot be attained by imperative means, as is the case with the planning of scientific research and the management of business cycles. Partly, also, it is because different social processes rightly continue to be protected from political control, and enjoy constitutionally guaranteed autonomy. Yet even where imperative control is possible and legally admissible there is often such a strong need for consensus that the state prefers indirect to imperative means of control. In contrast to order and compul-sion, this of course leaves those addressed with the freedom of decision. In its concern for the public good, the state thereby becomes dependent on the willingness to obey of particular interests. Given sufficient powers of veto, those interest groups can then make their obedience conditional upon state concessions. As a reaction to this development, the state has established sophisticated negotiation mechanisms between public and private interests on which many of its decisions today depend.

Both these developments have consequences for the Constitution. Wherever the law determines the activities of the state only vaguely, public administration loses not merely democratic legitimacy, but also its constitutional commitment and control. Specific procedural requirements have not so far proved capable of filling this gap. Negotiating political measures allows for the involvement of certain groups in the state's decision-making process, which are not subjected to the constitutional requirements for legitimacy and responsibility. Furthermore, such a process also produces decisions evading procedural precautions, which the Constitution prescribes for collectively binding decisions. However, it cannot be concluded that the state should abandon those activities which are not subject to constitutional control. This would not only mean a loss of legitimacy; it would also conflict with another constitutional directive, the principle of the welfare state. Instead, the attempt has to be made to adapt the constitutional requirements to the changed circumstances. This is not an easy undertaking, and jurisprudence has not so far provided convincing solutions. However, the constitutional commission does not seem even to recognize the problem.

4

Listing the loss of constitutionally relevant issues has illustrated the connection between procedure and result. Where the constitutional consultation does not follow political upheaval but is left up to the players in day-to-day politics, it will be conducted according to the conditions governing day-to-day politics. Experts who are called in cannot change this, since they are unable to determine the issues to be discussed and merely answer questions arising from a given agenda. The chance has been missed to elevate the constitutional consultations, which originated in reunification, out of this sphere. The next question is whether or not the players in day-to-day politics should also remain exclusively responsible for the ratification of their own reform recommendations. Already one can predict that this question will once again reopen the fundamental differences which have characterized the constitutional debate since

1990: revision of the Constitution as part of routine parliamentary operations, or the passage of an act with which the people give legitimacy to a revised basic order after the secular event of reunification?

There are several arguments in favour of a referendum on the revised Basic Law. A plebiscite is a valid form of providing oneself with a constitution. It was only the special circumstance of Germany's division which prevented its use in 1949. The authors of the Basic Law naturally assumed that reunification would entail a plebiscite on the all-German constitution, and expressed—though they did not prescribe—this option through Article 146. The promise was to be fulfilled after the disappearance of the obstacle. Yet this does not represent illusions of direct democracy. The Basic Law, in particular, has demonstrated that the legitimacy of a constitution is not dependent on a plebiscite: constitutions have to be based on a lasting consensus, and past plebiscites are therefore of limited persuasive power. None the less, it makes sense to use this procedure now. Even if the population of the old Federal Republic has accepted the Constitution without a referendum after a prolonged process of testing its value, there has been no such acceptance on the part of the population of the former GDR. It would be appropriate to allow those who have to carry most of the burden of change explicitly to declare themselves in favour of the Constitution under which they will live in future.

That constitutions are enacted by plebiscite not only corresponds to traditions arising from the revolutions of the late eighteenth century; it also possesses an intrinsic rationale, which originates from the function of constitutions. They express the consensus on the basis of which society agrees politically, and on which it also settles its differences of opinion and interests. Therein lies a fundamental difference between constitutions and mere acts of power. The constitution has priority over the latter. Claims on power and resulting acts are only legitimate on the basis and in the framework of a constitution. Hence the constitution cannot be the product of the very same process it is meant to authorize and to structure. By allowing the rulers themselves to change the conditions of rule, one therefore places at risk the legitimizing and limiting functions of the constitution. Against this risk, the Basic Law protects itself with the insurmountable obstacle to change as laid down in Article 79, paragraph 3, and with the requirement of a qualified majority. As long as no party controls two-thirds of the votes in both the *Bundestag* and the *Bundesrat*, government and opposition will have to agree on changes in the Constitution.

These protective measures may be sufficient for those specific corrections which from time to time become necessary in a relatively detailed and relatively precise constitution. However, it is already apparent that the recommendations of the constitutional commission will have a wider dimension. The constitutional reform of 1993 will be the most comprehensive and far-reaching in the history of the Basic Law, which will eclipse even the significant constitutional changes which had to be made on the occasions of rearmament, the emergency legislation, and the financial reforms in the federal system of 1969. Not least with regard to European unification, it will represent more than just a change within the system. The forthcoming constitutional reform comes close to a change of the system itself.[15] Changes of such magnitude must not be granted by players and members of political institutions to themselves; they ought to be sanctioned by the people to whom they owe their mandate. It might even be worth considering whether it would not help to maintain awareness of the distinction between constitution and the institutions of executive government, the *pouvoir constituant* and the *pouvoirs constitués*, to subject all future constitutional changes to referendum.

Notes

1. See U. Thaysen, 'Der Runde Tisch oder: wo blieb das Volk?', in *Der Weg der DDR in die Demokratie* (Opladen: Westdeutscher, 1990); H. J. and R. Will, 'Die Verfassungsfrage in der DDR auf dem Weg zur deutschen Einheit', in *Kritische Vierteljahresschrift für Gesetzgebung und Rechtswissenschaft* (1990), 157; also contains the draft constitution, p. 167. On the latter see P. Häberle, 'Der Entwurf der Arbeitsgruppe "Neue Verfassung der DDR" des Runden Tisches', *Jahrbuch des öffentlichen Rechts der Gegenwart*, Neue Folge Band 39 (1990), 1; see also the articles by W. Templin, U. K. Preuss, G. Roellecke, K.-H. Ladeur, T. Ansbach, T. Böhm, and E. Fischer, in B. Guggenberger and T. Stein (eds.), *Die Verfassungsdiskussion im Jahr der deutschen Einheit* (Munich: Carl Hanser, 1991). On the constitutional question after the events of 1989 in general see U. K.

Preuss, *Revolution, Fortschritt und Verfassung. Zu einem neuen Verfassungsverständnis* (Berlin: K. Wagenbach, 1990); K. N. Rozner, *Der Verfassungsentwurf des Zentralen Runden Tisches* (Berlin: Duncker & Humblot, 1993).

2. See A. v. Mutius and T. Friedrich, 'Verfassungsentwicklung in den neuen Bundesländern', *Staatswissenschaften und Staatspraxis*, 2 (1991), 243; E. Röper, 'Verfassungsgebung und Verfassungskontinuität in den östlichen Bundesländern', *Zeitschrift für Gesetzgebung* (1991), 149; R. Steinberg, 'Organisation und Verfahren bei der Verfassungsgebung in den Neuen Bundesländern', *Zeitschrift für Parlamentsfragen*, 23 (1992), 497; P. Häberle, 'Die Verfassungsbewegung in den fünf neuen Bundesländern', *Jahrbuch des öffentlichen Rechts*, Neue Folge Band 41 (1993), 69; H. v. Mangoldt, *Die Verfassungen der neuen Bundesländer* (Berlin: Duncker & Humblot, 1993).

3. See K. Stern and B. Schmidt-Bleibtreu (eds.), *Verträge und Rechtsakte zur deutschen Einheit*, 3 vols. (Munich: C. H. Beck, 1990).

4. See P. Quint, 'The Constitutional Law of German Unification', *Maryland Law Review*, 50 (1991), 475; H. H. Klein, 'Verfassungskontinuität im revolutionären Umbruch. Die Verfassung der DDR zwischen dem 7. Oktober 1989 und dem 3. Oktober 1990', in *Festschrift für P. Lerche* (Munich: C. H. Beck, 1993), 459; B. Schlink, 'Deutsch—deutsche Verfassungsentwicklungen im Jahre 1990', *Der Staat*, 30 (1991) 163; H. Quaritsch, 'Eigenarten und Rechtsfragen der DDR-Revolution', *Verwaltungs-Archiv*, 82 (1991), 314.

5. This discussion is documented in Guggenberger and Stein, *Die Verfassungsdiskussion im Jahr der deutschen Einheit*; on the present state of the German Constitution see also *Veröffentlichungen der Vereinigung der Deutschen Staatsrechtslehrer*, 49 (1990).

6. See D. Grimm, 'Zwischen Anschluss und Neukonstitution', *FAZ 5/4* (1990), reprinted in *Kritische Vierteljahresschrift für Gesetzgebung und Rechtswissenschaft*, iii (1990), 148, and also in Guggenberger and Stein, *Die Verfassungsdiskussion im Jahr der deutschen Einheit*, 119.

7. See P. Häberle, 'Die Kontroverse um die Reform des deutschen Grundgesetzes', *Zeitschrift für Politik*, 30 (1992), 233; P. Badura, 'Die Verfassungsfrage im wiedervereinigten Deutschland', in *Bitburger Gespräche, Jahrbuch 1991/92* (Heidelberg: Müller, 1991), 27; P. Kirchof, *Brauchen wir ein erneuertes Grundgesetz?* (1992); R. Scholz, 'Aufgaben und Grenzen einer Reform des Grundgesetzes', in *Festschrift für P. Lerche*, 65, with further references.

8. See D. Grimm, *Die Zukunft der Verfassung* (Frankfurt a. M.: Suhrkamp, 1991), 313.

9. For a more detailed discussion of this problem see D. Grimm, 'Die politischen Parteien', in *Handbuch des Verfassungsrechts* (Berlin: de Gruyter, 1983), 317.
10. See W. V. Simson and J. Scharze, *Europäische Integration und Grundgesetz. Maastricht und die Folgen für das deutsche Verfassungsrecht* (Berlin: de Gruyter, 1992).
11. This was demanded by H. Wieczorek-Zeul, *Das Parlament* (23 Oct. 1992), 4; see also W. Möschel, 'Fünf Optionen für Europa', *FAZ* (12 Sept. 1992), 13.
12. See R. Wildenmann (ed.), *Staatswerdung Europas?* (Baden-Baden: Nomos, 1991), esp. the contribution of M. R. Lepsius, p. 19; see also D. Grimm, 'Der Mangel an europäischer Demokratie', *Der Spiegel* (19 Oct. 1992), 57.
13. For further detail see D. Grimm, 'Subsidiarität ist nur ein Wort', *FAZ* (17 Sept. 1992), 38; M. Jachtenfuchs, 'Die EG nach Maastricht', *Europa-Archiv* (1992), 279.
14. For the following see Grimm, *Die Zukunft der Verfassung*, 31, 397.
15. On this point see E. G. Mahrenholz, *Die Verfassung und das Volk* (Munich: Carl Friedrich von Siemens Stiftung, 1992); D. Murswiek, 'Maastricht—nicht ohne Volksentscheid', *Süddeutsche Zeitung* (14 Oct. 1992), 11; H. H. Rupp, 'Muss das Volk über den Vertrag von Maastricht entscheiden?', *Neue Juristische Wochenschrift* (1993), 38.

7

The Constraints on Constitutional Change in France

GUY CARCASSONNE

The Constitution of the Fifth Republic is the sixteenth France has adopted since 1789.[1] The first Constitution lasted one year; the second was never enforced; while the remainder have varied in duration from twenty-one days[2] to sixty-five years.[3] The multitude of constitutions arises on the one hand from a combination of the French taste for geometrical architecture and written law and, on the other, from an ideological conception of what a constitution is. Those characteristics led each political faction to have its own idea of what a constitution should amount to, each of them assumed to be both complete and rational. Thus, any change in political forces throughout the nineteenth century almost inevitably produced a new supreme law. The consequence of such practices has been that it has taken more than a century and a half for the French people and their political representatives to understand and accept that a constitution should be the definition of common rules rather than a partisan weapon.

The political legitimacy of the Fifth Republic itself was heavily contested initially, a state of affairs which continued for years. Popular acceptance and adaptation was achieved long before political acceptance.[4] Amongst left-wing parties, reform of the Constitution has been a central proposition for two decades. However, once the Left gained power in 1981, such calls for change seemed to vanish as the Left found the institutions of government as established by the Constitution to its liking. Thus France has acquired constitutional stability. Although still subjected to criticism, in general the Constitution has been accepted, with any references to earlier hostility towards the Constitution serving only to portray those involved as out of date. However, a possible negative effect of this is the degree of reverence which the Constitution has received in certain circles, especially amongst the Gaullists, given that the Constitution was the creation of de Gaulle.[5] This has led to a few ritualistic speeches about reform, but prevented actual initiatives. The Constitution was introduced at a time when political stability began to seem possible in France also. For the first time in French history, parties operated as disciplined forces in parliament, with the result that governments began to last much longer in office than had been the case previously,[6] and the French Republic ceased to practise political instability as a traditional national sport.

Naturally, there is a close link between the development of constitutional and political stability: political stability was made easier, if not in fact created, by the constitutional system, with the effect that the achievement of political stability brought prestige to the Constitution, and thus lessened desires to change it. This is not to argue that the Constitution was suddenly immune from criticism, nor that the emergence of political stability was necessarily seen as a good thing. On the contrary, the strength of the presidency has been denounced repeatedly as despotic,[7] while the emergence of disciplined groups in parliament has been interpreted as discrediting the chambers,[8] and the support of an automatic majority for the government has been seen as suppressing normal democratic controls.[9] The memory of former political struggles that were confused but lively, and the relative torpidity of the Fifth Republic in comparison, nourished feelings of boredom and nostalgia in sections of public opinion and especially amongst certain politicians. Quite naturally, in searching for remedies for the observed defects of the system, many politicians were prompted to suggest amending the Constitution as a solution. Even amongst supporters of it such reform proposals were to be heard. A further impetus to the discussions on the need for reform was the experience of the political Right in opposition: some of its spokesmen began to wonder whether institutions that could give such firm power for such a long time to their adversaries were so desirable after all. The result of these views on the Constitution has been continual calls for change since 1958, with a no less vociferous lobby opposing such changes. These will be examined in turn in the next sections.

1. CHANGING THE CONSTITUTION

For about fifteen years the position of each party had been relatively predictable—total support for the Constitution from the Gaullists, total rejection by the Communists and a few other individuals, amongst whom Mitterrand was most active,[10] and, for those occupying the political ground in between these two extremes, a broad acceptance of the institutions combined with a rather paradoxical denunciation of the personal power of the President.[11] During the 1970s, however, these divisions began to lose their distinct party lines.

On the Left, a young socialist leader and public law teacher, André Laignel, was one of the first to praise the virtues of those institutions,[12] precisely on behalf of the ideals of change which were, then, those of the Socialist Party. The Constitution could secure stable power, which the Left had always lacked previously. Such stability could make possible the radical reforms which the Left intended to promote. Thus, the conclusion of this new syllogism was that those institutions could serve the Left. Naturally, such a conclusion was not unanimously accepted. The author himself presented his arguments cautiously, while the weight of traditional dogma prevented them from being immediately adopted. Only time and, above all, the exercise of power would be able to demonstrate the ease with which the Left would accommodate itself with the Constitution against which its most prominent leaders had fought.

Yet, imperceptibly, a first substantial change had occurred. In the absence of a considered alternative, the Left had, in fact, accepted the direct election of the president, or at least had resigned itself to it.[13] Therefore, its acquiescence to this central issue, albeit implicit, prevented it from proposing radical change. Consequently, the Left contented itself with proposals for minor change. Around the same time, an almost symmetrically opposite phenomenon was experienced by the French Right. Gaullism and 'Pompidolism' had been able to unite the traditionally divided French Right. As soon as Georges Pompidou died in April 1974, the quarrels re-emerged, symbolized by the immediate competition between Valéry Giscard d'Estaing and Jacques Chaban-Delmas, both of whom were candidates at the first presidential ballot in 1974, and followed very rapidly by the bitter struggle between Giscard d'Estaing and

Jacques Chirac, between the UDF (Union pour la Démocratie Française) and the RPR (Rassemblement pour la République).

It is no surprise that this struggle had its roots in institutional factors. The RPR vacillated between pursuit of its vocation of watchful guardian of Gaullist constitutional dogmas and pursuit of its immediate interests, which no longer included the pre-eminence of presidential power as the RPR no longer held this position. The 'Giscardian' movement, by contrast, simultaneously demonstrated a certain reformist audacity[14] with a reaffirmed vigilance concerning the issue of presidential pre-eminence. In fact, the positions of both the Right and the Left illustrated perfectly Olivier Duhamel's theory according to which the doctrinal load in the constitutional positions of the actors is in inverse proportion to their distance from power.[15] Thus the closer a party is to power, and *a fortiori* when a party has power, the more constitutionally pragmatic it becomes; the further a party is from power, and *a fortiori* when actually excluded, the more constitutionally doctrinaire the party's position. Consequently, it is quite logical that during the seven years from 1974 to 1981, which saw Gaullism, 'Giscardianism', and socialism succeed each other, positions on constitutional change moved perceptibly. Moreover, as will be discussed below, the new terms of the debate delimited the possible amendments.

1.1. The Terms of the Debate

The complexity arises from the fact that personalities hostile to each other on all other grounds found themselves sharing common positions in defence of common constitutional proposals. There were three themes in particular in the debate: (i) a return to a purely parliamentary system; (ii) a shift to a presidential system; and (iii) maintaining the existing system with substantial modifications.

The Communist Party (PCF) was really the only French party to favour a return to a parliamentary system, and it did so for three reasons. The first was that, having no possibility of exercising power or winning a presidential election,[16] maintaining such a doctrinal position posed no obstacle to the PCF's immediate political interests. The second reason is the long tradition of the Left in equating democracy with a parliamentary system.[17] Finally, having been at the zenith of its influence under the Fourth Republic,[18] the

PCF had a certain nostalgia for the institutions to which it attributed its past splendour. In fact, the Fifth Republic has been particularly harsh for the PCF. From the outset in 1958 the PCF, with approximately the same number of votes as the Gaullist party at the first ballot, won only ten constituencies at the second ballot while the UNR (Union pour la Nouvelle République) by then had 199 deputies. Since then, the triple effect of the PCF's ideology, of its own mistakes, and of the institutions has continuously reduced its influence. As the Party refused to recognize the first two of these as problematic, it blamed the institutions for all its problems. This is what drove it to denounce constantly, and in vain, the whole structure of the Constitution in addition to each of the elements of rationalized parliamentarism. Yet, victim itself of the general reverence for the Constitution, the PCF did not propose to name a Sixth Republic but sought to amend the Fifth to such an extent that it would be changed beyond recognition. The most complete expression of its position concerning the institutions is to be found in its 1971 programme for government.[19] It proposed to weaken significantly the power of the president,[20] to alter radically the relationship between government and parliament to the advantage of the latter, and to 'establish the sovereignty of the French people', by which it meant introducing proportional representation.

After more than thirty years of the Fifth Republic, proponents of the traditional parliamentary system remain present in the debate, but hardly as what could be described as a real political force. None of their proposals has ever been put on the parliamentary agenda, nor even examined in committee. This experience, however, is not unique to the defenders of the pure parliamentary system; those supporting a presidential system, although better distributed across the political spectrum, have had no greater success.

The logic of those seeking a presidential system is apparently rigorous. In so far as the head of state dominates the executive power, and in so far as the prime minister is subordinate to the head of state, and in so far as parliament is diminished, and the combination of all three leads to a system of unlimited presidential power, in order to establish an equilibrium it is necessary to sever all links between the legislative and executive powers. In essence, France would adopt a system inspired by that in the United States.

One of the first, and most eminent, to propose this was a professor of law, Georges Vedel.[21] Quite quickly, some politicians picked up the idea and gave rise to an active group who defended the proposal dogmatically, although Vedel had merely proposed it as one possible solution from many. Since the end of the 1960s a constant flow of constitutional draft bills have adopted this proposal and still do. Their authors come in particular from the centre of the political spectrum, those for whom the present bipolar trend is the most uncomfortable and who, being sincere democrats, would wish to avoid both systematic allegiance and systematic hostility towards governments. Followers are also to be found within the socialists and amongst deputies of the classical Right, both of whom are frustrated with the operation of the chambers to which they belong.

Yet, though the theme of a presidential system reappears periodically, even in public opinion, it never seems to gain any ground. The reason lies not in the strength of the objections to the proposed system, but in the fact that there is no cause to debate the proposal, given the inertia generated by the current consensus as to the acceptability of the existing institutions. Consequently, to the extent that reform of the French Constitution is seriously mooted, such discussions are to be found mainly in relation to particular amendments to the existing institutions.

Apart from a few rather isolated personalities and old-fashioned Gaullists,[22] all the political leaders, influential columnists, and most academics recommend a number of alterations to the Constitution. Everybody is aware that the Fifth Republic has given to France a stability and, to a certain extent, a degree of efficiency that should not be damaged or even threatened by inappropriate changes. However, the constitutional system also bears responsibility for the widening gap between the people and the political system. The loss of influence by MPs has weakened a useful link between the population and the central power. The existence of disciplined groups in parliament gives the impression that there are no more checks and balances, that the government can impose its will while itself being a mere screen behind which the president freely pulls the strings. This lack of presidential accountability is certainly the principal reproach addressed to the institutions, and it has become more intense as the presidential term of office goes on.

The above are what may be called the common-sense grievances. Most are also shared by politicians, at least when they are not in positions of power themselves. Even here, however, Mitterrand can be an exception, as in his declaration that the institutions were bad before his accession to power and would be bad again following his departure.[23] The model being provided by the President himself, it is not surprising that other leaders criticize aspects of the Constitution and propose methods by which to improve it. Yet the whole enterprise of reform is further complicated by a general belief amongst politicians that it is not so much the institutions themselves which are at fault, but the method of their implementation.[24] Thus most of their suggestions and proposals centre on implementation rather than on amendments to the text of the Constitution. Furthermore, many of the suggestions are but manifestations of good intentions rather than precise propositions for reform. None the less, it is still possible to discern what the possible constitutional amendments could be.

1.2. The Possible Amendments

The opposing criticisms from the supporters of a purely parliamentary system and from those supporting a presidential system have encouraged a sort of half-way position which may lead to concrete achievements. The different amendments which might be successful can be gathered around three complementary aims, which would be (a) to render the president more accountable, (b) to render the parliament less constrained, and (c) to cause the citizens to become more involved.

Rendering the president more accountable.   When reading the text of the Constitution, the different powers given to the president appear as rather important without being overwhelming. Above all, the main feature of his powers, except in foreign affairs, is that they give him the power, not to take decisions, but to decide who will take decisions: the president appoints the prime minister (Article 8) but, afterwards, the prime minister is, legally, the principal decision-maker in terms of French policies; the president can call a referendum (Article 11) but it is the people who provide the answer to the question; if there is a crisis between the executive and the legislative powers, the president can dissolve the Assembly (Article 12), but once again it is the people who arbitrate; the president can appoint three members of the *conseil constitutionnel* (Article 56) and submit treaties (Article 54) and bills (Article 61) to its review but does not decide the result himself. Those are almost the only powers the president can exercise without any countersignature.[25]

None the less, although his legal powers are limited, the president gives more than an impression that the limits do not operate and that no one can resist his will. This evidently comes from the way he is elected: the direct decision of the people, in addition to the double ballot system which means that whoever wins will have gained the support of more than 50 per cent of the whole French electorate, give a tremendous personal legitimacy to the president. His political significance is thus far more than his legal powers would justify. It is the second ballot of the presidential election which determines, in fact, the two political tendencies which will struggle in parliament until the next presidential election. When the majority in the Assembly is of the same political persuasion as the president, which has occurred up to now for thirty-two out of thirty-six years, it is not the leader of the majority who is appointed prime minister by the president; it is the prime minister appointed by the president who becomes leadeı of the majority. Thus there is little point in attempting to diminish the president's powers as expressed in the Constitution, given that the source of the president's strength lies outside the Constitution, being a result of the manner in which the system reacts to the way the president is elected. As far as this element cannot be reconsidered politically, the only possible alternative would be to shorten the presidential term of office.

Such an idea is not new. The seven-year term is a legacy of history. In 1958 de Gaulle was indifferent to the duration of the term of office, believing that it would be uncertain in any event: his intention was to retire if ever his recommendations were not followed by the electorate, irrespective of the moment or topic, and so he did.[26] One decade later, the problems inherent in such a long period of office were accepted by Pompidou, who decided to reduce the term to five years. A constitutional draft bill was adopted by both chambers in 1973. However, the necessary ratification, either through a referendum or a qualified (three-fifths) majority vote of

Congress, never took place, partly on account of the Left which, although in favour of the reform, opposed it on the grounds that it was insufficient.[27]

Since then the issue has periodically re-emerged. Opinion polls show a majority in favour of the reform. Many political leaders also favour it, and even the president has shown a certain acceptance of the idea. None the less, the idea retains its opponents, most of whom consider that such a reform might prove to be the first step towards a presidential system or, at least, be a way of weakening the power of the head of state, which they oppose.

If, for legal and logical reasons, the president cannot be better accountable, he must become more frequently accountable, by facing the electorate every five years instead of every seven. A complementary proposal is to limit by law the number of times a particular individual can hold the office of president, the preferred limit being for two terms. Another proposal is to require presidential and legislative elections to be held at the same time. It remains to be seen whether such proposals will be achieved, but there is little doubt that the electorate favours a reduction in the duration of the term of office, whatever may be the limits on repeated service.

Rendering parliament less constrained.   In 1958 no one imagined that one day France might have disciplined groups in parliament and a homogeneous majority. That is why all possible steps were taken in the Constitution to provide the government with stability and ability to act. However, as early as 1962, a majority was found in the Assembly. This has been an important element of modernization, but has not been without its inconvenience. The combination of a majority and of the provisions designed to deal with the hypothesis of a lack of such a majority has created an uncomfortable situation in which parliament has been constrained. For years MPs have complained about their relative weakness. Both opposition and government deputies feel powerless to influence the decisions of government. Several provisions in the Constitution are criticized for allowing this to occur, and are consequently the centre of attention in terms of proposals for reform. The aim of such reforms would not be to give new powers to parliament, but rather to withdraw some facilities which government is seen as abusing.

The first issue is to lengthen the sessions of parliament: at present, they are limited to eighty days from October to December and ninety days from April to June. It is proposed to create a single session that could begin around mid-September and last up to the end of June. This would give the chambers more time both to examine the drafts and to control the government. The second issue is that MPs want a minimum right of control over their own agenda,[28] which might result in the reservation of one meeting a week to give priority to the reading of private member's bills. The third issue is the enlargement of the number of permanent committees and an increase in their powers. On all of these issues a consensus could probably be obtained, but would still leave unresolved the main difficulty caused by Article 49, paragraph 3. By this provision, the prime minister has the right at any time[29] to call a vote of no confidence linked to a draft bill. The effect is that the reading of the bill immediately stops and if, within twenty-four hours, no motion of censure is registered, the text is adopted without a vote. If a motion of censure is registered within the twenty-four-hour period, its discussion is placed on the agenda after another two days. Then, either the motion of censure is adopted,[30] the government is overthrown, and the text rejected, or no vote is held on the confidence motion and the text is considered adopted.

Initially, this system had been seen as a means of enabling a government without a stable majority to go on working as long as it was not overthrown.[31] However, between 1962 and 1988 governments which had the support of an absolute majority abused this facility to solve internal political problems. Although fewer than forty bills have been adopted by this method, the result has been a rise in feelings of parliamentary impotence, shared by MPs and the public. That is why some politicians have suggested limiting the use of this method of enactment to three or four times per year.[32] Others have proposed to restrict its use only to the most important bills, the obvious difficulty being to identify these types of bill in advance. A more recent proposition is to give the Assembly itself the power, under certain conditions, to refuse the dilemma 'accept the text or dismiss the government'.[33] Whatever solution is finally chosen, it is certain that, if only for psychological reasons, it will be necessary to modify this system. If this is not done in time, the greatest danger is that one day this article may be abolished, which would be a disproportionate response to a provision which incorporates an important principle, albeit one the excessive use of which must be resisted.

Causing the citizens to become more involved.   Like many political systems, the French does not adequately provide for citizen participation. While it seems improbable that textual additions to a constitution can inspire persons to participate in political life, none the less, for those already predisposed to such participation, two procedures may improve their involvement. The first is the referendum, which has been opposed historically for two reasons—the Bonapartist use of the plebiscite, and the personalization of issues which were the subject of a referendum by de Gaulle, who portrayed the referendum as a test of public confidence in him rather than a vote on the substantive issue. For sixteen years following the feeble performance of the 1972 referendum called by Pompidou,[34] no referendum was called. In 1988 this situation changed, due to developments concerning the future of the territory of New Caledonia. A second referendum was held in November 1992 concerning ratification of the Maastricht Treaty. Here, however, the victory of the 'yes' vote was made possible precisely because the President had stated that he did not view the result as having any personal significance in terms of confidence in his ability or policies.

The referendum may be a useful way to invite the people to decide upon matters of importance. At present, this procedure is only possible to ratify certain treaties or to adopt bills relating to the organization of public powers. This means that social or political questions cannot be put to a referendum. This is one of the reasons why in 1985 Mitterrand unsuccessfully tried to amend Article 11 in that direction. It has also been suggested that the question to be put to a referendum should be subject to the prior control of the Constitutional Council in order to ensure that it respects the supreme text.[35] A rather recent tendency is consideration of a possible popular initiative, as already exists in Switzerland. While the first proposition to amend Article 11 to allow for a referendum on social and political matters is broadly accepted and depends only on an opportunity to have it adopted, debate on the popular initiative has only just begun, and rather discreetly at that.

Another reform which might be taken into consideration is to introduce a consultative referendum, as exists in Scandinavia. A version of this could take a form which would enable the president to put a simple question to a referendum, provided that, afterwards, parliament would draft and pass the corresponding bill, knowing the people's will. In this way, all would fulfil their roles: the president, who decides to consult the electorate; the people, who decide about their own future; and the MPs, who enact the laws. In any event, whether of a consultative nature or not, the referendum is one of the possibilities accepted as serving to promote a higher involvement, even if only occasional, of the citizens in public affairs.

Another possibility would be to allow citizens to bring matters before the Constitutional Council. This Council, created in 1958, was largely inactive for over ten years, prior to a surge of activity at the beginning of the 1970s, as a result of which, by proving its independence, it gained prestige in public opinion. A very important step forward was taken when the right to submit a bill to the Council was accorded to the opposition in 1974.[36] However, the bills subjected to this particular form of judicial review continue to be limited to those that are not yet promulgated and are often submitted by public authorities. A further extension was proposed by Mitterrand in 1989. A constitutional draft bill provided that all bills could be submitted to the Council, and that anyone who thought that a bill was contrary to the Constitution by restraining his liberty would be able to refer the bill to the Council. Adequate procedures were to be introduced to prevent frivolous applications.[37] Although opinion polls showed much support for this reform,[38] it turned out to be one more failure, and once more for political reasons which had little to do with the topic. What is most surprising is that, officially, this reform project had very few opponents; if nothing else, this favours its approval in the future. Giving the right to citizens to defend their interests and beliefs before the most prestigious institution in the country would undeniably be viewed as significant progress.

In addition to the above proposals for amendment, there is an emerging debate concerning the status of the judiciary. As with the judiciary in other countries, the French have also experienced a deep crisis. Yet it is unclear to what extent constitutional amendments alone will remedy this situation. The debate is just beginning.

As can be seen, the debate on constitutional change in France is still lively, and the proposals which could justify amendments are numerous. A consensus amongst leaders of all parties might even be possible on a certain number of them. Many of the reforms have strong public support also. How, then, is it that the reforms have not been achieved? The explanation is quite simple: up to now, the calls for change have been generally less powerful than the impediments to change. It is to these impediments that the discussion next turns.

2. THE IMPEDIMENTS TO CHANGE

Since 1958 the Constitution has been amended eight times, which proves that change is possible. However, five attempts, following presidential initiatives, have failed, which proves that change is difficult to achieve. Naturally, both successes and failures have explanations; yet the explanations for the successes keep changing, whereas those for the failures are almost always the same.

Acceptance of the Constitution as providing the rules of the game and, consequently, consensus that it should not be altered without the agreement or acceptance of a broad majority of the players has amounted to significant progress for French public law. However, this reluctance to change the Constitution is so ingrained in political consciousness now that even reforms broadly supported or accepted have been impossible for over sixteen years, apart from the very specific amendment recently arising from the Maastricht Treaty.[39] In order to understand this situation, analyse its causes, and try to forecast its likely development, one has to take into account the existence of structural and circumstantial impediments to constitutional change.

2.1. *Structural Impediments*

Of the structural impediments, inertia is the first. All countries have many problems to solve, such that constitutional issues, except in very special circumstances, are seldom considered urgent enough to be placed at the top of the political agenda. Moreover, given political struggles between government and opposition, any proposal concerning reform of the Constitution is ritually criticized as a diversion from the 'real problems' facing the country. This is not unique to France, and has had far greater consequences in countries such as Italy. Bearing in mind this traditional inertia, the success of any initiative requires a combination of many factors in order to overcome the first two obstacles to change: the divisions within and between parties, and the constitutional requirements for change themselves.

The divisions within and between parties. The way the Constitution was amended in spring 1992 illustrates the difficulty perfectly. When the Maastricht Treaty was signed, in accordance with Article 54 of the Constitution the President submitted it to the Constitutional Council to determine whether the Treaty respected the supreme law or whether amendments were necessary to the Constitution prior to ratification of the Treaty.[40] The decision of the Council focused on three elements which were not compatible with the Constitution[41] and required constitutional amendments in order to allow ratification to occur. A bill was introduced accordingly, and was finally adopted by Congress on 23 June 1992. The interesting point is that, of the groups supporting the bill, none could manage to vote unanimously. The Socialist Party supported Mitterrand's amendment, yet eight of its deputies and two of its senators refused to vote in favour. The same thing happened to the groups attached to the UDF, and even the 'centrist' groups, which have made the European ideal the first element of their political identity, were not able to achieve total unanimity. As for the Gaullist groups, they were not even able to define a position and decided to leave their members free to vote as they chose.[42]

This example may seem exceptional on account of the fact that the intrinsic difficulty involved in changing the Constitution was complicated further by the debate on the future of Europe. However, it would probably be a mistake to consider those divisions as being linked only to the specific European nature of the matter. On the contrary, the last previous attempt to alter the Constitution to allow citizens to refer bills to the Constitutional Council, a far less controversial issue than the Maastricht Treaty, resulted in a similar political débâcle. A majority in the National Assembly could be achieved only on account of divisions within the three right-wing opposition parties, which resulted in their splitting their votes.

Ordinarily, the discipline that exists within the groups gives the government the possibility either of certainty as to its own absolute majority or, if no such majority exists, the opportunity to negotiate and compromise with the opposition in order to obtain the necessary support. Agreements reached in such circumstances are usually respected. On constitutional issues, however, no such certainty is possible. Not only has consensus between the groups never been obtained so far, but one can observe a strong trend towards division inside each group (with the exception of the Communists, and even this may not last) which makes it impossible for their whips or spokesmen to commit all the votes of their members, or for the government to be sure that they will be able to fulfil their commitment. This obstacle is all the more important given that the requirements to amend the Constitution are quite demanding.

The constitutional requirements for change. In terms of legal theory, the way to amend the Constitution is set out in Article 89. According to this, the initiative for an amendment may come either from the president, upon a proposition made by the prime minister, or from any member of parliament. If the draft bill is put on the agenda, which only occurs when the initiative comes from the president, each chamber must adopt it in the same form. When this is done, the bill must still be ratified by referendum, unless the president chooses[43] to submit it to the Congress (a joint meeting of senators and deputies), which must ratify it by a qualified majority of three-fifths. In the case of ordinary legislation, a joint committee tries to reach a compromise over any lasting disagreements and, if it does not succeed, the government may ask the deputies to make the final decision. In the constitutional amendment procedure, however, a joint committee does not exist and the two chambers have equal powers. In effect, this means that the Senate has a power of veto over any constitutional changes, a power which it exercises.

As a result of the electoral system, the composition of the French Senate is such that traditionally conservative rural populations are over-represented. Thus, the Senate is instinctively averse to change. Moreover, as senators had the same powers as deputies during the Third Republic, they have never really accepted the subsequent supremacy which the National Assembly received under the Fourth and Fifth Republics. This is why the Senate tries to benefit from any attempt to amend the Constitution by seeking to appropriate more powers to itself, and does not shrink for that purpose from resorting to a sort of blackmail made possible by its right of veto. This is just what it did in 1989, adopting the constitutional draft bill after having modified it in a way that was acceptable neither to the government nor to the National Assembly, even those on the right-wing benches.[44] In this way it tried to impose its own conditions, while not appearing responsible for the failure of a popular amendment. Again in 1992, the Senate managed to reduce slightly the supremacy of the National Assembly on grounds which had nothing to do with the Maastricht amendment.[45] After a public manifestation of bad temper during which Mitterrand appeared to indicate that he might not accept the Senate's measure and resort instead to a direct referendum, the President finally had to accept the will of the Senate, as the Maastricht Treaty was at stake if he refused.

This does not mean that amending the Constitution is impossible. Rather, it means, first, that such amendment will always be more difficult for the Left than for the Right; and, second, that amendment is possible only if the Senate either has an interest in the change or, on the contrary, is not concerned at all, as was the case in October 1974 and June 1976 respectively. As a result of this state of affairs, the hypothesis that there is a short cut to amending the Constitution has gained ground. This possibility first arose in 1962 when, in order to introduce direct election of the president, de Gaulle decided to amend the text not through the use of Article 89 but by calling a referendum directly under Article 11. Legally his decision was open to criticism on the following bases: (i) that Article 89 is included in a section entitled 'about amendment', while Article 11 is not; (ii) that Article 11 when written was never interpreted as being applicable to an amendment to the Constitution; and, finally, (iii) that it made no sense to provide for a complicated procedure of amendment in Article 89 which ended in a referendum, if it were possible simply to go direct to a referendum under Article 11.[46] De Gaulle, however, was able to reply that his choice of using Article 11 was perfectly democratic provided that the answer to any proposal for amendment would be given by the French people themselves. In any event, the referendum took place and was a success. However, use of the same procedure some six years later proved a failure, after which de Gaulle resigned.

Since then, the question of using Article 11 remains open. Ultimately, whether this short cut respects the Constitution is merely an academic question as, even if the procedure is contrary to the Constitution, it still results in a decision by the electorate. Neither Georges Pompidou nor Valéry Giscard d'Estaing needed to bother about the matter while in office. However, in March 1988 Mitterrand responded to a question as to whether Article 11 could be used in this way by saying that 'the custom established and approved by the people can from now on be considered as one of the possible ways of amendment, together with Article 89'.[47] This possibility was publicly called to mind in 1992 in discussions as to what would occur if the normal procedures failed on the Maastricht issue.[48] Not only does this short cut appear as a future eventuality, therefore; it is likely to be the only possible way from now on by which the circumstantial impediments to changing the Constitution might be overcome.

2.2. *The Circumstantial Impediments*

On 11 November 1991 the President announced his intention to propose in the autumn of 1992 several amendments to the Constitution which would include provisions on the length of the presidential term of office. Autumn 1992 came and went without any such proposals: once more 'real problems', such as Maastricht, Sarajevo, and unemployment, intervened. The fact is that the initiative probably came too late—or, indeed, perhaps too soon—as the relative popularity of any constitutional change is dependent upon a specific methodology of introducing it. These issues will be discussed below.

The popularity of proposals for change. While the Constitution may need improvements, it undoubtedly works as it is. Thus no change is particularly vital. Consequently, even if a proposal is broadly approved, such as that of the five-year presidential term in office, for example, it is generally not considered simply on its own merits, but is coloured by opinions about the person proposing it.

So far, Mitterrand has made three attempts to change the Constitution and announced a fourth. The first attempt took place in 1984, at a time when both he and the parliamentary majority were very unpopular.[49] Faced with a crisis concerning the status of private schools, Mitterrand tried to deal with this through a change of government, replacing Pierre Mauroy with Laurent Fabius, and by introducing an amendment procedure which would allow a referendum on the topic.[50] Even if the idea itself was good, the move appeared to many as a political ruse, and the Senate accordingly felt it legitimate to block the process a year before a likely change in the political composition of the government and the defeat of the President, which in fact was to occur in 1986. With Mitterrand's proposal being viewed as a political manœuvre, the response to it also assumed a tactical political character.

The second attempt in 1989 aimed to give citizens the opportunity to refer bills to the Constitutional Council. Once more, the Senate caused this initiative to fail, apparently on the grounds that it could not participate in a measure which would be interpreted as a success for a left-wing president. The third attempt was the sole success, but this was because the constitutional issue involved was of secondary importance, the main concern being to enable ratification of the Maastricht Treaty rather than to alter the existing distribution of powers. The fourth proposal announced presents a dilemma for the President. The experience of the previous three proposals for amendment demonstrated the futility of resorting to parliament. It also appears that any referendum to change the Constitution would not succeed unless linked to a proposal to reduce the presidential term of office to five years. Yet the President could hardly achieve such a reform and himself remain in office afterwards; having shortened the term of his successors to five years, it would seem incongruous that he should remain in office after more than twelve years.

One can further understand Mitterrand's hesitancy given his unprecedented low levels of support as measured by public opinion polls: at the end of the summer of 1992, polls showed a confidence rating of less than a third of those polled. Indeed, the desire to see him resign might prove to be the decisive factor in motivating the 'yes' vote if a referendum were held. The situation being as it is, the announcement made in November 1991 will probably not be followed up unless Mitterrand should decide to resign, an unlikely possibility. An option, however, would be to take the initiative right before the end of his term, around the autumn of 1994, when the question of resignation would not be an issue. The opportunity of promoting constitutional change in the coming years seems slight. Yet it would probably be a mistake to interpret this state of affairs as a mere reaction to the present political situation. After all, Pompidou was unable to do much better, and to the extent that Giscard d'Estaing had more success, this was due to the fact that he respected what may be termed a specific methodology of introducing reform.

The methodology of introducing reforms.   In 1976, on a very technical question—what would happen if a presidential candidate disappeared during the process—the Constitution was slightly amended by parliament and congress. It seemed wise to provide for such a situation: moreover, the reform neither gave nor withdrew power from anyone, and both chambers had a majority of the same political persuasion as the incumbent president. It was, apart from the particular case of the Maastricht amendment, the last successful attempt to introduce constitutional change through the parliamentary procedure. The conclusion to be drawn is that the parliamentary procedure needs one necessary, but in itself insufficient, condition to be successful: that the amendment should involve a change of very little political interest.

This is why it is possible to predict without hesitation that this procedure will fall into disuse. Unless the Senate itself is reformed first, no president in the future, of whatever political persuasion, will accept the hazardous veto of the Senators and, in general, the complexity and dangers of the parliamentary procedure. If ever the Constitution is amended, it will be through a direct referendum. But this implies another element. The only way a president can be sure of a victorious vote is by organizing such a referendum at the very beginning of his term, during what is called 'the state of grace'. It is relevant to note that the only significant amendment adopted after the Gaullist period was the reform brought about by Giscard d'Estaing less than six months after his election, through the parliamentary procedure which was still fit for use at that time.

The crucial condition for constitutional change is a direct referendum, organized very soon after a presidential election. The debate was opened a long time ago and it is now time for a conclusion, which might occur sometime in 1995 with the next presidential election. The candidates will have to take policy positions on the duration of the term of office, in addition to some or all of the previously mentioned issues. A direct referendum could be called within the year following the election, whoever should win. Naturally, such a prediction does not pretend to be iron-clad, but rather is presented as the logical result of the foregoing analysis. In the meantime, two other problems, partly related, will feed the debate: the ongoing quarrel concerning electoral law, and the question of the constitutional consequences of Europeanization.

One of the main arguments of the supporters of proportional representation is that it exists in all European countries with the exception of the United Kingdom and France. Yet, given that those who complain most about the electoral law are precisely those who cannot manage to win enough constituencies—the National Front on the extreme right wing, the Communist Party on the extreme left, and the Greens—they do not have enough influence in parliament to obtain a reform which is contrary to the short-term interests of the larger parties. As long as there is no strong public pressure for the introduction of proportional representation, the most that can be expected is the introduction of some form of mixed system.

Concerning Europeanization, the only real question is whether or not it has any direct consequences for national constitutional systems. In France, the answer is no. The European Community may bring many common policies, but the negotiation and execution of such policies remains an issue of national competence. As far as European integration goes, it is generally considered that even in the event that a federalist hypothesis was an option to be pursued, there would still be an absence of demand for any sort of unification of the twelve constitutional systems. Hence, if constitutional change occurs in France, it will be important but limited and occur immediately before or after the next presidential election.

ADDENDUM

Since the above text was completed, the situation in France has changed, at least in its external manifestations. In November 1992, François Mitterrand announced his intention of making new proposals. To this end, he created a Consultative Constitutional Committee and asked it to prepare some propositions upon various elements of the Constitution. The Committee, sixteen members of which were appointed by the President, consisted mainly of lawyers (eight professors, five senior judges, one barrister) but also included one former minister of General de Gaulle, Pierre Sudreau, and one former Left Prime Minister, Pierre Mauroy. The Committee, created on 2 December,[51] was chaired by Professor Georges Vedel. The Committee worked hard and quickly, and did not hesitate to exceed the limits of the terms of reference set by the President. Its report was published on 15 February 1993.[52] The proposals in the report are organized around three themes: that the power of the executive should be better defined; that there should be a more active parliament; and that citizens should play a greater role in the political system.

In relation to reform of the power of the executive, the Committee was divided on the question of the length of the presidential term of office. Ten supported the existing seven-year term, while six favoured a five-year term. The Committee was also divided on the question of renewal of the presidential term of office. The majority of members who favoured a seven-year period of office were unable to agree on this issue. The consequence was that six members of the Committee favoured limiting the renewal to one term, while seven favoured no limits being imposed. Since no clear majority could be obtained, the Committee made no final recommendation in its report; instead it set out the arguments for each position. One recommendation which the Committee did agree upon was that the presidential term of office should end on a precise date (probably 15 March), in order to avoid complications.[53] Beyond these issues, the Committee made some useful recommendations aimed at clarifying the competences of the president and of the government. It proposed, for example, that the president should appoint fewer senior civil servants than is at present the case; that members of the government should be legally more accountable than at present; and, in addition, that any newly appointed prime minister should, in the fortnight following his appointment, obtain a vote of confidence from the National Assembly.

Concerning the activities of parliament, the Committee's recommendations were largely technical. It suggested that the parliament should debate welfare expenditure, and be informed immediately of any armed intervention abroad and be able to debate it. Of greater significance was the recommendation that parliamentary sessions should be lengthened: in contrast to the existing two three-month sessions, under the terms of the recommendation there would be a single session lasting from the beginning of October until the end of June. The Commission also proposed to make membership of parliament incompatible with the simultaneous occupancy of most important local elected offices. This particular idea is certainly to be approved, but its translation into practice is far too timorous: most of the difficulties with which the French parliament has to deal arise from the fact that its members are not available and present often enough; and the main reason for their absence is their involvement in local government.

The Committee also proposed that members of parliament should be able to decide on the parliamentary agenda at least once a week. At present, the government has complete authority over this. However, as a counterweight to this, it felt that it was necessary to extend the procedure under Article 49-3 to possibilities of rejection (of a draft bill adopted by the National Assembly at the meeting at which it decides the agenda) rather than only approval. This is the only modification proposed for a provision which is already highly criticized in its present shape. Finally, another recommendation was made, which may be considered a minimum requirement in a modern democracy: that the opposition should be able not only to propose but also to obtain the creation of parliamentary committees of inquiry.

Concerning the role of citizens in public life, the Committee envisaged a procedure of minority-initiated referendum. Under the terms of the recommendation, one-fifth of the members of parliament (both chambers) would be empowered to propose that a referendum be held. The proposal for a referendum would then be submitted to the Constitutional Council for verification of its compatibility with the Constitution. On the basis that the proposal was found to be compatible and also enjoyed the support of one-tenth of the electorate, then if parliament, after a four-month delay, did not adopt the bill, a referendum would be organized by the Constitutional Council. Further recommendations by the Committee included a proposal to revive the procedure which allowed citizens to appeal direct to the Constitutional Council, and changes in the composition of the superior council of magistracy in order to make the latter more independent. Finally, the Committee envisaged, quite logically, a procedure for amendment of the Constitution which would deprive the Senate of its current right of veto. Under this proposal, after a constitutional bill had received two readings in each chamber, the president could organize a referendum where the constitutional bill was adopted by one chamber by a three-fifths majority, even if the other chamber had not agreed.

The report of the Committee contains some very good proposals. It can be argued, however, that it lacks both imagination and daring on several important elements, such as Article 49-3. The President adopted some of the proposals, added one of his own (on the suppression of Article 16 about exceptional circumstances), and officially presented a constitutional bill just before the general elections he knew he would lose.

Since March 1993 the Constitution has been amended again on two occasions, both after initiatives taken by the Government and accepted by the President. The first modification gave more independence to judges (July 1993), while the second, minor if not superfluous, affected the right of sanctuary (November 1993). More important reforms remain, therefore, on the agenda.

Support for a five-year presidential term was expressed by the Prime Minister, Édouard Balladur. However, after becoming a presidential candidate in early 1995 and at a time when his rating in the opinion polls was high, he began to talk again about keeping the seven-year term. This is both a spectacular confirmation of Olivier Duhamel's theorem and a good summary of the constraints on constitutional change in France. There is a right moment for important amendments—straight after a presidential election—and often there is a willingness to accept such changes. Unhappily, so far, the willingness vanishes when the right moment has come, while the right moment has usually gone by the time the willingness reappears.

Notes

1. Taking into account the so-called constitutional bill of 10 July 1940 and the constitutional bill of 2 Nov. 1945.
2. The Additional Act to the Constitution of the Empire which was adopted on 23 Apr. 1815, and which ceased with the defeat at Waterloo.
3. The Third Republic was born in 1875 and disappeared *de facto* in 1940, *de jure* in 1945.

4. In the referendum of 28 Sept. 1958 adopting the Constitution, those in favour amounted to 66.4% of the electorate and 79.2% of those actually voting.
5. See O. Duhamel, *La Gauche et la Vᵉ République* (Paris, 1980), 187.
6. From 1958 to 1992, France has had 12 different governments, which gives an average duration of over 34 months. By comparison, during the Third and Fourth Republics, the average was around 7 months.
7. 'The provisions of the Constitution which have helped the settlement and abuse of personal power must be suppressed or amended'; *Programme commun de gouvernement du parti communiste et du parti socialiste* (Paris, 1972), 150.
8. The most biting criticism of the institution came from François Mitterrand in *Le Coup d'état permanent* (Paris, 1964).
9. A Gaullist back-bencher, Hector Roland, once declared that he and his fellow members of the majority were the 'hobnailed boots' of General de Gaulle.
10. Together with Pierre Mendès France, whose opposition was such that, unlike Mitterrand, he never accepted the idea of being a presidential candidate.
11. See Duhamel, *La Gauche et la Vᵉ République*, 160.
12. 'La Gauche socialiste face au fait majoritaire' (thesis, Univ. of Paris I, 1975).
13. See Duhamel, *La Gauche et la Vᵉ République*, 247.
14. By fixing the age of majority at 18 and by reforming the Constitutional Council.
15. Duhamel, *La Gauche et la Vᵉ République*, 548.
16. De Gaulle had deliberately avoided a system of direct presidential election in 1958 for fear that a communist candidate might be elected thus. By 1962, this fear had vanished.
17. This tradition took root in the way that both the Second Republic ended and the Third Republic began, following the crisis of 1877.
18. The worst level of performance during the Fourth Republic was 25.7% of the vote in legislative elections in 1956. This figure was 3 times the rate achieved in subsequent elections.
19. PCF, *Changer de cap: Programme pour un gouvernement démocratique d'union populaire* (Paris, 1971).
20. The president would have kept only the right to appoint the prime minister, and would have lost his symbolic power of arbitration.
21. G. Vedel, 'Le Régime présidentiel', *Revue des travaux de l'Académie des sciences morales et politiques* (Paris, 1957), 261.
22. The most prominent being Michel Debré, the first Prime Minister of the Fifth Republic, who wrote most of the Constitution as Minister for Justice in the last government of the Fourth Republic.
23. C. Nay, *Les Sept Mitterrand* (Paris, 1988), 171.

24. See Duhamel, *La Gauche et la Ve République*, 169.
25. Two other powers can be used without countersignature. One is to send messages to the parliament, the other is to use the 'crisis powers' of Art. 16.
26. On the evening of 27 Apr. 1969, when it became clear that opponents of decentralization and reform of the Senate would win the referendum, de Gaulle announced his resignation, to take effect at noon the following day.
27. The Socialist Party demanded that the government should add an amendment limiting a president to two terms in office.
28. In fact, they already have one which they seldom use, and it is subject only to priority being given to government legislation.
29. The only condition is that the cabinet should have considered it first.
30. This requires an absolute majority of deputies, with only votes in favour of censure being registered.
31. The system was the French adaptation of the German constructive motion of censure.
32. However, except for Jacques Chirac, no one has ever used this provision more than 3 or 4 times a year.
33. See G. Carcassonne, 'La Règle du jeu', *Le Monde*, 27 Feb. 1992.
34. The rate of abstention was almost 40%, while only 36.1% of the electorate voted in favour.
35. The proposition was included in an amendment to the 1985 constitutional draft bill, which ultimately failed to be adopted.
36. Constitutional Bill No. 74-904, 29 Oct. 1974, amended Art. 61 and enabled 60 deputies or 60 senators to submit a bill, after its adoption but before its promulgation, to the Constitutional Council.
37. The reference to the Constitutional Council would only occur following examination by the ordinary courts and either the Conseil d'État or the Cour de Cassation.
38. Some 71% of the public were said to be in favour, according to *Le Parisien*, 12 Oct. 1989.
39. This amendment only succeeded owing to the personal commitment of leaders of the opposition.
40. According to Art. 56, if the Constitutional Council decides that a treaty is incompatible with the Constitution, it cannot be ratified unless the Constitution is first amended accordingly.
41. The 3 elements were European monetary union, the possibility of European citizens other than those of French nationality having the right to vote and be candidates in local elections, and a minor point concerning visas to enter France.
42. At the meeting of Congress, most Gaullist MPs did not take part in the vote.

43. According to Art. 89, when the president is the initiator of the procedure, he may choose either Congress or a referendum. On the contrary, if the initiative comes from the parliament (which has never happened so far), the only method of ratification is by referendum.

44. The Senate already has a veto over organic bills where it is directly concerned. It wanted to extend this veto right to all organic bills.

45. An organic bill being necessary to organize the participation of non-French EC citizens in French local elections, the Senate managed to assume a right of veto over this organic law by means of what is now Art. 88-3 of the Constitution.

46. Art. 89 had established an equilibrium so that neither executive nor legislature could achieve constitutional reforms without the input of the other. Use of Art. 11 broke this equilibrium.

47. Interview in *Pouvoirs*, Mar. 1988.

48. *Le Monde*, 19 June 1992.

49. Only a minority showed confidence in the President in polls. See 'Popularités 1981–1988', in *L'État de l'opinion 1989* (Paris, 1989), 149.

50. As the question of the status of private schools does not concern the 'organization of public powers' or an international treaty, the referendum procedure in Art. 11 does not apply.

51. 'Décret no. 92-1247 du 2 décembre 1992 instituant un Comité consultatif pour la revision de la Constitution' (*Journal officiel*, 3 Dec. 1992).

52. 'Rapport remis au Président de la République le 15 février 1993 par le Comité consultatif pour la revision de la Constitution' (*Journal officiel*, 16 Feb. 1993), 2537.

53. France still follows the presidential calendar based on President Pompidou's death. If he had died in July instead of Apr., all the subsequent presidential elections would have had to be organized in Aug. If the normal end of term occurs in Mar., the election will always take place at the end of Feb. and beginning of Mar. Moreover, if ever, either by death or resignation, a presidential election had to be organized at another time of the year, it would be only for one occasion, and the ordinary calendar would begin again the next time.

8

Lions Around the Throne: The Expansion of Judicial Review in Britain

GEOFFREY MARSHALL

A major feature of post-war constitutions in Europe has been the adoption of judicial review of legislation, and rejection of the unchallenged sovereignty of elected majorities. Germany and Italy, and later Spain and Sweden, followed this pattern. France was—with the United Kingdom—an exception, but in the 1970s the *Conseil constitutionnel* began to use the principles of the 1789 Declaration of the Rights of Man as a guide to its control of Assembly measures before promulgation—a development called by one observer a 'repudiation of Montesquieu'.[1] Since then France has begun to move more explicitly in the same direction. In 1990 the Assembly debated a constitutional amendment and an organic law to extend the jurisdiction of the Constitutional Council, enabling it to rule on the constitutional propriety of laws after their promulgation on a reference from the ordinary courts.[2] This, if adopted, would certainly breach the tradition historically buttressed by the Montesquieu-ian doctrine that the judicial branch is 'next to nothing'.

In England from the time of Bentham until perhaps the 1960s we find an equally abiding mistrust of 'Judge and Co.', and a tradition of judicial restraint and abnegation. In the United States the judicial deference to state and congressional legislatures that began in the late 1930s took a different course in the 1950s, and it is tempting to speculate that the liberal transmogrification of the Supreme Court under Chief Justice Warren may have had something to do with the revival of judicial review in Europe, at least at the level of human-rights protection. In Britain, different and more particular forces were at work; none the less, a judicial revolution occurred on a minor scale. Speaking in the House of Lords in 1985, Lord Roskill said that:

as a result of judicial decisions since about 1950, both in this House and in the Court of Appeal there has been a dramatic and indeed a radical change in the scope of judicial review . . . described, but by no means critically, as an upsurge of judicial activism.[3]

The reference here is, of course, to review of administrative action. The upsurge can be attributed in some degree to the example and impact of particular judges (particularly in the 1960s Lord Reid, and perhaps later Lord Diplock). Why they were moved when they were, and by what elements of the *Zeitgeist*, may be undiscoverable.[4] But when we reflect on the way in which expansion of judicial authority has been brought about in England at various periods in the absence of any formalized constitutional principles and in the face of a sovereign Parliament, we can perhaps see the importance of certain common-law devices, particularly a willingness to manipulate the concept of jurisdictional control, and the various presumptions about parliamentary intention. One could almost say, looking back into the distance, that constitutional liberty in the United Kingdom has been preserved by a handful of maxims of interpretation and rules of public policy. This of course reinforces the point made by Maitland and others about the unconfined character of constitutional law.

The English constitution is at once everywhere and nowhere; in other words by no sort of refinement can one isolate it from Common law and Equity. . . . The constitution of one of the two Houses of the legislature is unintelligible without a knowledge of the law of incorporeal hereditaments . . . while the right of redress for unlawful arrest by officers of the Executive is merely an aspect of the law of trespass.[5]

This is one reason, amongst many, why the project of codifying the constitution (ours or anybody's) is unmanageable—the object being, like the universe, finite but unbounded.

1. RESISTING UNFETTERED DISCRETION

Willingness to manipulate the jurisdictional principle to resist attempts by Parliament to confer judge-proof powers on executive bodies was seen with particular clarity in the *Anisminic*[6] case in 1969. In the Foreign Compensation Act of 1950 Parliament had attempted to protect the findings of a compensation committee. The Act said that any determination by the committee should not be called in question in any court of law. The House of Lords decided that if a decision rested on a mistake of law it was a nullity and no determination at all. So there was no decision to be protected by the parliamentary ouster clause and the court could declare that to be the case. Parliament could in theory, no doubt, forbid even jurisdictional review and create an entirely unfettered discretion. But the statutory language necessary to achieve that result would have to border on absurdity by endeavouring to give effect to anything that purported to be a decision, by someone or something purporting to be a particular body—an exercise that would strain the rule of law to breaking-point.

A similar judicial approach has been taken where attempts have been made to confer broad discretionary powers on ministers and local-government bodies. It has been insisted that, even where decision-making powers have been conferred in what appear to be unrestricted terms, they should be exercised in accordance with the principle and purposes of the empowering Act,[7] or in accordance with natural justice, or fairly or reasonably. Where, as in the *Tameside*[8] case in 1977, a minister is empowered to act if he is satisfied as to the existence of particular facts, the courts may inquire whether the facts are such that the minister *could* be satisfied. Until the 1960s natural justice had been regarded as an obligation resting on bodies whose duty was to act judicially and not administratively. But that principle was rejected in *Ridge* v. *Baldwin*[9] (a case involving the dismissal of Brighton's Chief Constable). A right to have notice of charges and to be heard in answer to them now appears in a wide range of cases where established interests are threatened by the actions of public, and in some cases private, bodies. There has also been a significant expansion in the notion of what constitutes a protected interest. Some licences or benefits that may previously have been treated as being conferred in the exercise of a policy discretion may be held to be claims that give rise to legitimate expectations.[10]

The ambit of legitimate expectation is unclear. It may on a wide interpretation imply that a public authority that has followed a particular policy is estopped from changing it to the disadvantage of individuals affected by it. On a narrower view, legitimate expectation may only mean that those affected must be given a hearing and the merits of their arguments be considered before their expectations are dashed.[11]

2. NARROWING STATE IMMUNITIES

Recent years have seen a diminution in the extent to which the prerogatives and immunities of the Crown escape judicial review. The Crown's evidential privileges have been subsumed under the concept of public-interest immunity, whose operation is not at the disposal of the Crown but under the control of the courts.

In 1985 in *Council of Civil Service Unions* v. *Minister for the Civil Service*[12] it was said that some aspects of the prerogative could be subjected to review. In one sense this has always been true, since the courts have been willing (as with parliamentary privilege) to inquire whether a particular prerogative or privilege exists and what its limits are.[13] Regulations governing the civil service may be issued under prerogative powers; but a mere assertion that a regulation is made by virtue of the prerogative cannot in itself be sufficient, whatever its content. A regulation could hardly, for example, provide for solitary confinement or whipping as a mode of civil-service discipline. The Canadian courts have also held that the Crown's exercise of prerogative powers is reviewable even in matters of defence and foreign affairs, such as the deployment on Canadian soil of American cruise missiles.[14] Neither the British nor the Canadian courts, admittedly, have been keen to exercise their powers where issues of national security are alleged to exist. In the *CCSU* case Lord Roskill said that considerations of justiciability would place outside the scope of judicial review prerogative powers such as treaty-making, appointment of ministers, creations of honours, and the dissolution of Parliament. But it is possible that even these actions could involve abuses of power (indeed, they commonly do). Individual rights could be involved in questions such as whether (and how) the armed forces should be used in the United Kingdom, or whether the honours list has been used for corrupt partisan purposes. The evidential issues in such cases are not incapable of judicial weighing and resolution.

A further question of Crown immunity, recently resolved by the House of Lords, is whether the Crown and its ministers are subject to the contempt jurisdiction of the courts. The Court of Appeal held in 1991 that the Home Secretary, Kenneth Baker, had committed contempt of court by refusing to obey a judicial order to return a deported immigrant, claiming refugee status, to the jurisdiction. The Home Secretary originally declined to obey the order on the ground that the judge who issued it had no authority to do so and that he was about to apply to have the order set aside. This he did, but the Court of Appeal held that the judicial order, whether irregularly made or not, had to be obeyed until set aside, and that it was a serious contempt on Mr Baker's part not to do so. The Home Secretary argued that as a minister of the Crown he could not be held in contempt, and that mandatory injunctions could not be made against the Crown or Crown servants. The Court of Appeal took the view that this had no bearing on the ability of a court to find that a minister is in contempt. The Crown—that is to say, ministers—then shamelessly, and without any parliamentary protest, appealed (at our expense) to the House of Lords to establish the proposition that they could commit contempt whenever they felt inclined. Happily the attempt failed and it is now clear that ministers in their official capacities are not beyond the reach of injunctions or contempt proceedings.[15]

3. EXPANDING THE GROUNDS OF REVIEW

In *CCSU* v. *Minister for the Civil Service* Lord Diplock summed up the grounds on which administrative action is subject to review, as being 'illegality', 'irrationality', and 'procedural impropriety'. He added:

Further development on a case to case basis may . . . in course of time add further grounds. I have in mind particularly the possible adoption in the future of the principle of 'proportionality', which is recognised in the administrative law of several of our fellow members of the European Economic Community.[16]

The relation between the three grounds of review is not as clear as it might be. The second and third, if they provide grounds for quashing decisions, are themselves forms or subcategories of the first. Procedural impropriety may include, but is not confined to, breach of the common law, rules of natural justice, or statutory rules of procedure. Illegality embraces a variety of acts that are *ultra vires*, or done without jurisdiction, all of them involving wrong or improper use of the powers conferred, or a failure to use powers conferred. Irrationality is not mere unreasonableness, but the special variety known, since the *Wednesbury* case,[17] as Wednesbury unreasonableness. It ought in principle to be rather rare. It has been described as 'something so absurd that no reasonable person could ever dream that it lay within the powers of the authority'. But some of its alleged constituents, such as taking extraneous matters into account, acting in bad faith, and ignoring relevant considerations, are not particularly uncommon, and indeed are activities on which many local authorities seem to spend a large proportion of their time.

Irrationality, in fact, seems in some ways too extreme a criterion and in other ways not sufficiently wide-reaching. If it means hare-brained decisions of an entirely arbitrary kind, courts will be reluctant to deploy it as a tool of review. On the other hand, it fails to capture certain types of fault that touch on constitutional propriety. This point has been argued by Jeffrey Jowell and Antony Lester,[18] who see in the rationality criterion the possibility of protecting, at the administrative level, a range of human rights and freedoms. Violations by governmental officers of equality or privacy rights or principles of freedom of expression are suggested as examples. Thus *Wheeler* v. *Leicester City Council*,[19] where the council refused to license a rugby club because some of its members had taken part in a tour of South Africa, could be explained as protecting a principle of free expression or freedom of conscience. Alternatively it might be said to involve the use of unfair means to attain the council's legitimate ends—something that, as Jowell and Lester point out, comes near to breaching the principle of proportionality.[20]

4. THE USES OF PROPORTIONALITY

Proportionality itself needs some analysis. It may in one guise be merely another way of describing a misfit or lack of proportion between a given action and a permitted objective, that may be brought about by self-misdirection, by use of delegated powers for an inappropriate purpose, or by misuse of such powers in bad faith. It may signal a lack of fairness or equity in weighing evidence or in imposing a condition or penalty. In this sense it seems merely a sub-category of pure or impure unreasonableness, showing itself by the absence of a sense of proportion—as where a government department allows only four days to make objections to a statutory scheme.[21] In Community law such disproportionateness may be invoked to condemn laws or regulations that are over-broad or sweeping in their application. So protection of public health against food additives may not justify a complete ban on all food containing additives.[22] In recent British decisions there has been some reluctance to accept proportionality as a ground of review. In *ex parte Brind*[23] the Master of the Rolls (Lord Donaldson) implied that it might threaten the role of judicial review as a supervisory rather than an appellate remedy. That distinction, it must be said, is not as plain as it once may have been. The line between mistake of law within jurisdiction and jurisdictional error is not clear-cut, and its importance is disputed. It has been suggested that the rule now emerging is (as to errors of law) that decisions may be quashed for any decisive error either because all errors of law are now considered jurisdictional or because it is the business of the court to remedy all such errors.[24]

The view of proportionality taken by Lord Donaldson was endorsed in the House of Lords[25] by Lord Ackner, who thought that in order to apply the proportionality test the court would have to 'step into the realm of appellate jurisdiction' and substitute its view of the merits of the case. This, he suggested, was necessarily implied by 'the European test of whether the interference complained of amounts to a pressing social need'. But that confuses the proportionality issue with the quite different initial question which a court such as the European Court of Human Rights puts to itself in weighing whether an apparent breach of the Convention's limitations is justified as a legislative provision necessary in a democratic society. The proportionality test relates to a different and subsequent inquiry—namely, whether the *means* adopted by the legislature are over-broad or disproportionate to the objects that the legislature is seeking to promote. It is true that, in asking the initial question about the compliance of legislation with a pressing or substantial social need, a constitutional court has to pose a question about merits. That is one reason why the distinction between a supervisory and an appellate role, familiar in English decisions on the review of administrative action, has no real part to play in the constitutional review of legislation. If the distinction has a counterpart there, it lies in the contrast between a higher or more intense and a lower or more restrained standard of review; that is to say, in the distinction between a minimal rationality test (or a considerable margin of appreciation for legislative judgment) and an active imposition of the court's own balancing of the issue.

We need therefore to distinguish the use of proportionality as a near-synonym for ends–means rationality in administrative review from its use by European and other constitutional courts (for example in Canada) as an ends–means test applied to the relation between permitted legislative purposes and the particular means adopted to further them. In its constitutional role, the invocation of proportionality is increasingly familiar. It contains an obvious attraction for a reviewing court, as a formula that appears to eschew interference with the merits of legislative policy. It is none the less a flexible instrument for controlling the merits. Its potentiality stems from the fact that the purposes of legislative measures are not always unambiguously clear on their face, and can be formulated in broader or narrower terms. By stating a statute's purposes broadly (or sometimes narrowly) it can often be shown that they could have been achieved by a differently drafted enactment, and the measure in question can thus be presented as disproportionately broad or narrow in relation to the imputed purpose. Thus in *Dudgeon* v. *The United Kingdom*[26] the European Court of Human Rights found that the prohibition of all adult consenting homosexual activity was a disproportionately broad means for protecting vulnerable members of society such as children. If that could properly be said to be the statute's purpose, then no doubt it was over-broad. The same technique can be seen in some of the decisions of the Canadian Supreme Court applying the provisions of the Charter of Rights and Freedoms, for example the equality guarantee. Requiring all lawyers in a province to be Canadian citizens may be a disproportionately broad method of securing efficient legal services.[27] The elements of constitutional proportionality in Canada have been categorized as including fairness, rational relationship between ends and means, minimal interference with rights, and avoidance of over-severe impacts on those affected by legislation.[28] If the United Kingdom enacts a Bill of Rights, or imports the European Declaration, the House of Lords would find proportionality a useful device. Imputing irrationality to Members of Parliament is likely to attract criticism, especially from that not inconsiderable number of elected members for whom the label 'Wednesbury unreasonable' might have been specially invented.

5. PUBLIC LAW AND PUBLIC POWERS

Judicial review is a public-law remedy; so its scope is determined by the boundaries of public law. It has sometimes been said that there is no fundamental distinction between public and private law in the UK, but that is in some ways true and in some ways not. For pedagogical purposes administrative, constitutional, and criminal law are commonly termed public-law subjects, perhaps because they involve relationships between citizens and government. But criminal law involves relationships also between private citizens: and some relationships between citizens and governments (Crown liability, for example) are part of the civil law of tort and contract. In practice, the public/private division for purposes of judicial review is measured by the availability of remedies. Decisions that can be contested, or duties that can be enforced by applications for the traditional prerogative remedies of *certiorari*, prohibition, and *mandamus* are within the public-law field. What this field is, or should be, is a question that has been posed both by internal procedural changes and by developments in Community law.

The procedure for obtaining the various existing orders was rationalized in the late 1970s and is contained in the Supreme Court Act of 1981 and Order 53 of the Rules of the Supreme Court. Relief of the appropriate kind can be obtained by an application to the High Court, and the applicant is permitted to join with his application a claim for damages.[29] Various administrative changes have resulted in applications for judicial review together with other cases of an administrative kind being heard by a special group of Queen's Bench judges—establishing in practice a sort of specialized administrative court, 'albeit one that lacks the distinctiveness and constitutional status of the Conseil d'Etat'.[30] Applications for judicial review may not now be entirely confined to those issues that could have been reviewed by the old prerogative orders,[31] but such applications[32] are in principle designed to be available only against bodies that are carrying out activities of a public character—whatever that may be. In *ex parte Datafin*[33] it was said by Lord Lloyd that judicial review was available when a body was performing a public-law function. One criterion for the exercise of such a function is the source of the deciding authority's power. If it lies in statute, or subordinate legislation, or the prerogative, or if it derives from 'the authority of government', then the body in question will be subject to judicial review. If the source of power is contractual, then it will in principle not be. Lord Lloyd rejected this source-relative approach, however, saying that the distinction must lie not in the source of the power or the source of funds expended[34] but in the nature of the duty carried out. If it were a public duty the body would be subject to public law.

There are clearly some difficulties about the sources-of-power approach. It neglects perhaps the possibility of there being alternative criteria for considering a body to be exercising public power. For example, there is the question of subjection to or independence of control or direction by government. Moreover, the existence of contractual relationships may not be inconsistent with the carrying out of public (in the sense of governmental) duties. There is no doubt that in employing civil servants, ministers of the Crown are engaged in carrying out a public duty. But if it is the case that, as Sir William Wade has argued, Crown employment is not an aspect of the prerogative,[35] and if civil servants have contracts of employment,[36] then the employment relationships of Crown servants who have such contracts will lie outside the sphere of public law. Cases in which judicial review has been refused to the employees of bodies such as local health authorities[37] illustrate the proposition that employment by a public authority does not bring all resulting employment disputes into the area of public law.[38] Yet no one would deny that a health authority is carrying out a public duty and has that duty imposed on it by statute.

The root of the difficulty (or some part of it) is that in England, and perhaps elsewhere, the public/private distinction has been used in two distinct but easily confused senses and for a number of different purposes. One sense of 'public' draws a line between persons and bodies who are to be treated as within the sphere of government or exercising the authority of the state. 'Public' here means governmental or official. But another public/private distinction sets off what concerns citizens in general from matters that concern only particular individuals. In that sense, 'public' relates to people in general or the community at large, not the government. It is in that sense that public houses or public libraries or taxis or brothels provide a public service. It may well also be in the public interest that there should be such services. But none of that means that they are engaged in public in the sense of governmental operations. Indeed, 'public' in the second sense can be used more or less as a synonym for 'private'. So Maitland could say that 'in England we have public prosecutions for any member of the *public* may prosecute'. He meant to say that *private* persons might prosecute. 'Abroad', he added, 'they have state prosecutions or official prosecutions.'[39]

To draw the boundaries of public law, therefore, on the *Datafin* criterion of performance of a public duty may be to court confusion. If the purpose of defining the domain of public law is simply to determine the appropriate remedies, then it may be a matter to be settled by considerations of procedural simplicity and convenience. And, indeed, there are some who think the division from that point of view is irrational and could be eliminated.[40] On the other hand, the distinction between the public or governmental and the private sphere is important for many other constitutional purposes. There is, for example, the question of the eligibility of public bodies to share in the statutory immunities of the Crown. In the early cases involving exemptions from rates and taxes, phrases were used such as 'purposes required for the government of the country'[41] or 'part of the public government of the country'.[42] Later on, phrases such as 'emanation of the Crown' were used, though in *BBC* v. *Johns*[43] that term was rejected as being 'of no assistance whatsoever'. It may be, though, that some word is needed to cover what Crown servants, agents, and officers have in common for this particular purpose.[44]

A different purpose for which it may be necessary to draw a dividing line between the sphere of government and private activity is that of determining whether certain EC directives can create directly enforceable individual rights in the United Kingdom against bodies that may or may not be a part of government. Under Article 89 of the Treaty, the binding nature of a directive exists in relation to each member state, and there should not be any so-called horizontal direct effect so as to impose an obligation on individuals who are not acting as, or as part of, the state or government. So what for this purpose is to be brought within the sphere of public or governmental authority? Can the various directives against discrimination in the employment field, for example, create of their own authority directly enforceable rights against the very large number of what we term quangos, that is to say quasi-autonomous *non-governmental* bodies? Not, it would seem, if that label is an accurate one. But UK courts and the European Court of Justice have reached different conclusions about the criteria. Under British constitutional principles, for example, the police are certainly, in terms of control, not servants of the state or government.[45] But in *Johnson* v. *Chief Constable of the RUC*[46] the European Court held that, whatever its relations with other organs, the police service was an organ of the state and a public authority. In *Foster* v. *British Gas plc*[47] it was said that a body, whatever its legal form, which has been made responsible, pursuant to a measure adopted by the state, for providing a *public service* under the control of the state, and which has for that purpose special powers beyond those which result from the normal rules applicable in relations between individuals, is included among the bodies against which the provisions capable of having direct effect may be relied on. Some of this phraseology, however, merely restates the problem. The notion of providing a public service is dangerously ambiguous in the way we have already noticed. In the sense of service by the public (government) rather than *to* the public (people), 'public service' is merely a synonym for whatever is counted as official or government activity, and provides no help in defining it.

In the wider constitutional frame there exist still more contexts in which the rights of individuals depend upon the delimitation of public and private spheres. In the USA the application of the Fourteenth Amendment equal-protection clause required the Supreme Court to determine the criteria that bring the behaviour of persons or organizations within the concept of state action. Government financing or licensing (but not every kind of licensing[48]) have been important factors. In the matter of defining organizational characteristics the Supreme Court has not been noticeably

successful, often relying on phraseology such as 'powers traditionally exclusively reserved to the state'[49] or saying that where private
individuals are endowed by the state with powers or functions
'governmental in nature' they become agencies or instrumentalities
of the state and subject to its constitutional limitations.[50]

Similar problems occur in the application of the First Amendment free-speech guarantees which limit the extent to which defamation law can restrict criticism of *public officers*. How is this
particular unprivileged category of persons to be defined?[51] Moreover, how far can constitutional free-speech rights be exercised in
private places as distinct from public forums, and how far may the
right to free expression be exercised in relation to private (non-
public) matters and non-public persons?

These are aspects of a question sometimes posed in more general
terms about the extent to which constitutional rights should have
direct effect on private-law relationships within a particular legal
system. In Canada that question arises because the Charter of
Rights and Freedoms is limited in its application to the parliament
and government of Canada and the legislatures and governments of
the provinces. This produces characteristic problems about the
sphere of government. In *McKinney* v. *University of Guelph*,[52] in
which academic mandatory retirement provisions were attacked as
violating equality rights, it was held that the university bodies in
question were not within the governmental sphere, largely because
they were autonomous and not subject to governmental direction;
but a minority of the Supreme Court thought that other criteria
such as government funding should have been considered.

To enumerate the various contexts in which it is necessary to
define the limits of public, in the sense of governmental, action is
perhaps to contemplate what one American commentator has
called a conceptual disaster area.[53] It may be that the different
purposes for which the public/private dividing line has to be drawn
(judicial review, governmental immunities, Community directives,
defamation law, the sphere of constitutional protection) suggest
that no single or simple set of criteria can be made generally
applicable. But it would be a mistake to conclude that the public/
private distinction should be treated as infinitely plastic or as having only semantic importance. In different ways the placing of the
boundary line shifts the balance between public obligations and
individual liberties.

6. THE EUROPEAN IMPACT: COMMUNITY REVIEW

A number of additional grounds for challenging the validity of both executive measures and Acts of Parliament have come into existence since 1972. The upshot of the European Communities Act of 1972 is that all UK laws bearing on matters within the scope of the Treaty may need to be interpreted or disregarded if they conflict with Community provisions, objectives, regulations, or directives, and under Article 177 of the Treaty the European Court of Justice has jurisdiction to rule on the interpretation of the Treaty, or on the validity and interpretation of acts of the Community institutions.

The results of this have been seen most obviously in employment law, equal pay, pensions and retirement legislation, sex discrimination, value-added tax, and even in local-government, environmental, and road traffic regulations.[54] There is an impact also on the law of judicial review itself, as appears in *Johnson* v. *Chief Constable of the RUC*. A provision of the Sex Discrimination (Northern Ireland) Order 1976 made a certificate signed by the Secretary of State conclusive as to whether an act was done for the purpose of safeguarding national security, public safety, or public order. The European Court held that this deprived the applicant of an effective judicial remedy to determine whether her dismissal had been discriminatory—a right protected by a Community directive on equal treatment in employment.

It could be said that in relation to matters covered by treaty the British Parliament is already subject to an economic Bill of Rights: Article 119 of the Treaty and the various Community directives on pay and conditions are in effect a series of guarantees of equal protection in the economic sphere. There are, in addition, reflections of economic rights into the social and political sphere. The freedom to supply information about abortion services, for example, involves a free-speech right. Community law may also require British courts to hold that provisions of British Acts of Parliament are of no force or effect. In the House of Lords in the *Factortame*[55] case, Lord Bridge referred to the duty of a UK court to override any rule of national law found to be in conflict with any directly enforceable rule of Community law. In addition, the European Convention on Human Rights is a source of limiting principles that may be applicable in British courts. Although the Convention is not part of UK law, British courts have to interpret Community law, and that law has been said by the European Court of Justice to recognize the principles stated in the Convention. So from the European Court's standpoint the Convention places limits both on Community law and on national law. When national laws are not made in order to implement Community law and are outside the scope of the Treaty, the Court of Justice has no power to determine whether national legislation is within the rules of the Convention; but when national law is made to implement Community obligations, it seems that it can, in respect at least of some of the rights in the Convention (for example those that deal with respect for family life).[56] If this is so, it has a consequence of some significance for the possible future adoption of a Bill of Rights in the United Kingdom. Most of the legislative proposals that have been made for the enactment of a Bill of Rights by incorporation of the European Convention in a British statute have included a provision for what in Canada is known as the legislative override—that is to say that the adopting statute would provide that any subsequent Act of Parliament could oust or exclude the application of a provision of the Bill of Rights by an express declaration to that effect. But the effect of such an override provision would be to oust the jurisdiction of the courts in relation to the particular legislative provision that is made subject to the override or notwithstanding clause. So, in so far as such an override clause prevented the courts from adjudicating on the compliance of a statute with any part of the Convention that bore on matters within the scope of the Treaty, or Community regulations or directives, it could be held to deny the rights of affected individuals to a hearing before an independent tribunal for the determination of their civil rights and obligations— a right guaranteed by Article 6 of the Convention.

Parliament could, of course, make it plain by express words that the override provision should take effect notwithstanding anything in the Convention or in the Treaty or in sections 2 and 3 of the European Communities Act. That would raise a deep-lying issue about the basis of Community authority that the British courts have so far avoided. The European Court has repeatedly alleged that a national court which is called upon within the limits of its jurisdiction to apply provisions of Community law is under a duty to give full effect to those provisions, if necessary refusing of its own motion to apply any conflicting provisions of national legislation, even if enacted subsequently.[57]

But, assuming that this is a proposition of Community law, a British judge who is faced with it cannot avoid the question why the Community is entitled to make laws that are applicable in the United Kingdom. The answer to that in UK law is plain. The Community was given that authority by the European Communities Act of 1972, and an express amendment to section 2 of that Act could extinguish or limit that authority. Nothing in the 1972 Act even purports to entrench or limit amendment or repeal of section 2. The Community theory, on the other hand, is that the Community and its law-making bodies together with the national legislatures now constitute a new legal system whose central organs are entitled to make their legislation prevail *sua sponte*.

One legal analogy that might be prayed in aid to support such a claim is the doctrine of legal and constitutional autochthony invoked by some former British colonial territories in order to claim that their independent constitutions have a new root or basis which is not legally derived from the British legislation that provides the historical source of their constitutions.[58] But autochthonous lawmakers, so-called, at least do not assert the right to legislate for the territories from whose legal root they claim to have severed themselves. Perhaps theories of this kind could be metaphorically represented in cosmological terms as big bang theories of legal creation. Their plausibility is much the same.

An alternative explanation of the Community's origin that preserves legal continuity (a continuous creation cosmology?) might be that the legislatures of the constituent member states unconditionally abdicated their own legislative powers after passing the empowering Community legislation. But a difficulty in that supposition would be that, if it is true, it must have been true at the time of that legislation and before the Community and its legal system came into being. It must therefore be not a Community doctrine, but a theory or possibility inherent in the national legal systems. Whether a member state's legislature is capable of doing what is postulated would depend upon its own constitution. Some may have been so capable; but the UK Parliament clearly was not. It is said to be capable of legislative suicide; but it is not capable of abdicating legislative power in and over the United Kingdom whilst it remains in existence. That was Dicey's formulation,[59] and no British court has yet repudiated it.

Until such time as the UK Parliament unambiguously asserts its authority, however, we have a system of review of administrative and legislative action that is increasingly European and may become more so. As one judge of the European Court of Justice has said, 'We are bound to come to one European system . . . the evolution of one system of law is a necessity . . . As economic, social and cultural relations between European states intensify, legal evolution will be less and less dependent on political decisions alone.'[60] Evolution in these relationships, that is to say, will be, to an increasing degree, judge-driven. We are going to be regulated in many ways by—as Bentham might have put it—International Judge and Co. That has its benefits. But, like harmonization of legislation, harmonization of judicial methodology can be an inconvenient taskmaster. In a federal set of communities, there should be room for juridical as well as political subsidiarity. In the variety of public-law problems—in the boundaries between public and private power and in the varying role that different societies might wish to allot to judicial discretion, and the varying preferences they might wish to indulge in relation to statutory interpretation (amongst other doctrines)—there should be room for different communities to behave differently. Mr Justice Hercules—the ideal and unbiddable judge who figures in Dworkinian jurisprudence—may suit some national tastes and not others. But if all that is to be possible it will require the development in the Community of theories of judicial review still to be worked out. It may be that some assistance for a single Europe is to be found in the experience of judiciaries in North America and the Commonwealth who have been longer at the federal game.

7. CONSTITUTIONAL REVIEW IN THE UNITED KINGDOM?

A question remains to be asked about the impact of Community law and the expansion of the judicial role in Britain. Is it likely to be extended still further to embrace judicial review of legislative action, stemming from the adoption of a domestic Bill of Rights placing limitations upon the legislative authority of Parliament? The Bill of Rights debate has been rumbling on since the 1960s, with its proponents making little headway. The history of the reform campaign has been one of repeated but doomed attempts to introduce into Parliament bills to incorporate in statutory form the

European Convention on Human Rights. The members of the Lords Select Committee on a Bill of Rights in 1977 were in favour of that course of action if a Bill of Rights were to be adopted, but not unanimous as to whether it should be. Nor has there been agreement on the desirability, or possibility, of entrenching a Bill of Rights against future repeal by simple majority. The 1977 Select Committee thought (though on inadequate consideration) that it could not be done. Most sponsors of House of Commons bills also have taken a cautious—or timid—view of the matter and proposed a version of the Canadian Charter's override or 'notwithstanding' clause that would allow express exclusion of the Bill of Rights by any legislation enacted after its adoption. Most recently the argument has been imprudently diverted by attempts to promote more wide-sweeping reform proposals (including changes in the electoral system and the second chamber) to be embodied in a new so-called written constitution. In 1991 Mr Tony Benn published his Commonwealth of Britain Bill, a comprehensive new quasi-republican constitutional instrument. In the same year the Institute for Public Policy Research published a draft United Kingdom Constitution running to 129 articles and six schedules. Both contained a newly drafted Bill of Rights—in the latter case attempting to combine elements of the European Convention with the International Covenant on Civil and Political Rights. These general flights of constitutional fancy may have delayed matters somewhat. Nevertheless the specific arguments for a Bill of Rights remain to be faced. British judges now may be heard arguing the case for action. Amongst recent judicial advocates has been Lord Justice Bingham. Speaking at the 1992 Bar Conference (and shortly before taking up his appointment as Master of the Rolls) he suggested that the present situation had three undesirable consequences. There was considerable delay and expense involved in the recourse to Strasbourg. The absence of incorporation of the Convention led in effect to frequent reversals of UK judicial decisions by an international tribunal. As a result the confidence of the public in the British court system was weakened.

Those who oppose incorporation talk of politicization of the judiciary and the danger that British judges will become more like American judges (not to say Canadian, New Zealand, German, Italian, and Spanish judges). But in some degree, and almost invisibly, they already have. They would suffer no great crisis of identity if asked to move still closer in their juridical stance to the Commonwealth and to Europe.

Notes

1. M. Cappelletti, *The Judicial Process in Comparative Perspective* (Oxford, 1989), 190–211. In bk. xi, ch. 6 of *L'Esprit des Lois* Montesquieu remarked that 'Of the three powers, the judiciary is in some measure next to nothing'; *The Spirit of Laws*, trans. Sir Thomas Nugent (London, 1878), i. 167.
2. See 'L'Exception d'inconstitutionnalité: le projet de réforme de la saisine du Conseil constitutionnel', *Revue française de droit constitutionnel*, 4 (1990). What is envisaged is not exactly a right of individual access for citizens but a 'procédure de renvoi' in which judicial bodies rather than individuals invoke the jurisdiction of the Constitutional Council.
3. *Council of Civil Service Unions* v. *Minister for the Civil Service* [1985] A.C. 374.
4. It has been suggested that what led Lord Diplock in a progressive direction was his interest in French administrative law (Lord Wilberforce, 'Lord Diplock and Administrative Law' [1986] *Public Law* 6). It may also be significant that between 1959 and 1962 there was a considerable change in the composition of the House of Lords. In that period seven members retired, perhaps bringing about a more flexible approach in the public-law field.
5. J. H. Morgan, 'Remedies against the Crown', in G. E. Robinson, *Public Authorities and Legal Liability* (London, 1925), p. lxxiii.
6. *Anisminic Ltd.* v. *Foreign Compensation Commission* [1969] 2 A.C. 147.
7. *Padfield* v. *Minister of Agriculture, Fisheries and Food* [1968] A.C. 997; *Laker Airways* v. *Department of Trade* [1977] Q.B. 643.
8. *Secretary of State for Education and Science* v. *Tameside Metropolitan B.C.* [1977] A.C. 1014.
9. [1964] A.C. 40.
10. *Schmidt* v. *Secretary of State for Home Affairs* [1969] 2 Ch. 149.
11. See e.g. *Re Findlay* [1985] A.C. 318; *R.* v. *Secretary of State for Health ex parte United States Tobacco International Inc.* [1992] 1 Q.B. 353.
12. [1985] A.C. 374.
13. *A.G.* v. *De Keyser's Royal Hotel* [1920] A.C. 508. The same is true of the doctrine of Act of State: *Nissan* v. *Attorney-General* [1970] A.C. 179.

14. *Operation Dismantle Inc.* v. *The Queen* [1985] 1 S.C.R. 441.
15. *M.* v. *Home Office* [1993] 3 W.L.R. 433.
16. [1985] A.C. 374 at 410.
17. *Associated Provincial Picture Houses* v. *Wednesbury Corporation* [1948] 1 K.B. 223.
18. 'Beyond Wednesbury: Substantive Principles of Judicial Review' [1987] *Public Law* 368.
19. [1985] A.C. 1054.
20. See also J. Jowell and A. Lester, 'Proportionality: An Emerging Ground of Judicial Review', in J. Jowell and D. Oliver (eds.), *Judicial Review* (London, 1988).
21. *Lee* v. *Department of Education and Science* (1967) 66 L.G.R. 211.
22. *Commission* v. *Federal Republic of Germany* [1987] E.C.R. 1227.
23. [1990] 1 All E.R. 469.
24. See ch. 9 of Sir W. Wade and C. Forsyth, *Administrative Law*, 7th edn. (Oxford, 1994), esp. the summary at pp. 319–20.
25. *Brind* v. *Secretary of State for the Home Department* [1991] 1 All E.R. 720.
26. 1982, 4 E.H.R.R. 149.
27. *Andrews* v. *Law Society of British Columbia* [1989] 1 S.C.R. 143. Cf. *Ford* v. *A.G. Quebec* [1988] 2 S.C.R. 712; *Devine* v. *A.G. Quebec* [1988] 2 S.C.R. 790 (far-reaching ban on use of English-language signs in Quebec a disproportionate method of protecting French language and culture); and *Morgentaler* v. *The Queen* [1988] 1 S.C.R. 30 (disproportionate impact of criminal-law provisions on women seeking abortion). A result similar to that in *Andrews* was reached in *Reyners* v. *Belgian State* [1974] E.C.R. 631.
28. *R.* v. *Oakes* [1986] 1 S.C.R. 103 at 138–9.
29. Supreme Court Act 1981 s. 31.
30. Louis Blom-Cooper, 'The New Face of Judicial Review: Administrative Changes in Order 53' [1982] *Public Law* 250 at 259–60.
31. See *R.* v. *BBC ex parte Lavelle* [1983] 1 W.L.R. 23 at 31.
32. The number of applications increased considerably during the 1980s. A study published in 1991 showed the following distribution: Benefits (including housing benefits): 40; Trade, commerce, company affairs: 33; Professional discipline (including NHS): 15; Education: 42; Family cases: 24; Employment: 26; Health: 35; Homeless persons: 177; Housing: 206; Immigration: 419; Licensing: 41; Local government/rates: 58; Planning/public health: 135; Prison cases: 16. (*Source*: M. Simkin, 'The Judicial Review Case-load 1987–1989' [1991] *Public Law* 490 at 492.)
33. *R.* v. *City Panel on Takeovers and Mergers ex parte Datafin* [1982] Q.B. 815.
34. The source of funding provides a very different criterion. Many bodies

derive their funds from government, but do not act under the authority of government. Universities are only one example. Do they carry out public duties? Do Oxford colleges? What 'deriving funds from government' means is also not entirely clear. Almost everybody derives some funds from government.

35. See 'Procedure and Prerogative in Public Law' (Child & Co. Oxford Lecture 1985); see also Wade and Forsyth, *Administrative Law*, 7th edn., 248–9.

36. As appears from *R.* v. *Lord Chancellor's Department ex parte Nangle* [1992] 1 All E.R. 897.

37. *R.* v. *East Berkshire Health Authority ex parte Walsh* [1985] Q.B. 152.

38. See also *Doyle* v. *Northumberland Probation Committee* [1991] 1 W.L.R. 1340; and *R.* v. *Crown Prosecution Service, ex p. Hogg, The Times*, 14 Apr. 1944, C.A.

39. F. W. Maitland, *Justice and Police* (1885), 141.

40. e.g. H. Woolf, 'Public Law–Private Law: Why the Divide?' [1986] *Public Law* 220.

41. *Coomber* v. *Berkshire Justices* (1883) 9 App. Cas. 61, 71.

42. *Metropolitan Meat Industry Board* v. *Sheedy* 1927 A.C. 899, 903.

43. [1965] Ch. 32 at 73.

44. For various other purposes they are not identical. Not all agents of the Crown are servants, and some who hold offices under the Crown are neither servants nor agents (cf. *Lewis* v. *Cattle* [1938] 2 K.B. 454, 457). S. 2(6) of the Crown Proceedings Act provides that officers of the Crown for purposes of that Act must be persons paid in respect of their duties wholly out of the Consolidated Fund or moneys provided by Parliament or other funds certified by the Treasury.

45. See *Marshall* v. *Southampton and South West Hampshire Area Health Authority (Teaching)* [1986] 2 All E.R. 584 (E.C.J.); *Duke* v. *Reliance Systems Ltd.* [1988] 1 A.C. 628. As the result of the *Marshall* case the European Equal Treatment Directives were implemented by UK legislation (in the Sex Discrimination Act 1986).

46. [1987] Q.B. 129.

47. [1991] 2 W.L.R. 258.

48. The issue of liquor licences, for example, or the provision of police and fire protection does not implicate the state in private action; *Moose Lodge No. 107* v. *Irvis* 407 U.S. 163 (1972).

49. *Jackson* v. *Metropolitan Edison Co.* 419 U.S. 345, 352 (1974).

50. *Evans* v. *Newton* 382 U.S. 296, 299 (1960). Do some or all public utility services come within such a description, especially where the supply of services traditionally supplied by state agencies has been privatized?

51. The Supreme Court has widened this category at times to include public figures: since 'many who do not hold office are nevertheless intimately involved in the resolution of important *public questions*' (*Associated Press* v. *Walker* 388 U.S. 130 at 163–4 (1967)).

52. [1990] S.C.R. 229. The private action issue has also been considered in relation to the Charter's free-speech guarantee, which was held not to apply to the issue of an injunction to prevent picketing directed against a private employer (*R WDSU* v. *Dolphin Delivery Ltd.* [1986] 2 S.C.R. 573). The question whether constitutional rights create obligations in the sphere of private relations seems to be crucial in relation to free-speech, free-association, and equal-protection rights, perhaps because in these cases there are conflicts between constitutional rights that are difficult to resolve and are reflected in a tension between communal and private or libertarian values.

53. Charles Black, 'State Action, Equal Protection and California's Proposition 14' 81 *Harvard Law Rev.* 69 at 95 (1967).

54. e.g. in *R.* v. *London Borough Transport Committee ex parte Freight Transport Association* [1990] 3 C.M.L.R. 495 (validity of heavy goods vehicle silencer requirements) and [1991] 1 W.L.R. 828 (requirements held consistent with Community environment policy).

55. *Factortame* v. *Secretary of State for Transport* (No. 2) [1991] 1 All E.R. 70.

56. In relation to Art. 8 (respect for private and family life) see *EC Commission* v. *Germany* [1987] E.C.R. 1263, and the decisions noted in N. Grief, 'The Domestic Impact of the European Convention on Human Rights as Mediated through Community Law' [1991] *Public Law* 555.

57. *Amministrazione della Finanze dello Stato* v. *Simmenthal* [1978] E.C.R. 629: *Costa* v. *ENEL* [1964] E.C.R. 585.

58. K. C. Wheare, *The Constitutional Structure of the Commonwealth* (Oxford, 1960), 89: 'They wish to be able to say that their constitution has force of law . . . through its own native authority and not because it was enacted or authorised by the Parliament of the United Kingdom. They assert not the principle of autochthony only; they assert a principle of something stronger, of self-sufficiency, of constitutional autarky . . . a principle of constitutional autochthony (from the Greek—sprung from that land itself O.E.D.).'

59. A. V. Dicey, *Introduction to the Study of the Law of the Constitution*, 10th edn., ed. E. C. S. Wade (London, 1959).

60. T. Koopmans, 'European Public Law: Reality and Respects' [1991] *Public Law* 53 at 62.

9

Constitutional Developments in the Netherlands: Towards a Weaker Parliament and Stronger Courts?

MICHIEL SCHELTEMA

1. INTRODUCTION

In 1983 a completely redrafted Constitution came into force in the Netherlands. The old Constitution, dating from 1815, had been amended several times—the amendments of 1848 were the most important ones—but a complete revision had never been undertaken before. During the process of rewriting the document, issues of substantive constitutional importance had been under discussion. Some issues had been given special attention, such as the introduction of some kind of referendum, the need for judicial review of Acts of Parliament—not existing in the Netherlands—and the introduction of elections for the mayors of cities and towns to replace the existing system of appointments by the Crown.

In spite of the discussions, however, major changes were not made. While the text of the new Constitution is both more modern and shorter, it did not change the fundamental rules of the system of government or the division of powers between parliament, the executive, and the judiciary. Mayors continue to be appointed by the Crown, and the possibility of a referendum has not been introduced. It is of interest that in the decade since 1983 the discussion of more fundamental changes has received a new impetus. In the 1989 elections the question of judicial review formed part of the political debate. In 1990 the second chamber of parliament established a committee to study a number of questions relating to constitutional reform, questions which were thought to have been settled in 1983. The cause of those recent discussions has been a series of developments at both the national and international, more especially European, levels.

In this chapter I shall deal with the position of the courts in relation to parliament and to the administrative authorities. The courts have assumed a more important role due to a large extent to international developments, especially developments in European law. The influence of European law can be seen also on other constitutional issues: thus fundamental rules in the Netherlands which clearly differ from those prevailing in most European countries have been subjected to criticism.

2. THE DUTCH TRADITION IN ADMINISTRATIVE LAW

Before the influence of European law is addressed, some background should be provided about the Dutch judicial system, especially in the field of administrative law. In the Netherlands a fairly strong tradition has consistently opposed the introduction of judicial review of administrative action. Consequently, the present Dutch system is the result of a slow and piecemeal development instead of the elaboration of a clear theory about the relationship between the executive and the judiciary. In 1994, however, a new system was introduced that put an end to this situation.

Since 1887 the Constitution has included a provision that opens up the possibility of introducing separate administrative courts. The advocates of that provision were aware of the developments in France: in that country the council of state had become an administrative court in 1872. A similar court was planned for the Netherlands. In 1901 a bill was introduced to establish a high administrative court for a great number of administrative cases. However, the bill was not adopted.

The opposition came from two sides. In the first place, the administration itself, naturally enough, did not favour the introduction of independent courts. But in academic circles also a strong opposition existed. Professor Struycken in Amsterdam was especially influential. In his opinion, independent administrative courts would be dangerous in a real democracy. Since the administration is under constant parliamentary control, abuses of power can be prevented by an active parliament. But if complaints against administrative decisions can be brought to a court, the courts acquire control over the administration at the cost of the democratic control by parliament. For that reason, an appeal within the administration should be preferred. Such an appeal is, in Struycken's opinion, also advantageous for the complainant. If the administration has discretionary powers, a court cannot do more than control whether the decision violates a statutory clause. But in the case of an internal appeal to a higher administrative body, that body can decide that the discretion of the administration should be used in a different way from that of the original decision.

Struycken's ideas have had great influence. Administrative courts with a general competence were not established in his time. Preference was given to a system of appeals within the administration, a system that originated in the nineteenth century. The most important of those appeals was the appeal to the Crown. In practice, this meant that an appeal against an administrative action could be brought before the council of state, which gave its advice to the government. However, the advice was not binding: the minister could decide otherwise. This was the system of *juridiction retenue*, also known in France but abolished in that country in 1872.

For some special areas, however, administrative courts were set up from time to time. At the beginning of this century tax courts already existed, and courts for social security cases soon followed. In 1930 special courts were set up for civil servants with complaints against their employer; and in 1956 a court for economic decisions was created. But there still remained some categories of case for which a special administrative court was lacking. In a number of those cases an internal appeal was possible, but in others this did not apply. It is interesting to see how the ordinary courts have filled the gap. In a long but consistent process the supreme court has extended its competence in the field of administrative law. At the end of the last century—at the time of the discussion about administrative courts—the supreme court abstained from dealing with cases of public law. But when it became clear that the bill of 1901 would not be successful, it changed its attitude. In 1916 it decided[1] that the ordinary courts are competent to hear any case where the claimant asks for the protection of his property rights or for damages against the administration.[2] And in 1924 it held[3] that the provisions on torts in the civil code can also be applied if the administration violates a provision in a statute dealing with public law. But the ordinary courts refrained from declaring illegal administrative decisions that were based on discretionary powers. So they respected the intention of parliament not to give too many powers to the courts. And they also respected the competence of the administrative courts: if such courts were set up, a case could not be brought to the ordinary courts.

3. CHANGES IN THE LAST TWENTY-FIVE YEARS

Over the past few decades, especially in the last twenty-five years, important new developments can be seen. One of them was the establishment in 1976 of a judicial branch of the council of state. It was the answer to the unsatisfactory situation whereby administrative courts existed for some special areas but not for others. In the latter case the ordinary courts were competent, but these courts did not apply the same standards as the administrative courts did.[4]

The council of state as a new administrative court has become competent to deal with appeals against administrative decrees—i.e. decisions in an individual case like a licence, a subsidy, or an exemption—provided that no other administrative court is competent to hear the case. On the one hand, this new court made the system of administrative courts even more complicated, since its competence was complementary to that of the already existing administrative courts; on the other, it was the first court that was not specialized in one area but dealt with different types of case. It was, for that reason, best situated to develop general concepts of administrative law; and it has done so in practice.

The second important development is that the attitude of both the administrative and ordinary courts has changed to a large extent. The reluctance of the courts to deal with questions where issues of a political or a discretionary nature are at stake has diminished, as well as their preference to base their judgments on statutory law. Consequently, the courts no longer review administrative decisions only on the basis of the statutes that have granted the power to the administrative authority. Now they also apply unwritten law such as the principles of fair administration, developed in the case law of the administrative courts. Those principles play an important role in cases where the authorities have been granted full discretion: in essence, the result is that administrative action has come under much stricter judicial control than was the situation thirty years ago. This kind of development runs in parallel with changes in other Western European countries, and has certainly been influenced by French and German law. In the Netherlands an important stimulus was the establishment, already mentioned, of the judicial branch of the council of state in 1976.

At about the same time the supreme court adopted the doctrine that the ordinary courts should set the standards for judicial review of administrative action. The supreme court has clearly departed from its former, rather reserved position in laying down those standards. Since the ordinary courts are, on the basis of the judgment in the *Guldemond* case,[5] competent to deal with administrative cases, they are in a position to decide whether they will abstain from admitting a case if an appeal to an administrative court or an internal administrative body is provided for. In a number of cases the supreme court made it clear that the ordinary courts should do so only if the kind of protection that is offered by the administrative court or appellate body is adequate in all respects. Whether an adequate protection is offered is to be decided by the ordinary courts. The consequence of this doctrine is that in administrative cases an action can be brought before an ordinary court not only where no administrative court is competent but also where the competent administrative court does not offer adequate protection to the citizen.

This development was an important step towards the creation of clear and uniform rules for administrative review. Uniform rules could not be developed by the administrative courts themselves, since the system of administrative courts is complex, with many different courts existing to deal with special matters without the possibility of an appeal to one final administrative court. Unlike the situation in France, the Dutch council of state does not act as the supreme administrative court. As was mentioned before, the new doctrine as set out by the supreme court provides that any person who cannot obtain adequate judicial protection by bringing an action before an administrative court may resort to the civil courts to obtain relief. As many of the statutes establishing the administrative courts fail to provide these courts with full powers of enforcement, this development is of importance. In many cases, no action was possible before the administrative courts, for example, where the administration simply does not answer a request: only an explicit administrative decision could be subject to review. Consequently, the administrative courts responsible for social-security matters had no competence to deal with cases in which the administration did not react to a request for a benefit. As a result of the supreme court's decision, however, in such cases the applicant may take the case to an ordinary court.[6]

It is relevant to mention that the consequences of the doctrine of the supreme court are not always in conformity with the legislation enacted by parliament. Some of the statutes establishing the administrative courts do not grant powers to the courts because parliament preferred not to do so. But the result is that those powers are now exercised by the ordinary courts. In recent years the supreme court has increasingly used Article 6 of the European Convention for the Protection of Human Rights and Fundamental Freedoms as the basis for its decisions to be applied in judicial review of administrative action, demonstrating the importance of that Convention for Dutch national law. But at the same time this argument strengthens the position of the court *vis-à-vis* parliament: since Acts of Parliament must be in conformity with the Convention, provisions in statutes that are held to violate it are not binding.[7]

4. THE POSITION OF THE COURTS TOWARDS STATUTORY LAW

The more prominent role adopted by the supreme court can also be seen by means of an examination of the changed attitude of the court towards statutes and their interpretation. In the past the supreme court took the position that important amendments to the law should be made by Acts of Parliament. It was not supposed to be a task of the courts to change the law as the Dutch courts had not, in their own opinion, the powers of courts in common-law countries. Accordingly, in 1980 the president of the supreme court called upon the legislative bodies to give more guidance in developing the law, as otherwise the courts would be obliged to answer questions of a political nature, a task considered inappropriate for the judiciary.[8] Using the issue of the right to strike as an example, the president emphasized that the legislature, and not the courts, should lay down the rules.

In some respects this position conformed with public attitudes towards the courts at that time. Especially at the end of the 1960s, the courts had been the subject of considerable criticism: not only were they accused of consisting of older, conservative, upper-class people, but the old-fashioned values of these people were said to be represented in the courts' judgments. On the other hand, politicians were much more admired at the time. Parliament and the politicians within the government were seen as the appropriate people to change society. Their decisions were legitimated by a democratic process, and controlled by the voters in elections. In public esteem, politicians rated much higher than the judiciary; consequently, their claim to change the law was better founded.

In such a situation it is wise for courts to adopt a prudent position, and the Dutch supreme court did so. However, times have changed, and many people are now somewhat disillusioned with politics. The way politicians deal with problems does not always seem to be the best way, especially when they resort to short-term solutions advantageous to their political party over long-term solutions which take the interests of all concerned into account. In comparison with the way courts deal with their cases, it is no longer evident that the courts' solutions are that much worse than those of politicians. Rather, the courts seem to solve disputes in an unbiased, rational way, giving full attention to the arguments of all parties concerned, whereas politicians do not always do so. Moreover, the courts have responded to the previous criticism: although judges are still appointed for life, they now seem to be more aware of developments in society and to take these into account in coming to decisions. In such circumstances the courts have greater freedom to address the problems the legislature has left unresolved. These days it would be quite unlikely that the president of the supreme court would ask for more guidance from parliament: rather, the courts are of the opinion that they are quite well prepared to develop the law in all cases where this is needed.

This more independent and self-aware position also means that the courts feel less constrained in adopting positions which are not in full conformity with the law as it was enacted by parliament. The extension of the jurisdiction of the ordinary courts into the administrative law area, mentioned above, is an example of this. While this development was not necessarily foreseen by the legislature, there are cases where the supreme court has in essence contravened parliament's intention: although the statutes concerned specifically refrained from granting certain powers to the administrative courts, the supreme court has in effect reversed this position. An example is that of cases concerning aliens: the administrative court was not permitted to annul a deportation order in a summary procedure because the government and parliament did not wish such a power to be in the hands of a court. Yet the supreme court ruled that this situation would result in a gap in the system of legal protection which was not acceptable in a modern state. Consequently, it held that the ordinary courts should fill this gap by assuming the powers that were withheld from the administrative courts.

5. THE INFLUENCE OF EUROPEAN AND INTERNATIONAL LAW ON THE QUESTION OF JUDICIAL REVIEW OF ACTS OF PARLIAMENT

As was previously mentioned, judicial review of Acts of Parliament is forbidden by the Constitution. When this principle was discussed in 1983, no changes were introduced; yet a doctrine that appeared stable only a decade ago is now under intense discussion. It is of interest to inquire into the causes of this change.

In the following discussion it will be shown that an important factor has been the development of European law and also of other international legal instruments. In order to understand the relevance of these influences, it should be pointed out that the Constitution already provides for one exception to the doctrine forbidding judicial review of statutes (Acts of Parliament). This exception occurs where a statute is contrary to a self-executing provision in an international treaty; in such circumstances the statute can be declared non-binding by the courts. Before 1980 little case law existed in which articles in a statute were held to be contrary to an international treaty. Since that time, however, a whole body of case law has developed in which statutes were held to violate treaties. The

European Convention for the Protection of Human Rights and Fundamental Freedoms is an important source of this case law, as is the law of the European Community. Thus the existence of international courts in Luxembourg and Strasbourg, and their case law, have been important for this development. The result is rather strange. A provision in the national constitution guaranteeing a fundamental right cannot be invoked against an Act of Parliament. Yet if the same fundamental right is provided for in the European Convention, it can provide the basis to set aside an Act of Parliament. It is a somewhat awkward situation that the national constitution cannot guarantee fundamental rights while a treaty can do so.

Membership of the European Community has brought further changes. Within the Community, both the European Court of Justice and the courts of the member states are required to ensure that EC law prevails over national law, including Acts of Parliament. This has placed the national courts in a stronger position *vis-à-vis* parliament than they were accustomed to in the national context. Cumulatively, all of this leads to a situation in which the courts have become more accustomed to reviewing statutes than they were before 1980. From judicial review at the European level, it seems to be but a small step to accepting judicial review at the national level also.

6. A REMARKABLE SUPREME COURT CASE

Two factors were mentioned above which have changed the position of the courts in their relationship with parliament. The first is the stronger position the courts now hold in public opinion as compared to the situation two or three decades ago, and the simultaneous decline in public esteem of the political bodies. The second is a series of international developments which have given the courts power to scrutinize parliamentary action, a power they never possessed before. None the less, it came as rather a shock to Dutch lawyers when in 1988 the president of the Hague court declared a statute void in a summary procedure. The statute withdrew certain rights of students with retroactive effect. The president held that this was contrary to the principle of legal certainty. It is interesting that the Constitution does not even contain a provision dealing with legal certainty. As the basis for his decision, however, the president found a totally forgotten clause in a charter set up to unify the Netherlands with its former territories overseas. Since Indonesia and Surinam have left the kingdom this charter has no great importance, but officially it is still in force.

When the case came to the supreme court,[9] it discussed the question whether judicial review of statutes on the basis of the Constitution or on the basis of general legal principle could be accepted. The court stated the arguments for both positions, and it can be concluded from the opinion that the arguments in favour of judicial review were deemed to be stronger than those against. However, given that parliament had discussed the question as recently as 1983, it was difficult for the court to decide in favour of judicial review only a few years later. This was an especially difficult decision given the lack of consensus amongst legal authors on the issue.

It is interesting to note that one of the strongest arguments in favour of judicial review mentioned in the opinion was represented by the international developments described above. Another argument in the same direction was of interest also. The court referred to authors who have observed and criticized the process of enacting statutes by parliament. Their main point is that statutes are almost always prepared within the ministries, and for that reason are much better suited to the resolution of the problems of ministries and their bureaucratic organizations than to dealing with the problems that the citizens might have. Especially in the field of administrative law, the demand has been made that, where statutes regulate the relationship between public authorities and citizens, they should not be made unilaterally by one side in that relationship. Yet in fact this is the case to a large extent: the influence of the ministries in the process of legislation is strong. Although it is for parliament to enact the bills introduced by the government, parliament does not always have sufficient knowledge to exercise adequate countervailing power.

Furthermore, there is another reason why parliament sometimes is unable to criticize bills. It has become quite common for government policy to be discussed in parliament before important decisions are made or before bills are introduced. Twenty or thirty years ago, it was the rule that ministers had to defend their decisions only after they were taken, and discussions about bills were held only after they were introduced. In contrast, under the new situation, when ministers and the majority of parliament have adopted a certain policy, and this policy has to be completed by new legislation, parliament is no longer free to take a fresh stand concerning the bills that are introduced. The fact that parliament and the government co-operate so much in formulating government policy, together with the fact that ministers and the majority of the members of parliament belong to the same coalition of political parties, means that the rights of the citizens are no longer as well protected by parliament as they were in earlier days.

Since the *Harmonisatiewet* case some new developments should be mentioned. During the 1989 elections the issue of judicial review received more attention in the programmes of the political parties than ever before, and important parties moved in the direction of accepting the principle. The new government promised to come up with a proposal on how judicial review could best be introduced. A much-debated question in this respect is whether all courts should have the power to declare a statute void, or whether this power should be vested in the supreme court alone or, alternatively, in a special constitutional court. The government asked a number of constitutional specialists to give their opinion on the question, and it is interesting to note that the result was a greater consensus in favour of judicial review than had ever previously existed. Nevertheless, it is by no means certain that the Constitution will be amended in the near future. Although the present minister of justice is in favour of reform, many politicians are reluctant to proceed. Accordingly, it will be difficult to obtain the two-thirds majority in parliament needed to amend the Constitution.

7. THE ABOLITION OF THE APPEAL TO THE CROWN

On one important issue the influence of European law has been decisive: the abolition of the appeal to the Crown. Although some discussions had been held on the question whether the institution of the appeal to the Crown should not be replaced by appeal to an administrative court, in 1985 a judgment of the Strasbourg

European Court of Human Rights finally put an end to the old tradition.[10] It held that Article 6 of the Convention was violated because the Crown could not be considered as an independent court. The Dutch supreme court had not taken the position that the appeal to the Crown offered inadequate protection to the citizen, but after 1985 it did.

The Strasbourg judgment gave a strong impetus to the modernization of the whole system of administrative law. That modernization had started with a new clause in the Constitution of 1983, providing for a General Administrative Law Act. Since 1983 a royal commission had been preparing a draft for that Act. In 1989 a bill, based on the draft, was laid before parliament. It was adopted in 1992[11] and came into force on 1 January 1994.[12] It provides for uniform rules on the relationship between administrative authorities and citizens, including the principles of proper administration and a number of procedural rules for the administration (such as the rule that the administration should decide on an application by a citizen within eight weeks in normal cases). The Act has a broad scope: it governs the work of all administrative authorities and pertains to all fields of administrative activity like social security, environment, housing and planning, and taxation.

During the preparation of the statute a discussion came up whether the General Act could be handled by the many existing administrative courts. Would the uniform rules of the Act be interpreted in a uniform way by so many different courts? At this time the Strasbourg judgment made it clear that the existing system had to be changed anyhow. This argument favoured the position of the advocates of a reform of the whole system, and their view prevailed. Consequently, on 1 January 1994 a chamber for administrative cases was set up at all nineteen ordinary courts, and those chambers are given a broad competence in administrative cases. Many administrative courts were abolished. (The system of appeals is still regulated on a provisional basis: appeals in social-security cases are dealt with by an appellate court in Utrecht, and other appeals are decided by a division of the council of state.) All the statutes providing for the rules of procedure before the various administrative courts were abolished. The new, uniform rules of procedure for administrative cases are included in the General Administrative Law Act.[13]

8. CONCLUSION

Looking back over the developments of the past decades, it is clear that the position of the courts has become much stronger *vis-à-vis* the legislature and the administration. European law has contributed to this to a large extent. However, the influence of European law strengthened a national development in the same direction. For that reason, the influence of international law is more welcome than it would have been in the time when Struycken's ideas were still dominant. It has become clear that the ideal of democratic control over government is not the same as giving all powers to politicians. The political system has its own defects. For that reason the strengthening of the role of the courts as a decision-making system which concentrates on rational problem-solving and which takes seriously the arguments put forward by all parties seems to conform with the wishes of the general public. In any case, it seems clear that in a democratic society a system of checks and balances is always needed.

The outcome of the political process is not always as democratic as it should be. This is especially true for the process of taking decisions at the European level. When the defects of the political process become more apparent, the courts can feel more free to function as a countervailing power. This process can be seen clearly in the Netherlands. Yet, without the developments at the European level, and especially without the relatively strong position of the judiciary at that level, this tendency would not have gone so far.

Notes

1. HR (Supreme Court) 31-12-1915, *Nederlandse Jurisprudentie* 1916, 407 (*Guldemond* v. *Noordwijkerhout*).
2. This also pertains to the government. A doctrine like 'The King cannot do wrong' has never existed in the Netherlands.
3. HR 20-11-1924, *Nederlandse Jurisprudentie* 1925, 89 (*Ostermann*).
4. It must be said that differences existed also among the administrative courts themselves.

5. HR 31-12-1915, *Nederlandse Jurisprudentie* 1916, 407 (*Guldemond v. Noordwijkerhout*).
6. Under the new General Administrative Law Act, these irregularities have disappeared; the competence of the administrative courts is laid down in a small number of rather simple rules. See later on in this chapter.
7. See later in this chapter.
8. Open letter in the daily newspaper *NRC-Handelsblad*, 10 May 1980.
9. Judgment of the Supreme Court of 14 Apr. 1989, *Nederlandse Jurisprudentie* 1989, 469 (case of the 'Harmonisatiewet').
10. ECHR 23 Oct., 1985, Benthem case, CEDH, series A, vol. 97.
11. It can be compared with the German *Verwaltungsverfahrensgesetz* or the Administrative Procedures Act in the USA, but it is intended to be more comprehensive.
12. A translation into English of the Act can be obtained from the Ministry of Justice in the Netherlands, PO Box 20301, 2500 EH The Hague (fax 070 3707910).
13. It is clear that international developments have contributed to the development of Dutch administrative law. But the contrary can also be true: 'Brussels' is providing for many rules in all fields of governmental activity, but those rules are not harmonized at the European level. So different administrative procedures may be prescribed for different activities, where the General Administrative Law Act and similar Acts in other countries provide for uniform rules for all administrative activities at the national level.

10

Implementing the Spanish Constitution

ASCENSIÓN ELVIRA PERALES

In 1992 the Spanish Constitution, drawn up in 1978, celebrated its fourteenth birthday—quite a short life-span, but one which has brought about considerable changes in the socio-political sphere and a reaffirmation of the meaning of the Constitution, which was almost certainly not foreseeable during the *iter constituyente* (constitutional process). It is not the aim of this chapter to undertake an in-depth analysis of the Constitution, nor of its evolution. Rather, the more important aspects of its development will be outlined, on the one hand highlighting the extent to which the constitutional brief has been fulfilled and on the other demonstrating the incidence of change in the Constitution itself.

1. POLITICAL TRANSITION AND THE CONSTITUTIONAL PROCESS

Spain lived through a dictatorship from the civil war of 1936–9 until the death of General Franco on 20 December 1975. Franco's death led to a series of other events which resulted in the democratic elections establishing a parliament whose duty it became to draw up a democratic constitution. Even though the need for institutional reform was obvious from the start, the first attempts, overseen by the then president of the government, Carlos Arias Navarro, were shown to fall far short of the desires of the majority of the population. This resulted in the appointment of a new president of the government, Adolfo Suarez, who became the first architect of the transition.

Little by little new laws were introduced, allowing basic rights which up until then had been denied,[1] such as the right to hold political meetings, the right to strike, and the right to freedom of expression. Many of these laws were introduced in the form of decree laws because of the risk that they would not otherwise be passed by a parliament which still consisted of members from the Franco era, known collectively as *democracia orgánica* at the time.[2] However, the most important and influential piece of legislation introduced was the Political Reform Law which allowed the election of a new democratic parliament. This law was peculiar in that it was passed by the old Franco *Cortes*, and thus gave rise to a lot of talk of *hara-kiri* by that body as it stepped aside to allow the arrival of democracy. A referendum was held soon afterwards, and the wording of the law was approved by a majority of the electorate.[3]

The basis of the law was the adoption of a popular monarchy, the restoration of universal suffrage, the implicit recognition of a multi-party system, and the introduction of a bicameral system, which the Constitution would later introduce with the special feature that the king could name some of the senators. Recognition was also given to the principle of the democratic nature of the state; supremacy of the law was established; and recognition was given to basic rights as inviolable and binding on all organs of the state. The Political Reform Law was subsequently modified by the Royal Decree Law of February 1977 in relation to political meetings. After this came the decree of March 1977 on the system of general elections. Along with this type of measure, the legalization of the Spanish Communist Party (which had played an important underground role in the struggle against Franco) contributed further to the democratization of the system and the holding of general elections in June of 1977, which brought about what later came to be the *Cortes Constituyentes*.

It is also worth outlining the repercussions which all this had later, such as the recognition of the demands of the autonomists in the form of the Royal Decree Law of October 1976 (this repealed a decree of 1937 which had deprived Vizcaya and Guipuzcoa of their special economic and administrative status), the Royal Decree Law of 1977 which ruled on the governing bodies of Guipuzcoa, Vizcaya, and Alava, and the Royal Decree Law which recognized the 'pre-autonomous' state of the Basque country or, in the case of Catalonia, the decree which provisionally re-established the *Generalitat* of Catalonia.[4] All these decrees laid the foundation for what would later be the different systems of government of the autonomous communities. These regions were given their own organs of government and certain powers as a way of meeting the demand for autonomy. In this way the text of the Constitution itself was influenced.

Once the parliament had assembled, in July 1977, it soon became apparent that, while some members favoured drafting a series of constitutional laws which would develop the basic aspects of the new political system, a majority preferred to draw up a constitution proper. The lower house of the parliament consequently appointed a Committee for Constitutional Affairs and Public Liberties, from which a working committee (*Ponencia*) was formed, composed of three members of the UCD (Democratic Union of the Centre, the governing party), one member of the PSOE (Socialist Workers' Party of Spain), one from Alianza Popular, another from the PCE–PSUC (Communist Party of Spain–United Socialist Party of Catalonia), and one from Convergencia i Unio as a representative of regional minorities. This working committee created a draft constitutional text which, due to a leak, appeared in the press in December 1977. Subsequent demonstrations about the contents of the draft led to its being radically changed before it officially appeared as a draft bill on 5 January 1978. Several amendments were proposed and studied by the working committee before a final report was presented for debate in the Parliamentary Committee for Constitutional Affairs and Public Liberties. Finally, the latter drafted a report which was published in the official state bulletin of the parliament in July 1978 before being passed on to the congress for debate.

The text which was approved by the congress was submitted to the Constitutional Committee of the senate and subsequently approved by the senate itself. Because of discrepancies between the texts approved by congress and the senate, a joint senate and congressional committee was formed. Its report, concluded on 28 October 1978, was passed by both houses separately and a referendum was held on 6 December when the new Constitution was accepted.

Despite the fact that this constitutional process was neither always easy nor free from dispute, what is certain is that there was an overall 'consensus', that is, a need felt by all the politicians to reach agreement, not only because none of them could count on an overall majority but also in order to avoid old historical traps. In short, there was a desire to write a 'Constitution for everybody'.[5] In what follows I intend to adhere as far as possible to the structure of the Constitution in order to show its basis and development.

2. BASIC RIGHTS

In relation to basic human rights, the changes which occurred as a result of the Constitution taking effect are obvious. Despite the fact that some basic rights were acknowledged during the period of political transition, a comprehensive list of constitutionally recognized and guaranteed rights was only drawn up when the Constitution took effect. Whilst this may seem unimportant in countries with a long tradition of constitutionality, it is obviously of great relevance in countries such as Spain which have lived through a dictatorship. In this situation both citizens and the legislature want basic human rights to be formally established within the law as quickly as possible, and to see the legal structure to protect these rights come into operation very quickly.

In the title (part) of the Constitution concerned with basic human rights, the influence of the German Constitution is very apparent, especially in the establishment of guarantees for these rights, as in the statement of the necessity of respecting the 'essential content' of the law. At the same time as protecting basic human rights, those drafting the Constitution also ensured that they provided protection for more modern rights, such as protection of the environment (a social claim), and regulations on the use of computer technology (a new fundamental right, very closely linked to the right to personal privacy). Such rights tend to be found in the newer constitutions, and in particular are included in the Portuguese Constitution. It was evident that the aim of members of parliament was to provide more than a mere list of rights which would enhance the Constitution, even though guarantees of some rights (human rights in general) were postponed for future development. At the same time, the balance between social demands and the economic situation of the state was taken into account.

Yet the development of human rights has been very uneven. The Constitution has introduced many new laws, such as the *Ley*

Orgánica (LO) 1/1980, for Religious Freedom, the LO 1/1982, on the right to one's good name and to personal and family privacy, LO 9/1983, protecting the right to assemble, and LO 6/1984, regulating the process of habeas corpus; but in other areas, laws which were drawn up before the existence of the Constitution are still in operation and, as can be imagined, are in many respects inadequate. Examples include Law 191/1964, regulating the right to association, or the Royal Decree Law 17/1977, which regulates the right to strike and to take industrial action in the workplace. In relation to the latter, it appears that particular problems at issue may soon be rectified by legislation to be introduced as a result of the gravity of the strikes which took place during the first months of 1992. In general, it appears that the legislature has enacted laws on a pragmatic basis, in response to the requirements of the socio-political situation, rather than by working according to a systematic plan[6] and time-frame to develop those rights which are guaranteed by the Constitution. This situation, which seemed justifiable shortly after the Constitution took effect, is less understandable at this stage. The consequences are that, on occasion, parliament passes laws which merely respond to a political problem, often drawn up on the spur of the moment rather than representing the best that might in theory be possible.

An example of such concerns is the recent LO 1/1992 on the *Protección de la seguridad ciudadana* (Guarantee of safety on the streets/urban safety), the aim of which is to alleviate the problems of drug-trafficking and the lack of safety on the streets. Even while this law was being drawn up it provoked opposition in some sections of the community, because of the fear that some of its sections could contravene basic constitutional precepts. As a result of the ambiguity of the terms in which the law has been drawn up, it is possible to imagine that, albeit in a very extreme situation, the law could be used to infringe basic human rights which are guaranteed by the Constitution. On the other hand, it is necessary to differentiate the various rights which are guaranteed in Title I and the various types of guarantee. Within Title I two sets of rights will be discussed: those which are very strictly protected, and those rights at the opposite extreme which are given the least protection.

The most important rights are the acknowledgement of fundamental rights in the strict sense, that is to say Section I, Chapter 2,

Title I together with Articles 14 (Equality) and 30.2 (Conscientious Objection). These are capable of providing specific guarantees through preferential and expedited procedures before the courts or individual appeal (*recurso de amparo*) before the Constitutional Court. As to the first of the above-mentioned guarantees, this has not been further developed by the legislature, given that the law which is still applicable to this type of proceeding is that of 62/1978 for the legal protection of the rights of the individual. That is to say, it is a law with a very limited range of legal protection,[7] which was drawn up before the Constitution came into effect and which was later extended by the Constitutional Court in its second *Disposición Transitoria* to include all the rights encompassed in Article 53.2.

As to the rights of individual appeal when brought before the Constitutional Court, this has become a guarantee liberally applied[8] both in jurisprudence and in the theory of basic human rights. In effect, the jurisprudence of the Constitutional Court has influenced that of the ordinary courts, and has also had an influence on the theory of basic human rights or, to be specific, of some basic human rights. The scope that constitutional jurisprudence encompasses is so great that this, on the one hand, emphasizes the respect in which this institution is held but, on the other, restricts the possibility of theoretical studies[9] and the means by which these could provide a support to a subsequent constitutional jurisprudence.

At the other extreme we find that the rights in Chapter 3, Title I are not even designated as such, but rather appear as 'governing principles of social and economic policy'. These rights appear to be the Cinderella of constitutional law. Nevertheless this must not obscure the fact that they are norms which are applicable to and, where appropriate, essential when establishing possible unconstitutionality in the development of rules and regulations. In fact, the extent to which the introduction of these social rights has been achieved is due to the social sensitivity of the issues concerned, given that they deal with controversial topics such as ecology or issues relating to specific social groups (e.g. the disabled, or senior citizens). The application of these Chapter 3 laws has even been considered by the supreme court, which is traditionally conservative and resists innovation.[10] But obviously these social claims depend on political discretion and availability of resources, as opposed to the previously mentioned rights, the essential content of which is guaranteed regardless of economic and social circumstances.

Within the sphere of basic human rights it is also necessary to consider the role of the *Defensor del Pueblo*, the Spanish equivalent of the Swedish Ombudsman. This institution was established despite the scepticism of many sections of society who felt that such a magistracy was something more appropriate to Nordic than to Latin countries. Yet during its ten years of existence this institution has had a very positive impact, not only in achieving resolution of complaints filed by individuals, but also in the analysis of greater problems, such as the investigation of the state of Spanish psychiatric hospitals,[11] in which the system's deficiencies were stated and recommendations made as to the changes required to remedy the situation. It is in precisely this way that effective use of public powers can be achieved and improvement in constitutionally recognized human rights brought about. Currently, a reform of the *Ley Orgánica* is under consideration, in order to make the institution more effective in the light of experience.[12]

In terms of human rights the work of the *Defensor del Pueblo* has been very positive, not only because it safeguards them through actions implemented by the different public authorities, but also because there is widespread support amongst the public for these same human rights.

3. THE MONARCHY

The important role played by the monarchy in the development of the constitutional system during the transition must be emphasized. There are many factors which contributed to this. First, the monarchical institution, in the person of Juan Carlos I, provided a link between the former and the present regimes. It was General Franco who named Juan Carlos successor to the throne, thus creating a link between the monarchy and his own regime. As a result Juan Carlos won the support of certain sections of the population, notably the military. Second, the legitimacy of the Borbón dynasty was restored by the abdication of Don Juan de Borbón, father of the present king, in May 1977, shortly before the first democratic elections were held. Finally, Don Juan Carlos's personality won widespread popular support. As a result, the anti-monarchical reaction which could have developed, and which in fact did become apparent in the constituent parliamentary debates (even if, on occasion, this amounted only to rhetoric), proved to be of little significance.

Nevertheless, once the Constitution was in place and the political situation was stable, it is worth noting that the monarchy has played merely a symbolic role—which is its proper function within the Spanish system—leaving responsibility in the hands of politicians. The only function in which the king has the power of decision is in the naming of a candidate for presidency of the government (Article 99 CE). However, even in this case the king only has the power to name a candidate when there is no clear majority in parliament and where a coalition has not agreed on a candidate. In any event, parliament's choice of candidate will always take precedence over that of the king.[13]

4. LAS CORTES GENERALES

Of the different institutions of the state, the *Cortes Generales* (parliament) merits special attention. The parliament consists of the *Congreso de los Diputados* and the *Senado*, two separate houses, each carrying out different parliamentary functions, such as the enactment of legislation, approval of budgets, and government control. In carrying out these functions each house enjoys administrative and financial autonomy, and has the capacity to make its own rules.

Certain areas of the legislative function merit particular attention, especially given the extent to which they differ from other systems. With regard to legislative initiatives, it must be emphasized that the Spanish Constitution (Article 87) provides for certain possibilities. To be precise, as well as the traditional sources of government initiative a proposal for legislation may come from the congress or the senate (in this case, on the proposal of a group of deputies or senators or, indeed, a parliamentary group), and it is also possible for a proposal to come from an autonomous community[14] and even from popular demand. This, however, is very restrictive, in so far as the most important procedures and subjects are excluded and, in addition, a minimum of 500,000 signatures is required.[15]

In relation to the legislative power generally, it is necessary to stress first the superiority of the congress. This house can overrule the veto of the senate by means of an absolute majority or, after two months have elapsed, by a simple majority. In the same way, any amendments to a law passed by the senate will only be included in the final draft if they are also approved by congress. Second, there exists under Article 75 of the Constitution the possibility that legislation can be dealt with at committee level, i.e. without coming before a full plenary session at all. However, constitutional reform, state budgets, organic or basic laws, and international affairs are not included in this. This facility to approve law at committee level is a copy of something which exists in the Italian Constitution and which gives rise to what are called *leggine*. It is worth pointing out, however, that a plenary session can be held at any time to reclaim the right to deal with the legislation in question. Third, the Spanish system allows for variations in the legislative procedure. Such is the case, for example, with the *Leyes Orgánicas*, which require the approval of an absolute majority in the plenary session of the congress, and the same in order to overcome the veto of the senate. The *Cortes Generales* appears, therefore, to be a complex body in which the inequality of powers between the two houses is very apparent, and it is this fact which requires more attention.

On the one hand, it is essential to point out how the Constitution provides for situations in which the two houses must act together, for example in relation to the exercise of non-legislative powers concerning the monarchy (the swearing in of the king or the heir to the throne, the appointment of a 'Tutor', a guardian of the king). In other cases there is provision for the creation of joint committees of both congress and senate, for example, in accordance with Article 167 CE, or to reach an agreement to authorize international treaties (Article 94.1 CE). This task would be carried out separately in both houses if agreement were not otherwise forthcoming between the two. There also exists a joint investigative committee (Article 76 CE) and, according to the recent modification of the *Defensor del Pueblo* law,[16] a joint committee to deal with reports of that institution. However, most Acts require separate participation of both houses, and in these cases the congress is clearly predominant.

The electoral system rests on the basis of electoral districts, and for the election of the deputies is based on proportional representation as defined by the d'Hondt method. There is a list system, under which the voters cannot change the order of the candidates or choose between the candidates of different lists (*listas cerradas y bloqueadas*). The election of senators (except for those elected in the autonomous communities) is carried out on the basis of the 'revised majoritarian system' (*sistema mayoritario corregido*), in such a way that, of the four elected in each province or electoral district, each voter can choose a maximum of three candidates. However, the final results are very similar, because on the one hand each province has a minimum of three seats assigned to it and on the other many provinces elect fewer than six deputies, which in practice does not make the result very proportional.[17]

The structure and functioning of parliament is affected by the fact that in the creation of the upper house totally opposing ideas were involved. There were those who supported the idea of a traditional type of second chamber, whilst others wanted a federal-type senate. No doubt the latter were influenced by the territorial division of the country which the Constitution had imposed. The final result is the hybrid with which we are now familiar: one house is responsible for 'territorial representation', but its functions are a copy of those of the congress. It also has a final decision-making process which corresponds to that of the congress, but overall enjoys less authority than the congress.

When considering the authority of the senate, one notices a secondary role in most areas, even in connection with the autonomous regions, where equality with the congress can only be seen in relation to some aspects of Article 150.3. The only case in which the senate decides with complete autonomy relates to the approval of government proposals concerning the use of emergency measures in an autonomous region. While this is an issue of considerable importance, it is one which in normal circumstances is unlikely to arise.

When discussing reform of the powers of the senate, a majority of teachers of constitutional law show a preference for constitutional reform by legislation, which would undoubtedly allow for a more thorough reform. Politicians, in contrast, would prefer to introduce reform by means of elaborating new standing orders for the senate in which the participation of the autonomous communities is increased. This might be achieved—to give a concrete example—by the creation of a commission of autonomous communities, which would have a decisive input in any matters related to those communities.[18] This preference for taking the indirect route to reform reflects a fear of constitutional reform on two accounts: first, fear that opening up the Constitution to reform may provide a means to undermine the current contents of the document, which has hitherto served Spain well and which represents the political consensus in the post-Franco era; second, fear that reform of the senate could be used to try to change other aspects of the Constitution, specifically to modify all the regulations having to do with autonomous communities. Nevertheless, as is apparent, a reform introduced by means of a change of the standing orders of the house cannot effect an in-depth reform because it would be limited by the terms of the Constitution, where the system of representation chosen ('majority system', apart from those nominated by the autonomous communities) determines the result.

Looking to another area, we must mention the fact that the constitutional provision to produce standing orders for the *Cortes Generales* which would regulate the situations mentioned in Article 74 of the Constitution has not been fulfilled. This regulation affects, especially, Acts which have to do with the monarchy (proclamation and oath of the king, crown prince, regent, etc.). The fact that this provision has not been fulfilled assumes some importance on account of various problems connected with Prince Felipe, the heir to the throne, and because of the recent difficulties in the British royal family.[19] On a more general level, there is much talk of a 'parliamentary crisis' (which, for the person on the street, can be taken to mean the absence of deputies and senators from the debates in the houses of parliament). However, this phenomenon is not an exclusively Spanish problem, but one which is internationally widespread, amongst other factors resulting from the role played by the houses of parliament in relation to the government. Underlying this notion of parliamentary crisis is a latent danger that politically inexperienced sectors of society could confuse this crisis (parliamentary) with a democratic crisis owing to the relative novelty of the democratic process. In addition, the political behaviour of certain parliamentary representatives or party leaders who are not at ease in a party system nor within the general rules of democracy does nothing to help alleviate these fears. This observation does not, however, refer to matters of law, but rather to social and political problems.

5. THE GOVERNMENT

The constitutional design of the Spanish government is, to a large extent, based on the German one, and the similarities between the two have increased in practice. Indeed, it has been said that the Spanish presidency has taken on a chancellor-like role. In effect, the prominence of the president within the government has increased, especially since the Socialists came to power in 1982. Felipe Gonzalez's personal charisma has meant that the government identifies very closely with him. This has possibly been accentuated by the poor quality of opposition leaders, and by the support of an absolute majority in the first two governments which he led. Nevertheless, governmental regulation has not been supported by the creation of a legal framework for the government. In fact, the only ruling dealing with this area, and inadequately at that, is Law 10/1983, on the *Organización de la Administración Central del Estado*. Consequently, it is often necessary to have recourse to pre-constitutional laws such as the *Ley de Régimen Jurídico de la Administración del Estado* of 1957, which in many cases, instead of facilitating the task, makes it more difficult to clarify the process to be followed by government, or the nature of the relationship between government and state administration.[20]

The difficulties of analysing the government arise from its composition, because the Constitution, apart from recognizing the president, vice-presidents,[21] and ministers, opens the door of government membership to 'the rest of the members who establish the law' (Article 98 CE). In effect, questions arise as to whether or not parliamentary secretaries are members of the government in a juridical sense. The favoured reply is negative, based on the fact that these posts were created by decree, not by law, and that such persons participate in cabinet meetings in an informative role only.[22] On the other hand, the working of the government is very varied, and even if the main organ of implementation is the cabinet, there also exists the possibility of an 'emergency cabinet' which is made up of a reduced number of members depending on the area of emergency—for example, there was an emergency cabinet throughout the Gulf crisis.

Although individual decisions may be made by a minister within the department of which he/she is in charge, as was mentioned earlier, there exists a whole series of situations where either the president alone has to endorse these decisions or the cabinet has to do so, keeping in mind that the president is exclusively responsible for these cabinet decisions. Within the area of the responsibilities of the president, what is noteworthy is the president's autonomy in fixing the government's programme (Article 99.2 CE), in appointing, allocating, and removing ministers (Article 100 CE), and in the management and co-ordination of government action. One area which requires consultation with the cabinet is that of dissolving the parliament (Article 115 CE).[23]

6. THE CORTES AND THE CONTROL OF THE GOVERNMENT

The methods of control over the government are those typical in a parliamentary system: questions, interpelations, committees of inquiry, and motions of censure. The government, on the other hand, can dissolve the Cortes and ask the congress for a vote of confidence. Nevertheless, these methods of control have only a qualified effectiveness because of the parliamentary majorities. It is usually public opinion and a general election which lead to a change of government.

It is easier for a government to remain in power than for the opposition to bring it down. In a vote of investiture of the president of the government (Article 99), the candidate in a first vote needs an overall majority of the members of congress; but in a second vote a simple majority of those voting is enough. A simple majority is also what is needed for a government to win a vote of confidence. A motion of censure can only be passed by an overall majority in the congress, and it is necessary to propose a candidate for the office of president of government, who would become president if the motion of censure were passed.[24] All this means that the role of the government is greater than the role of the Cortes, although parliamentary discussion is still important, particularly as a means of informing public opinion. For example, the motions of censure put forward so far have served more to publicize a particular party's policies than actually to control the government.

Finally, it is necessary to remember that government responsibility is always the responsibility of the government as a whole: the responsibility of an individual minister is decided by the president of the government.

7. JUDICIAL POWER

The judiciary, as some authors have said, is so called in the Constitution because it is the only branch which is not considered to be a genuine power; yet it is without doubt one of the parts of the institutional system into which most effort has been and continues to be put, albeit with very little to show for it. None the less, it is necessary to point out that the level of mistrust of the judiciary inherited from the Franco era was very high. Consequently, the judiciary's evolution has been swifter and much more positive than originally expected.

The structure of the judiciary rests on two basic principles: the independence of the judiciary, and the right to be tried by a judge who was appointed by law and the jurisdictional area, i.e. in accordance with the principles of any democratic state.[25] The first fact meriting attention within the Constitution is the creation of a *Consejo General del Poder Judicial*,[26] based on the Italian *Consiglio Superiore della Magistratura*, a governmental branch of the judicial system. This body has generated much controversy due to various factors; one of them was the passage of the *Ley Orgánica* 6/1985, on the *Poder Judicial* (LOPJ), under which the method of election of the members of the judicial council was reformed in such a way that all members had to be elected by parliament. When this occurred there were accusations that the council was being politicized, since prior to the reform the majority of those elected were usually elected by the magistrates themselves. The majority of the council has been criticized for its tendency to approve government directives and because of its ineffectiveness in regulating the judicial system. Yet a central problem may be the lack of communication between the council and the ministry of justice.

On the other hand, two serious problems for the Spanish system of justice are the build-up of cases outstanding in the majority of the courts and tribunals, and the failure to modernize judicial premises. Procedural laws also need to be brought up to date, not only to make them more effective but also because this would result in more effective judicial protection. In the light of all this, the reform and modernization of the Spanish justice system remains one of the most important and outstanding issues to be addressed.

8. THE CONSTITUTIONAL COURT

Separate from the ordinary judiciary but within the sphere of justice, the Constitutional Court stands out in the way it supports the system from within, safeguarding the values of the rule of law through the use of checks and by means of the right of individual appeal (*recurso de amparo*). The jurisprudence of the Constitutional Court is, as I have stated before, the focus of attention for many scholars and for the rest of the courts, who base their own interpretations of the law on those interpretations expounded by the Constitutional Court itself.

Constitutional jurisdiction in Spain has claimed a fundamental role in constitutional development. The Spanish Constitutional Court has followed those European models which appeared after the Second World War, especially the Italian and above all the German model. It has distanced itself from the Court of Guarantees of the Second Republic which, because of certain problems, both structural and relating to the times in which it operated, was not successful. The Constitutional Court exercises an abstract control over the norms which have the status of laws, based on Kelsen's classic model.[27] Recourse to challenging a law on grounds of unconstitutionality is limited to the president of the government, groups of 50 deputies or 50 senators, and the *Defensor del Pueblo*. In special cases the legislative assemblies of the autonomous communities may initiate a challenge, if it is a case of norms which affect them. On the other hand, control in specific cases has been developed by the Constitutional Court when the question of unconstitutionality is raised. This can be invoked by any judge and court if it is considered that a norm or regulation which is applicable to the case and has the status of law is unconstitutional.

Within the area of relations between the state and the autonomous regions, or that of relations between regions, 'conflicts of jurisdiction' (*conflictos de competencia*) can arise. These may be positive, in so far as each party claims authority, or negative, where neither of the two assumes responsibility. In this last case, the issue of conflict can be raised by an individual or by the central government. Another example of this 'conflict of jurisdiction' is that which occurs between different 'state bodies', i.e. between any of the following: government, congress of deputies, senate, general council of the judiciary (Arts. 59.3 and 73 LOTC).

In relation to guarantees of basic human rights, the tool which can be used by the Constitutional Court is that of the individual appeal (*recurso de amparo*). Any individual with a legitimate interest, or the *Defensor del Pueblo*, or the public prosecutor, is entitled to have recourse to this remedy, after having exhausted all other judicial procedures. Along with these main responsibilities, it is also the duty of the Constitutional Court to be familiar with questions affecting the compatibility of international treaties with the Constitution and, therefore, with the challenges that the government can make to measures and resolutions taken by the autonomous communities.

Rather than carry out an analysis of the different functions of the Constitutional Court, it is of more interest here to outline the role that this body has played, and continues to play, in Spanish constitutional development. First, it is necessary to outline how the Constitutional Court contributed to the consolidation of the Constitution as a real judicial norm. That the Constitution was such a judicial norm was brought to light by legal scholars quite soon after its adoption, but this opinion was not accepted so quickly in judicial circles. However, the first rulings of the Constitutional Court, especially those on basic human rights which had not yet been formulated in statutes, came down heavily in favour of the application of these basic rights not only on a subjective basis, but also on an objective one.[28] This compelled the courts, including the supreme court, to admit this characteristic, so that it came to be recognized as a general principle. Second, the concept of constitutional justice can form a certain guarantee against possible abuses of power. This is especially necessary in the case of governments which hold absolute majorities in parliament. This particular guarantee is very noticeable in Spain owing to the right of the *Defensor del Pueblo* to appeal against alleged unconstitutionality. Third, to a large extent the building of a state with autonomous communities has been the work of the Constitutional Court through its work in the resolution of conflicts of authority and through jurisprudential definition of the complex system of sources of authority which the Constitution establishes.

As is the case with the other courts, the Constitutional Court also finds itself with a great backlog of work, especially because of the large number of appeals alleging an infringement of Article 24 of the Constitution (the right to effective judicial protection), followed by cases concerning the right to equality, and cases on conflicts of authority between the state and the autonomous communities. These conflicts abound on account of the absence of a system of concurrent jurisdiction.

One risk run by the Constitutional Court is that of becoming politicized. However, the real problem may be the political image that certain sectors of opinion have tried to give it, and which could damage its prestige in the eyes of the public. Such critics ignore any constructive criticism which might be helpful to the Court, as well as to jurists and politicians, in the enormous task that it undertakes. It would certainly be to the benefit of the Court to distance itself from any partisan struggles.

9. THE AUTONOMOUS COMMUNITIES

The subject of autonomous communities is characterized by the distinctions that exist between historic communities and Andalucía (known as the autonomies under Article 151 CE) and those communities that followed the way of Article 143.[29] The former communities have a greater degree of autonomy, whilst the latter have less jurisdiction; however, this distinction is only the beginning of the complexity in this area. Certainly the Navarran Autonomy must be given special attention because of its adherence to the *Ley Orgánica de Reintegración y Amejoramiento del Régimen Foral de Navarra*. On the other hand, there are the historic regions of Catalonia, the Basque country, and Galicia (although of a different character and less marked in its demands and differentiation from the rest than the other two autonomies mentioned). Lastly there is Andalucía, which followed the path outlined in Article 151 of the Constitution.[30] In the remaining autonomies, that is in those with less jurisdiction such as Valencia or the Canary Islands, the difference lies in the fact that they saw their legal competences augmented when both laws were transferred in 1982.

The state of autonomous communities is based on the principle of unity (Article 2, in relation to Article 1.2 CE), solidarity (Articles 2 and 138.1 CE), equality (Articles 138.2, 139.2, and 149.1), freedom of movement and residence throughout the entire Spanish territory (Article 139.2), and freedom of movement of goods (Article 139.2). On the one hand, one must realize that not only is the autonomy of the regions recognized, but the Constitution also makes reference to the autonomy of town councils and provinces (Article 137 CE). The difference between the autonomy of the regions and the autonomy of the town councils and the provinces is based not only on the level of autonomy, but also on the fact that the autonomous communities have the right to set out norms which may become law within the area of their authority.

The distribution of authority between the state and the autonomous communities is based on Articles 148[31] and 149[32] of the Constitution. Here it is necessary to emphasize that the Constitution does not establish an a priori division between the state and the autonomous communities, nor which responsibilities each one must assume. Secondly, at first glance it would appear that the responsibilities connected to Article 148 are those of the autonomous communities and those of Article 149 the ones which remain in the hands of the central state. However, on closer examination one will notice the provisions of Articles 151 and 148.2, which allow the autonomous communities to assume responsibilities within the framework of Article 149.1; that is, the only responsibilities which are excluded are those which have been marked 'exclusive' to the state. Finally, responsibilities listed outside these two lists can be assumed by the autonomous communities, if they are included in their statutes of autonomy. As a result of this, the authority of the autonomous communities is—or can be—very wide. It is, therefore, necessary to outline how problems can arise. Many arise from attempts to define the limits of authority of both sides, especially trying to define what should be understood by *lo básico* (the basics) and how far the authority of each can stretch, a task which will be carried out by the Constitutional

Court. And one should not forget that the right of the state is supplementary to that of the communities, which leads to the conclusion that the right of the state, if in conflict with one or several autonomous regions, while not being non-existent, will simply not be applicable.[33]

On the whole, the relationship between autonomous communities and the state has been notable for its contentiousness, resulting to a large extent from the absence of concurrent jurisdictions in the Spanish legal code, which in practice leads to an abundance of conflicts of jurisdiction and appeals of unconstitutionality[34] being brought before the Constitutional Court. But we must also point out that, in practice, autonomy in the historical communities has worked well, while in those that are not historical communities it is clear that more time is needed. Nevertheless, the Constitution has foreseen the possibility of increasing the autonomous communities' jurisdiction through Article 143 after five years (Article 148.2). This move towards greater autonomy is the aim of these communities, and the two major political parties, PSOE and PP, have endorsed this through joint agreements.

Initially the additional jurisdiction being handed over to these communities will be implemented by the *Leyes Orgánicas de Transferencia*,[35] and only afterwards will an appeal be made to the statutes of autonomy (*Estatutos de Autonomía*). An agreement has already been made on matters concerning health and education. The last government (prior to the 1993 general election), for its part, approved the return to parliament of the *Ley Orgánica de Transferencias a las Comunidades Autonomas*[36] for debate, which means that once it is approved in parliament, there will be more equality between autonomous communities as of 1993. The whole issue of autonomous communities remains very controversial for a variety of reasons, not least of which is the role of the European Community; this has resulted and will further result in a loss of jurisdiction for the autonomous communities, since many of their functions have passed or will pass to the EC. The end result of this will be that in some cases the role of the autonomous communities will simply be to carry out decisions made elsewhere.

At the same time, another major issue concerning the autonomous communities is that of the *hecho diferencial* (distinguishing factor), i.e. the whole area of ideological-nationalistic characteristics which distinguishes one autonomous community from another. This distinguishing factor is especially prominent in the case of the Basque country, Catalonia, and, to a lesser extent, Galicia, because of a long tradition of autonomy and the existence of their own languages (Euskera, Catalan, and Gallego), as well as better levels of economic development (at least in Catalonia and the Basque country).

It is precisely this 'distinguishing factor' clause which makes the achievement of greater equality as between the different autonomous communities and the possible reform of the senate difficult. It is also problematic in the case of the reform of Title VIII of the Constitution,[37] since it is judicially difficult to translate into law, and even its political acceptance is doubtful because of the changes which would become necessary owing to a new approach to the territorial organization of the state, which has already been chosen.

10. CONSTITUTIONAL REFORM

The possibility of constitutional reform must be tackled from the point of view of the constitutional mechanisms provided. The procedure for reform favoured by the constituent body makes actual reform very difficult to carry out, especially through the provision of Article 168 CE, for the reform of the *Título Preliminar* (Introductory Part), Section I of Chapter 2 of Title I, or Title II, or for the complete revision of the Constitution. To carry out such a reform it is first of all necessary to obtain the approval of two-thirds of each house, after which the houses must be immediately dissolved. Second, the new houses, after ratifying the decision, may proceed with the process of reform, which has then to be approved by a two-thirds majority of each house; finally, the approved text must be submitted to a referendum.

The other procedure for reform requires the approval of both houses by a three-fifths majority. If this is not reached, a joint working committee may be charged with trying to reach an agreement. If this is not reached, reform may be carried out by obtaining an absolute majority in the senate and a two-thirds majority in the congress. With this procedure a referendum is optional, but could be held on the request of at least one-tenth of the members of each house. This mechanism for reform, while not as complicated as the previous one, still makes it very difficult for a minority to instigate reform. In this way, it appears that the aim is for only those reforms which are supported by the majority of the political parties to be successful.

The desire of the members to preserve the constitutional text as it is means that reforms which could actually improve the current system are delayed or postponed, as is happening with the hypothetical reform of the senate. Other possible reforms such as that of Title VIII, as has been previously mentioned, have been defeated on purely political grounds due to the lack of agreement between the various political groups involved, whether they are political parties of national standing or parties from specific autonomous communities.

11. SPAIN AND THE EUROPEAN COMMUNITY

Spain's integration into the EC, which it joined in 1985, has not given rise to any constitutional problems, apart from the previously mentioned loss of power by the autonomous communities. Furthermore, the Constitutional Court has shown itself ready to accept the supremacy of rulings of the EC Court of Justice, which means in effect that it is this court, and not the Constitutional Court, which would have jurisdiction should any conflicts arise.[38] However, the Treaty of Maastricht, and particularly the results of the Danish referendum, gave rise to some debate as to Spain's position *vis-à-vis* the EC, and has led to voices being raised for and against the European union.

The Maastricht Treaty was submitted to the Constitutional Court for examination on grounds of compatibility with the Constitution.[39] The decision taken by the court (24 July 1992) was that it is necessary to reform the Constitution to give citizens of other EC countries resident in Spain the right to vote. Following this decision, the government announced that it would call on the support of all the parliamentary groups in order to bring about the necessary reform. This has meant that the process of constitutional reform is initiated not by a government proposal (*proyecto*) but by a proposition underwritten by all the parliamentary groups, so that the constitutional 'consensus' is being renewed.[40] In addition, the procedure to bring about the reform was put into effect at a time which was in fact outside the normal working sessions of the parliament. The reform was approved in July 1992, and the new text appeared in the *Boletín oficial del estado* soon after.

Nevertheless, we must underline the fact that the scope of the reform is quite limited because, in fact, it simply adds the term 'and passive' to Article 13.2 of the Constitution.[41] This new right will be appended to the right to vote in municipal elections which foreigners resident in Spain already enjoy—when and if a treaty or agreement, based on reciprocity, has been drawn up between Spain and the country of origin of the foreign resident.[42] It should also be noted that the reform was introduced through Article 167 of the Constitution in such a way that it caused as little disruption as possible.

In relation to other areas of the Maastricht Treaty constitutional reform is not necessary, as the Treaty does not conflict with any of the provisions of Article 93 of the Constitution:

Authorization may be granted by an Organic Act for concluding treaties by which powers derived from the Constitution shall be transferred to an international organization or institution. It is incumbent on the *Cortes Generales* or the Government, as the case may be, to ensure compliance with these treaties and with resolutions originating in the international and supranational organizations to which such powers have been so transferred.

This article was introduced specifically to deal with Spain's entry into the European Community. This had already been applied for, and it was felt that, once democracy was well established in Spain, it would be forthcoming. Because of that, constitutional reform was avoided on being accepted as a member of the EC and, it must be added, Spain very quickly adjusted to the new demands, and was particularly successful in immediately adopting EC law. The legal mechanism used was LO 10/1985, authorizing Spain's membership of the EC.

12. CONCLUSION

The evolution of the Spanish Constitution seems to prove the assertion that 'Spain considers itself a social and democratic state', though this does not mean that everything has been done nor that there are not areas that could be improved. In general, however, it can be said that constitutionalism has taken root, despite the doubts which existed while it was being established. This uncertainty was the consequence of a turbulent history and the many years of dictatorship which the country experienced. That the Constitution has rooted itself firmly can be appreciated from the frequent repetition of the popular phrase 'this is unconstitutional', used on the streets when there is a possible infringement of human rights, or when state policies are unpopular. The Constitution has become the property of the people and has helped to create a political consciousness which was sadly lacking before.

Nevertheless, there is still much to be done as far as constitutional development is concerned, giving special attention to those areas pertaining to basic human rights, economic rights, the improvement of the system of autonomous communities, and achieving full conformity of the administration and the courts to a new legal reality. These are issues not only for which it is necessary to provide further theoretical guidelines, but which also need to be made more applicable in practice. This means full conformity with the existing constitutional reality, and alignment with socioeconomic, political, and constitutional evolution in other European countries. It is, perhaps, also necessary to make the political class more aware of the problems which affect other sectors of society.

I have drawn attention to some of the possible reforms which would make the Constitution more effective—a goal which is, of course, desirable. Acceptance of these reforms, however, causes anxiety because of the changes to Article 13 which they imply. However, if generally accepted, the reforms would in effect guarantee the Constitution, in the sense that once they had been ratified everyone would have to adhere not only to the original document of 1978 but also to the entire constitutional system.

Notes

1. Even though some basic human rights were nominally included in the so-called Fundamental Laws of the Franco period, they were never actually put into practice.
2. In these *Cortes* the family, the local government, and the workplace were represented, but without any true democratic participation.

3. During the campaign leading up to the referendum a large section of the old anti-Francoist opposition was in favour of abstaining from the referendum in the belief that a complete break with the past was necessary, and that the proposed reform was therefore not sufficient.

4. Both Catalonia and the Basque country had been autonomous regions during the Second Republic in Spain, hence the allusions in all of these laws to 're-establishing' autonomy.

5. An excellent history of the transition period, particularly for foreigners, is R. Gunther, 'El Proceso constituyente español', *Revista española de estudios políticos*, 49 (1986), 33–55.

6. As would have been achieved by drawing up a calendar in which priority would be given to developing the most important rights, or those rights which were insufficiently developed when the Constitution took effect. For example, the regulation of the right of association is still embodied in a law enacted in 1964, which restricted the right of association very severely and is obviously contrary to the present legal system.

7. The rights protected were: freedom of expression and freedom to assemble, freedom of correspondence and to privacy of correspondence, religious freedom, guarantee of the inviolability of the home, and judicial protection against illegal arrest. To these were added protection against sanctions which might be imposed on issues concerning public order.

8. In fact the greatest number of appeals before the Constitutional Court are to do with judicial protection.

9. Judicial literature has followed the jurisprudence of the Constitutional Court, without offering any alternative interpretations. In effect, the Constitutional Court very rarely looks to Spanish judicial literature for support, as opposed to what happens in the German Constitutional Court on occasions.

10. As an example of the direct application of these rights by the supreme court (*Tribunal Supremo*), see judgment of 25 Apr. 1989.

11. Defensor del Pueblo, *Informes, estudios y documentos. Situación jurídica y asistencial del enfermo mental en España* (Madrid, 1991).

12. See *Diez años de la Ley Orgánica del Defensor del Pueblo. Problemas y perspectivas* (Madrid, 1992).

13. In relation to studies written on the Spanish monarchy it is worth mentioning M. Aragon, *Dos estudios sobre la monarquía parlamentaria en la Constitución española* (Madrid, 1990); Ignacio de Otto, 'El mando supremo de las Fuerzas Armadas', *Revista española de derecho constitucional*, 23 (1988), 11–43; M. García Canales, *La monarquía parlamentaria* (Madrid, 1991).

14. To be precise, Art. 87.2 of the Constitution offers two paths towards the initiative by autonomous communities; the first consists of asking the government to formulate a proposal of law, the second involves the sending of three members of the autonomous assembly to the congress to defend a previously formulated proposal of law. In fact, only the second option can be considered a mechanism for the initiation of the legislative process.

15. This was developed by Law 3/1984 which regulates popular initiatives. Excluded from popular initiatives are subjects dealt with by *Ley Orgánica*, those of an international character, and those referring to the prerogative of pardon, and in addition any other matter which might have been the subject of a proposal of law by one of the houses of parliament. On the other hand, the number of signatures demanded was very high. Because of all the limitations provided for, real effectiveness of this type of initiative is very rare.

16. LO 2/1992, modified from LO 3/1981, with regard to the *Defensor del Pueblo*.

17. See Arts. 68 and 69 of the Constitution and LO 5/1985, relating to the general election system, Arts. 161–6.

18. On the reform of the senate, see *Anuario de derecho constitucional y parlamentario*, 13 (1991), 179–232.

19. All these topics have been covered by the mass media, e.g. *El Mundo*, 30 Jan. 1993.

20. At the moment it seems that a proposal to modify this last-mentioned law is being studied, which would undoubtedly facilitate a greater knowledge of how it functions.

21. The Constitution does not establish the exact number. At present there is only one vice-president.

22. See the analysis offered by A. Bar, 'La estructura y funcionamiento del gobierno en España: Una aproximación analítica', in *El gobierno en la constitución española y los estatutos de autonomía* (Barcelona, 1985), 19 ff.

23. See A. Bar, *El presidente del gobierno en España* (Madrid, 1983).

24. See Arts. 112 and 113 of the Constitution.

25. See I. de Otto, *Estudios sobre el poder judicial* (Madrid, 1989). L. M. Diez Picazo, *Régimen constitucional del poder judicial* (Madrid, 1991).

26. In relation to this body, see M. J. Terol Becerra, *El consejo general del poder judicial* (Madrid, 1990).

27. The abstract control of norms, i.e. an examination in abstract of the possible unconstitutionality of a norm independent of any specific case, is submitted to the Constitutional Court. This type of control can only be sought by the higher institutions of state.

28. The importance of basic human rights was made clear in the first rulings, STC 5/1981, of Feb. 1981.
29. Art. 143.1: 'In the exercise of the right to self-government recognized in Article 2 of the Constitution, adjacent provinces with common historic, cultural, and economic characteristics, insular territories, and provinces with a historic regional status may obtain self-government and form autonomous communities in conformity with the provisions contained in this title and in the respective statutes.' Art. 151 establishes a different procedure and more competences for some regions.
30. We must note that in the previous referendum, when they did not get the majority required by the province of Almería, they proceeded with the reform through LO 12/1980, which allowed Andalucía access to this kind of autonomy.
31. Art. 148 develops the competences which the autonomous communities *may* assume (22 in all) and states in subsect. 2: 'After five years, autonomous communities may, by amendment of their statutes, progressively enlarge their powers within the framework laid down in Article 149.'
32. Art. 149: '1. The state shall have exclusive jurisdiction over the following matters: ... [32 in all] 2. Without prejudice to the jurisdiction that may be assumed by autonomous communities, the state shall consider the promotion of culture a duty and an essential function and shall facilitate cultural communication between autonomous communities, in co-operation with them. 3. Matters not expressly assigned to the state by this Constitution may fall under the jurisdiction of autonomous communities by virtue of their statutes of autonomy. Jurisdiction on matters not claimed by statutes shall fall to the state, whose laws shall prevail, in case of conflict, over those of the autonomous communities regarding all matters in which exclusive jurisdiction has not been devolved to the latter. State law shall in any case be supplementary to that of autonomous communities.'
33. As regards those aspects related to the systems of jurisdictions along with the principles which guide the autonomous communities, see I. de Otto, *Derecho constitucional: Sistema de fuentes* (Barcelona, 1988), ch. 12. In general, in relation to the complex area of autonomous communities it is worth consulting E. Aja *et al.*, *El sistema jurídico de las comunidades autónomas* (Madrid, 1985), and *Informe sobre las autonomías* (Madrid, 1988); S. Muñoz Machado, *Derecho público de las comunidades autónomas*, 2 vols. (Madrid, 1982, 1984).
34. Conflicting jurisdictions if they arise in relation to provisions without force of law, and appeals to unconstitutionality if they arise in relation to provisions of a legal nature.

35. This open-door policy towards the *Leyes de Transferencia* has been studied by law scholars. The biggest disadvantage of a possible solution for our autonomous communities rests in the fact that the jurisdiction for these laws lies exclusively in the hands of the state legislature, which is the only legislature with the power to reform or abolish them. However, because of the political cost this would entail it does not seem feasible to do so unless a prior agreement has been made with the autonomous community in question.

36. *El País*, 4 July 1991.

37. In relation to this matter see J. Perez Royo, 'La reforma de la constitución', *Claves de la rázon práctica*, 20 (Mar. 1992), 9–15.

38. In relation to this, see amongst others STC 28/1991.

39. The Constitution expressly provides for this in Art. 95: '1. The provisions of any international treaty containing stipulations contrary to the Constitution shall require prior constitutional amendment. 2. The government or either house may request the Constitutional Court to declare whether or not there is an inconsistency.'

40. In relation to this question, consult *El País*, 2, 4, and 8 July 1992.

41. 'Only Spaniards shall be entitled to the rights recognized in Article 23 (participation of citizens in public affairs), except in cases which may be established by treaty or by law concerning the right of active and passive vote in municipal elections, and subject to the principle of reciprocity.'

42. The extent of the effect of conceding the vote to EC citizens, resident in Spain, remains to be seen. It could have a great effect in certain areas, specifically the Mediterranean coast and the Canary Islands where there are large settlements of northern Europeans, many of them retired people. During the municipal elections held in 1991 there were protests by Danish and Dutch citizens who were not allowed to vote, despite agreements signed with Denmark and Holland, owing to the fact that the general election *Ley Orgánica* was not adhered to.

PART V

CONSTITUTIONAL REVIEW AND CHANGE II: THE CENTRAL AND EASTERN EUROPEAN EXPERIENCE

11

The Relevance of Western Models for Constitution-Building in Poland

WOJCIECH SOKOLEWICZ

1. WHY A NEW CONSTITUTION?

Occupied during the Second World War, Poland was reborn within a much-altered territory and with its sovereignty limited by the USSR: the state was dependent on its eastern neighbour politically, ideologically, and economically. The permanence of dependence on the USSR was guaranteed by the Communist Party, which bore the name of the Polish Workers' Party until 1948 when, having absorbed a number of members of the essentially social democratic Polish Socialist Party, it was renamed the Polish United Workers' Party. Over the decades until 1989, the Communists had the decisive influence over the exercise of state power; its constitutional framework was shaped according to their political strategy and sometimes even tactics.[1] Starting from 1947, all political opposition was banned and persecuted by law among other measures.

Admittedly, in the years 1944–7 the validity of the so-called 'democratic principles' (rather an ambiguous notion in itself) contained in the 1921 Constitution[2] was restored; yet what in fact provided the constitutional grounds for the exercise of state power was the new legislation on people's councils, inspired by the slogan proclaimed in the USSR, 'all power to the councils'. The so-called Little Constitution of 1947 restored, transitionally and formally, the principle of separation of powers, and even incorporated a number of provisions of the 1921 Constitution. Paradoxically, this happened in the days of increased Stalinist terror and eradication of all the remaining democratic forms of social life. The paradox can easily be explained if one realizes that the constitutional solutions were nothing but a façade to conceal the actual monopoly of Communist power.

Just a few years later, on 22 July 1952, a day which was to be celebrated for many decades to come as an official holiday, the Constitution of the Polish People's Republic was promulgated. It was quite openly characterized as one of 'the socialist type' (and at the same time the state's name was changed from the former 'Republic of Poland', a name restored since late 1989). The so-called 'socialist' nature was most distinct in the following guiding principles:

1. the unity and uniformity of state power;
2. the political monopoly of the Communist Party (PZPR), initially implied and then explicitly guaranteed in the Constitution by an amendment in 1976;
3. an economy planned centrally by state authorities, based on state ownership of property established by the Constitution;
4. the guarantee of civil rights in accordance with Marxist conceptions of those rights,[3] entailing the priority of social and economic rights over personal and political rights; of the so-called material over procedural (formal) guarantees; and of collective over individual rights. Above all, the Marxist concept of rights permitted and even assumed limitations of civil rights if such limitations were motivated by 'class' interests or political reasons.

The amendments—of which there were as many as sixteen before the 1989 transformation, with the broadest and most far-reaching one being passed in 1976—in no way changed the properties of the 'socialist' Constitution of 1952 outlined above. Some of them, however, did result in a mitigation of the repressive regime, and facilitated its subsequent opening to democratic transformation. Here I am referring first and foremost to the amendments influenced by the political crisis of 1980[4] which gave birth to 'Solidarity'. At that time—or at a somewhat earlier date—a number of institutions were established designed to guarantee the constitutional and legal functioning of state authorities. This was done by way of constitutional changes (which, for example, created the constitutional tribunal[5] and the tribunal of state in 1982) while martial law was still in force. In some cases, though, the changes were also introduced by ordinary legislation (e.g. creation of the chief administrative court in 1980, and of the institution of the commissioner for the protection of civil rights in 1987;[6] this latter institution was confirmed constitutionally two years later). Obviously, in the context of a communist state, all the above institutions could play but a limited role in practice; yet they represented and in some degree anticipated the future 'democratic state ruled by law' in that they provided, among other things, for patterns of social behaviour within a framework of law.

The 'socialist' Constitution's transformation into a democratic one in Poland was done peacefully, by gradual evolution and in accordance with the principles of legality.[7] The changes were initiated by an agreement negotiated during the round table conference between the communist government and the democratic opposition. The results were then translated into law by the constitutional amendment of 6 April 1989. This enabled the organization that same year of partly free parliamentary elections. Moreover, the amendment created the office of president to replace the collegiate council of state, and the senate as the second house of parliament, thus introducing some elements of separation of powers into the state's political system.

The six constitutional changes to follow in 1989–91 took that process further, significantly transforming the contents of provisions of what was still formally called the 1952 Constitution. In its present wording, the Constitution has the following effects:

1. It replaces the principles of unity and uniformity of state with some elements of the separation of powers, e.g. institutional guarantees of independence of the judiciary introduced by an amendment in 1989; election of the president by popular vote by an amendment in 1990; and organization of a genuine local government according to principles specified in another amendment in 1990.

2. It expresses the principle of political pluralism, providing a simple procedure for the legally effective formation of political parties and equality of parties before the law, in contrast to the previous 'exceptional' legal situation of the Communist Party.

3. It proclaims a free market economy and freedom of economic activity of the citizens, as well as guarantees of private ownership which are absolute and not relative as previously.

4. It expresses the universal conception of human rights, based on principles of international law instead of the Marxist conception of civil rights and liberties (whose strong impact still remains, however).

As a result mainly of the changes introduced in 1989, the Constitution of 1952 underwent a radical transformation, changing from a 'socialist' into a democratic one, and getting the chance of becoming also a living constitution. None the less, most Polish politicians and scholars are still of the opinion that an entirely new constitution is needed. The most frequent arguments for that solution are as follows.

First, even with recent amendments, the 1952 Constitution cannot possibly perform the function of integrating a society which still remembers how it came into being. The Constitution is burdened with the original sin of having been promulgated non-democratically, when the Stalinist terror was at its most severe and with the personal contribution of Stalin himself. That promulgation can hardly be said to have legitimacy; what is worse, though, is that a constitution of this kind cannot become the symbol of a reborn and sovereign Poland. Its disgrace, so to speak, is its birth certificate.

Second, even after the introduction of changes, the present Constitution still contains traces of its original conception of the unity of state power. They can be found first of all in the provisions that locate the Sejm (lower house) above all the remaining state authorities. In the current state of political pluralism, proliferation of parties, and extensive exercise of democratic freedoms, this results in a dysfunction of relations between the various state authorities. In particular, the actual powers of the president are limited (elected since 1990 by popular plebiscite and thereby having democratic legitimacy). In addition, the cabinet seems too dependent on the will of the Sejm. The Sejm being fragmented as it is, adjustment of its common will involves considerable difficulties: this sometimes presents a threat to the stability of the government, but always weakens the power and authority of the state. Devoting much of its time to unproductive disputes, the Sejm dangerously approximates to the pejorative stereotype of the 'Polish parliament' as some nations still remember it today. Briefly, what is needed is rationalization of the state structures based on a better balance of the separate segments of state power, with competences delimited according to the principle of the separation of powers.

Third, the Constitution in its present wording insufficiently develops the guarantees of civil rights with respect to personal and political rights. Instead, it promises too much in the sphere of socio-economic and cultural rights, which are formulated in accordance with the implied conception of the 'socialist welfare state'. Such guarantees are inconsistent with the operation of a market economy and the new interpretation of the role of state in society.

Fourth, as a result of numerous changes introduced at different times and for different purposes, the wording of the Constitution is far from coherent. This incoherence hampers the work of the constitutional tribunal and to some extent impairs its ability to ensure the constitutionality of laws.

In this situation, the need for a new constitution is generally accepted. The task of preparing one was initially undertaken by the parliament of 1989–91. Two draft constitutions, very different from each other, were prepared (one by the Sejm, the other one by the senate);[8] yet neither was eventually promulgated. It was found that a parliament formed in elections that had been only partly free lacked the democratic legitimacy to decide on matters as fundamental as the political system of the state and the legal situation of individuals who come under that state's jurisdiction. Nor did the former parliament pass the so-called Little Constitution (despite the fact that the required legislative procedures had already been initiated). The Little Constitution was designed as a constitutional statute which would regulate—with the binding force of a constitution—the system and functioning of some of the chief state organs only (parliament, president, and government); it was to have remained in force until a new, complete constitution could be promulgated.

The parliament elected in the free and democratic elections of 1991 made significant progress on the road to a new constitution. First and foremost, in the constitutional statute of 23 April 1992, published in the *Journal of Laws*, 67, as item 336, it defined the procedure for preparation and promulgation of the Constitution. A specially appointed body was charged with the task of preparing a draft—the constitutional commission of the national assembly, i.e. of the two parliamentary chambers in joint session. The commission is composed of forty-six deputies appointed by the Sejm and ten senators appointed by the senate. They are to prepare the draft either on their own initiative or based on proposals submitted by at least fifty-six members of the national assembly (that is, by one-tenth of its total membership) or by the president. In either case, the constitutional commission is the only body authorized to submit a draft constitution to vote by the national assembly. The assembly promulgates the constitution by a majority of two-thirds of its votes with at least a half of its total membership present. Next, the assembly accepts or rejects suggestions submitted by the president, whose powers approximate to a suspensive veto also in the case of the constitution. The promulgated constitution is then to be signed by the president, but only acquires validity after going successfully through the test of a referendum. The constitution is considered ratified if the majority of those participating in the referendum vote for its adoption (in contrast to other cases of national referendum where the majority of persons with the right of vote is required).

What is worthy of notice is the president's control over the legislative process, which is somewhat less than in the case of ordinary statutes: for the president's suggestions to be rejected, an ordinary majority suffices and not the qualified majority of two-thirds of the votes. Instead, the senate's control has been increased. Senators enjoy rights equal to those of deputies as participants in the national assembly's legislative work, though admittedly they are outnumbered by the deputies (100:460). In addition, parliament modified somewhat the system of state institutions in that it promulgated a so-called Little Constitution, i.e. the constitutional statute of 17 October 1992 on the relations between the legislative and the executive authorities of the Republic of Poland and local government (*Journal of Laws*, 84, item 426). The Little Constitution—an unofficial but common name—proclaims and introduces the separation of powers based on a relatively strict differentiation between the legislative, executive, and judicial functions. At the same time, it removes from Polish constitutional law the provisions that declared the general supremacy of the parliament (or the Sejm, to be exact) in the system of state organs. This solution in itself strengthens the position of the executive authority as an equal partner of the remaining two 'powers'.

The executive authority has been strengthened not only in the new general constitutional principles but also in the more specific institutional changes. The most spectacular of these include, first, the president's increased control over the appointment and dismissal of the government as a whole and of its separate members, with overthrow of the government by the parliament made more difficult; second, the admission of decree laws passed by the government duly authorized by the parliament by way of an ordinary statute, which brings to an end the former legislative monopoly of the parliament.

The Little Constitution preserved the validity of those provisions of the 1952 Constitution (with subsequent changes, of course) which concerned matters outside its area of regulation, amongst other things the judicial authority and the basic rights and duties of citizens. A change of political importance in this respect is that such provisions are now valid by force of an explicit statement of Article 77 of the Little Constitution and not by will of the political authority that had once introduced them. Therefore, the 1952 Constitution is no longer valid *as such*. Also, those of its provisions temporarily preserved can reasonably be expected to lose their force gradually. Still, in 1992 President Lech Wałęsa took the initiative by submitting a draft constitutional statute entitled the Charter of Rights and Freedoms. Turned over to the parliament and submitted to the legislative procedure, the draft meets European and international standards. If promulgated, the Charter will replace the relevant chapter of the 1952 Constitution, preserved by the Little Constitution. Therefore, the Polish Constitution of today resembles a triangle, with the Little Constitution as the base, and the two other sides being the preserved provisions of the 1952 Constitution and the Act on the procedure for the preparation and promulgation of the new Constitution.[9]

Without attempting to prejudge the ultimate effect of the above actions, the following can now be stated quite safely:

1. The need for a new constitution is still generally recognized by all the political parties of consequence and by a large part of the academic community.
2. The preparation of a draft new constitution is still at the preliminary stage: it has to be added, however, that the seven drafts prepared during the preceding parliamentary term are binding for the present parliament.
3. The parliamentary work aimed at preparation and promulgation of a new constitution will not soon be completed, and their actual results are unpredictable, which is due among

other things to the arrangement and distribution of political forces in parliament and also the requirement of a two-thirds majority to promulgate the new constitution.

For this reason, theoretical reflection—however limited in scope—on constitutional legislation in general, and on that of Poland in particular, may also prove of some importance for directing the legislative works now in progress.

2. THE PAN-EUROPEAN MODELS

A constitution should fit the social setting in which it is to function: it should correspond to existing social relations and consciousness; it should include the nation's historical traditions. Beside all its other functions, the constitution must symbolically express the common aims and interests of the nation that has laid that act down by its own sovereign will, either directly or through its representatives. These statements are widely accepted in modern doctrine,[10] and nothing speaks for their general revision.

Yet the insistence on these opinions is not tantamount to exclusion of all foreign influences. First, such exclusion is impossible because of international law which is binding on the entire international community. Second, and to a greater extent still, the domestic legislator has necessarily to include the state's regional obligations that follow from its accession to the relevant supranational structures.[11] Third, owing among other things to the now accelerated integration processes, we deal—especially in Europe—with interpenetration of constitutional solutions, and the pace of that interpenetration is likely to increase.[12] Further, the Polish constitutional legislator is additionally stimulated to become open to the outer world by the frequently proclaimed slogans which are a response to the recent past: of 'coming back to normal' or 'borrowing from the tested models'. Meanwhile, Poland can neither simply return to its pre-communist normalcy nor—generally speaking—borrow from its own constitutional models, as few of them have really proved viable in the historical perspective.

The May Constitution of 1791, appraised as a legal act according to modern criteria, proves strikingly outdated:[13] and suggestions that the names of state organs from the days of the First Republic should now be restored do nothing but demonstrate the nostalgic disposition of one of the political formations.[14] The March Constitution of 1921 soon revealed all its weakness once it was applied in practice, and was then broken by Piłsudski's coup. The semi-authoritarian April Constitution of 1935 was criticized from the beginning by progressive circles in Poland and abroad. It cannot possibly be included in the democratic political tradition, despite the efforts made now and then to do so. The question arises—asked pertinently by a foreign researcher[15]—whether 'normalcy' can be measured at all on the scale of 1921 or 1935. Or—let us add—1791. Which of those political models should be considered tested? Probably none. This is why it seems so important to give some thought to the possible outside contributions to the work of creating the Polish constitution.

The belief is now becoming more and more widespread that the most reliable and also tested measures of normalcy are the so-called European standards[16] formulated in the documents of the Council of Europe, the broadest and at the same time the least formal structure of European integration. By becoming a member of the Council, Poland undertook to observe its standards. The obligation should be met the more scrupulously as Poland has also united—by a treaty of association for the time being—with the European Community, a more advanced though smaller structure of European integration. Article 68 of the treaty stipulates that 'it is the essential preliminary condition of Poland's economic integration with the Community that existing and future Polish legislation should be assimilated with that of the Community members'. By entering the European club, Poland has to recognize its norms and realize the extent to which special attention is paid to the conduct of a new member. Thus, so far as European standards (in the above sense) are concerned, their inclusion in domestic law is the Polish constitutional legislator's duty and not an option to be accepted at his own discretion.

At this level of European integration, this should present no difficulties. As will be shown further on, the European standards define the system of values and set the aims, but do not impose any definite constitutional model corresponding with those values and aims. The domestic constitutional legislator still has a broad—though not unlimited—range of possible constitutional solutions from which to choose. For this reason, respect for European standards is not necessarily in conflict with the quite justifiable trend towards a constitutional expression and guarantee of national identity.[17]

3. STANDARDS OF THE COUNCIL OF EUROPE

The (pan-)European standards seem to include (a) a democratic system of state organs, (b) guarantees of human rights, (c) recognition of the law as the main regulator of state–citizen relations (a state ruled by law), and (d) guarantees of a market economy.

The minimum of democracy expected from member states of the Council of Europe is the election of a parliament (the 'legislative body') in free elections. As can be implied from the importance attached to free parliamentary elections as the measure of democracy, it is also expected that the parliament should have a prominent position in the system of state institutions. Otherwise, compliance with that requirement would not be essential for a given system of government to be regarded as democratic. On the other hand, it would be an exaggeration to conclude from the imperative of free elections that the system is expected necessarily to be purely parliamentary, with either the assembly or parliament-cum-cabinet in power, and any form of presidential or semi-presidential system being excluded. Another measure of democracy that follows from the documents of the Council of Europe is the handing over of a broad section of public matters to local authorities. As with the case of parliamentary elections, so in this instance no detailed solutions are imposed: it is not specified whether the local government should handle some or all matters of local importance, or how the competences should be divided between central and local administration.

It seems, though, that Western observers give the post-communist states a specific warning. Choosing between democracy in the spirit of Locke (which stresses individual rights, the pluralism of associations, and 'procedural' justice) and that inspired by Rousseau (with a stress on majority rule, the collective interpretation of human rights, and 'material' justice), the post-communist states should not be too uncritical in deciding upon the latter variant. Rousseau's version of democracy is more easily assimilated in such states owing to its paradoxical convergence with the influence exerted for many centuries by the Churches (Catholic and Orthodox) and also, during the past forty years, by the Marxist-inspired authorities. In contrast to that approach is the idea of an open society[18] which in its essence expresses the liberal conception of a political system and constitution, with a 'procedural' constitution defining merely the rules of the game and not the tasks of the prospective winners. It is often stressed at the same time that respect for the rights of those who find themselves—permanently or transitionally—in the minority is an important measure of democracy, although such respect implies neither political stability nor prosperity.[19]

Neither the choice of a form of democracy nor of the general principle of a democratic construction of power is by any means self-evident and uncontroversial for the Polish legislator. Experiences so far may make sections of public opinion impatient with waiting for the demonstrable material effects of democratic rule: such groups create climates conducive to deviations from the rigours of democracy. It is thus important to bear in mind that Europe does expect, and will certainly demand, a definite minimum of commitment to such democratic requirements.

While, as can be seen, the pan-European standard of democracy proves to be most general, standards of human rights are more distinctive and involve fuller guarantees of control and procedure under international law. Developed from the earlier European Convention for the Protection of Human Rights, in time the standards became part of the generally recognized norms of international law, in particular of the subsequent Covenant on Civil and Political Rights. Some member states of the Council of Europe, such as Austria, made the Convention part of their constitutions, applying its provisions directly and with equal effect to the other domestic norms of constitutional law.[20] It is less important from the present viewpoint whether the technique actually applied is that of incorporation or transformation: what matters is that the Polish legislator will have to come to terms with the constitutional need to guarantee personal and political rights, at least to the extent contained in the Convention, *inter alia* by ensuring the effectiveness of the norms of international law in domestic legal relations.

By contrast with civil and political rights, social, economic, and cultural rights are of less importance. While the European Social

Charter has been in force since 1965, it is formulated as a programme rather than a directive. Although it does involve certain duties for states, those duties do not have to be performed by and in the constitution—ordinary legislation is quite sufficient here, and which of the Charter's provisions is to be included has been left for the separate states to decide in accordance with their respective material conditions and philosophy of development. States can accede to the Charter selectively, assuming the obligations that follow from some of its provisions only (but exceeding the minimum specified in the Charter itself). Moreover, the mechanism for controlling the performance of even those obligations is considered imperfect.[21]

Despite all the reservations which have to be made, it still seems obvious that membership of the Council of Europe and accession to the Social Charter (which can hardly be avoided by Poland) will by themselves stimulate a definite trend in Polish constitutionalism. With due regard to all the legal doubts, it implies future inclusion in the constitution of not just civil and political but also social, economic, and cultural rights, even if these are not to be directly translatable into the subjective rights of individuals. This trend is supported by a considerable part of public opinion,[22] and even from a theoretical perspective, were we to criticize its concurrence with traditional socialist thought, we would still have to take into account its adequacy for a constitutional model motivated by Catholic personalism.[23] At this point of the discussion it must be said that, by joining institutionalized Europe, Poland would find the theoretical model of a liberal constitution confined principally to procedural provisions rather difficult to accept.[24] In any case, the future constitution should not create legal obstacles to the guarantees of human rights in their pan-European interpretation: rather, such guarantees are the absolute minimum of what should be expected of such a constitution.

Closely related to the guarantees of human rights is still another pan-European standard, which consists of a duty by the state scrupulously to observe legal provisions in relations between the state and persons under its jurisdiction. However, the actual way of meeting that demand is something which can only be decided by the author of a national constitution. Should it be patterned after the German doctrine of the *Rechtsstaat*, which means a more formalized ('juridical') formulation of the procedural guarantees, and a broader formulation (which might be called 'material') of the substantive criteria? Or should the model be the Anglo-Saxon approach, the core of which is the principle of the rule of law, along with formal rules of procedure which take extra-legal values into account such as good faith, reasonableness, and justice? Or perhaps it is best to choose one's own solution, based on some elements of each of the above? After all, cultural differences conditioned the great variety of constitutional solutions to the problem in the different European states.[25]

The principle of the rule of law is intended to prevent political instrumentalization of law.[26] It is dependent, however, on the judges entrusted with power having high professional and moral qualifications, and on flexibility in examining cases.[27] It seems, therefore, that in creating a state ruled by law in Poland we are likely to encounter fewer threats if we sensibly proceed along the road marked by foreign experience of the practice of the *Rechtsstaat* principle. Left out of account here will be the opinions of those theoreticians[28] and practitioners[29] who suggest—partly in the name of a preferred priority of natural law, and partly to accelerate transformation of the system—that the realization of any version of a state ruled by law should be held back, at least for some time. Such opinions are obviously incompatible with pan-European standards.

The standards discussed here also include the free market, based on private ownership of property. While protection of private ownership seems self-evident (guarantees of the right to private property exist in the Constitution), it remains controversial whether the Constitution should establish norms making it possible for and perhaps even obliging the state to intervene in the economy, and, if the answer is yes, how this should be done. In this area, the practice of European states varies according to the programmes of the political forces in power. The Polish constitutional legislator should learn from this state of affairs, at least to the extent of not trying to prevent such variations appearing in Poland as well through the imposition of undue constitutional restraints on the activity of the state. A certain degree of state intervention is in fact required by the standards of social rights discussed above. Thus, in spite of quite justifiable aversion, we can only speak here of a constitutional formulation—even if it is by no means rigid—of a social market economy in opposition to that of a centrally planned system.[30] What favours this formulation is the fact, mentioned above in a somewhat different context, that the legislator is inspired by personalism which, with respect to the market economy, prescribes solutions other than those suggested by liberalism.[31]

4. THE PROSPECT: EUROPEAN UNION

The pan-European standards become more intensive, and acquire greater force, in structures and forms of integration higher than that of the Council of Europe. The European Community has been transformed into the European Union, whose legal foundation is the treaty signed in Maastricht in 1991. As the Treaty limits the sovereignty of states that accede to it, its ratification gave rise to a stormy debate in many European states.[32] It can be assumed that by becoming associated with the EC, Poland will aim at full membership of the Union in spite of all the resulting difficulties. Thus the future constitution should specify, amongst other things, the procedure of handing over legislative, administrative, and judicial competence to EU authorities as well as the principles and procedure of application of the law of the EC in internal affairs.[33] As with other European states, Poland will face the unprecedented phenomenon recently termed constitutional pluralism,[34] which stands in sharp contrast to what is popular in our part of the continent: the tendency to think mainly in terms of national sovereignty, self-definition, and often even the homogeneity of a national state.[35]

The Maastricht Treaty (hereinafter 'the Treaty') influences the constitutions of its signatory states in two ways: directly, by replacing their national regulations for specific areas, and indirectly, through the obligation to adjust such regulations. Whether this implies a political obligation alone or a legal obligation remains controversial.[36] For this reason, the Treaty is sometimes called the 'constitution of Europe': hence also the thesis of constitutional pluralism which it is to introduce. In its regulation of constitutional matters the Treaty introduces common citizenship of the Union, changing the present nature of citizenship as a definition of the individual's relation to the state under public law and depriving that notion of all of its ethnic elements.[37] Further, it incorporates the European Convention for the Protection of Human Rights, assuming a direct protection of individual rights in supranational procedures and creating for that purpose the office of the European Ombudsman. Finally, it institutionalizes the European political parties (i.e. those operating on the European scale).

Indirectly, the Treaty obliges states to shape their respective constitutions so as to prevent them from hindering policies of stable prices and balanced budgets; of markets based on principles of appropriately regulated free competition; and of priority given to monetary policy (which follows from the adoption of a common currency) within the framework of overall economic policies, with monetary policy promoted by central banks required to be autonomous in relation to national governments. The powers of the EU are to be either exclusive or joint, in the sense that the Union would exercise them in co-operation with its member states, based on the principle of subsidiarity. EU authorities will also be competent to decide on matters of defence, foreign policy, administration of justice, and even public order of the separate member states. What is assumed here is the growing importance of the European Parliament, as well as the participation of representatives of governments in the EU executive authorities. It is provided that the legislatures concerned should speed up the process of adjustment of domestic laws to the law of the EU,[38] which enjoys supremacy.

As can be seen, once signed and ratified by Poland the Treaty will have far-reaching consequences for Polish constitutional law. In a sense, its provisions influence the interpretation of the contents of practically all the pan-European standards discussed above. The situation may prove particularly complex with regard to standards of democracy. On the one hand, we deal with the requirement of free elections and of local government: on the other hand, the need arises to provide the democratically legitimated executive participating in important political decisions within the EU authorities with sufficiently broad powers and competences. Thus, whilst Hungary, for example, hopes that the influence of European integration might balance what some find to be the undue predominance of the prime minister in the Hungarian state,[39] the Dutch and Italians wonder whether their versions of parliamentarianism can be modified, and the government strengthened instead.

The regulations for elections to the European Parliament, while preserving a considerable degree of national autonomy, nevertheless aim at unification based on the proportional system. Though we cannot be absolutely certain, this is most unlikely to exert an influence on assessments of the electoral regulations applying to levels of representation within a given state and, consequently, on the constitutional regulation of the principles of elections in general. What can also be expected is that influential personalities representing the European institutions will exert pressure (whose actual effectiveness remains uncertain) favouring the adoption in constitutional works of their specific conception of democracy as containing forms of direct citizen participation not just in the political but also the economic and social spheres.

As important as the legal changes will be the adjustment of the East European political culture—still based on the majoritarian principle, collectivist and tribal in a sense—to European norms with their respect for pluralism, individualism, and tolerance. Different institutional solutions can well function successfully within one and the same political culture—yet one and the same institution functioning in the environment of different cultures may have entirely different effects.

As has been mentioned above, there will be a considerable 'internationalization' of the guarantee mechanisms in the area of human rights. It thus seems advisable, for example, that Poland also should look in advance to the introduction of more consistent guarantees of the citizen's right to a fair trial in all civil, criminal, and administrative cases in accordance with the most explicit provisions of the European Convention. European union can also be expected to result in a greater attention being paid to the degree and method of guarantee of social rights, if for no other reason than the freedom of movement within the Community of persons into different trades and professions. The possibility of the above-mentioned supremacy of EU law opens a new perspective on the question of the 'state ruled by law'. It is enough to mention here that, when establishing relations between Polish and EC law, any idea of natural law being in competition with that proclaimed by the will of man has to be rejected. In this way, insoluble contradictions can be prevented.

As far as the market economy is concerned, there can be no doubts in the light of the discussion so far as to its interpretation as a social market economy with a considerable degree of intervention on the part of the state. Were Poland, upon its accession to the Treaty, simultaneously to adopt in its future constitution a ban on state intervention, the national economy would be subjected to influences with no counterweight whatever, the direct influence of the EU authorities, and the indirect influence of the states represented in those authorities.

The discussion so far has concerned either obligatory inclusion by the Polish constitutional legislator of certain values and, in principle, only those aims that follow from the external obligations already undertaken, or the possible and desirable steps that might be taken in advance of Poland's accession to the EU: synchronization of Polish constitutional law with the system of pan-European law which is now becoming distinct. Yet, as is well known, all constitutional legislators are guided in their work also by foreign national models of government, constitutional solutions, or separate institutions. A thoughtful legislator performs his task with the utmost care, attentive to the peculiarities of his own country. Such attention is often considered a necessary and essential condition of effective application of the general principles and models that have been tested elsewhere. Let us therefore first unravel the Polish peculiarities, and then consider their consequences for the possibilities of reception of foreign models of government and constitution.

5. POLISH PECULIARITIES

This discussion of Polish peculiarities will concern only those major features that are relevant for the present subject. To some extent, most will prove common to other European states with past experience of communist totalitarianism and authoritarianism similar to that of Poland.[40]

Let me start the review with the effects of that very heritage. It leads to the aim not only of making the newly created institutions as different as possible (in terms of contents, form, and even name) from the former institutions associated with the past, but also of shaping them so as to make them prevent any recurrence of that past.[41] This fact has further consequences, some of which will now be mentioned.

Special importance is attached to the preservation of political pluralism, even at the expense of the effectiveness of the institutions in which that principle can find a fuller expression (e.g. parliament). If this fact is ignored, it is difficult to understand the insistence of so many opinion-makers on the principle of elections according to proportionality.

There is strong opposition to all manifestations of the personalization of state authority which was associated with the immense power of party leaders under the former regime, and at the same time perceived as a potential threat to the newly won democracy. For this reason, one can hardly agree with the simplified account (formulated, for example, in press statements by Deputy L. Mazewski and Senator J. Stepien) of the current relationship between the mode of election of the holder of authority (e.g. the president) and his powers, nor with the conclusion, drawn from different positions, as to the supposedly 'inevitable' transformation of the Polish state system into a presidential one.[42] Heavy stress is laid in Poland on the principle of a triple separation of powers, in contrast to the former principle of unity and uniformity. However, this is related to the above-mentioned insistence on political pluralism, which in turn results in the need to preserve a high status for parliament in the state structure.

What seems to be yet another peculiarity of the Polish situation is a low level of constructive political participation in society. The reasons will not be analysed here: what matters most is the effect of this situation. A typical symptom is the alarmingly low turn-out at the parliamentary elections of 1991 (43.2 per cent of those with the right to vote) as well as of 1993 (52.08 per cent) and lower still at the local by-elections. This is particularly striking given extensive social participation in democratic and anti-totalitarian movements in some periods of their struggle for power, and also given the quite considerable attendance at a variety of current public protest manifestations. What is of importance for the present discussion is the effect of this situation: the weakening of the democratic legitimacy of the eligible organs of public authority, and the fact that groups in society (of whose size and nature little can be said) remain unrepresented, whether in parliament or in any other formal structures of government. What should be mentioned separately, though, is the fact that—in contrast with the former mass participation of citizens in routine public life—the present freedom includes freedom *not* to participate also. This should be borne in mind by the legislator when specifying the conditions of validity of voting in elections or referendums.

The next issue to be raised is the weakness of the traditions of democracy in public life. Political élites lack the habit of functioning within such an environment and, especially, of acting in accordance with the procedures typical of democratic systems.[43] This is revealed in the submission of collective representations (e.g. when deputies submit so-called statements instead of interpolations or questions), but also in the dispute between president and the government concerning the extent of control over the army. Examples are numerous.[44] The essential point here is the conclusion that, in a situation where democratic custom is still in the making, the range of acts regulated by provisions of law has to be broader. If, for instance, the law fails to ban combinations of certain posts or types of activity, very foolish ideas are likely to emerge, frequently defended with considerable effect by the refrain: 'What I'm doing is nobody's business, since the law doesn't prohibit such conduct.'

The low level of constructive political participation in Polish society is one of the reasons for the underdevelopment of the party system. Of over 200 political parties which notified the courts of their formation (and not even an estimated number can be quoted of those that never even applied for registration and legal personality), only six have representatives in parliament. This manifests either lack of ambition of many parties to play a part of their own in the political arena, or their constituents' lack of support for such an ambition. Instead, represented in parliament there are trade unions as well as associations that basically do not claim the functions of political parties. This makes the party system chaotic and formally ambiguous; the repercussions can be seen in the contents of the electoral regulations. What is probably more dangerous than chaos in the formal and organizational sphere is the confused representation by the parties of definite social interests, expressed also in their political programmes. The parties differ in their specific appraisal of the past, personal preferences, and professed moral values rather than in terms of programmes based on various interests. The fact is that the programmes are far from consistent and precise, and all attempts at including the parties that operate in this situation to the Left, Right, or Centre yield but moderate effects, the divisions being largely conventional. Not just the fragmentation of the party system, but also the reluctance to compromise on the part of parties already organized and operating hampers the functioning in Poland of effective parliamentary government, which, after all, requires a stable and clear party system as its precondition.[45]

A peculiarity of Polish public life is the extensive participation in it of the Catholic Church, and its ambition to influence constitutional solutions. The system of Christian values—interpreted authoritatively by the church hierarchy—is to serve as the normative foundation of the entire system of law, with the Constitution included as the crown of that system, according to a recent statement.[46] The church authorities assess the work of state organs—e.g. the commissioner for civil rights protection—directly and almost arbitrarily, guided by their own hierarchy of values. Yet that hierarchy is next-to-incompatible with the pan-European standards discussed above (as demonstrated by the problem faced by Ireland because of its anti-abortion law).[47] What is more, the hierarchy creates additional criteria for the appraisal of the adaptability of foreign models or institutions. As can be expected, the Church is hardly likely to promote with any greater ardour Poland's integration with Europe. The executive in the present political arrangement seems to be quite susceptible to influence from the episcopate (as demonstrated by the mode of introduction of religious instruction in schools); this considered, only the legislature can be expected to put up any greater opposition. This is an additional argument for the preservation of its broad powers, including those of control.

Finally, what should be treated as still another Polish peculiarity is the specific situation in which the economic changes are being introduced. A planned economy based on state ownership is being replaced with a free market based on private ownership. This involves the essential tasks of privatization of former state property, restructuring of industry, and securing social protection for the economically weakest. However, the entire operation proceeds in conditions of profound economic crisis, recession, and inflation—still present, even if subdued. The situation requires vigorous intervention on the part of the state, and that depends amongst other things on efficient operation of the professional administrative machine.

Obviously, all the above (and probably also other) peculiarities of the Polish political, social, and economic situation, tradition, and heritage can be taken into account by the constitutional legislator considering the use of foreign models. The range actually included can be broader or narrower; this depends on the legislator's rationality, on his following the presumptions of the rational legislator, to use the well-known term introduced by Prof. J. Wróblewski. It is highly probable, though, that the legislator's actual decisions will be determined largely by subjective, irrational prejudices. The right choice depends on re-interpretation, in the context of the integration processes, of the basic conception ('philosophy') of state, and that requires steps that are both difficult and often quite painful.[48]

In the end, it is to be feared that the actual choice will be determined not by theoretical reflection and rational reasoning but by an entanglement of the current interests of the political groups influential at that very moment, as has often happened before both in Poland and elsewhere. This would not be too dangerous in itself were it not for the fear that, should the events coincide unfavourably, the road to European democracy may lead through authoritarian regimes of the South American type.[49]

6. POSSIBLE APPLICATIONS OF THE MODELS TESTED ELSEWHERE

The problem of application of foreign models—their admissibility, limits, and helpfulness—differs depending on a given model's degree of generality. Despite what can be supposed at first sight, the complications by no means show a linear decrease as the level of abstraction grows.

Theoretically, the legislator can be assumed to make choices at the following three levels of generality:

1. in the macro-scale—between different types of system of government, i.e. between democracy and autocracy, anarchy etc.; this question seems settled and leaves no room for doubt, at least not in this interpretation;
2. in the medio-scale—between different forms of a given system, practised in different states, i.e. between monarchy and republic, parliamentary, semi-presidential, or presidential republic—in the shape assumed by those forms in the separate states;

3. in the micro-scale—between different institutions installed, in one form or another, within one or more national state systems.[50]

It is the latter two levels of generality that require a more careful discussion. The hypothesis is that, despite the appeals of persons who sometimes enjoy supreme authority (such as politicians, scholars, or both), a wholesale reception of a single system of government is impossible in Polish conditions even if that system has been tested with good results elsewhere. Thus the constitutional legislator should not aim at applying a definite form of democracy exactly in the shape in which it functions—and succeeds—in some other state. What can serve as a warning here is the mistrust, detected by local researchers, with which the former East Germans treat the West German legal order imposed on them by the union of Germany. The present state is accepted by 81 per cent of the population of West Germany, but by as few as 47 per cent of the East Germans,[51] and that in spite of the most favourable conditions in which the change proceeded!

The problem of the re-introduction of a monarchy can safely be considered to be of no great practical importance. In Polish conditions all declarations for this solution are but evidence of political exotics. Similar proposals put forward in some other post-communist states of Southern Europe (Romania,[52] Bulgaria, perhaps also Serbia) are perhaps of greater significance; but their political and especially cultural contexts are different. In some of those cases, monarchy might be a factor to integrate a society which has slender traditions of democracy and has experienced a rather rapid transition from personal dictatorship (particularly oppressive in the case of Romania) to freedom: the ability to 'self-organize' is even lower than that of Polish society.

Yet the sum of differences creates the situation where the authors of the future Polish constitution will not be in a position to adopt either as a whole or at least in general outline a definite single model of government in any of the national variants that have succeeded in Western republics. One can hardly be guided by the pure model of parliamentary democracy as the rule of an assembly, nor probably by the classical parliament-cum-cabinet structure. With the low political participation of citizens and the proliferation of parties, a parliament following the principles of that system would be unable (as has already been shown by experience so far) to form an executive efficient and stable enough to cope successfully with the task of introducing a market economy, of contributing effectively to the overcoming of economic crisis, and also of organizing the state's accession to European structures and properly representing it within those structures. This type of parliamentarianism would have to be rationalized cautiously.

The need for caution is what I wish to stress here. Even deviations towards a chancellorship—which is otherwise an attractive system, partly because of its success in neighbouring Germany—may lead back to the visions of enlightened and reforming dictatorship. Such fears are sometimes voiced in Hungary[53] in response to the strong position acquired there by the prime minister through the new constitutional solutions. Its only moderating factor is the president, whose personal authority allows him to exceed the extremely limited powers granted to that office by the Constitution.

What gives rise to many more reservations, though, is the widely recommended formation of a presidential republic imitating the United States of America (proposed less often), or even a semi-presidential system modelled after the Fifth French Republic or modern Finland (which is suggested more often). Let us now concentrate on this latter suggestion, the most attractive at first sight. It has emerged in the climate of social impatience at the slow 'maturation' of the party system and parliamentarism, followed by discouragement with what looks like political weakness. At the same time, the proposal is maintained by favourable opinions about presidential systems operating in entirely different conditions and, as it may be supposed, by undue trust in law's effective role in relation to politics (through helping, for example, in the 'natural selection' of political parties). Moreover, the suggestion under discussion follows from the belief that the countries undergoing the hard—but, let us hope, beneficial—surgical procedure, the transformation to a different system, ought democratically to entrust the scalpel to one person, at least for the transitional period. That person would be the guarantor of changes, responsible for their proper direction:[54] at the same time, he would share with the government both the strictly executive authority and the responsibility for its exercise. Already at this point, a reservation appears: a solution designed for a transitional period that entails a prolonged process may well become solidified: vested with supreme authority, the president may one day start hampering the transformations instead of promoting them. Further, who is to decide that the period of temporary strengthening of the executive power should come to an end? And will the holders of executive authority be appreciative of such a proclamation—made by parliament, for example? These are only some of the doubts.

Bearing in mind the Polish peculiarities discussed above, the dangers of a state system which locates the president at the centre of power can easily be detected. With weak democratic traditions, failure on the part of the flimsy political parties to fulfil their function of restraint, and also the impaired democratic legitimacy of parliament, such conditions may open the road to personal autocratic rule exercised over the head of parliament and the parties. His own legitimacy acquired in general elections, the president would have no difficulty in using the populist bent of a considerable portion of a politically passive and ideologically confused society by appealing to its tribal and fundamental inclinations.[55] It would be enough to establish and skilfully use channels of direct communication with society, more or less institutionalized (referendum v. mass meetings or the media). Certain signs of this turn of affairs were to be noticed in recent events; for example, in the president's initial standpoint on the draft constitutional act about the mode of preparation and promulgation of a new constitution. As shown by experience (admittedly, not Polish experience so far), a president who is not subject to proper control tends to respect the constitution less, along with the rules of the political game expressive of the very essence of constitutionalism. That would pose a threat to a state ruled by law which is based precisely on constitutionalism.

Finally, there is another most important matter. In planning to build a system of government based on political pluralism, one should realize that the fullest expression of that pluralism in a state system is a parliament elected in proportional elections. As Michel Crozier wrote, it follows from the president's strategic position that in order to consolidate his power, he will appeal rather to the nation's unity and seek the most persuasive formulation of that ideal of unity.

For all the above reasons, it has to be assumed that the best solution for the Polish constitutional legislator is to elaborate his own indigenous model of the system, naturally in keeping with the pan-European standards (those already binding for Poland and those others that can justifiably be expected to become binding in the future). He should also use carefully, selectively, and critically foreign experience at the level of 'micro-choices' (concerning the separate institutions and detailed solutions). The actual form of the system should, however, be 'local' and original. The 'medio-choice' should be made in favour of an appropriately corrected parliamentary model, as despite all the reservations this offers the least threat to the overriding values.

However naïve this may sound, the indigenous model would best be created by a legislator able to maintain a distance from current party and political disputes, to associate long-term aims and major interests, and to weigh the rational arguments. The choices made in the process of its creation will necessarily be political in their essence, yet they will have extremely broad and far-reaching national repercussions, and will sometimes amount to choices between nearly equal values, i.e. between (a) the representativeness and effectiveness of parliament, (b) free enterprise and an adequate level of social security, (c) representative democracy in a pure sense and different forms of civic participation, whether formalized or informal, and (d) national, state sovereignty and full participation in the integration of Europe and—in a broader sense—of the modern world, i.e. between tradition and modernization.

The importance of knowledge of the constitutional models of other countries is beyond dispute, if just to add to the arguments when considering definite options. Such models should, however, be treated not as dressmakers' patterns, to be copied mechanically, but as the source of intellectual inspiration and—this has to be stated clearly as well—as the context of the system of government, indispensable for appraisal of the separate institutions.

As regards the example of such separate institutions, the Polish legislator has always referred to it readily and repeatedly, and is likely to do that in the future as well. It has even been remarked in the literature on the subject that all the new institutions introduced during the constitutional reforms of the 1980s were in fact modelled on the example of other states, the only native element being the symbols.[56] This opinion seems generally correct, if a little exaggerated. It would be difficult to invent today an entirely novel institutional expression of general and universally accepted principles. To some extent, however, the state of affairs described resulted also from weakness and lack of imagination in the Polish approach to constitutional law. Anyway, as has been stated above, this can hardly be a matter for grave reproach.[57]

Here we reach the last problem. Both in the case of the 'medio-choice' (the entire system inspired by foreign models) and of the 'micro-choice' (imitation of the separate selected institutions), profound knowledge of the subject of this discussion is necessary. Since this aspect is often neglected in practice, it seems worth stressing the point once again, even if statements that are well known and established in the methodology of comparative constitutional law have to be quoted.

7. THE NEED FOR ADEQUATE APPRAISAL OF 'TESTED' MODELS

At the lower levels of generality, we deal with the realization of specific values (which more or less correspond with those expressed in the pan-European standards) in the context of the constitutional solutions of the individual West European states and—much less frequently—of the new democracies of Eastern Europe. We deal, therefore, with many different solutions that can serve as examples, but sometimes also as warnings. The post-communist European states—among which Poland is no exception—are usually and quite comprehensively fascinated with the models of larger and more prosperous states.[58] And yet—no doubt the truism can be excused—each model is a definite idealization of the reality it represents.[59] In order to appraise the actual usefulness of its whole or parts for the constitutional construction achieved, one should, therefore, perform what might be called 'de-idealization', aimed at a better recognition of the functions actually performed by such a model in both the given social organism and the legal context. Below, the succeeding elements (stages) of the intellectual process of 'de-idealization' are set out.

Knowledge of the historical origin of the given system (institution) makes it possible to separate out the chance or unique causes. For example, the model of the Fifth French Republic cannot be reasonably considered or judiciously appraised without regard to the strong personality of General de Gaulle, the war in Algeria, and the related state of mind of the army. At the same time, a given model should be seen as a link in the historical process, and thus also in reference to the preceding situation. Monarchy evolved differently in Great Britain, in the Scandinavian countries, in Benelux, or—again because of a different origin—in Spain. The factor of tradition is so strong as to become sometimes the only reason for preservation of some provisions or even of entire institutions.

This leads to the absolute necessity of taking the dynamics of the models examined, their changes, and the social, political, and cultural causes of those changes into consideration also. This is all the more essential as intensification of changes can be expected, influenced by the EU and the 'interpenetration' of the national constitutions in Europe,[60] resulting from the countries of the British Commonwealth gaining independence in the sphere of constitutional law. Most changes concern separate institutions within a given system and have no greater impact on the nature of that system as a whole; in themselves, however, they are an interesting manifestation of the trends of modern constitutionalism, whether on a national or more general scale. What can be mentioned here by way of example is, in France, the development of local government or consolidation of the function of jurisprudence of the Constitutional Council which assimilates that body to constitutional courts; in Sweden, abolition of the bicameral structure of parliament; and in a number of countries, the spread of the institution of ombudsman.

The dynamics discussed become the more explicit the greater the insight into the actual functioning of a given model. For example, only a careful examination of actual political relations makes it possible to reconstruct the true structure of interdependence between president and prime minister in the Fifth Republic, which was actually much more complex than is generally believed.[61] Reconstruction of a model from the legal provisions only would be an idle pastime for the Polish constitutional legislator. In the extreme case, it would lead—as we know from experience—to a specific constitutional nominalism, which consists in drawing conclusions from the very name of an institution. An example of this approach is the opinion that the senate as such, from its very nature, should have extensive powers to contribute to the shaping of state foreign policy. Another example is the isolation of norms from their context and their interpretation like other norms which sound the same but function in an entirely different context.[62]

It is important to be familiar with the discussion and opinions on the given model or its role in academic discussion in the country where it is applied. By way of contrast with the former period, where at least the public criticism of the Western models was unduly sharpened for political reasons, we now deal in Poland with an alarming inclination to approve such models quite indiscriminately. Yet some institutions persist by force of inertia (and tradition) only, and cause no great harm simply because they function in the context of the conditions of the entire system. None the less, such institutions are sometimes submitted to critical analysis and radical reform proposals. Even in the most developed Western democracies there are few institutions which are immune to criticism. Thus there is no single ideal model of electoral regulations. While the Italian proportional system has been effectively criticized, the opposite trend can be found in France and still persists in Great Britain. In general, opinion on the superiority of either of those two electoral systems is most divided.[63] In the USA, practically every presidential election in turn is preceded by a recurring wave of criticism of the institution of electoral colleges, which at least formally preserves the indirect nature of those elections.

The position within the system of the republican head of state is the subject of heated discussions in countries of the British Commonwealth which have weakened their ties with the UK: Canada, New Zealand, and particularly Australia.[64] For entirely different reasons, the position of the president of Italy has been questioned: two-thirds of the respondents in a public opinion survey have favoured the introduction of direct presidential elections,[65] which is in keeping to some extent with the practice of the exercise of power by the last holders of that office and coincides with the trend towards consolidation of the executive and the president's office within it. Many debates concern the so-called upper house of parliament. In Italy and Spain, it is proposed that the upper chambers should be transformed into bodies representing regional authorities (as in the German *Bundesrat*), which is related to consolidation of the position of regions as such. In Great Britain, it is repeatedly suggested that the House of Lords should be modernized (through the introduction of elections) or even abolished. Though the Polish legislator used it as the basis for one of the models, the Italian national council of the judiciary is much criticized in its own country for both theoretical and practical political reasons.

Some of the states that practise the principle of the rule of law still do without constitutionally specified guarantees of human rights. Still waiting to be implemented are the proposals put forward in Great Britain for many years now, and repeated by the Labour Party in its campaign of 1992, for a coherent and comprehensive charter of civil rights similar to that passed in Canada and to some extent also in New Zealand.[66]

Finally, when examining a given model, one should take into account the interrelation and interaction between its separate elements (internal arrangements) and between that model and its broadly conceived surroundings (external arrangements). In the internal sphere, the important points are, of course, the relations with the other elements of the whole, and also with the rest of the system. As has already been mentioned, an institution seen in itself may be found outdated or accidental. But even then it is not necessarily dysfunctional, either in relation to the whole or as a whole. In a specific situation, its usefulness can be conditioned by its relations with the other institutions or elements of the state system. What can serve as an example here is the second chamber of a parliament. Its functions in a federation differ from those in a unitary system; it is also different in nature if elected in general and direct elections, as contrasted with indirect election or appointment.

The external arrangement consists of the relations between a given system or form of government and its separate component institutions, on the one hand, and the social and political environment on the other hand. Practically all the Western models of government function in an environment already shaped and more or less stable politically. The party systems are relatively permanent and, therefore, only occasionally corrected. They define to a large extent the importance of the separate institutions of the legal system. This concerns above all the institution of electoral regulations which has already been discussed. However, the so-called constructive vote of censure of the government can have different meanings in practice, depending on the composition of parliament: large party blocs as against considerable fragmentation, where all at-

272 THE CENTRAL AND EAST EUROPEAN EXPERIENCE

tempts at forming the majority to suggest an alternative to the prime minister in office meet with serious difficulties. In Hungary, for example, the constructive vote of censure is thought to have shaken in practice the constitutionally assumed balance of powers in favour of the government.[67] The absence of civil society results also in the state being forced to provide its own organs with the necessary competences and material means, and to undertake tasks which would and should be otherwise delegated to organizations of citizens.[68] This means overgrowth of the executive functions and consequently also of the state control structures.

As has been shown, the use of foreign patterns in the formation of the state system and its institutions prompts many doubts. But the difficulties would be much greater had anyone attempted to graft foreign party systems on to Poland. The example of the European parties seems to suggest, however, that such attempts cannot be excluded.

Notes

1. M. K. Dziewanowski, *The Communist Party of Poland*, 2nd edn. (Cambridge, Mass., 1976).
2. K. Działocha and J. Trzciński, *Zagadnienie obowiązywania Konstytucji Marcowej w Polsce Ludowej 1944–1952* (The Problem of Validity of the March Constitution in People's Poland 1944–1952) (Wrocław, 1977).
3. W. Sokolewicz, 'Über die sozialistische Auffassung von den Grundrechten und -pflichten', *Jahrbuch für Ostrecht*, 19 (1978), 111–42.
4. W. Sokolewicz, 'The Contemporary Polish State: Structures and Functions', in L. S. Graham and M. K. Ciechocińska (eds.), *The Polish Dilemma: Views from Within* (Boulder, Colo., 1987), 37–68.
5. W. Sokolewicz, 'Constitutionality as a Precondition of the Rule of Law: A Certain Dilemma of a Socialist State', *Archiv für Rechts- und Sozialphilosophie*, 41 (1990), 190–208.
6. S. Gebethner, 'La Nouvelle Institution du défenseur des droits civiques en Pologne', *Droit polonais contemporain*, 1/2 (1988), 21–34.
7. I have discussed the process in detail in 'The Legal-Constitutional Bases of Democratisation in Poland: Systemic and Constitutional Change', in G. Sanford (ed.), *Democratisation in Poland 1988–90: Polish Voices* (London, 1992), 69–97.

8. Z. Czeszejko-Sochacki, 'Projekty nowej konstytucji (Przegląd zagadnień węzłowych)' (The Draft Constitutions (A Review of the Crucial Problems)), *Państwo i Prawo*, 7 (1991), 3–14.

9. W. Sokolewicz, 'The Polish Constitution in a Time of Change', *International Journal of the Sociology of Law*, 20 (1992), 29–42.

10. For remarks on the constitutions of European post-communist states, see e.g. A. Pradetto, 'Postkommunismus, Kooperativismus und gesellschaftliche Autonomie', *Osteuropa* (1990), 1214.

11. For the interpretation of the term 'supranational' (as opposed to 'international'), see J. Barcz, 'Organizacje ponadnarodowe' (Supranational Organizations), *Sprawy Międzynarodowe*, 7–8 (1991).

12. S. Cassese, 'The Impact of European Political Union on National Constitutions', paper presented at the conference on Constitutional Policy and Changes in Europe, Oxford, 2–5 Apr. 1992, 10–14.

13. Particularly if its style, vocabulary, and precision of the language (not to mention the merits) are compared with the practically contemporary US Constitution of 1787.

14. See 'Projekt Konstytucji RP' (Draft Constitution of the Republic of Poland), in *Program Trzeciej Rzeczypospolitej* (The Programme of the Third Republic) (Warsaw, July 1991).

15. A. Komorida, ' "Revolution by the Constitution" and "Revolution in the Constitution": Some Remarks on the Cases of Poland and the Soviet Union', paper presented at the 3rd AIDC Congress, Warsaw, 1991, 5.

16. In this context, A. Wasilkowski mentions 'certain already shaped and further developed values and systemic solutions that guarantee the respect of those values'; see A. Wasilkowski, 'Konsekwencje stowarzyszenia z WE dla porządku prawnego Polski' (The Consequences of Association with the EC for the Legal Order of Poland), typescript (Warsaw, 4–6 June 1992), 1.

17. Which is feared by U. K. Preuss, 'Patterns of Constitutional Evolution and Change in Western and Eastern Europe', paper presented at the conference on Constitutional Policy and Change in Europe, Oxford, 2–5 Apr. 1992, 1. The fears are also shared by some Polish authors. The need for a new approach to the problems of sovereignty has been stressed in a press interview by A. Wasilkowski, 'Konstytucja RP a integracja europejska' (The Constitution of the Republic of Poland and European Integration), *Rzeczpospolita*, 25 June 1992, p. ix.

18. See R. Dahrendorf, 'Historia bez końca' (A Story with No Ending), interview in *Polityka*, 14 Mar. 1992, 10.

19. See K. Auchincloss, 'Demokracja cudów nie czyni' (Democracy Does No Wonders), *Newsweek*, repr. *Gazeta Wyborcza*, 20 Feb. 1992, 8.

20. For discussion of some of the related legal complications, see T. Öhlinger, 'Austria and Article 6 of the European Convention on Human Rights', *European Journal of International Law*, 1/1–2 (1990), 286–91. See also J. Barcz, 'Ochrona praw zasadniczych w ramach Wspólnoty zachodnio-europejskiej (W sprawie kompetencji FTK RFN)' (Protection of Basic Rights in the European Community (On the Competences of the West German Federal Constitutional Tribunal)), *Zeszyty Niemcoznawcze PISM*, 1/4 (1989).

21. T. Öhlinger, 'Die Europäischen Sozialrechte', in M. Nowak *et al.* (eds.), *Festschrift für F. Ermacera* (Kehl am Rhein, 1988); idem, 'Die Europäischen Sozialrechte', in F. Matscher (ed.), *Die Durchsetzung wirtschaftlicher und sozialer Grundrechte. Eine rechtvergleichende Bestandsaufnahme* (Kehl am Rhein, 1991), 335 f. See also the most sceptical opinion of J. Jończyk, 'Co to jest europejskie prawo socjalne?' (What Is European Social Law?), *Rzeczpospolita*, 2 June 1992, p. x.

22. As remarked e.g. by Preuss, 'Patterns of Constitutional Evolution', 9. A similar conclusion can be drawn from an article by K. Łojewski, 'Czy w Polsce istnieje jeszcze Konstytucja?' (Does Poland still Have the Constitution?), *Rzeczpospolita*, 4 Feb. 1992, p. vii, who points to the violation in practice of the social rights that are still guaranteed by the present Constitution.

23. See R. Papini, 'Introduction à une théorie des constitutions d'inspiration personaliste', and J. Cavero Lataillade, 'Observations préliminaires'; both delivered at a scientific conference on Democracy and Constitutional Reform in Central Europe, Budapest, 10–13 Oct. 1991. See my report, *Państwo i Prawo*, 1 (1992), 110 f.

24. Although this very approach is recommended by a group of influential Anglo-Saxon authors (e.g. N. Johnson, 'Constitutionalism: Procedural Frameworks and Political Ends', paper presented at the conference on Constitutional Policy and Change in Europe, Oxford, 2–5 Apr. 1992, 6) and the Polish lawyers under their influence.

25. See Preuss, 'Patterns of Constitutional Evolution', 15.

26. Johnson, 'Constitutionalism', 9–11. It has to be mentioned that our interpretation of the *Rechtsstaat* and the rule of law includes the evolution of those formulas, and therefore does not always agree with that of the other authors. See e.g. K. Hatanaka, 'The "Rule of Law" State Notion in the USSR and Eastern Europe', *Ritsumeeikan Law Review*, 6 (1991), 2 f.

27. G. Marshall, 'Lions Around the Throne: Summary', paper presented at the conference on Constitutional Policy and Change in Europe, Oxford, 2–5 Apr. 1992, 1.

28. e.g. K. Wrzesiński, 'Państwo i prawo a społeczeństwo obywatelskie'

(State, Law, and Civil Society), *Studia Filozoficzne*, 4 (1990), 117 ff., argues that priority of the natural over the proclaimed (positive) law is indispensable for civil society.

29. e.g. A. Strzembosz, 'Prawo i sprawiedliwość. Jak eliminować normy totalitarne' (Law and Justice: How the Totalitarian Norms Can Be Eliminated), *Rzeczpospolita*, 4 Nov. 1991, p. iv. Also characteristic is the opinion of M. Boni: 'Adherence to the letter of the law should not block transformation in Poland', *Gazeta Wyborcza*, 12 Feb. 1992, 3.

30. M. Lakatoš, 'Die Demokratie und die Verfassungsreformen in der CSFR', duplicated typescript of conference paper (Budapest, 10–13 Oct. 1991), 14; according to some opinions, at no time or place did the centrally planned economy actually become social.

31. Papini, 'Introduction à une théorie des constitutions d'inspiration personaliste', 10 f.

32. For discussion of the situation in France, which is complex both legally (the double procedure—changes of the Constitution and the ratified Treaty based on the results of an announced referendum) and politically (struggle between the Leftist president and Rightist opposition), see 'Maastricht pod francuską lupą' (The Maastricht Treaty Closely Investigated by the French), *Rzeczpospolita*, 11–12 Apr. 1992, 3.

33. See J. Barcz, 'Konstutucje państw członkowskich a stosowanie prawa wspólnot zachodnioeuropejskich w sferze wewnętrznej państwa' (Constitutions of the Member States and Application of the Law of European Communities in the Internal Sphere of the State), *Biuletyn Rady Legislacyjnej. Tworzenie Prawa*, 6/23 (1990), 27–55.

34. Cassese, 'The Impact of European Political Union', 4 ff.

35. Preuss, 'Patterns of Constitutional Evolution', 5.

36. See my report on the discussion of that problem, 'Polityka ustrojodawcza i zmiany w Europie' (Constitutional Legislative Policy and Changes in Europe), *Państwo i Prawo*, 6 (1992).

37. Preuss, 'Patterns of Constitutional Evolution', 4 f.

38. R. Sadurska, 'Reshaping Europe—Or "How to Keep Poor Cousins in (Their) Home": A Comment on the Transformation of Europe', *Yale Law Journal*, 100/8 (June 1991), 2505.

39. A. Ágh, 'The Permanent "Constitutional Crisis" in the Democratic Transition: The Case of Hungary', paper presented at the conference on Constitutional Policy and Change in Europe, Oxford, 2–5 Apr. 1992, 16.

40. For an extensive comparative analysis, see M. Wyrzykowski, 'Recepcja w prawie publicznym: Tendencje rozwojowe konstytucjonalizmu w Europie Środkowej i Wschodniej' (Reception in Public Law: The Tendencies of Development of Constitutionalism in Central and Eastern Europe), *Państwo i Prawo*, 11 (1992), 23.

41. Instead, one could hardly agree—without the author's additional explanations—that the heritage of communism includes a more general inclination to limit state authority (as a response to the omnipotence of the communist state) or a stress on the guarantees of human rights (as a response to the former limitations of those rights), as argued by J. J. Hesse, 'Constitutional Policy and Change in Europe', paper presented to the conference on Constitutional Policy and Change in Europe, Oxford, 2–5 Apr. 1992, 4.

42. B. Nowotarski, 'Przesunięcie władzy. Ewentualne konsekwencje systemu prezydenckiego w Polsce' (The Shift of Power: The Possible Consequences of the Presidential System in Poland), *Polityka*, 7 (16 Nov. 1991), 3.

43. Vice-President of the French Institute of International Relations D. Moisi has even stated in a press interview that 'it would perhaps be more advantageous from the Western point of view if the Polish institutions were less democratic but the political culture—more democratic instead' (*Rzeczpospolita*, 27 May 1992, 6).

44. Many of them have been contrasted and interestingly analysed by M. Kruk-Jarosz, 'Kultura polityczna a konstytucyjne problemy funkcjonowania organów władzy państwowej' (Political Culture and the Constitutional Problems of the Functioning of the Organs of State Authority), duplicated typescript of conference paper, Bratislava, 4–7 Nov. 1991, and 'Kilka uwag w sprawie najpilniejszych problemów prawa konstytucyjnego' (Some Remarks on the Most Urgent Problems of Constitutional Law), undated paper prepared for the legislative board attached to the Prime Minister.

45. Thus Preuss, 'Patterns of Constitutional Evolution', with respect to all the European post-communist states.

46. e.g. the sermon of Bishop L. S. Głódź of 3 May 1992; see *Rzeczpospolita*, 4 May 1992, 1.

47. In the interview quoted in n. 43 above, D. Moisi makes what he himself finds a rough remark: 'the choice is between Europe and the ban on abortion'.

48. See Hesse, 'Constitutional Policy and Change in Europe', 4; Ágh, 'The Permanent "Constitutional Crisis" ', 2.

49. Ágh (ibid. 11) warns against that, advising not to deviate from rigorous observance of the principles of democracy.

50. The above classification has been based on the methodological suggestions of Áhg, ibid. 2.

51. A. Heldrich, 'Die Wiedervereinigung Deutschlands als Experiment einer Verfassungsreform', duplicated typescript of conference paper, Budapest, 10–13 Oct. 1991, 4.

52. See e.g. the interview with D. Cornea in *Rzeczpospolita*, 1 Oct. 1992, 5.
53. Ágh, 'The Permanent "Constitutional Crisis"', 10.
54. S. Bartole, 'Transitional Constitutions in the Eastern Europe Countries (with Special Regard to the Danubian-Baltonic Area)', duplicated typescript of conference paper, Warsaw (1991), 6. Further on, the author does voice some reservations concerning the prospect of personalization of power.
55. Dahrendorf, 'Historia bez końca'.
56. M. Wyrzykowski, 'Reflections on Some Recent Constitutional Developments in Eastern Europe', *Tilburg Foreign Law Review*, 1/1958 (1992), 171–3.
57. The above statement seems to correspond with the more general postulate of M. Gulczyński ('Polska znów na rozdrożu' (Poland at the Crossroads Again), *Nowa Europa*, 10–12 Apr. 1992, 20), for 'openness to all the functional methods and forms of organization of social life'.
58. See Hesse, 'Constitutional Policy and Change in Europe', 3.
59. Let me once more quote Dahrendorf, 'Historia bez końca'.
60. Hesse, 'Constitutional Policy and Change in Europe', 2.
61. See J. V. Poulard, 'The French Double Executive and the Experience of Cohabitation', *Political Science Quarterly*, 105 (1990), 243–67.
62. Which happens not only to the authors of academic works but also to the organs that apply the law, e.g. the constitutional tribunal in its grounds of a decision passed in 1992.
63. Which has been reflected in the international conference on Electoral Systems in Central Europe, Budapest, 30 July–2 Aug. 1991. See my report, *Państwo i Prawo*, 10 (1991), 105 f.
64. See C. Saunders, 'The Historical Evolution of Anglo-Saxon Constitutional Systems', paper presented to the conference on Constitutional Policy and Change in Europe, Oxford, 2–5 Apr. 1992, 6 f.
65. See *Bulletin of the Polish Press Agency* of 28 Dec. 1990, 15.
66. To some extent only, as the Charter of Rights passed in New Zealand in 1990 was given the form and rank of an ordinary statute.
67. See Ágh, 'The Permanent "Constitutional Crisis"', 7–9.
68. Cf. Pradetto, 'Postkommunismus', 1220.

12

Constitutionalism and Constitutional Change in Czechoslovakia

DUSAN HENDRYCH

After November 1989 there was a general awareness that a humiliating period of Czechoslovakian history had ended and that a new era was beginning. This feeling was prevalent still in 1990, when the idea of an open democratic society, together with the transformation of the economy from state control to a market model, informed the political programmes of most election groups and coalitions. Moreover, the electoral successes of those who had emphasized such solutions testified to the fact that such programmes were favoured by a large section of the citizens of Czechoslovakia. However, even at that time it was possible to note some different currents which—either openly or still covertly—preferred other values than those of a civil society with a market economy. Generally speaking, they were represented by the following political groups:

> the Communist Party, which participated in the 1990 elections still as a uniform party for the whole of Czechoslovakia, under a programme which made cautious links with the period of attempted reform and of democratic socialism of 1968;

> the Slovak National Party, which went to the elections with a policy based on the establishment of an independent Slovak state; in this process the more radical section of the party drew upon the tradition of the Slovak state during the period of the Second World War, a state which had originated and existed with the support of Nazi Germany;

> the Movement for Self-Government and Democracy–Association for Moravia and Silesia, which tried to assert, on the basis of historical law, self-government for Moravia and Silesia and the

achievement of the same status of 'Land' as Bohemia and Slovakia enjoyed.

The election results achieved by these three political groups[1] testify to the fact that the ideas promoted by them had found a generally favourable response, which also manifested itself later on, in the 1992 elections. This was particularly evident in Slovakia, where a significant shift occurred towards nationalism and nationalism with a socialist component, in addition to the inclusion of a programme of Slovakian independence in the programmes of all Slovak political parties (although the differences in the ways of achieving this goal and the sequence of consecutive steps cannot be overlooked). These parties and movements in Slovakia promoting the preservation of a strong and functional federation and a common state suffered a crushing defeat in the 1992 elections.

Soon after the 1990 elections it was obvious that a marked political differentiation and change of the political scene would take place. The most marked changes took place in the victorious movements in the Bohemian Lands and in Slovakia, which split to give rise to several new political subjects. Instead of federal political parties, covering the territory of the whole state, the regional and national character of political forces increased. These changes necessarily influenced attitudes to the constitutional issues of the then federal state. Nationalist partisan criteria prevailed over the modern and desirable integration criteria (Dahrendorf, 1990).

The escalation of national problems evident throughout Eastern Europe after 1989 did not bypass Czechoslovakia. Although it had been a democratic state on a European and world scale from its foundation in 1918 until 1948, it could not avoid national problems in the course of its history because of its geographical position and the multinational structure of its population. History has shown that at that time national conflicts could not be resolved on the basis of humanist ideals emphasizing primarily the value of the individual. National problems twice caused the collapse of Czechoslovakia: the first time in 1939 (Watson, 1943), the second in 1992.

At the outset a strong democratic unitary state was seen as the most suitable constitutional solution. According to one of the leaders of the October 1918 *coup d'état*, Alois Rašín, the creation of a unitary state was the only way of overcoming differences of historical development, and of enhancing a homogeneous state administration. That was the reason for the refusal to grant autonomy to the individual lands, contrary to the practice under the Austro-Hungarian system. However, the adequacy of a unitary state had been questioned from the very beginning. Opposition was voiced by the German population of Czechoslovakia, at that time numbering more than 3 million, as well as by Slovak Catholic autonomist circles and by some Czech political parties of a regionalist orientation. The Pittsburgh-based Czechoslovak National Council, one of the associations of American Czechs, also reminded politicians that the Constitution should respect the 'Pittsburgh Agreement' of 30 June 1918, concluded between the American Czechs and Slovaks, in respect of autonomy for Slovakia.

During the review of the 1920 Czechoslovak Constitution in the parliament, Dr Bouček, rapporteur for the Constitution, declared the intention of the government coalition to push the unity of the state to the extreme and to eliminate anything that could bring about national disunity. On this occasion he said that 'there was not the slightest basis for federalism in our country in recent history' (Tobolka, 1946; Broklova, 1992). Although it is possible to understand the reasons underlying such an extreme attitude by the government coalition (post-war revolutionary upheaval, the unpreparedness of Slovakia for autonomy, etc.), this attitude created, at the very beginning of the existence of the state, a certain schizophrenia which the state was never able to rid itself of. However, general consensus on the issue of a unitary state has not been reached. On the one hand, the idea of a unitary state and a unitary Czechoslovak nation has been defended together with the civic principle; on the other hand, the hankering for national autonomy extending as far as sovereignty has been preserved and gradually increased. The struggle of both tendencies, however differently motivated, has always formed part of any constitutional change in Czechoslovakia. This applies particularly to the constitutional relations between the Czechs and the Slovaks.

In connection with the so-called Prague Spring of 1968, the issue of the right to self-determination of nations arose simultaneously with the requirement of radical democratization of public life. While the citizens of the Czech Lands preferred democratization, including the incorporation of human rights in the Constitution and legislation of the state, the citizens of Slovakia emphasized to an ever-increasing extent the right to self-determination and the consistent and definite solution of the national problem in the constitutional system of Czechoslovakia. Slovak pressure resulted in the federalization of the Czechoslovak state under Constitutional Act No. 143/1968 on Czechoslovak federation. However, the 1968 federal system was criticized as an unsatisfactory solution, as it concealed centralism and the leading role of the Communist Party in the state and society, as established in the 1960 Constitution. Amendments of the Constitutional Act on Czechoslovak federation made in 1970 served only to confirm this criticism (Jičínský, 1991). It is not surprising, therefore, that finding a constitutional solution to the nationalist problem became the central issue in Czechoslovak policy from 1990 to 1992, in spite of the partly successful endeavour to generate a functioning civil society based on the rule of law.

1. CONSTITUTIONAL TRADITION

In 1989 the idea of returning to constitutional tradition was voiced frequently. Yet it was not clear what this tradition amounted to. Most people living in this geographical area had been citizens of different states several times in their lifetime without moving from their domicile. The Czechoslovak Republic existed for seventy-four years, during which time its existence was interrupted for six years (1939–45). During that period one part became a German protectorate, the other a German-dependent state. In particular, the creators of the Slovak state sought different constitutional traditions from those advocating a Czechoslovak state. This difference of constitutional traditions and their assessment was obvious also later on, in the period of real socialism, when one group categorically denied its own constitutional traditions as bourgeois and obsolete while the other group overestimated them uncritically in the name of humanist democracy. The Czechoslovak constitutional tradition was of relatively short duration and of a contradictory character. However, it was connected with the constitutional tradition of Austro-Hungary and was heavily influenced by the constitutional traditions of Western democracies. In this broader aspect this tradition is relevant. To understand better some of the constitutional problems of recent times, it will be useful to recall the constitutional development of Czech and Slovak society by a brief characterization of the central historical periods.

1. Of fundamental significance for modern constitutional development in Central Europe is the Austro-Hungarian settlement (*Ausgleich*) of 1867. Under this settlement, Czechs and Slovaks continued to live in a common state, but that state was federalized: the dominant position in one part, called Transleithania, was occupied by Hungary, while Austria was dominant in the other, called Cisleithania. The Kingdom of Bohemia, the Margraviate of Moravia, and the Duchy of Silesia (i.e. approximately the present-day Czech Republic) formed parts of Cisleithania, while the present-day Slovak Republic which, naturally, did not form any autonomous or administrative unit, was under the Hungarian Crown. The differences between both principal parts of the then monarchy were manifest not only on the constitutional level but also in the different legal systems. In Cisleithania, in contrast to those areas under the Hungarian Crown, tendencies towards democratic development manifested themselves with ever-growing frequency in public life, in particular through a relatively strong system of self-government of the individual Lands, guaranteed by the Land Constitution. In that period also the Czech nation experienced its national revival in a European context.

2. Most important for the Czechoslovak constitutional tradition is the period from the origin of the Czechoslovak state in 1918 to September 1938. This period was dominated by two significant events. The first was the reception of Austro-Hungarian law in the territory of the state. This was effected as early as 28 October 1918, by an Act providing that 'all Land and Realm laws remain temporarily in force'. As has been mentioned already, there was no uniform law in Austro-Hungary. For that reason it was necessary to provide for the reception of two laws: the Cisleithanian law for the Czech Lands and the law of the Hungarian Crown for Slovakia and Sub-Carpathian Ruthenia. Elimination of this legal dualism was sought gradually (albeit with difficulties) during the whole period of Czechoslovakia's existence, and yet unification of the legal systems had not been achieved completely by 1992.

The second significant event was the Czechoslovak Constitution of 1920 (replacing the so-called Provisional Constitution of November 1918), which actually fulfilled the function of a type of organic law. The Constitution of the Czechoslovak Republic was

democratic and legally valid. It was inspired by the then constitutions of European democracies, particularly the French. However, other models were carefully studied also, especially the
Constitution of the USA, the Swiss Constitution, and the Weimar
Constitution of Germany. Attention was paid to the Westminster
model also. The Constitution of the Czechoslovak Republic was
based on the traditional separation of powers, but preferred the
system of a parliamentary democratic republic with two houses of
parliament, a weak president, and a government accountable to the
parliament. Particularly appreciated was the constitutional system
of judicial power guaranteeing the independence of the courts from
both the legislative and the executive powers (Adamovich, 1929).

3. The period of the so-called Second Republic (1938–9) was
short, but rich in events. It can be characterized by the following
facts: on the basis of the Munich Accord, a part of the territory
was annexed by Germany, while Slovakia and Sub-Carpathian
Ruthenia, until then Lands of a unitary state, obtained autonomy
by Constitutional Acts. Further interference with the 1920 Constitution due to the critical situation was caused by a Constitutional
Act empowering the president to amend the constitutional charter
by decree, and affording the government an extraordinary power of
prescription. Also at this time the name of the state was changed
from the Czechoslovak Republic to the Czecho-Slovak Republic.

4. In March 1939 Czechoslovakia became factually extinct:
Slovakia became an independent state; the Czech Lands became a
part of the German Reich under the name of 'Protektorat Böhmen
und Mähren'; and Sub-Carpathian Ruthenia and a part of Slovakia
were annexed by Hungary. From the constitutional viewpoint two
facts are of interest: the first being the Slovak state, the second being
the provisional state system of the Czechoslovak Republic, established in exile.

According to its constitutional documents, the Slovak state was
based on Christian, national, and estate principles as a republic, but
not a republic of a traditional parliamentary type. The Slovak state
was a single-party dictatorship. Moreover, it was only formally
sovereign: in essence, it was a vassal of the German Reich.

At this time, a provisional state representation of the Czechoslovak Republic was established abroad on the basis of the will of
most Czechoslovak citizens. The representatives of this state-in-
exile expressly declared the constitutional and legal continuity of

the First Republic (1918–38). This was proclaimed by the constitutional decree of the president of the republic of 15 October 1940 on the provisional exercise of legislative power. This constitutional decree (reprinted under No. 20/1945) made it possible for the president to exercise legislative power in the form of decrees for the period in which the legislative body, constituted in accordance with the 1920 Constitution, could not exercise its legislative power. This decree, together with subsequent decrees issued in exile, was subsequently called 'the London Constitution', in accordance with their place of origin. Although this constitutional decree was approved by the provisional national assembly immediately after the war in 1946 and retrospectively declared a Constitutional Act from its very origin, the question of whether this constitutional decree, violating as it did—albeit in a state of emergency—the 1920 Constitution, was merely a declaration of the continuing validity of the legal system of the First Republic, or whether it was an act conceiving a new state system with the reception of the legal system of the First Republic (Budník, 1947) has never been answered explicitly. Subsequent political developments seemed to favour the second alternative.

5. After the Second World War there was a short period in Czechoslovakia, from 1945 to 1948, which was characterized—in comparison with other Eastern Bloc countries—by a relatively high standard of democracy and of constitutionality. It was known as the period of restitution of legal order. This meant that continuity of the legal system of the First Republic was affirmed and that the legal rules adopted between 10 September 1938 and 4 May 1945 were not considered a part of the Czechoslovak legal system.

The presidential decrees issued both in wartime and in the postwar period, as well as other constitutional regulations issued immediately after the war, substantially changed the 1920 Constitution in many respects, for example by the introduction of a single-chamber parliament, the establishment or, to be more accurate, approval of Slovak autonomous organs, the restriction of the number of political parties, far-reaching nationalization, and the establishment of National Committees (Hendrych, 1993). Practically a new constitutional system began to be established, executing the so-called Košice government programme, which was adopted by the new Czechoslovak government as a result of the compromise between the London and Moscow *émigrés*.

6. The period from 1948 to 1968 is marked by three constitutional documents: the 1948 Constitution, the Constitution of the Czechoslovak Socialist Republic of 1960, and Constitutional Act No. 143/1968 relating to the Czechoslovak Federation, substantially amending and supplementing the 1960 Constitution. This period was characterized primarily by contempt for law and for human rights and freedoms. It was also the period in which the principle of a unitary state was rejected as the adoption of the Constitutional Act on Czechoslovak federation constituted a new tradition, which lasted until the dissolution of Czechoslovakia in 1992. However, the national problems were not solved; time has shown that they were merely shifted to another level.

The 1948 Constitution, adopted shortly after the Communist Party and its allies had taken power, retained certain democratic features and characteristics of European constitutionality. However, the Constitution very soon ceased to be respected, and a number of subsequent political trials testified to the concept of law as an instrument of class struggle. The 1960 Constitution amounted to a political proclamation rather than a set of directly applicable legal norms. With reference to constitutional development, it should be noted that it was this Constitution which confirmed the leading role of the Communist Party in society and state, and established Marxism-Leninism as the state ideology (Articles 4 and 16 respectively).

The federalization of Czechoslovakia effected in 1968 was modelled on Soviet nationality policy. It is something of a historical irony that the constitutional equalization of nations and the expression of their right to self-determination as far as secession was legalized at the cost of suppression of human rights and basic freedoms in Czechoslovakia. Such a federation, combined with rigid centralism of management, opposed the European idea of federalism as co-operation, unification, and equilibrium between the limited sovereignty of member subjects and their participation in the power of the federal state. The socialist federation could never have amounted to a true and real federation, as it lacked the necessary pluralist political system. It is no wonder, therefore, that the critics of the 1968 federal system, even after the 1970 modifications, continued to see in it the 'Prague centralism' connected with the rule of the Communist Party and its 'normalization' measures.

2. CONSTITUTIONAL CHANGES AFTER NOVEMBER 1989

After November 1989 a number of substantial changes were made to the existing constitutional legislation, the aims of which were threefold: the restoration of traditional values of democracy and a state based on the rule of law; the revision of the federal organization of Czechoslovakia to increase the autonomy of the member states; and, finally, the achievement of such changes in the legal system as would allow the full development of a market economy, including tax legislation.

Of the most important legislative measures at the federal level, mention should be made of at least the following.

The revision to the Constitution which eliminated some of its unacceptable principles (e.g. the leading role of the Communist Party in the state and society) or allowed the transition to an open society and the generation of democratic institutions (e.g. communities as self-governing units with individual legal subjectivity). Another significant change to the Constitution guaranteed to all types of property the same status and protection (constitutional amendments of property rights). Of great importance for the structure of public administration were the provisions of the Constitution on the division of powers between the federation and the republics. However, the politically accepted constitutional changes of 1990 do not represent the most favourable solution, and the distribution of powers later become a source of conflict between the federation and the republics. This was manifested in the preparation of the new constitutions, and in the deliberations over the form of the common state of both nations—Czechoslovakia. A very important constitutional change was the establishment of the constitutional court. Constitutional Act No. 23/1991, which introduced the Bill of Basic Rights and Freedoms, thereby amending the Constitution significantly in the field of human rights, also contains provisions of substantial relevance to the whole legal system (Hendrych, 1993).

Following the 1990 elections, the preparation of new Constitutions for the CSFR, the Czech Republic, and the Slovak Republic in mutual co-ordination became one of the first tasks of the newly elected federal parliament and of the parliaments of both member republics. The programme declaration of the then new federal government of 3 July 1990, submitted to the federal assembly, stated:

Our common mandate, derived from the first free elections after 44 years, is limited to two years. The culmination of our legislative work will be the new Constitutions of the Federation, of the Czech Republic and the Slovak Republic. They will codify the rights and freedoms of the citizens to the full extent of international documents on human rights. They will define also the mutual competences of the republics and the federation so as to correspond with the interests of both of our nations . . .

Therefore, all three supreme representative bodies primarily exercised the function of constitutional assemblies. For this purpose, these bodies established expert and deputy commissions for the preparation of the individual Constitutions. The federal assembly occupied a specific position in this process, particularly with reference to co-ordination. For this reason, the work of its deputy and expert commissions was participated in to a significant extent by the members appointed by the Czech and Slovak supreme state institutions. The work of the federal commissions was marked from the very beginning by disagreements between the Czech and the Slovak political representations in respect of the fundamental principles of the new federal Constitution in basic outline. The second draft submitted to the deputies was prepared by President Havel. Neither draft was accepted by the commission of deputies and actually reviewed as a whole.

The stalemate in the proceedings of the federal commission of deputies for the preparation of the Constitution, and, subsequently, a partial stalemate of the proceedings of the federal assembly as a whole and of both of its chambers, led the decisive political forces to shift the focal point of the discussions on political consensus to the presidiums of the national councils of both republics. The presidiums were to try to achieve an agreement which would form the basis for further progress of the proceedings in the federal assembly. The hope was that this would result in a simultaneous expression of sufficiently strong identical political will on the part of both national representations concerning the future form of the federal constitution. The number of fundamental disputable issues included the new division of powers between the organs of the federation and those of the republics, with particular reference to government and administrative powers. It was agreed that the new division of powers must aim at the increase of the powers of the republics and their greater incorporation into the decision-making processes of federal authorities and the formulation of federal policy. However, ideas as to the methods and procedures of achieving this, without the CSFR losing at least the fundamental attributes of a state, were becoming increasingly different on the Czech and the Slovak sides. Suspension of these negotiations until the end of the election period (June 1992) was considered even at that time as a significant signal not only of the fact that the constitutional bodies would be unable to fulfil their principal task but also of a real danger of extinction of the common state. This anxiety was justified shortly after the elections, when the Czech polity could not find a partner on the Slovak side who would identify with the principle of federal organization and with the preservation of the common state as a legal subject. On the other hand, the idea of confederation or of another form of looser association of two sovereign states did not find understanding on the Czech side.

What were the ideas and standpoints of the leading personalities on the Czech and Slovak sides before the 1992 elections? Of fundamental significance from the very beginning was the name and the character of the agreement to be reached by the presidiums of both national councils. The decisive part of the Slovak representation always insisted that the result of the negotiations must be expressed in the form of a state treaty between the two republics which would be legally binding for the federal assembly in the matters of the new Constitution. They accentuated the fact that the treaty would be concluded between two sovereign states which would agree in that very treaty about the division of powers between the federation and the member states, and on the structure of organs of the common state. On the Czech side, on the other hand, the federalist standpoint prevailed, viz. that the conclusion of any agreement was superfluous and at variance with the existing valid Constitution. According to the Czech party, the standpoints of both parties could be satisfied sufficiently in the preparation and adoption of a new federal constitution in the federal assembly, particularly in the House of Nations, which could contravene any essential decision aimed against one of the member republics.[2] Later on, the Czech party modified this uncompromising attitude and adjusted it to the

Slovak requirements by expressing its consent to the conclusion of a political agreement between both national councils as the expression of their joint will concerning the principles of federal organization.

The differences between both national representations, which manifested themselves in all three legislatives bodies, were rooted also in the problem of whether the agreement or treaty should constitute a new state, or whether the existing CSFR should continue to remain the sole subject of international law, albeit with a different internal structure. From the very beginning of the negotiations this was connected also with the question of whether the common state should prefer national or civil principles.

Although an agreement had been reached finally in the matter of division of powers between the federation and the republics, and the last meeting of the representations of both republics in the spring of 1992 resulted in a general agreement, it turned out to be a pyrrhic victory, because the presidium of the Slovak national council subsequently failed to accept the agreement with the Czech side concluded by their plenipotentiaries with a close majority. This rejection by the Slovak party was also the formal reason for the suspension of further talks, and resulted in a further considerable weakening of the Slovak government coalition parties.

In the 1992 election considerable polarization occurred between voters in the Czech and Slovak Republics over both political and economic issues. The elections also gave expression to the citizens' ideas of the future constitutional organization to a considerable extent. For most Slovaks—supporters of Mečiar's Movement for Democratic Slovakia, the Party of the Democratic Left, and the Slovak National Party (together accounting for almost 60 per cent of the votes in the elections to the Slovak national council)—the yearning for an independent state was connected not only with national ambitions but also with the desire for better social conditions to be provided by the state. Thus it came to light that the hypothesis about a pro-federal majority in Slovakia was entirely false; hence also the success of the parties of nationalist orientation.

On the other hand, a major part of the Czech population (of which 42 per cent voted for right-wing parties) preferred such values as a civil society, a democratic state, a market economy, etc. The new Czech representation had no reason to make any concessions in these matters to the Slovak party in exchange for the promise of some unspecified and vague form of confederation or union. Naturally, there were pro-federal forces in Czech society even after the 1992 elections: some liberals, social democrats, communists. However, their motives for the preservation of the Czechoslovak state differed, and they did not represent a sufficiently strong group in parliament. Moreover, Slovak policy after the 1992 elections convinced the citizens of the Czech Republic to an ever-increasing extent that the split of Czechoslovakia into two independent states was preferable to the uncertainty of further constitutional development.

From the number of acts of Slovak policy in that period, two in particular should be mentioned: the first was the adoption of the declaration of the Slovak national council of 17 August 1992, on the sovereignty of the Slovak Republic. This was seen as a serious political signal as to the negation of the previous agreement by both republics to live in a common state. The second was the adoption of the Constitution of the Slovak Republic on 1 September 1992 (Constitutional Act No. 460/1992), which proclaimed, despite the existence of the CSFR, the superiority of Slovak law over federal law—although in specified cases only. This was at variance with the very nature of federal organization, and this act of the Slovak national council could have been considered as a secession of Slovakia from the common state. However, it was probably politically wise that the Czech political representation did not take such a rigid attitude, and left the extinction of the common state to the discretion of the federal assembly. Slovak legislators also expressed distinctly their renunciation of Czechoslovak constitutional tradition and the participation of Slovaks in the foundation of the Czechoslovak state in 1918. On the other hand, they emphasized their centuries-long experience with the struggle for national existence and the natural right of the nation to self-determination. All of this clearly expressed the discontinuity in their relations with Czechoslovakia and its legal system which necessarily brought about the appropriate political and legal measures on the Czech side also.

The principal political agreement on the break-up of Czechoslovakia was concluded between the representatives of the two strongest political parties in the Czech Republic and the Slovak Republic—the Civic Democratic Party and the Movement for

Democratic Slovakia, respectively. This agreement, as well as the secession measures accomplished by the Slovak parliament, represented the factual decision about the fate of Czechoslovakia. All subsequent measures also aimed at making the separation peaceful and also politically and economically acceptable for both parties. It was also necessary to agree on the further function of all federal organs, on the one hand as guarantors of Czechoslovak statehood, on the other hand as the organs capable of effecting the extinction of the state in a constitutional manner. The fact that these objectives were attained does not mean that it was an easy task. The extinction of the Czechoslovak state on 31 December 1992 was constitutionally effected by Constitutional Act No. 542/1992 on the extinction of the Czech and Slovak Federal Republic, adopted on 25 November 1992, after complex and repeated negotiations, reconciliation procedures, and voting by the federal assembly.

A full analysis of the significance of this Act is beyond the scope of this chapter. Nevertheless, it is necessary to outline its content briefly. First, the Act states the date of extinction of the CSFR. Secondly, it provides that the successor states of the CSFR are the Czech Republic and the Slovak Republic, to which pass all powers previously exercised by the CSFR on the basis of Constitutional and other Acts. Thirdly, this Constitutional Act provides that on the date of extinction of the CSFR all bodies and authorities of the state, all federal state organizations (of both a profit-making and non-profit-making character), and the army and the federal armed security corps become extinct. Fourthly, it contains a problematic provision which neither successor state finally respected: that beginning on 1 January 1993, legislative power in both successor states would be exercised by legislative bodies consisting of deputies elected in the 1992 elections both to the federal representative bodies and to the representative bodies of the republics. In this way the Constitutional Act intended to bind the existing legislative bodies of both member republics to respect the legitimacy of their colleagues from the federal assembly, which had become extinct on 31 December 1992, in the legislative bodies of the successor states.

Next, the Constitutional Act contains provisions concerning the transfer of the powers of judicial organs of the federation to the judiciary of the successor states. In concrete terms it concerned the supreme court of the CSFR and the constitutional court of the CSFR. Finally, the Act contained two significant provisions enabling a continuous transition to new constitutional conditions: it established the power of the parliaments of both member states to adopt, even before the extinction of the CSFR, Constitutional and other Acts in order to ensure the proper exercise of powers by each successor state and from 1 January 1993 at the earliest, and to provide for the Czech Republic and the Slovak Republic to conclude on their own behalf treaties with third parties even before the extinction of the CSFR, with the proviso that they would enter into force after the extinction of the CSFR.

The most important agreements concluded between the Czech Republic and the Slovak Republic include the agreements on customs union, payment union, and common currency.[3]

The above-mentioned Constitutional Act is closely related to Constitutional Act No. 541/1992 on the division of property between the member states and its transition to the Czech Republic and the Slovak Republic. The solution to this problem was requested by numerous deputies as the necessary precondition for the adoption of the Constitutional Act on the extinction of the CSFR. For that reason it was submitted for voting earlier, and its adoption finally concluded the constitutional extinction of the CSFR.

The idea of a unitary state, which has always represented one of the constitutional traditions for the Czech part of the common state, ceased to be realistic with the extinction of Czechoslovakia. Moreover, the idea of a federalized state (in the end recognized and supported in both parts of the state) has lost its meaning. It is too early to assess whether the split of a state in which the interests of two state-forming nations were gradually diverging was good for the future of both new states and for the stability of the Central European area. None the less, the first steps of the successor states, however awkward, seem to afford hope of positive development.

3. THE CONSTITUTIONAL SITUATION IN THE CZECH REPUBLIC

Following the adoption of the Constitution of the Slovak Republic as an independent, sovereign state, it was necessary to accelerate the process of preparation of the Constitution of the Czech Republic, also as an independent, sovereign state. It must be admitted that the Czech side, in contrast to the Slovaks, had always had a somewhat dilatory approach to the preparation of the Constitution of the Czech state. Without a doubt this was due to the fact that the Czech Lands have always directed their efforts primarily towards the preparation of the federal Constitution as the basis for the Constitutions of both member states. This idea formed the basis of both initial expert drafts of 1990 and 1991, as well as the drafts prepared by the individual political parties in the same period. That was also the reason why these drafts could play merely a subsidiary role in the preparation of the Constitution of the independent state.

There was relatively little time left for the preparation of an official draft of the Constitution of the Czech Republic and the preparation of alternative drafts. Undoubtedly, this situation influenced the whole concept of the Constitution, which was based consistently on the idea that the Constitution itself created directly applicable law and that all law in the state was based on it. At the same time, however, the Constitution endeavoured to express only fundamental politically indisputable solutions which would enable the consensus of decisive political parties in the Czech national council to be obtained and, consequently, the adoption of the Constitution before the date of extinction of Czechoslovakia. Applied to the drafting of the Constitution, this resulted in a solution which bases the foundations of the Constitution broadly. Thus Article 112 of the Constitution of the Czech Republic defines the constitutional system as follows:

The constitutional system of the Czech Republic consists of this Constitution, the Bill of Basic Rights and Freedoms, the Constitutional Acts adopted under this Constitution and the Constitutional Acts of the national assembly of the Czechoslovak Republic, the federal assembly of the Czechoslovak Socialist Republic and of the Czech national council, codifying the state boundaries of the Czech Republic, and the Constitutional Acts of the Czech national council adopted after 6 June 1992.

In the drafting of the Czech Constitution, an agreement was reached that this fundamental law of the Czech Republic would not deal in detail with the consequences of the extinction of the CSFR and the measures to be taken in this context. I am convinced that it was sensible to separate these matters from the Constitution, although these specific constitutional provisions could not be excluded from the constitutional system in the meaning of Article 112 of the Constitution of the Czech Republic. The Czech national council reacted to the federal Constitutional Act on the extinction of the CSFR by the adoption of the Constitutional Act of the Czech National Council No. 4/1992 on the measures connected with the extinction of the CSFR. This Constitutional Act is significant particularly for its assertion of the legal continuity of the legal system of the CSFR. Although some provisions of this document were amended subsequently by the Constitution, it does not change the fact that the Czech Republic, as a successor state of the CSFR, clearly proclaimed its continuity with the CSFR and that federation's legal system, and also claimed its international rights and obligations. However, the Czech national council based its considerations consistently on the idea that the Constitutional Act on the extinction of the CSFR, adopted by the federal assembly of the CSFR, binds this Czech legislative body only as long as it does not interfere with its sovereign status and powers. It stated this view expressly in Resolution No. 5/1992, expressing its exclusive right to the modification of constitutional conditions of the Czech Republic and permitting no doubt as to the continuity of its legislative power.

References

Adamovich, L. (1929), *Grundriss der tschechoslowakischen Staatsrechtes.* Vienna.

Broklová, E. (1992), *Československá demokracie* (The Czechoslovak Democracy). Prague (English summary).

Budník, J. (1947), *Prozatímní státní zřízeni Československé republiky* (Provisonal State System of the Czechoslovak Republic). Prague.

Dahrendorf, R. (1990), *Reflections on the Revolution in Europe.* London.

Hendrych, D. (1993), 'Transforming Czechoslovakian Public Administration: Survey of Reform Steps Taken', *Public Administration*, 71–2.

Jičínský, Zd. (1991), 'Grundlegende Entwicklungsprobleme der tschechoslowakischen Föderation', in J. J. Hesse and W. Renzsch (eds.), *Föderalstaatliche Entwicklung in Europa.* Baden-Baden.

Tobolka, Zd. (1946), *Jak vznikla Ústava Československé republiky z roku*

1920 (How the 1920 Constitution of the Czechoslovak Republic Originated). Prague.

Watson, S. E. W. (1943), *A History of the Czechs and Slovaks*. London.

Notes

1. The Communist Party 13.47%, the Slovak National Party 12.45%, and the Movement for Self-Government and Democracy–Association for Moravia and Silesia 8.96% on average.
2. In the House of Nations of the federal assembly, being the upper house of a senate type, prohibition of outvoting was applied. Both member states were represented by equal numbers of directly elected deputies. In the cases enumerated in the Constitutional Act on the Czechoslovak Federation, a resolution in the House of Nations could be adopted only if a majority of all deputies elected in both the Czech and Slovak Republics voted for the resolution, unless a qualified majority was required. As the adoption of the federal Act itself was conditional on the affirmative resolution of both houses, neither the Czech nor the Slovak representations could be harmed.
3. The agreement on common currency was abolished on 8 Feb. 1993. Separation of currencies was established in the form of an Act both in the Czech Republic and in the Slovak Republic.

13

The Permanent 'Constitutional Crisis' in the Democratic Transition: The Case of Hungary

ATTILA ÁGH

In the autumn of 1991 there was an overt 'constitutional crisis' in Hungary concerning the role of the president of the republic, a crisis which was subsequently more or less settled. In fact, the whole history of the democratic transition has been a permanent constitutional crisis. The constitution-making process as a method of establishing the fundamental rules of the game in politics and as a constant redefinition of the concept of the state has always been central in the transition. Consequently, the major political disputes have centred on the issue of constitution-making. This process, however, has its own internal coherence and cannot be reduced to the history of political or party struggles, although their very important role for this process comes directly from the nature of the systemic change. Similar occurrences are to be seen in Southern Europe (SE) and in East Central Europe (ECE), namely in Poland and Czechoslovakia.[1]

The differences between ECE countries, however, are as important as the similarities. The characteristics of the constitution-making process in the democratic transition appear in the most marked way between the other ECE countries and Hungary, because of Hungary's earlier start, more developed party system, and the centrality of the legalist-constitutionalist transition. Thus, Hungary now has a new democratic constitution which has transformed its predecessor fundamentally, while in Poland and Czechoslovakia there have been but a series of amendments, as yet neither co-ordinated nor developed into a new constitution. An example of this difference is the operation of the constitutional court (CC). In Hungary, it began its work in January 1990 and has since accumulated much experience, but in Czechoslovakia a CC was established only in February 1992. Historically, the constitution-making process has not ended in either country, but the newly emerging problems may have some relevance for the other ECE countries.

The political disputes in Hungary since 1988 have taken the form of constitutional debate. Thus the constitutional crisis can be analysed in successive periods, with its major actors being parties of different constitutional traditions and orientations. Perhaps the most important aspect of these disputes from a political-science perspective, if not that of lawyers, is that there has been no abstract legal or political rationality to these political disputes or periods of constitution-making, such as some difference of opinion over some general idea of democratization or Westernization. Although all ECE countries have borrowed a lot directly from Western constitutional solutions and 'legal means of regulation', nevertheless in each period quite definite political aims have informed the proposed or formulated constitutional changes of the decisive actors. Sometimes these aims have been very short-sighted and counterproductive, violating the concept of legal 'rationality'.

Instead of the most rational or Westernized constitution, the major actors want a constitution which suits their political needs best. Consequently, our story is about the most feasible, as opposed to the most perfect, constitution. Accordingly, the question concerning the process of constitution-making has to be formulated as follows:

1. What has been the political role of the constitutional debates in the democratic transition?
2. What have been the major concepts of the state underlying the conflicting process of constitution-making?

The preliminary answer is, first, that there has been a process of choices at the following levels: (1) macro-choice between political systems, (2) meso-choice between parliamentary or presidential forms of government, and (3) micro-choice of regulation of the polity by the legislature.[2] Second, the new front line in the political debate is that there is: (1) a traditionalist-conservativist concept of the state involving concentrated paternalistic powers, a concept which currently threatens to re-emerge; and (2) a new perspective based on the concept of the 'European' state with its real division of powers and trans-national perspectives, a concept which has recently emerged on the horizon. These two concepts of the state provide the essence of and reason for the recent constitutional debates.

1. THE POST-WAR CONSTITUTIONAL HISTORY

The post-war consolidation of the young Hungarian democracy led to an early formulation of a constitution by the parliament elected in 1945. Act I of 1946 established a republic as the form of the state, in contrast to the previous monarchy. The act had a special political function at that time, emphasizing the irreversibility of the democratic transformations. In its actual form the act was only an interim constitution, the result of a political compromise, and as such was meant to regulate the country only until a new, comprehensive constitution could be formulated. The 1946 Constitution, however, proved to be a 'final' one. In the short-lived post-war Hungarian democracy there was no other opportunity to create a more comprehensive constitution. The 1946 Constitution itself remained valid only until 1949, when a new constitution of the 'people's democracy' superseded it.

The 1946 Constitution has three major features. First, it is a political compromise which contains many signs of the early post-war period; above all, it concentrates on preserving the new political stability by safeguarding the republic. Second, it is a very characteristic summary of Hungarian legal traditions, expressed mainly by the predominance of parliament. The parliament in this constitutional solution has more rights than elsewhere in Europe, with the exception of the UK. Consequently, the president of the republic and the government have fewer rights: the president is elected by the parliament and excercises his functions through the parliament. The responsibility of the government to the parliament is also very accentuated. Third, this constitution fulfilled the function of importing international standards of human rights and democratic constitutional devices, and paved the way for international acceptence of the young democratic state. Although the first of the above-mentioned features vanished soon after the historical situation of the post-war consolidation, the second and third features, i.e. the successful combination of Hungarian traditions with international standards, have resulted in the 1946 constitution being seen as a model of Hungarian constitutional thinking.

In 1949, as a result of the 'transition to socialism', a new constitution was formulated. It reflected many characteristics of the 1936 Constitution of the Soviet Union and also borrowed the latter's structure. The 1949 Constitution brought three major changes: (1) it introduced the principle of the unity of state power in contrast to the division of powers, and all the other statements (the monopoly rights of the ruling party etc.) stem from this; (2) instead of a presidency, it established the collective central organ of the presidential council as a 'transmission belt' between party decisions and state legislation operating through decree laws; and (3) it lowered the constitutional status of the parliament to a nominal-symbolic level, keeping parliament merely as a democratic façade for state socialism.[3]

In Hungary the 1949 Constitution was the only 'socialist' constitution, but it underwent some major amendments. The most extensive changes occurred in 1972, when the results of the 1968 economic reforms were included in the Constitution (the relative independence of state enterprises, the equality of the different forms of property, etc.). In 1976 Hungarian adherence to international agreements on human rights was included, and in 1983 the new election law made competitive elections mandatory, requiring at least two candidates in every constituency. In general, the amendments moved in the direction of liberalization, but until the late 1980s the Stalinist character of the 1949 Constitution remained unchanged. In reformist political thinking the 1946 Constitution became more and more an ideal standard for Hungarian constitution-making and, as a reaction to the 'façade parliament', the supremacy of the parliament appeared as the best constitutional solution for the democratic state and rule of law.

In the late 1980s the struggle for political reform, i.e. the extension of socio-economic liberalization to political democratization, took the form of constitutional debates in which proposals for the abolition of the 1949 Constitution and the re-establishment of the 1946 Constitution became the dominant issue. In the series of political compromises, in fact, a very strange contradiction emerged: the general structure of the 1949 Constitution was preserved by these 'amendments' (the 1989 and 1990 Constitutions) but the amendments were, in fact, radical changes, which used the principles and the text of the 1946 Constitution. In that very rare historical moment, in 1989–90, when constitution-making was both possible and necessary again, an 'interim' constitution emerged in two steps. Although forced into the structure of the 1949 Constitution, it none the less revived the spirit of the 1946 Constitution.

Because of this contradiction some argue that the Stalinist Constitution is still valid in Hungary, while some others—and they are the sober majority—point out that actually more than 90 per cent of the text of the Constitution was changed; the only unchanged sentence from the 1949 Constitution is 'The capital of Hungary is Budapest'.

The rare historical moment of constitution-making is over. Yet again the 'interim' constitution has proved to be a 'final' one. Nowadays there is no consensus among the major political forces represented in parliament concerning the principles of a newly written, comprehensive constitution. None the less, the existing Constitution, despite all its shortcomings, may be accepted as an appropriate constitution for a democratic-legal state, as it meets all the major requirements of European standards. Smaller changes can be expected even in this deadlocked situation, and the debates among experts continue with a view to introducing a new constitution, possibly after the 1994 elections in the second half of the 1990s.

The real constitution-making was a process of democratic transition, and its major stages have to be described with their characteristic actors and achievements. In the following discussion an attempt is made to present both the political fights and the constitutional substance of the given period. After the 'final' point of the fundamental changes, an overview of the present situation and an outline of the prospects and requirements for further change is provided.[4]

2. THE MAJOR STAGES OF CONSTITUTION-MAKING

2.1. 'No Pact—No Constitution' (May 1988–June 1989)

After the dismissal of Kádár, party leader of the state socialist regime, the reform process accelerated both in the field of legislation and in that of constitution-making. The legitimation crisis of existing institutions, actors, and legal regulations became manifest.[5] In an ambitious project a new constitution-making process began and the concept of a 'European-type' constitution was accepted until the end of 1988, when proposals were rejected by the opposition, not because of their shortcomings *per se*[6] but because the opposition did not consider the incumbent institutions, including the parliament, to be legitimate bodies to adopt a new constitution. The principle was: 'No Pact—No Constitution', i.e. first a pact was needed concerning democratic elections, after which a newly elected democratic parliament could deal with the new constitution. Hungary was obsessed with the Spanish negotiated transition; both party reformers and opposition leaders called for a 'Moncloa Pact' during the process of Hungarian democratization.

Yet the proposal for the 1988 'constitution that never was' played an important role in 1988–9 once published. It very much influenced subsequent constitutional developments, as mostly the same constitutional experts took part in the formulation of the new variants. Moreover, an active legislative programme in the 'old' parliament prepared the way for a peaceful transition. Great strides were made in the enactment of economic legislation until, at the end of 1989, conformity or structural compatibility with a market economy had been reached in the most important cases.[7] As far as political legislation is concerned, the bugbear was the presidential council. In passing decree-laws, it had been a substitute for parliament for thirty years, but it came under attack only in 1987. In December 1987 the parliament amended the Constitution and simultaneously passed a law on the enactment of legislation, which allowed it to regain its own monopoly over legislation from the presidential council. Although the presidential council was abolished only by the new 1989 Constitution, its political role disappeared much earlier, and it made way for the enactment of political legislation by the parliament.[8]

After so many months, the most significant result was the law on free associations (including the formation of political parties) passed by the parliament in early January 1989 and completed by a new law on the workings and finances of political parties in October 1989. During 1989 the newly emerging parties became the central actors of the political transition, not only *de facto* but also *de jure*. The central committee of the ruling Hungarian Socialist Workers' Party accepted the principle of a multi-party system in

February 1989. In March the opposition round table was organized with eight members (a ninth joined later), and in June 1989 official negotiations started in the national round table between the ruling party and the opposition. The deadlock of 'No Pact—No Constitution' was over.[9]

2.2. *The September (1989) Pact*

The national round table talks rejected the Polish compromise of limited competition and accepted an election law with full competition between all parties. In accordance with Hungarian tradition, there was a clear preference for a parliamentary over a presidential system. All participants agreed upon the need for a very strong parliament and they established the constitutional court (CC), endowing it with comprehensive rights of control over all political actors and institutions. The political strengths of the participants in the coming elections were completely uncertain, and all therefore wanted at least to retain some controlling power in the parliament and an indirect control over their partners through the CC. Faced with this uncertainty, a compromise was reached on all these matters—election law, free competition, strong parliament, CC—with relative ease because all wanted this oversized set of 'checks and balances' as a constitutional solution. The leading representatives of the major parties (Antall, President of the Hungarian Democratic Forum and Prime Minister, Tölgyessy, the President of the Alliance of Free Democrats, and even some leaders of the Alliance of Young Democrats) began their political careers as constitutional experts by translating the conflicting party demands into the language of the constitution-making process.

Nevertheless, the pact was not signed on 18 September 1989 by all the participants. The AFD and Fidesz did not veto it, but refused to sign it because of a major conflict concerning the election of the president. In general, the provisions of the 1946 Constitution were repeated, which provided for the election of the president by the parliament; however, according to the compromise which was accepted by the majority of the round table, the first president would have been elected by direct popular vote prior to the general elections. While the liberal parties raised constitutional arguments, in fact their fear was that Pozsgay, then by far the most popular figure, would be elected president.[10] Therefore, the major issue was the nature of the direct political transition and not the long-term constitutional formulations. The liberal parties wanted a more radical and speedy transition of power, which would have meant sharper confrontation with the reformists of the ruling party. The HDF, in turn, was considering a slower and more gradual transition, including a coalition with the reform wing of the ruling party (later reorganized as the Hungarian Socialist Party in October 1989). A four-party alliance (AFD, Fidesz, HSP, and ISP) called for a referendum, which they won in November by the smallest possible margin (a 50.14 per cent majority).

The November referendum decided that even the first president would be elected by the parliament, after the general elections. The September pact otherwise served as a basis for the elaboration of the new constitution. The old parliament passed the new constitution in October, and on 23 October 1989 the Fourth Republic of Hungary was declared with an interim president. To some extent the constitution-making process had been finished, but the vulnerable points ultimately became visible at the end of 1989. The first of these was the role of the (weak) president, whose position became much weaker after the November referendum, when all political actors turned their attention to the election campaign.[11]

The 1989 Constitution expressed the power transition with a political compromise concerning the nature of the state as Chapter I, section 2 underlines: 'The Republic of Hungary is an independent constitutional state where the achievements of both civil democracy and democratic socialism prevail.' However, section 3, replacing the paragraph on the leading role of the Communist Party, strongly emphasizes the freedom of political parties and their separation from the state:

The Parties shall not directly excercise public power. Accordingly, no Party shall have the right to guide any state body. In order to separate the Parties and public power from each other, the functions and public offices which shall not be held by a member or official of any Party shall be specified by law.[12]

These two paragraphs may be the most characteristic statements of the beginning of democratic transition in Hungary: the nature of the slow, balanced, and negotiated transition appears here quite clearly, *in statu nascendi*.

The introductory sentence to the new, interim constitution gives the essence of this transition very forcefully:

With a view to promoting a peaceful political transition to a constitutional state implementing a multi-party system, parliamentary democracy and social market economy, Parliament lays down—until the enactment of a new Constitution of the country—the text of Hungary's Constitution as follows.

Indeed, the 1989 Constitution proved to be an interim constitution valid for some months only, but certainly 'promoting' political changes as the introductory sentence conceived. The transitory character of this constitution appears in two major constitutional solutions: first in the predominant role of parliament in passing most laws with a qualified majority, which means in fact the establishment of a 'constitutional assembly' for managing the political transition, and, second, going beyond Hungarian constitutional traditions in respect of the rights of the president, investing him with the role of safeguarding democracy. This extension of presidential rights to include 'negative' or controlling powers was preserved word for word in the 1990 Constitution, and it has played an important role in current political developments: 'The President of the Republic is the head of state of Hungary; he/she embodies the unity of state and watches over the democratic operation of the mechanism of State.'[13]

The September pact and the 1989 Constitution were great achievements, and milestones in the peaceful and negotiated democratic transition. However, by the autumn of 1989 the parties transformed the constitution-making process into an election campaign, and they concentrated only on concrete political matters. The national round table talks established special committees for economic and social policy, but their negotiations were neglected and sentenced to oblivion in an atmosphere of intensifying party conflicts. The socio-economic aspect of legislation and constitution-making was, therefore, forgotten; perhaps it is more accurate to say that such legislation was sufficiently advanced not to create any problem at the given stage of transition. Yet its neglect of a social pact proved to be the great disadvantage of the September pact, and by that neglect the political actors initiated a negative tradition which became the biggest burden for the democratic transition.

2.3. *The April (1990) Pact*

The spring 1990 elections produced a stable governing coalition in Hungary (HDF, ISP, and ChDPP) with the HDF and AFD emerging as the biggest parliamentary parties. After the elections these two parties, aiming at a short cut towards some kind of two-party system, concluded a pact on further amendments to the Constitution. The leaders of the two parties negotiated in complete secrecy and signed the pact on 29 April 1990, after which the pact became public and the new parliament amended the Constitution accordingly.[14]

The April pact met serious resistance from the other parties and from large sections of public opinion because of its 'élite (*kamarilla*) politics', its exclusiveness, and its content, i.e. the new constitutional solution. The political formula of the September pact was completely reversed: instead of a strong parliament with a weak president, a strong government and a slightly stronger presidency were established with a much weaker parliament. In the September pact most of the laws were of constitutional force (i.e. with a qualified, two-thirds majority); according to the April pact, their number was reduced to twenty. Consequently, the 'constitutional-assembly-type' parliament was, by that action, reduced to a 'normal' parliament where, even in respect of fundamental laws determining the fate of the nation for decades, a simple majority could be decisive. However, the major change was the introduction of the German constitutional solution for stable government: the constructive no-confidence vote. As a result, the government became very strong, but without proper checks and balances.[15]

The Free Democrats have paid a heavy price for the April pact, and they have not so far recovered from the losses. They gained the presidency by the April pact for once, and the AFD President, Árpád Göncz, was elected by the parliament on 3 August 1990. Yet the *kamarilla* politics created resentment even within their own party; their parliamentary group became troubled by the bargaining process and was not able to find the role of a new opposition party for a long time. Moreover, later on they realized that, in the rush to conclude the pact, they had forgotten to include the most important laws in those 'twenty' laws of constitutional force. These 'forgotten' or neglected laws concerned economic and social policy (privatization, compensation, etc.). As a result, the AFD was plunged into crisis and has had second thoughts about the April pact. A sad reminder of political history is that the AFD began to advocate the need for a stronger presidency in the autumn of 1990, as a necessary part of a system of 'checks and balances' against an over-strong government.

The 1989 Constitution expressed the results of the pre-transition crisis as the point of departure for the real power transition. After the free and competitive general elections in spring 1990, the process of power transition came to an end and a new political compromise was born. The features of this particular political compromise are clearly imprinted on the 'final' constitution as well, but the 1990 Constitution in general has been a correct constitution, meeting European standards. Still, it was meant to be an 'interim' one, to be replaced by a completely new and coherent constitution soon after the power transition. The historically rare moment of consensus disappeared after the first months of the new regime, and this 'interim' constitution serves rather well as far as the democratic foundations of the state and the rule of law are concerned; on the other hand, it functions rather poorly in a series of particular matters, at least partly because of its internal contradictions and unfinished character.

The most important novelty in the 1990 Constitution has been the constructive motion of no-confidence, which has created a prime-ministerial government and has redrawn fundamentally the relationship between the centres of power. The 1990 Constitution states (Chapter VII, Section 39/A):

A motion of no-confidence may be submitted in writing against the Prime Minister, with the indication of the person nominated for the office of Prime Minister. This shall be agreed upon by at least one-fifth of the representatives. A motion of no-confidence submitted against the Prime Minister shall be considered as a motion of no-confidence against the Government. If, in consequence of the motion, the majority of the National Assembly representatives express their no-confidence, the person nominated for the office of Prime Minister shall be considered to have been elected.[16]

The constructive no-confidence vote as a legal device renders the government stable, enhancing the governability of the country. It gives special rights to the prime minister, since ministers are individually responsible only to him and not to the parliament. The prime minister is reponsible for the whole government collectively to the parliament, and he can dismiss ministers at will. By this legal

device the 150-year-old Hungarian tradition of individual responsibility of ministers to parliament was discontinued, and a teasing
contradiction emerged between the poor performance of some ministers and the maintenance of their tenure in office. The whole
impact of prime-ministerial government on political life may be
seen as the loosening of parliamentary control over the executive
powers, above all over the huge concentration of powers in the
prime minister's office.

The majority of constitutional experts, and also of the public,
consider that the April pact was in some ways detrimental to
constitutional developments.[17] The rights of the parliament were
curtailed and those of the government extended. Thus the prime
minister emerged as the only real power centre. The use of a simple
majority in parliament pushed aside the role of parliament as a
constitutional assembly of the broadest national consensus. As the
history of the new parliament shows, the April pact excluded to a
considerable extent the three opposition parties (AFD, HSP, and
Fidesz) from creative participation in the legislative process. The
new constitutional situation later led the government to state, in
May 1991, that it was opposed to any kind of social pact which
would involve opposition parties and other social and political
actors.

The April pact has determined the fate and framework of subsequent political struggles. The HDF and the AFD have changed
their political courses completely: the HDF has been 'radicalized' in
its confrontation with the previous system, including the reform
socialists. The AFD, in turn, has opted for a more gradualist approach, criticizing the radicalism of the HDF, which has to some
extent turned out to be a form of right-wing populism.

2.4. The Strength of a Weak President

With a strong prime minister as the overwhelming element of the
Hungarian political system after May 1990, all the other political
actors began to look for those checks and balances which had been
established by the September pact. First of all, the CC gained an
eminent role in controlling the arbitrary simple parliamentary majority by declaring some laws passed by parliament to be unconstitutional. In public life, it was the 'weak' president who became a

very important 'strong' counterforce to the prime minister. In an effort to gain full powers, the governing coalition began to appropriate all positions not only in the political but also in the economic and social area. It expected the president to act as a 'rubber stamp', signing appointments by the prime minister without hesitation. The first conflict emerged between the prime minister and the president in the autumn of 1990, and since then it has been one of the major cleavages in the Hungarian political system.

Although the term 'constitutional crisis' was used first by representatives of the government only in the autumn of 1991, it applied even before then: the division of powers has not so far worked in ECE (and much less in EE, where there are presidential systems without any real counterbalancing powers).[18] Again, Hungary may be the best case compared to the 'semi-presidential' systems of Poland and Czechoslovakia, where presidents in some ways have uncontrolled power. Yet Hungary faces the same type of difficulty to a lesser degree, and it has to cope with its own problems.[19]

The common background of this drive for full powers comes from the traditions, routines, mentality, and practice of the previous one-party system, and at the same time it pre-dates state socialism in the form of the inter-war authoritarianism. The formalist façade of democracy with one overwhelming and uncontrolled power centre behind it is the most dangerous blind alley which the ECE countries have to avoid at this stage of the democratization process. Political transition, with all its difficulties and uncertainties, needs a stable government, but not as the only political actor, since this would be a return to the idea of the enlightened or reform dictatorship of the last period of the state socialist systems. Otherwise, while some constitutional devices such as the positive no-confidence vote can work properly in the consolidated democracies, in the emerging democracies there is the danger of a one-man show in politics.

Unexpectedly, Árpád Göncz, a not very well-known playwright, has turned out to be a charismatic personality as President. He is a modest, soft-spoken figure, and has human warmth and a capacity for direct, personal contact with the population. He contrasts favourably with the aggressive style of other politicians, and with the historical positioning and pathos of the new government. This is why the President has become the most popular figure and the Prime Minister much less so.[20] In late October 1990 the government mismanaged an increase in the price of petrol (issuing a sudden declaration of a huge price-rise much beyond real costs), thereby provoking a mass civil disobedience campaign which paralysed the whole country. When the government began to consider the use of the police and the military to restore 'law and order', the President declared that he would prevent it and asked the government for negotiations. The conflict was solved, resulting in a loss of prestige for the government and a gain in prestige for the President. Although the government raised doubts as to whether the President had been entitled to resort to this type of declaration, most legal experts indicated that the President simply used his constitutional powers as the commander-in-chief of the army. Here the story of the two major counterbalancing powers to the Prime Minister—the presidency and the CC—was coupled together: the Prime Minister and his ministers have asked the CC several times about the rights and duties of the President. These 'explanations' of the Constitution concerning the role of the presidency in concrete matters have been major political events, and have determined the institutional framework of the division of powers to a considerable extent.

As has been mentioned above, the first clash between the President and the Prime Minister took place in October 1990 over the so-called 'taxi-drivers strike' which paralysed the country. The role of the President in the management of the crisis raised the issue of his actual constitutional rights as the commander-in-chief of the army. Some months later, in February 1991, there was a meeting in Visegrád (Hungary) between the leaders of Poland, Czechoslovakia, and Hungary (with two Presidents, Wałęsa and Havel) which triggered a discussion as to who would be present from the Hungarian side. Although this problem was solved practically with the presence of both the President and the Prime Minister, the fundamental question remained manifestly unsolved, since the Constitution had a similar wording concerning the role of each in foreign policy. Chapter III, Section 30/A says:

The President of the Republic . . . shall enter into international agreements on behalf of the Republic of Hungary; if an agreement by its content falls within the competence of the legislature, the prior consent of the National Assembly shall be required for the conclusion of the agreement.

At the same time Chapter VII, Section 35 states that the Prime Minister shall 'participate in determining foreign policy; enter into international agreements on behalf of the Government of the Republic of Hungary'.

The Constitution's wording, indeed, is too vague to provide a definite answer for either question, international representation or command of the army. On 8 April 1991 the Minister of Defence turned to the CC on the latter issue, and in July 1991 a new, open conflict broke out between the President and Prime Minister in the 'media war': the President refused to countersign the appointments by the Prime Minister of deputy presidents of Hungarian radio and television. This time the Prime Minister turned to the CC for an interpretation of the Constitution. The ruling of the CC in all these matters concerning the role of the President came out on 23 September 1991. It confirmed the President's rights and duties concerning his central role in safeguarding the democratic workings of the institutions, but it specified and limited the President's power to veto appointments.

Both sides welcomed the resolution of the CC as an approval of the President's position. On 26 September 1991 the Prime Minister repeated his claim for the countersignature and received a new refusal. The stalemate has since held on all fronts, first of all in the media war, where the government has tried to fire the independent media presidents and to replace them with politically loyal party figures to control the electronic media. The new clash occurred with a renewed attempt by the Prime Minister to dismiss the incumbent media presidents, and the President's resistance to it, which led to a new ruling of the CC, on 8 June 1992, with almost the same formulations. This shows that the CC has reached its limit in the legal regulations between the political sub-centres. The lack of a breakthrough in the extension of the Prime Minister's power irritates the government more and more. The two most important laws for the government in 1991 (the compensation law of 13 May 1991 and the retroactive punishment law of 18 November 1991) were referred to the CC by the President and were annulled by it. Both the President and the CC have exercised their 'negative' power only in these cases, as a restraint and check on the overwhelming role of the government.

In Hungary a stable parliamentary system has been organized, and all political actors still agree upon the principles of parliamen-

tary democracy over presidentialism. The political disputes around
the role of the presidency have not meant that the opposition forces
want a change towards any kind of presidential system. All constitutional adjustments to and modifications of the role of the presidency in the political system which arose as explanations or
interpretations of the Constitution by the CC have not so far
touched the essential features of the parliamentary system. All the
disputes around the role of the presidency (and that of the CC) have
been at the level of the micro-choice, i.e. the smaller regulations
required in order to prevent asymmetry in the power structure.

Government stability is a priority during the political transition,
but it cannot be overstretched as the 'tyranny of the majority',
either by a simple parliamentary majority system or by the prime
minister. As a matter of principle, the simple majority system has
been legitimized by the election of a majority to govern the country,
but it is not expected to decide its fate for decades by passing
'fundamental laws' (laws of constitutional force, i.e. concerning the
essential features of the socio-political system) as a form of the
constant constitution-making process. In general, the majority has
its constitutional limitations even in the consolidated democracies;
in particular, it has to have them in a more marked way during the
political transition in the emerging democracies. These limitations
of counterbalancing powers (and the Europeanization process itself, which provides this model) can decide where the future of the
newly emerging ECE democracies lies between the alternatives of
the European and the Latin-American models.[21]

3. CONTROVERSIAL ISSUES IN THE PRESENT CONSTITUTION

Obviously, the roles of the parliament, president, and prime minister have been organically interconnected, but they have been
characterized somewhat ambiguously in the present Hungarian
Constitution. The CC is a more or less separate case, and its role
has been clearly specified in the Constitution. These controversial
issues are very specific in Hungary, but they are essentially similar
to those which have emerged in SE countries during their democratic transition, and in their parties' attitudes towards constitutional settlement.

As Pridham suggests, Spain followed a line of political consensus in the constitution-making process (changed from time to time to the government/opposition rivalry); Greece had a much more controversial confrontational process; Portugal accomplished an extensive constitutional revision; finally, in Italy the original national consensus turned into a rupture between left and right in the constitution-making process. In Hungary we can detect the same elements of consensus (September pact) and dissensus (April pact), and later the emerging rupture between government and opposition over the relevant constitutional matters. A new turning-point may come in the 1994 elections, and with a new government. In any case, the alternation of power between government and opposition seems to be a prerequisite of democratic consolidation and also a test case for the new Constitution. The European integration process will also be a test case, as Pridham describes it in Greece, where the external links for this 'penetrated system' had profound implications for the party system and the behaviour of parties towards the constitution-making process.[22]

Discussing the Spanish constitution-making process in a coherent theoretical framework, Bonime-Blanc emphasizes that it is one of the major activities of a transition to democracy. No political figure or party can avoid involvement in the following two constitutional issues: the political formula by which political élites decide on the limits and practices of the new government and regime; and the socio-governmental formula of the rights and duties of its citizens. She also points out the significance of consensual versus dissensual practices. A consensual constitution-making process takes place where most (if not all) political groups participate in the drafting of the constitution and the agreements are reached by compromise. Dissensual constitution-making is a process in which not all political actors participate, dogmatic solutions prevail, and, irresponsibly, the views of one or more major political parties are excluded from these solutions.

Bonime-Blanc widely illustrates her opinion that democratic constitutions are meant for the regulation of the division of powers and thus that they are also a technique of ensuring liberty. In this approach, it is very useful to distinguish the normative, nominal, and semantic types of constitution. The normative ones are those which in practice are fully activated and effective, the nominal ones may be legally valid but not implemented, and the semantic ones are only for legalizing the existing power configuration but cannot serve as the procedural framework for competitive power elements. It is evident from this analysis that the constitutional arrangements of ECE lie between the normative and nominal types nowadays, and those of EE are between the nominal and semantic ones.[23]

3.1. *The Classical Triangle of Powers*

In the classical triangle of powers it is certainly now the prime minister whose role has been most exposed in the political system in the disproportionate scope of his functions *vis-à-vis* the parliament and the president. As I have emphasized, it has been not a personal rivalry between the Prime Minister and President but a vital question of the balance of powers, specially tailored to Hungarian constitutional traditions and to the present stage of the political transition. Also, in the case of the parliament, the issue is about the constitutional powers of the simple majority over the qualified majority, i.e. about whether the alternative for the parliament is to become a 'co-ordinate' legislature (in a relationship of co-operation with the executive) or a 'subordinate' one (with a single cohesive majority party and a disciplined party fraction), or whether it deteriorates into a 'submissive' one (which is unable to set limits on the executive's discretion). For the 'normal' process of subsequent constitution-making we would need in Hungary a co-ordinate legislature, but the present one is in danger of regressing into a subordinate parliament through 'the tyranny of the majority'.[24] It must be stressed that the controversial issues in the constitutional debates do not originate from and are not caused by the contradictions between the amended and non-amended parts of the new Constitution (which may be the situation in Czechoslovakia or Poland). On the contrary, the present controversies are the result of the new Constitution itself—as the case of the positive no-confidence vote shows—which has produced a strong prime minister, with ministers not responsible to parliament, only to the prime minister, and with the drastic reduction in the laws requiring a qualified majority.

The major problem is that after the April pact the constitution-making process seems to have halted to a great extent. The coalition government has had much difficulty with those twenty laws earmarked by the April pact for a qualified majority, and in such a way some of the most important, fundamental laws (e.g. media law) have not been passed by the parliament because the government has not wanted to engage in a bargaining process with the opposition in order to create consensus, although it has happily engaged in confrontation when its simple majority was 'automatically' assured. The major exception was the issue of local governments, necessitated by the local elections which were due in the autumn of 1990. This fundamental law was passed in a very strange way. The conceptual part was acknowledged by the government as a law of the two-thirds majority and the other, more practical, parts were separated into independent laws (including the finances of the local communities) that required only the simple majority. The government made a similar attempt to break down the law on the media, which had also been earmarked by the April pact for the qualified majority. It sought to break up the law into some non-qualified laws and to pass these separately; however, owing to strong resistance, it stopped these preparations. What is more, in February 1992 the HDF put forward a proposal in parliament to limit the possibility of private motions or bills by opposition MPs, supposedly to save time for urgent government bills.

Again, this raises questions about the constitutional rights of the simple majority in parliament; whether the issue is about governing the country, or about monopolizing the constitution-making process. The prime-ministerial system of government provides a stable system for the political transition, but at the same time it produces a fusion of the government (executive) and parliament (legislature), and the result is that there will be no independent source of information and expertise for the parliament in the scrutiny of legislation.

The Spanish transition has gone through similar phases of compromise by the two dominating parties, which agreed first upon a compromise concerning a majoritarian and proportional representation system of elections and, second, upon the establishment of a strong prime-ministerial system. The most likely government parties (the UCD and PSOE, and in Hungary the HDF and AFD) pushed for the constitutionalization of a constructive motion of censure or positive no-confidence vote fashioned after the German Basic Law. The smaller parties in both countries have favoured the usual negative no-confidence vote but the big, would-be governmental parties have overpowered them. This has given a relative strength to the executive within the functional balance of power.

The prime minister has the right to select the cabinet after being confirmed by the parliament; thus he receives a critical amount of decision-making power. This somewhat cumbersome arrangement again represents (Bonime-Blanc argues) the product of compromise and the dominance of the two major government-minded parties.

Consequently, Bonime-Blanc concludes, the positive no-confidence vote has created a system with an over-powerful prime minister whose executive powers go beyond those typical of a purely parliamentary system. In Spain, however, the King has proven to be a sufficient counterbalance, together with the other social and political actors in the special circumstances of the negotiated transition. In the original German model, Bonime-Blanc underlines, the counterbalance was mostly external: there was an 'imposition of democratization' by victorious allied forces. Elections were not held for a constitutional assembly; instead, the provincial legislatures (*Landtage*), never too far from allied supervision, appointed members to the 'parliamentary council', which became the constitution-making body.[25] It is no accident that in Hungary, with a triangle of powers modelled after the German Constitution (and not having a 'Spanish king', only the popular president), the political actors, feeling the dominance of an over-powerful prime minister, are also seeking a counterbalancing force in the European integration process, with its standards of political institutions and norms. This is why inside the country the CC has gained an extraordinary role and significance.

3.2. The Constitutional Court: Beyond the Classical Triangle

The controversial issues discussed above explain why the CC, established by the September pact, has gained an influential place in the division of powers and a vital role in political life. Indeed, the CC has become a 'key player', lying beyond the classical power triangle but fundamentally influencing its relationships, in accordance with the September pact, which assigned to the CC the task of 'contributing to the creation of a state built on the rule of law, protecting the constitutional order, and safeguarding the separation and balance of power'. In this spirit the CC has four major functions: (1) preventive protection of constitutional norms by means of prior review of draft legislation, (2) *ex post* protection of constitutional norms by means of review of laws passed by the parliament, (3) revelation of the unconstitutional character of parliamentary decisions caused by neglect or failure on the part of the legislators, and (4) explanation or interpretation of the Constitution. Of these functions the second and fourth have proved to be very important, although the others also have come to the fore on several occasions.[26]

The CC has been overburdened with issues and motions since its foundation; in 1991 alone it received 2,302 motions. Its first function, that of preventive norm control, or the control of draft bills, has arisen least frequently but remains the most controversial. The three motions for preventive control (which can be proposed only by the parliament, government, or president) raised controversy not only because of the rulings of the CC but because of the function itself. Provision for constitutional examination of draft legislation exists only in a few countries (Portugal and, to some extent, France), for it has the potential to threaten the principle of the separation of powers; in essence, the CC would replace the legislature by seriously interfering in its work during the legislative procedure. Those cases referred to the CC so far have been, in fact, political issues between the ruling parties. In the autumn of 1990 the Prime Minister sought examination of two bills only to avoid political conflict with his coalition partner. The CC solved the issue when it declared the draft to be unconstitutional, instead of the Prime Minister doing so. Beyond this political contradiction (transferring the political responsibility to the CC) there is also a 'technical' one: a draft law may be sent to the CC at an early stage, yet later on in the legislative process the parliament can change the draft law fundamentally, while the ruling of the CC only applies to the earliest version. In any event, the CC has sought to get rid of this function because of the many contradictions which were manifested by the third case, when, in March 1991, fifty-two opposition MPs asked for preventive examination of the compensation law. The CC offered, on 18 April 1991, only a general explanation of the constitutional principles in that particular question, but it did engage in an analysis of the draft law, at the same time indicating its unhappiness concerning its involvement in the legislative process. Since then there have been no further motions for preventive control.

The second and 'classical' function of the CC has been a very important and very frequently used one (25 per cent of all motions in 1991). Motions concerning the unconstitutional character of laws and decisions of parliament can be initiated by anybody, but out of the many cases brought, the ruling of the CC has been in favour of the applicant in only thirteen cases, and among these only three were passed by the new parliament. These cases, however, especially two famous ones, have been crucial in the limitation of the arbitrariness of the simple parliamentary majority, and they have shown the CC in its role of safeguarding the democratic order and consensus. The CC annulled the compensation law on 29 May 1991 and the parliament had to reformulate it. The CC did the same later, on 3 March 1992, with the law on restrospective punishment or about the extension of the statute of limitations for certain crimes committed under the communist regime. The CC emphasized that the rule of law could not be secured by violating the rule of law, and that legal security and predictability were the first priorities in the democratic transition.

As to the third function, one has to mention independent actions of the CC, such as when it declared both the death penalty and the abortion law unconstitutional. In the case of the abortion law and also in the other cases, the CC gave deadlines for parliament to finish the proper legislation and to amend the existing unconstitutional laws. The fourth function of the CC has been in the forefront of our analysis, with the interpretation of the Constitution in the series of clashes between the President of the Republic and the Prime Minister. I have described these developments as leading to a political stalemate; but this fourth function of the CC will clearly be the decisive one in the immediate future, i.e. until 1994. The statements of the CC have confirmed the strictly parliamentary character of the Hungarian political system, with its unity of executive power balanced by a control function assigned to the president, this emanating from the principle of separation of powers (checks and balances) in safeguarding the democratic workings of the fundamental institutions. The president, with his 'negative' rights, has established himself as an independent actor in Hungarian political life, and this has not proved to have damaged the parliamentary system through any form of movement towards a presidential system.[27]

The CC has a very positive role but it is also oversized—even according to its members, who have turned to parliament to reduce their functions and to make a clearer distinction between the constitution-making and the constitution-explaining processes. However, the law regulating the powers of the CC is itself a law of qualified majority, and it is not at all likely that the government and opposition parties will reach an agreement concerning its new, more modest role. Since the decisions of the CC have been quite manifestly to place restrictions on the powers of the simple parliamentary majority and on the prime minister, in governmental circles criticism of the CC has been very sharp (some MPs of the coalition parties attack the CC using populist demagogy, arguing that the CC damages the national interests). Indeed, the CC has represented the 'idealism' of constitutional regulations, in contrast to the 'pragmatism' of the incumbents, as its president has declared.[28]

The fundamental problem has been, in fact, that there have been contradictions and insufficiently elaborated regulations in the new constitution. Since 1989 it has been evident to all political actors that a complete, newly drafted constitution would be needed in the 1990s. Although the CC with its decisions has paved the way for this, the political disputes have created a temporary deadlock in this process, at least until the new elections in 1994.

4. HEADING FOR THE NEW CONSTITUTION

4.1. The Missing Links

In 1988–9 political scientists in Hungary suggested that an extraordinarily created constitutional assembly, with special rights and with a short duration period of, say, two years, should be elected. I still think it would have been the best solution for handling the constitution-making process. However, the major actors were in favour of the regularly elected parliament, which would give them comfort and stability for four years. This 'long parliament', with its sharp division between the government and opposition, has blocked the constitution-making process ever since the April pact. Before the new parliament, i.e. until spring 1990, the process of forging consensus went ahead on the basis of political bargains and compromises, and in the pre-parliamentary stage, was very dynamic and innovative. The consensus or compromise-making process in the new parliament has been a history of failures and deadlocks, first of all because of the attempts by the governing parties to obtain full powers according to the worst CE traditions. Before the new parliament, again, there were very active and highly critical debates over various constitutional drafts in both the legal and political sciences. In the period of the new parliament there have been competing party drafts on some questions, but they have been more or less completely separate from public discussions by the experts in the specialist periodicals.

The political and socio-governmental formulas of the new regime have deserved public discussion, but they have been introduced by the government without any prior consultation. The new governmental machinery reflects the new concentration of powers in the prime-ministerial office (increasingly similar to the central committee of the previous ruling party). For the socio-governmental formula the new governmental élite has tried to change fundamentally the state–church relationship and the system of education, health care, and social security, without seeking consensus and by circumventing constitutional regulations. Thus these issues also have become very controversial, quite apart from being vexatious questions in any political debate.

Consequently, the disputes over the Constitution are very far from coming to an end. There are two important missing links even for the normal, everyday workings of the political system. First, a social pact is missing which could arrange the constitutional role of the interest groups in political life in general, and in the pre-parliamentary decision-making process in particular. Connected with this issue, there is an open question as to whether to maintain the existing unicameral or adopt the proposed bicameral parliament, since the latter could be a solution for the representation of minorities and interest groups.[29] However, in the context of majoritarian over consensus democracy, the major challenge is whether the chosen system would allow the opposition to act not only formally but also substantially, even for the preparation of a smooth alternation in power between government and opposition. The second missing link is, therefore, the regulation of the activities of the opposition. For the parliament it would mean a new set of house rules, legitimizing the roles of the government and opposition and regulating the workings of the party factions in the legislative process. The old standing orders, albeit amended, are no longer adequate, but the introduction of new rules, being a matter for a law of qualified majority, has been as deadlocked as all the others.

4.2. Europeanization and Constitutional Stability

The illusion of the easy, quick democratic transition has disappeared. All the political actors know quite well now that the most difficult period of the transition—and of the constitution-making process—still lies ahead. The ruling coalition favours Hungarian traditionalism, with its concept of a state with a golden age that never was; the opposition parties, otherwise very fragmented, are united in their concept of a state involving subsequent (West-) Europeanization, although they have not yet been able to turn this concept into political action. Still, among the three ECE countries Hungary, with its parliamentary democracy, appears to be the most advanced in the Europeanization process, even in the field of constitution-making, and may be considered as a laboratory for the democratization of Central and East European countries.

The process of Europeanization, i.e. the structural adjustment and accommodation of Hungary to the EC, cannot be reduced to its economic dimension. The social accommodation, i.e. political, legal, and cultural accommodation, leading to structural compatibility of Hungary with the EC, may be even more important, as it is only firm commitment to the principles of the European type of democracy on the Hungarian side and assistance to its political-legal transformation on the EC side that can be the safeguard for democratization in Hungary. During this systemic change and democratic transition the 'permanent constitutional crisis' has been normal and unavoidable; it has been, in fact, a creative crisis, leading to the dynamic transformation of the Hungarian polity. The present constitution has functioned rather well, and the decisive impetus for constitutional reform is obviously lacking. The main political actors, despite all political fights and mutual accusations, have learned to live with the present constitution, and no radical departure can be expected from the newly established conventions and practices. Yet the direction of the necessary changes needs to be indicated, since there have been some serious problems with the Constitution within the last three years. Three major contradictions emerged which have to be overcome in order to reach a constitutional stability with its guarantees:

1. the contradiction between the previous, state socialist constitutional framework and the new democratic substance, i.e. the contradiction between the structure and content;
2. the contradiction between the conflicting short-term particular political demands of different political actors and the needs of long-term democratic consolidation;
3. the contradiction between the drive of the new government to obtain full powers and the democratic principle of the division and limitation of powers asserted in the Constitution.

A set of measures could be taken to overcome the present permanent constitutional crisis:

1. The political actors should return to consensus politics as opposed to the recent dissensus politics to re-create that rare historical moment for constitution-making as a political precondition for constitutional stability.

2. The social and political actors should agree upon the basic principles of social policy, defining the rules of the game in this field in the form of a social pact to secure social peace for the democratic transition as a social precondition for constitutional stability.

3. The constitutional experts should elaborate a completely new and coherent structure for the new constitution, based on current European models as the scientific background and precondition for constitutional stability.

4. The political community and the population should express their full support for the parliamentary over the presidential system ('meso-choice'). This fundamental feature should be formulated in the new constitution without any ambiguity, by preserving the strong government ('micro-choice') but with an articulated system of checks and balances as an inner, i.e. constitutional, precondition for constitutional stability.

In practical terms this means the following tasks for the constitutional experts:

1. removal of the existing contradictions in the present constitution, first of all concerning the classical power triangle (president, government, and parliament);

2. filling the gaps in the present constitution, above all in the field of social and human rights with their elaborated formulation in the text;

3. redressing the role of the CC, i.e. giving it a more modest but legally and politically more feasible role, which can be sustained in the long run;

4. rearrangement of the role and 'technics' of the legislation by new house rules for greater efficiency and more democratism, i.e. with better preparation of bills, more democratic discussions in the parliamentary committees, and less 'failure by neglect' to pass laws, by which not only the working of the 'law factory' but also its political image may be improved.[30]

The new constitution, of course, will only be the tip of the iceberg if one takes into account that huge mass of legal and political regulations which have to be adopted for structural compatibility with the EC to be achieved. In all countries during their transition period to membership of the EC, great efforts were needed to accomplish these deep changes in their polities, requiring a comprehensive research and action plan. This seems to be emerging now in Hungary as well, and constitution-making, with its guarantees for constitutional stability, appears to be one of the most important parts of these efforts to achieve structural compatibility with the EC.[31]

Notes

1. Ample literature exists concerning the parallels between SE and CE in the democratic transition. See esp. A. Bonime-Blanc, *Spain's Transition to Democracy: The Politics of Constitution-making* (Boulder, Colo.: Westview, 1987).

2. On the terms 'macro-', 'meso-', and 'micro-choices', see G. Pridham, 'Political Parties, Parliaments and Democratic Consolidation in Southern Europe', in U. Liebert and M. Cotta (eds.), *Parliament and Democratic Consolidation in Southern Europe* (London: Pinter, 1990), 226.

3. I give here a short summary of the constitutional developments, based on the book *Alkotmánytan* (Constitutional Law) (Budapest: Századvég, 1992), 31–42.

4. I cannot describe here the whole democratic transition process in Hungary. For a comparative view, see my 'The Transition to Demo-

cracy in Central Europe', *Journal of Public Policy*, 11/2 (1991). My department has edited every year since 1988 *The Political Yearbook of Hungary* (*PYH*) (Budapest, 1989–94) with all the documents and analyses, and in my introductions (published also in English in the volumes) I have summarized the political developments of the given year in Hungary.

5. In 1987–8 some political scientists drafted semi-legal proposals for a new constitution. My own proposal was based on the radical reform of parliament; others wanted to reform the ruling party or to create a strong presidency for the transition period. It is important to emphasize that in the Hungarian democratic transition political science has played an eminent role, in contrast to Spain, where the constitutional law seems to have dominated over political science—see J. M. Valles, *Political Science in Spain: An Overview* (Barcelona: Instituto de las Ciencias Políticas y Sociales, 1989) and my 'The Emergence of the "Science of Democracy" and Its Impact on the Democratic Transition in Hungary', *Aula*, 2 (Budapest, 1991).

6. Until the end of 1988 I had been involved as an expert, with some other political scientists, in the preparations of the 'official' concept of the new constitution. This concept was written under the direction of Professor Kálmán Kulcsár, then Minister of Justice. There were also some drafts at that time about the bicameral parliament, with representation for the organized interests and/or the (ethnic, religious, etc.) minorities, and discussions are still continuing on this topic. In Feb. 1990 four co-authors of the Spanish Constitution visited Hungary for a two-day conference on the parallels of the constitution-making process in our countries. It was still the period in Hungary when the consensus approach dominated, but a year later the conflictual approach prevailed, and Hungary diverged sharply from the Spanish model, even in the constitution-making.

7. The market-oriented economic legislation reached a turning-point in Oct. 1988, when the law on companies and the law on taxation (personal and VAT) were passed by the parliament. The new economic legislation was summarized in the 1989 Constitution and further elaborated by subsequent laws.

8. The 1988 and 1989 volumes of *PYH* contain the last decree-laws of the presidential council.

9. The opposition round table was formed by the Society Bajcsy-Zsilinszky (SBZ), Alliance of Free Democrats (AFD), Independent Smallholder Party (ISP), Hungarian Democratic Forum (HDF), The Social-Democratic Party of Hungary (SPH), the Alliance of Young Democrats (Fidesz), and The Democratic League of Free Trade Unions (DLFTU). The Christian Democratic People's Party (ChDPP) joined later.

10. Pozsgay was an eminent leader of the Hungarian Socialist Workers' Party and the best-known political reformer, but at that time he represented too much continuity with the previous regime for the AFD and Fidesz.

11. A proposal for the direct election of the president re-emerged in a referendum in July 1990 but failed to secure enough popular support.

12. The text of the 1989 Constitution was published in the official journal, *Magyar Közlöny*, 74 (23 Oct. 1989). I quote here a semi-official translation, circulated as 'The Constitution of the Republic of Hungary' (in a uniform structure consisting of Act XX of 1949 and its amendments). On the basis of the 1949 Constitution, the structure of the 1989 Constitution is as follows: I, General Provisions; II, Parliament; III, President of the Republic; IV, Court of Constitutionality; V, Parliamentary Commissioner for Administration; VI, State Audit Office; VII, Council of Ministers; VIII, Armed Forces and Police; IX, The (Local) Councils; X, The Judiciary; XI, The Prosecution; XII, Fundamental Rights and Duties; XIII, Fundamental Principles of Elections; XIV, Capital and National Emblems; XV, Closing Provisions. The 1990 Constitution has retained this structure but has modified slightly the titles of the chapters.

13. The text of the 1990 Constitution was published in *Magyar Közlöny*, 59 (25 June 1990). I quote here a semi-official translation of this Constitution concerning the president. Ch. II, sect. 24 specifies the function of the 'law of constitutional force': 'A two-thirds majority of the votes of the members of Parliament shall be required for any amendment of the Constitution, also for enacting Acts of constitutional force.' The text of the Constitution indicates that this question should be regulated in detail by a law of constitutional force (e.g. human rights, Ch. I, sect. 8; the activities of MPs, Ch. II, sect. 20; the Constitutional Court, Ch. IV, sect. 32/A, etc.).

14. The formulation of the 1990 Constitution was a process of amendments, the major steps being Act XXIX (9 May 1990) and Act XL (19 June 1992); the text was finalized only with Act LXIII (2 Aug. 1992).

15. The text of the April pact and the 20 laws of qualified majority were published in the 1990 volume of *PYH*.

16. This model has evidently been borrowed from Germany, but the Basic Law applies in Art. 67 (vote of no-confidence) a simple and less complicated formulation: 'The Bundestag can express its lack of confidence in the Federal Chancellor only by electing a successor with the majority of its members and by requesting the Federal President to dismiss the Federal Chancellor' (*The Basic Law of the Federal Republic of Germany* (Ostfildern: Merkur-Druck Mayer, 1986), 41).

17. One of the leading Hungarian experts, who is also a member of the CC, has indicated the contradiction between the supremacy of parlia-

ment and the extended rights of the prime minister in the text of the 1990 Constitution. He has also pointed out the lack of regulation of the political responsibility of government before the parliament in the present structure. See P. Schmidt, 'The Constitutional Contradictions of Hungarian Parliamentarism', *PYH* (1992).

18. On 3 Sept. 1991 an HDF deputy, József Debreczeni, wrote an article in the daily *Magyar Hírlap*, attacking the President and publicly using the term 'constitutional crisis' for the first time.

19. The actual semi-presidential systems of Poland and Czechoslovakia (until the summer of 1992) show some historical continuity—with the Piłsudski-type 'dictatorship of patriotism' and with the Masaryk-type 'dictatorship of respect'. The missing constitutions and the difficulties of the constitution-making process in these countries have been described by Jiří Pehe and Anna Sabbat-Swidlicka, and also the contradictions of the Hungarian half-made constitution, by Edith Olthay, in a special issue, 'Toward the Rule of Law', of the *RFE/RL Research Report*, 1/27 (3 July 1992).

20. For 4 years the President has continuously headed the list of popular politicians in Hungary, and the Prime Minister (first Antall, then Boross) has been around position 14–16.

21. On the theoretical problems of constitutional limitations in the developed democracies, see J. Elster and R. Slagstad (eds.), *Constitutionalism and Democracy* (Cambridge and Oslo: Cambridge UP and Norwegian UP, 1988).

22. G. Pridham, 'Southern European Democracies on the Road to Consolidation', in Pridham (ed.), *Securing Democracy: Political Parties and Democratic Consolidation in Southern Europe* (London: Routledge, 1990), 30–4.

23. Bonime-Blanc, *Spain's Transition to Democracy*, 10–13. She quotes the definitions of the constitution by S. E. Finer ('Constitutions are codes of rules which aspire to regulate the allocation of functions, powers and duties among the various agencies and officers of government'), by C. Friedrich ('effective regularized restraint'), and by G. Sartori ('technique of liberty').

24. This terminology has been introduced as a typology of the parliaments of the political transition by U. Liebert in her paper 'Parliaments in the Consolidation of Democracy', in Liebert and Cotta, *Parliament and Democratic Consolidation in Southern Europe*, 249–65.

25. See Bonime-Blanc, *Spain's Transition to Democracy*, 76–81, 116–17.

26. See *Magyar Közlöny*, 77 (30 Oct. 1989), Act XXXII.

27. Z. Kerekes, 'Purposes and Facts: Reflections on the First Four Years of the Constitutional Court', *PYH* (1994), summarizes the CC activities. The CC has dealt in these first 4 years with about 7,000 issues, out of which only 18 have had direct political consequences, since these

CC decisions have cancelled partly or completely the Acts of Parliament.

28. The Declaration of László Sólyom in the weekly *HVG* (Budapest), 1 Feb. 1994. There are two theoretical and political problems which have been frequently discussed in the international literature, the presidency and the retrospective justice. See e.g. the two issues of *East European Constitutional Review* on 'Dilemmas of Post-Totalitarian Justice: Retrospective Justice and the Rule of Law in Hungary' and 'The Postcommunist Presidency' (1/2, summer 1992; 2/4–3/1, autumn 1993/winter 1994).

29. In July 1992 the government set out a draft law on the parliamentary representation of minorities. Although Hungary is almost completely ethnically homogeneous, still there are 13 small ethnic minorities, the gypsies being the largest (although very heterogeneous) ethnic group. The proposal suggested giving 14 seats in parliament to the minorities on their lists, which could solve the problem of the upper house in this respect. But the parliament has turned down this proposal, since it has found that in the form presented it is incompatible with the principle of party representation. There is also a national council for the conciliation of interests, and with the extension and consolidation of its rights the other problem of the upper chamber can be solved as well.

30. Our parliament has worked, in fact, as a law-making factory: in the 4-year cycle it has produced 219 new laws, 213 law amendments, and 354 other parliamentary decisions between May 1990 and Apr. 1994. The urgency of the situation, however, has brought about many failures as well (some laws had to be amended several times). There is a need now to switch from quantitative over-production to quality production.

31. The Hungarian Centre for Democracy Studies has edited a book on the Europeanization of the ECE political systems, particularly the parliaments, written mostly by local experts. This volume has been a result of regional co-operation, and in early 1994 a new Europeanization project was begun on the relationship between parliaments and the organized interests. See A. Ágh (ed.), *The Emergence of Democratic Parliaments in East Central Europe: The First Steps* (Budapest: Hungarian Centre of Democracy Studies, 1994).

PART VI
THE EUROPEAN COMMUNITY

14

On the Evolution of a European State: Reflections on the Conditions of and the Prospects for a European Constitution

GUNNAR FOLKE SCHUPPERT

1. THE DYNAMICS OF EUROPEAN CONSTITUTIONAL DEVELOPMENT

The evolution of a European state and the development of a constitution is a dynamic process. The European Community (EC) is always on its way to somewhere, although the direction it takes can vary and there may be advances and regression. The path for European integration was laid out in the preamble of the Treaty of Rome, which declared that the creation of a European Community was 'determined to lay the foundation of an ever closer union among the peoples of Europe'.[1] The Single European Act of 28 February 1986 reaffirmed this basic law of development in its preamble, and also, explicitly, in Article 1, where it states that 'the European Communities and the European Political Co-operation pursue the goal to contribute collectively to the concrete steps towards a European Union'.[2]

As the EC is constantly developing, any description of it can only serve as a snapshot. It is unclear where the route will finally lead, and whether the law of development has to be understood as a linear-progressive advance towards a European Union. Swings of the pendulum and regression cannot be ruled out, and it is not easy to judge whether a political arrangement like the EC can remain on the verge of becoming a federal state without developing in one or the other direction. This problem has best been expressed in the title of Rüdiger Voigt's contribution towards the future form of the European state order: 'Departure from the Nation-State: Return to the Nation-State'.[3]

1.1. Europe as a Dynamic System

Given that the question whether the EC is a 'pre-federal' or a 'quasi-federal' structure is, ultimately, a matter of terminology, it will not be discussed here.[4] Yet structural similarities with the organizational principles of federalism are undeniable. According to Renate Mayntz, federalism is defined as a state structure with multiple levels of decision-making, which are interdependent and often take decisions at the same time.[5] The problem common to both, the federal nation-state as well as the EC, lies in the allocation and balancing of the different levels of decision-making in order to create and maintain what might be termed a working multiplicity of levels.[6] If federalism means a distribution of powers, then the EC shares the basic problem of distinguishing between those decisions which are necessary for the furtherance of the Community's goal of integration and those powers which should remain within the competence of its member states.[7]

Therefore, if the EC shares the structural problem of the federal principles of organization—the balancing of different levels of decision-making—then it is of necessity a dynamic system. New research into federalism shows that the federal state order can only be properly understood as a dynamic system,[8] and that distinctions can and have to be drawn between different stages and phases of development of the federal system.[9] Significantly, these stages have found their reflection in the changes of the financial constitution.[10] It is not surprising, therefore, that co-operative federalism originated in Germany with the financial reform introduced by the 'Report on the Financial Reform in the federal Republic of Germany' as follows:[11]

The federal state structure is subject to changes in political, economic, and social conditions, and it cannot therefore be constitutionally fixed for the foreseeable future. . . . Hence, a form of federalism has to be developed which allows for a balanced and flexible system of order and co-operation between the federal government and the Länder. The federalism of today can therefore only be a co-operative federalism.

If its essentially federal structure requires Europe to be a dynamic system, then this is even more true because of its organizational purpose, and the resulting peculiarities of its constitution.

1.2. Programmed Constitutional Change: The European Constitution Geared towards Change

It is nowadays commonly agreed that the EC possesses something similar to a constitution. This consists of so-called primary Community law, as defined by the Treaties of Rome and subsequent alterations and additions.[12] It is furthermore accepted that, in contrast to constitutions of nation-states, the European Constitution contains singular peculiarities.[13] While constitutions of nation-states are said to balance elements of stability with dynamism, of rigidity with flexibility,[14] that of the EC is said to be necessarily dynamic and formulated with the expectation of change, since the organizational purpose of the Community consists in the progressive integration of Europe, which in turn implies changes in the Constitution. This view is correct. Not only is the European Constitution meant—like other constitutions[15]—to allow for political and social change to proceed smoothly, but it also has to mirror the progressive stages of integration: the organizational purpose of the Community implies the alteration of the Constitution in the form of programmed constitutional change.

If these reflections on Europe and on its Constitution as a dynamic system are correct, it should prove possible to distinguish certain phases of development in the process of European integration. An outline of these phases will now be given.

2. STAGES OF DEVELOPMENT OF EUROPEAN INTEGRATION

If the task is not only to describe the stages of development of European integration chronologically but also to explain and analyse them, one has to indicate the criteria used to recognize and define such stages.[16] Two criteria seem particularly relevant: first, stages of integration mirror those of the development of the European Constitution, as has been argued above. Secondly—and so far this is a working hypothesis only—the stages of development of integration are reflected in the definition of roles and identities of the different institutions of the EC.

2.1. Stages of Development of European Integration as Reflected in Changes of the European Constitution

In identifying the various stages in the development of the European Constitution, one may distinguish the phases discussed below, which were themselves the product of changing political attitudes towards European integration.

2.1.1. Phase I: Departure from the Nation-State: The Formative Years.

This first phase of European integration was marked by the ideal of superseding the nation-state after the Second World War. This ideal was supported by Winston Churchill in his famous Zürich speech of 1946. The underlying idea of the coming together of France and Germany as the nucleus of a United Europe was taken up by the so-called Schuman Plan, which envisaged pooling German and French coal and steel industries within a European community. The recipe for integration was made obvious here. The fusion of economic interests was meant to initiate a process of increasing sectoral integration, the economic compulsion and inner logic of which was to lead to spill-over effects, which in turn were to make a transformation from economic to political integration inevitable. The three Communities (ECSC, Euratom, and EEC) all subscribed to this ideal, which provided the basis for the integration efforts of the long-serving first President of the Commission, Hallstein.

2.1.2. Phase II: The Constitutional Crisis of the Community and the Luxembourg Compromise of 29 January 1966.

Since the EC is a dynamic political structure with different levels of decision-making, in which swings of the pendulum are predetermined, it should not be surprising that Hallstein's integration efforts should have given rise to counterforces, personified by the French President de Gaulle and his ideal of a Europe of nation-states.[17]

The declared French doctrine of the inalienable final responsibility of the member states came into conflict with those regulations of the Treaty which allowed for majority decisions to be taken in the area of agriculture from 1966 onwards (compare Article 43, section 2, subsection 3 with Article 8 of the EEC Treaty). France subsequently blocked the work of the Council through the so-called 'empty-chair policy'. Oppermann commented on this:[18]

Soon it became obvious that in reality it was a rejection in principle of majority decisions to be taken by the Council. Instead, it favoured the continuation of the principle of unanimity as well as the restriction of the Commission's room for independent political manœuvre. The conflict had fully emerged between the principles of European policy of a continuing process of pre-federal integration, on the one hand, and of the classic model of international co-operation under the conditions of full sovereignty on the other.

The French view largely prevailed in the Luxembourg compromise reached by the EEC's foreign ministers on 29 January 1966. This remains the most striking example of an 'agreement to disagree'.[19] Even though the Luxembourg compromise was not legally binding,[20] when put into practice it led to majority decisions being taken only when all member states agreed, or when they signalled that no 'vital interests' were at stake. The Luxembourg compromise[21] is noteworthy from two points of view. First, it is a perfect example of the importance of rules of decision-making in the political process,[22] and, above all, of the results which can be expected from a political process which is organized in a particular form. In his article on *Politikverflechtung*, Fritz W. Scharpf demonstrated the importance of the unanimity rule, particularly in the case of European agricultural policy.[23] He convincingly established that it systematically favours policy outcomes below the optimum. His definition of *Politikverflechtung* is even more explicit: he describes it as 'a decision-making structure which links two or more levels, and whose institutional logic systematically produces inefficient or unsuitable decisions'. I have added that 'if we take the butter-mountain as a symbol for unsuitable European agricultural policy, we can—with some exaggeration, but nevertheless relevantly— describe the butter-mountain as the result of the EC's institutional logic'.[24]

However, decision rules not only set the course for the results of political decision-making processes. They also inform us whether an organization like the EC, with the rule of unanimity, is rooted in classical international law or whether, by deviating from this 'institutionalized form of the consensual principle of international law',[25] the Community is on its way to a stage of integration which is qualitatively different. It is only against this background that the real meaning of the Luxembourg compromise becomes evident, and on which Walter Meng has commented:[26]

The agreement is an 'emergency break' on the road to an intensification of the degree of integration through procedural regulations. And it is exactly because it is not an act of any normative power that the agreement illustrates particularly well the conditions of this intensification: the value of co-operation within the organization must be greater to each individual member than the insistence on its own position concerning a particular problem. Whenever the relative values are reversed, then there is no need for a normative *actus contrarius* to turn back the wheel of this evolution through norms of procedure.

2.1.3. Phase III: The Introduction of European Political Co-operation.

The standstill in the process of European integration was overcome at the end of 1969 at the summit meeting of EC heads of governments in The Hague, after the resignation of de Gaulle. At this summit, on the occasion of the end of the twelve-year contractual transition period of the EC (see Article 8 of the EEC Treaty), it was agreed to further the harmonization of foreign policies of the member states by means of a political consultation and co-operation procedure. This was based on the realization that the process of economic integration 'demanded a minimum of conformity in foreign policy, since the common trade policy required a unified stance to be taken towards third countries',[27] illustrated particularly well by the example of the imposition of embargo measures.

This was the beginning of the so-called European Political Co-operation (EPC), whose organizational framework was first laid down in the Davignon report of 1970. In essence, it was an intergovernmental procedure of regular information and consultation in the area of foreign policy. In 1974, and largely on the initiative of Giscard d'Estaing, the Paris summit conference referred this task to a 'European Council' made up of heads of state and governments, the President of the Commission, and the foreign ministers of the member states, all of whom were to meet three times a year. This choice of organizational structure stresses the inter-governmental character[28] of policy co-ordination and demonstrates an essential, future-orientated extension of EC activities.[29] It did not, however, prove a further stage in the degree of integration. Rather the contrary, as will soon become clear.

2.1.4. Phase IV: The Introduction of Direct Elections to the European Parliament.

Until 1979 the European Parliament was composed of delegates from national parliaments. Thereafter, a decision by EC member states to invoke Article 138, section 3, which provided for direct elections, initiated—according to Oppermann[30]—'an institutional reform which was of great importance for European policy'. This importance was derived not from increased competences for the Parliament—it continued to have largely consultative competences—but from the immediate democratic legitimacy of its members. It lent weight to the decisions taken by the Parliament, and, furthermore, changed its role within the institutional structure of the EC.

2.1.5. Phase V: The Single European Act.

The Single European Act (SEA),[31] which came into effect on 1 July 1987, represents the most comprehensive revision of the Treaty of Rome to date,[32] of particular importance in five areas:[33]

> The SEA strengthens the position of the Commission within the institutional system by extending to it the right to delegate.
>
> It strengthens the European Parliament through the introduction of the co-operation procedure.
>
> It brings further areas of regulation (research, technology, the environment) into the competence of the Community.
>
> It provides EPC with a treaty basis.
>
> It lays down the concept of the single market.

The question of how far the SEA has changed the relations between the institutions of the EC will have to be discussed further below. At this stage, a brief outline of the treaty basis of the EPC and of the concept of the single market will suffice.

With the SEA, the EPC has been given a new legal basis and has been strengthened in its organization. The heads of governments in the European Council (who meet at least three times a year), and the foreign ministers in the Council (who meet at least four times a year), are the government bodies of the EPC. The organizational substructure has been described by Oppermann as follows:

Preparation is done by the political committee of the heads of political departments of the foreign ministries. Secretarial duties are performed by the 'group of European correspondents', which comprises experts on Europe from the foreign ministries. According to Art. 30, Sec. 9g SEA, a secretariat for the EPC has been set up in Brussels, which is responsible for preparation and administration. By formally placing the Secretariat under the control of the EC presidency, and by the participation of the Commission and the Parliament in EPC (Art. 30, Lit. 4 SEA), a strong EPC/EC link is envisaged.[34]

Two features are therefore noteworthy: the dominant role of the European Council as an institution of policy co-ordination, and the declared duality of the approach to European integration, apparent in the continuation of the three Communities with the addition of EPC.

The concept of the single market was embodied in the EEC Treaty through Article 13, SEA. According to that, the single market consists of a market free of internal borders, which ensures the free movement of goods, services, labour, and capital. The SEA also created 'the instruments for an easier realization of the concept. These include extensions in the possibility for majority voting (especially Art. 100a, EEC), the qualified participation of the European Parliament in the formulation of laws regarding questions of the single market (Art. 149, Sect. 2, EEC Treaty) and the broadening or clarification of Community competences (especially on environmental policy, Art. 130r, EEC Treaty).'[35]

2.1.6. *Phase VI: The Introduction of European Union.* The Maastricht Treaty on European Union of 7 February 1992 represents the latest move forward in European integration.[36] This is not the right place to discuss and evaluate the Maastricht Treaty in detail.[37] For our purposes of identifying phases of development, the question of immediate interest here is whether Maastricht represents a qualitative advance—as the term European Union appears to promise—towards a federal state. The answer has to be 'no'. Maastricht is not a *coup d'état*[38] and the qualitative advance is restricted to specific areas:

By introducing a common currency, the Maastricht Treaty creates a new quality in the economic development of Europe. The same can hardly be said for the political union. The treaty which was eventually negotiated does not represent a qualitative advance in the history of European Integration. Far from being a draft constitution, Maastricht rather limits itself—according to the approach chosen with the Single European Act—to the development or supplementing of basic structures already in existence. The competences of the Community remain—at least in principle—restricted to and aimed at specific functions, i.e. the creation and functioning of the Single Market and the European Union.[39]

The following points of view support this interpretation.

The Treaty of Union retains the SEA's distribution of the Union on two—albeit uneven—pillars, the European Communities and the EPC, the latter of which continues under a different name. Most regulations concerning the role of the European Council, the European Parliament, and the Commission have been substantially taken from the SEA. The position of the European Parliament remains principally unaltered (in particular there is to be no electoral reform); the hitherto existing regulations concerning hearings and co-operation have been copied and supplemented by a new procedure of co-decision (Article 139b, EEC Treaty). Despite all the innovations[40] resulting from the Treaty—new competences of the Community in the areas of culture, trans-European networks and industry, extension of co-operation even to areas like justice and the interior, introduction of a committee of the regions, of Union citizenship, etc.—the essential point should not be overlooked: the central authority of the European Union remains the European Council, which has to provide the necessary impulses and formulates the political goals. The central authority remains therefore an institution of representatives of member states (its competences are laid down in Article D of the Treaty of Union). The execution of common policies is also the responsibility of an authority representing the member states, the Council of the European Community.

In addition to these institutional regulations, it has to be emphasized that the principles of subsidiarity and of proportionality have been explicitly included in the Treaty. However, as Streinz has rightly pointed out,[41] all this can only 'come into effect if the European Court rethinks the definition of its own present role—which has been useful in the development of integration—and starts to act as a "constitutional court" guarding the principles of the relation between the Communities and the member states as well as the autonomy of regional entities'.

The catch-phrase 'definition of roles' leads us on to a different perspective from which to view the stages of integration.

2.2. Stages of Development of European Integration as Reflected in the Distribution of Roles among the Community's Institutions

Political processes can often be better understood and analysed if they are viewed as processes with different actors, who fulfil certain roles and, in doing so, act according to their own definition of these roles. The effectiveness of this approach, which assumes that organizations and institutions behave according to their own inherent logic (organizational behaviour),[42] has been demonstrated in what has become a classic study by Aaron Widavsky of the budgetary decision-making process, 'The Politics of the Budgetary Process'.[43] If one views the institutional set-up of the EC from this perspective—the European Parliament, the European Court, the Commission, and the Council/European Council—one will first of all easily ascertain that each of these institutions plays a certain role, and that each of them also has its own definition of this role. This fact can be clearly illustrated with the example of the European Court: its task has been to give shape to a Community based on the rule of law, and this has meant seeking to ensure that Community law takes precedence over national law.[44] In addition to this, it formulated general principles of law,[45] especially with regard to 'human rights'.[46] The European Court is commonly thought to have successfully carried out integration through law.[47] Yet there are calls for the European Court to alter the definition of its role to that of a 'constitutional court'.[48]

Additionally, one will find that the relation between the different institutions, especially between Commission, Council, and Parliament, are subject to continuous change, and that the relative weight of a particular institution varies. The thesis advanced here holds that there is more to be learned about the state of the European Community, and in particular the degree of integration, from an analysis of relations between institutions and of their changing relative weights than from an examination of the respective constitutional texts and programmatic rhetoric. In his textbook on European law, Thomas Oppermann has produced abundant material on which such an analysis of relations and changing relative weight can draw, and we can rely on his assessment in this matter.[49] A rough outline of the institutional structure would be as follows. First, there is the Commission, whose 'original' role and thrust as well as its relation to the Council has been described by Oppermann as follows:[50]

The provision of the EEC Treaty linking the Commission as an 'engine, guardian and honest broker of the treaty' (Walter Hallstein) to the final decision of the Council of Ministers, which was democratic at least at the national level, turned out to be politically fruitful from 1958 to 1965. Naturally, this lasted only as long as the Ministerial Council managed to act in line with the Community spirit. Accordingly, in the atmosphere of the early EEC years after 1958, and on the initiative of the Hallstein Commission, the establishment of free movement of goods in the Common Market and of a Common Agricultural Policy was accelerated. Furthermore, the free movement of labour within the EEC was secured, and the Community was enabled to represent a united approach to external relations . . .

Due to its function as the 'engine' of European integration, the Commission has often been labelled the 'genuine' European body.[51] Its purpose is to define the Community interest *vis-à-vis* member states' potentially differing conceptions. Its organization is geared towards this task. According to Article 10, section 2 of the so-called Merger Treaty, which combined the institutions of the three Communities,[52] members of the Commission excercise their functions 'completely independently for the benefit of the Communities', and they are explicitly freed from the member states' authority to issue directives.

Since the Commission aims to realize the interests of the Community, it becomes obvious that its relative weight is of decisive importance not only for the shaping of Community interests but also for the task of integration to overcome selfish nation-state attitudes. A loss of functions and importance would therefore not serve the ideal of European integration. Yet well-informed observers of the process of European integration agree that over time the Commission has lost influence, and that it has been relegated to second-class status *vis-à-vis* the European Council. This development is regarded as the real constitutional change of the EC. Oppermann describes this change, for which the crucial starting date was the Luxembourg compromise, as follows:[53]

For the time being, the establishment of the European Council has put an end to a momentous constitutional change within the EC. The previous 'philosophy of the Treaty', according to which the Commission as the 'engine of the Treaty' was meant to evolve into a European Government, has not been realized. Although the Commission remains essentially an independent body, and is to continue providing the impulses for Community action, the important directives of Community policy are meanwhile being issued by the European Council as the 'driving force' (Giscard d'Estaing). Decisive for the development of the EC will be the relative weights in the new balance between Council and the European Parliament as the primary political bodies of the Community. This constitutional change possibly signals an end to the vision of an ever-closer European federal state in favour of a 'European Union' in the sense of a para-state superstructure, which will of course be of greater intensity than classic international alliances.

If this analysis is correct—and there is every indication that it is—we can return to our initial reflections on Europe as a dynamic system and on federalism as balance. What appears crucial to the point of view of a European constitution is the balance between the institutions in so far as their organization is specific to their respective roles, and in so far as they act according to their own specific definition of these roles. This, in turn, means that it is less important whether the Community will be given new or more competences or whether or not the principle of subsidiarity, which is difficult to put into practice in any case, appears in the Treaty. Instead, emphasis is placed on the institutional arrangement which will make the decisions, and on whether there will be a tendency for the Community interest to prevail over those of the member states or vice versa.

What follows is a brief view of the Council, and its function as the European Council[54] in particular. Its dominant role is described by Oppermann as follows:[55]

The task of the European Council is above all one of a leading and inspiring body of the Community . . . It makes decisions of principle (for example about the implementation of direct elections to the European Parliament 1974/5, about the establishment of the European Exchange Rate Mechanism 1978, and about financial reform 1984) and issues, often in a solemn manner, communiqués to provide a guiding impetus. The communiqués of the European Council represent political directives to be followed in the work of the Commission (also according to Art. 152, EEC Treaty) and of the Council. The European Council can, furthermore, solve conflicts which were not overcome at the lower level (for example in 1976, about the distribution of seats in the European Parliament). In this sense, however, it is in danger of becoming a permanent arbitrator for ministerial councils plagued by indecision.

Reading the above, one might get the impression that the development of European integration has stalled, given the dominance of the Council/European Council which is controlled by member state governments. Or—as Oppermann put it[56]—that 'in addition to improvements of the decision-making process of the Council, there is a need for a genuine "European" counterweight among the EC institutions'. However, calling the European Parliament a democratic 'joker'—as Oppermann does in this context[57]—in my view misses the point. Every institution has its heyday, i.e. conditions under which it can give perfect, or near-perfect, organizational answers to certain problem areas. The heyday of the Commission lay in the formative years of the EC, in the development of economic integration. It appears to be no coincidence that, with the nation-state controlled institutions gaining in strength, there is also a greater intensity of integration as well as a broadening of Community competences over an ever greater number of policy areas. One might even regard this as the paradox of the development of the EC: the higher the intensity of integration and the more areas of policy being included, the more necessary it appears to transfer the leading-role status to an institution in which member states feel directly represented.

The heyday of the European Parliament has not yet arrived. This realization is of crucial importance, since it makes the possibilities of a genuine European development become apparent. That the heyday of the European Parliament has indeed not arrived so far has convincingly been demonstrated by Werner v. Simson,[58] and recently also by Dieter Grimm,[59] whose comments in this context deserve full approval:[60]

The European Parliament cannot transform itself into a real representative of the people without a European nation and without a European political discourse. Therein lies the fundamental difference between European integration in the twentieth century and the foundation of the German Reich in the nineteenth century. Owing to a uniform language and a common culture, a nation had already been formed in Germany, and had campaigned for a nation-state for more than half a century before it was eventually founded in 1871. Therein lies also the difference from the foundation of the United States of America, whose integral parts had never themselves been nation-states with different languages, traditions, and attitudes.

In Europe, in contrast, the Maastricht Treaty has opened the way for a European federal state, without the latter corresponding to a European nation or promising to do so in the near future. There may be a European electorate, but other than on election day itself it does not behave as such. Instead, in forming an opinion and in articulating interests, it will once again be fragmented into national parts. Owing to this, the European democratic deficit has structural causes and cannot therefore be solved in principle through institutional reform. The achievements of the democratic constitutional state can so far only be preserved in their entirety at the national level.

If these reflections are correct, a solution for further development of integration may be found neither in the resurrection of the Commission, nor in the 'joker' of the European Parliament, but only in developing existing institutional instruments in new ways. Two approaches may be suggested.

The first can be termed interconnection of existing institutions, and has already been pursued to some extent. Fig. 14.1 is self-explanatory.[61]

The second approach consists in accepting the Council as the engine of further integration, and altering its mode of decision-making, as has tentatively been suggested by the Union Treaty. Oppermann's comments point to the right directions:[62]

In the reality of the Community, the Council with its permanent members and its General Secretariat has, over time, evolved into a complex leading institution of the EC, which is, however, inscrutable given the frequency and varying compositions of its meetings. Complaints about the cumbersome decision-making process are frequent, but without the Council nothing can get done within the Community. Far beyond being merely a classic international conference, the Council has created an intimacy of daily contact and co-operation between heads of governments and ministers of foreign affairs, economics, finance, agriculture, employment, transport,

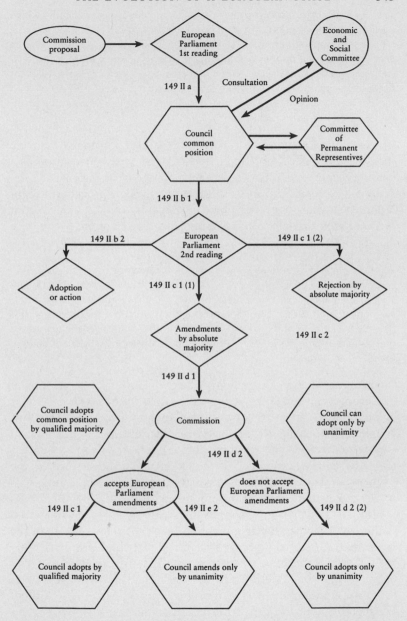

Fig. 14.1. Co-operation procedure

science, and justice as well as between the accompanying officials, which itself represents an important part of governmental Europe in the sense of a para-state superstructure. European policy in the Council is furthermore characterized by a multitude of changing, or sometimes more solid, constellations and coalitions between member states (for example the frequent Franco-German coalitions, or the special accord between the Benelux or the Mediterranean countries). The Council is therefore a Community institution, even in the real sense of the term.

If it is currently the heyday of the Council, or European Council, then there is a need, not for the creation of a new institution as a counterweight, but for a method which Meng has accurately described as 'intensification of integration through procedural regulations',[63] which refers to the supersession of the principle of unanimity by that of majority. It is instructive to quote Meng once again:[64]

All these phenomena indicate that the legal framework of international co-operation is in a phase of evolution, which manifests itself essentially in a shift in the balance between particular and common interests within international organizations. The measure for the particular conditions of this balance is hereby found in procedural regulations which set the norms for the formation of views in the making of those decisions which are binding for member states.

This completes our argument. The problem of the development of European integration consists in the balance between particular and communal interests. It has been shown that this is essentially a problem of the balance between the institutions[65] of the EC, in particular between the Council, the Commission, and the Parliament. Given the dominance of the Council/European Council, the problem shifts to the balance through procedural regulations. This marks the current stage of development.

However, this stage presupposes that the value of co-operation within the organization is greater for each member state than the insistence on its own position towards a particular problem. Only then is there a chance of success for the principle of majority decision-making. It should not be overlooked, however, that majority decision-making may find its limits in the further extension of EC membership. Majority rule becomes more difficult for states such as Great Britain, France, and the Federal Republic of Germany to accept, the more numerous and heterogeneous the group of member states becomes, since voting coalitions will no longer be 'calculable'. However, this would be yet another new phase of European development.

3. ATTEMPTS TO UNDERSTAND THE EVOLUTION OF A EUROPEAN STATE

It is not an easy task to understand the evolution of a European state, especially if one has to rely on an inherited terminology. One comes to realize that on the one hand fixed terms such as federation, federal state, unified state, or even state and non-state help in grasping organizational realities, but on the other hand they also render the completion of this task nearly impossible.

3.1. On the Inadequacy of the Inherited Terminology

The fundamental problem appears to be that, while the evolution of a European state is a dynamic process—as has been argued extensively above—the terminology of constitutional law is used to describe static conditions. This is particularly obvious in the case of the term 'state': from the legal point of view, an organizationally solid structure is either a state or it is not. If it is, then it possesses executive power, and the question of democratic legitimacy arises instantly and forcefully.[66] If it is not a state, because one or more of the classic criteria are missing (executive power, state territory, or a nation) the line of argument will be entirely different and much less dependent on the terminology of constitutional law than on that of political science, for example on the term 'private government'.[67] What is missing is a variable and graduated terminology, which is able to grasp transitions and gradual differences.

If this is the problem, an obvious solution may be to develop such a graduated terminology, which can grasp the intermediate stages and thereby also the borderline organizations. There are numerous examples of this in the area of administrative organization, in which the question arises of whether a particular organization—especially in the so-called 'third sector'[68]—is already, or is still, part of public administration. There is a large body of literature on 'para-governmental'[69] and 'quasi-governmental'[70] organizations as well as in the area of finance, on 'parafiski'[71] and 'intermediate financial authorities'.[72] However, these examples of 'quasi-' or 'para-' terminology already illustrate their limited explanatory power. Such terminologies are useful in order to describe and analyse intermediate stages of administrative or political science.[73] However, they can only fail as far as definite classification into categories is concerned, which is required of a national system of law. Given the strict distinction between actions of private and public law made in the German legal system, and given the problems of the course of law, of liability, and of jurisdiction which are associated therewith, the question whether a structure is or is not part of public administration cannot be left open.[74]

At the same time, a second fundamental problem of terminology for the understanding of the evolution of a European state has become apparent. It consists in the channelling and narrowing effect of a terminology which is grounded in the order of law of nation-states, and which may therefore be unsuitable for grasping the particularity of a supra-national organization. Herein, in my view, lies the principal precondition for understanding the evolution of a European state: it is of decisive importance whether one is looking at the EC from the point of view of national constitutional law, consequently missing the customary division of powers and a catalogue of human rights, only to proceed to complain about the much-quoted democratic deficit.[75] Or, indeed, whether one is searching for the conditions necessary for the constitution of a supra-national community to function. How it should not be viewed, and how a proper view of the problem can be distorted intentionally, has been demonstrated by the argument advanced by a *Spiegel* editorial about the future development of Europe:[76]

no European state which is constituted like the EC could become a member of the latter. Until today, EC politicians of all parties describe this state of affairs with the euphemism 'democratic deficit' as if it was a problem for constitutional purists.

Yet it is not about constitutional purism, and the EC cannot be viewed as an ideal mirror-image of national constitutional structures. The real nature of the problem has been explicitly stated by Frowein and Badura. Frowein observes:[77]

The use of the models and standards derived from the nation-state mis-judges the particular nature of European unification, which is not, like existing federal states, the consequence of historical processes, hegemonic structures, or outside pressures, but which has to emerge from a voluntary unification of independent states.

Badura comments:[78]

These arguments rightly warn that concepts and institutions of national constitutional law should not be transferred to non-state federations and communities, unless the existence of the political preconditions necessary for the working and success of democratic institutions is assured.

Only by adopting this approach, which frees itself from the nation-state perspective and is, furthermore, sceptical about the inherited terminology, will it be possible not merely to discern institutional pathologies and deficits in the organizational and constitutional structure of the EC, but to examine institutional competence,[79] which asks what the EC may be able to achieve at a given stage of integration. This is the only way to trace the line of European development and evolution. Badura regards it as 'the very achievement of the European Communities not to follow the abstract schemes of "federation" or "federal state" '.[80] He succeeds in grasping the distinct constitutional structure of the European Community as the organizational representation of its political maturation. The following passage deserves to be quoted in full:[81]

The Communities are characterized by the dependency of the Community executive on nation-states, ensured by the establishment, the composition, and the final decision-making power of the Council. It represents the political maturation of the European Communities. This organizational centre of the Communities' constitution yields the democratic legitimacy which originates in national governments due to their parliamentary accountability. The integrational form of democracy is naturally, and necessarily, governmental. However, this distinctive appearance of democracy is only the reverse phenomenon of the distinctive federative character of the European Communities. A substantial participation of the European Parliament in the Community's executive, or even its re-organization as a parliamentary legislature, would deprive the European sovereignty of its existing vital roots, and would require a new federal Community structure. 'Parliamentarization' of the European Communities thereby encounters its federative limits, even ignoring the question whether it is politically feasible to anticipate a nation of a

European federal state solely with the help of direct elections to the European Parliament.

3.2. On the Distinctiveness of the Process of Evolution of a European State

Following these reflections, we can draw the preliminary conclusion that the process of evolution of a European state can be properly grasped neither by contrasting the concepts of federation and federal state nor by applying the principles of national constitutional law. Instead, it has to be understood as an evolutionary process of a non-state association of states, which follows its own logic of development, thereby producing peculiar organizational and constitutional structures which are unique to the stage of integration of the day. If this basic thesis is correct, three central inferences can be drawn.

3.2.1. The EC as a 'Peculiar Type of Community in the Process of Continuing Integration'.
This description has been used by the Federal Constitutional Court to characterize the EC by emphasizing the peculiarity of this non-state association of states.[82] This correct and also widely held conviction is a direct invitation—and for jurists a convenient escape from difficult problems of qualification[83]—to view the EC as an 'intensive association of states *sui generis*'[84] with a distinctive constitutional order *sui generis* as a consequence.[85] This point of view tries to find a term for the specific accumulation and mixture of competences in the hands of the Community, and to emphasize the novelty of such a non-state association of states. Oppermann's comments are representative when he states that 'the European Community increasingly appears as a novel political superstructure which links its members with what is often more than a confederation, yet without completing the qualitative "leap" towards a comprehensive and superior European state structure and sovereignty'.[86]

The *sui generis* argument is, however, somewhat unsatisfactory, since the *sui generis* structure suddenly appears out of nowhere, instead of being understood as the product or a stage of a development process of the multitude of forms of international state associations. The most suitable characterization of the EC, in my view, is that of Rudolf Streinz,[87] which is based on the pioneering work of Meng.[88] Herein, the qualitative distinctiveness of the EC and its origin in international law are successfully combined:

Therefore, the European Communities have to be viewed as a developmental stage of the law of international organizations within the context of international law (see also Meng), albeit of a new quality. This is due to the special features distinguishing the European Communities which, though already found in other international organizations between states, have not hitherto existed in such cumulation, relative width, with such an inherent dynamic of integration, and the resulting, or at least possible, depth of integration. These include the separate lawmaking powers, the superiority of secondary, and partly also primary, Community law, the establishment of independent bodies and the possibility of majority decisions, all of which are features which establish and indicate the 'supranationality' of the Communities. The classification of Community law as international law is made possible by the dynamism this constitutional order has shown in other areas, and it also corresponds to the conceptions of law of member states, which is clearly apparent in the constitutional regulations with which some of these have created the legal basis for the ratification of primary Community law.

3.2.2. On the Osmotic Relation between Nation-State and European Community.

As already mentioned above, Rüdiger Voigt has attempted to conceptualize the dynamic of European development by presenting the two alternatives of development, 'departure from the nation-state' and 'return to the nation state'.[89] This idea of the pendulum is, however, of no great help, since the two extremes on the axis of development, the nation-state on the one hand and the federal state on the other, are themselves closed systems and cannot therefore account for the process of reciprocal influence of member states and the EC. This seems to me to be the decisive point, and I suggest that we characterize this process of reciprocal influence as *osmosis*.

Such an osmotic relationship is particularly obvious in the relation between national constitutional orders and that of the EC, which Georg Ress accurately described as follows:[90]

There has been talk about the linking of the Community to universal principles of law, and the question has been raised whether the member states too have to be bound by the EC's principles of law. This *reciprocity* becomes apparent when these EC principles are brought to bear on the realization of EC law and its application within the jurisdiction of a member state. These principles assert themselves in the different member states. For example, this process can be observed in the case of the universal legal principle of the proportionality of means, which is spreading like a fungus even in all those states which previously have hardly known of its existence. It is finding acceptance in the member states via the EC. *It is like osmotic reciprocal influence*, and not just a one-sided process of legal binding.

If this view is correct, and if reciprocal influence is the key to understanding the process of European development, it cannot be a case of either waiting for the EC to take the step of becoming a federal state or, alternatively, of anxiously observing the process of erosion of the nation-state in order not to miss the moment which finally marks the loss of sovereignty. Instead, one has to observe simultaneously on the one hand the intensification of integration of the Community and the corresponding step towards a new stage of development as an international organization and on the other hand the complementary transformation of the nation-state during the process of its assimilation in an international organization of high intensity.

3.2.3. On the Political Maturation of the European Community. It should now be sufficiently obvious that the EC is a distinctive type of community in the process of continuing integration, which can only be understood from a point of view and with a terminology which accounts for the peculiarity and the 'process-nature' of the EC. It is now necessary to understand the political maturation of the EC in order to discuss options of future development, and to reflect on institutional change as an organizational and constitutional phenomenon of the continuing process of integration. Only thus can the situation be avoided in which concepts lag behind actual developments. Hans Meyer has recently called for strategic planning to go further:[91]

It seems to me equally evident that now, after we have discovered the economy as a decisive instrument of political change and after we have brought about German reunification initially by means of the economy and the currency, the same way will be chosen in Europe. If, however, the bus of economic integration in Europe is about to leave, then we will be the last to catch it with our democratic structures and our human rights. I wonder whether the *strategic planning* should not rather be aimed at clarifying these important conditions for a stable economic system, before we lose our breath trying to catch the bus of economic integration.

If these reflections are correct, it is necessary to clarify two further points. What are the decisive axes of development, and what are the driving forces behind the process of integration? And in what way can such a development process be institutionally, and thereby also constitutionally, accompanied and secured? This, and not the drafting of an ideal European constitution, is the real task at hand. However, before these considerations are examined more closely, there will be a brief description of those options for development of the integration process.

4. IMPRACTICAL OPTIONS FOR DEVELOPMENT OF EUROPEAN INTEGRATION

In order to follow up the political maturation of European integration, it will be helpful to consider options of development which, on closer inspection, appear impractical. Two models will be considered here.

4.1. The Model of Specific Functional Communities for Different Sectors

4.1.1. The Basic Model of Functional Integration.
Hans Peter Ipsen has highlighted the characteristic of the EC as 'associations of functional integration' in his pioneering book on EC law.[92] In Ipsen's view, an association is the appropriate organizational structure for what he calls 'functional integration'. This functional integration is one which is specific to different sectors for which associations are indeed sufficient means.[93]

It is only meant to elucidate that its [the EC's] tasks are limited to practically orientated economic and social policies; that the direction of its purpose is one of sectoral functionalism. Herein, it is different from the nature of a state as a comprehensive intellectual and social reality with potentially unlimited competences of territorial and personal sovereignty. For what is characteristic of a practical association is the non-totality of its sphere of influence; its purpose being limited to specific practical problems which have been excluded from the competences of its founders, and for the realization of which the association requires neither territorial nor personal sovereignty.

It is clear that the EC has long since transcended the state of an association whose purpose of integration is limited to economic and social policy.[94] Its political finality has led to the incorporation of ever more areas of integration and co-operation, and it is on its way to a totality of sphere of influence, which illustrates its evolution from association to state. What is of concern here, however, is the original principle constructing *specific functional integration of different sectors*, with its expected and hoped-for spill-over effects.

4.1.2. The Refinement of the Basic Model by Schmitter and Wehner.

Assuming the basic model of specific functional integration of different sectors, it is not only a possible but an obvious task to distinguish different policy areas of different intensities of integration. While, for example, the area of economic policy is well suited to integration, since markets are not confined to nation-state territories, the integration of social policy is far more difficult, given the differing views on the necessary tightness of the social net. The areas of foreign and security policy, owing to the sensitive question of sovereignty, as well as that of educational policy, owing to the sensitive question of national identity, are, indeed, near-inconceivable as objects of integration. In other words, the present and the anticipated intensity of integration differs widely between specific sectors or policy areas. While the area of economic policy is already almost of a federal nature, in the area of foreign and security policy there are at the most signs of intergovernmental co-operation.

This interpretation has been taken up by Philippe C. Schmitter, who suggests the use of differentiating terminology for the labelling of different policy areas with different intensities of integration, by means of which the peculiarity and degree of co-operation and integration can be expressed.[95] This analytical framework has been applied by Schmitter to certain developments (enlargement) and policy areas (political co-operation, security policy) of the EC in order to examine which of these areas has a tendency to which of the different types of federative co-operation. Two examples will serve to illustrate this.

As far as political co-operation is concerned, the future development and the corresponding form of co-operation seems uncertain:[96]

If and when large-scale politicization does occur, its impact may not be what the neo-functionalists anticipated. Instead of providing the critical impetus for a definitive transfer of sovereignty to a supra-national state, it could power a nationalist reaction to it, leading to a confederation, or even sub-national or sectoral demands for something approximating a condominium or a consortium.

With regard to security, in contrast, there is a lot of evidence for the development of an integrated European army:[97]

Now that European security can no longer be taken for granted, i.e. now that new threats are surfacing that cannot be contained by existing NATO or bilateral commitments, only the emergence of something approaching a supra-national state will be able to accomplish the task. Even if a 'pluralistic security community' is firmly established among EC/EU members, it does not extend beyond their borders.

While Schmitter uses the types of federation he presents merely as instruments of analysis and predictions of future development, Burkhard Wehner proposes the more radical idea of integration communities which are specific to certain areas and functions: he suggests drawing *new state borders for new types of state*, thereby eventually superseding the nation-state.[98] Wehner's system of independent branch states is set out in Fig. 14.2.[99] A brief glance will reveal the consequences of the model for functional integration. If it is taken to the extreme in specific sectors, it would break up the existing nation-states as the vehicle for administration, solidarity, and cultural identity, and would thereby come into conflict with the central political maturation of European integration, namely the absolute necessity for member states to be tied together as nation-states.

4.2. The Model of Several Regionally Specific Integration Communities

A different model of development, though one born out of necessity, consists in the departure from the principle of uniform intensity of integration for all member states of the EC, and allows either for

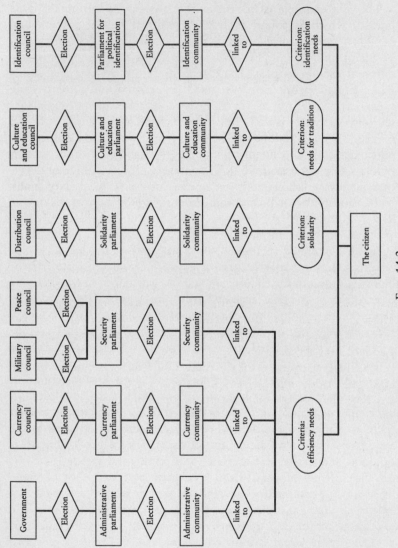

Fig. 14.2

the creation of sub-communities within the EC or for special conditions to apply for certain member states. There are examples for both these developments.

The first example is known as the 'two-speed Europe'.[100] This phrase, which is found mainly in political debate rather than being an official ideal of integration, implies that certain targets of integration of the EC will be reached at different times by different member states. There will, therefore, be member states which already work closely together in certain policy areas while others, which do not as yet fulfil the conditions for participation, will have to wait or will choose to do so. One example is found in the currency union which was agreed upon in Maastricht: participation is dependent on whether the candidate fulfils certain preconditions of economic stability during the third stage of development of the union, which is anticipated for 1999.[101] Not many member states are expected to fulfil these conditions on this target date.

While in this example the functional conditions of a working currency dictate programmed disparity, and while the latter appears surmountable by efforts of economic policy on the part of member states, in the following example a disparity in the intensity of integration is being accepted from the outset. The example is Denmark. After the Danish referendum had failed to produce a majority in favour of the Treaty of Maastricht, a typical EC compromise has been offered, granting Denmark special concessions in order finally to obtain the consent of the electorate in a second referendum. On closer inspection, this amounts to differentiation between member states according to their will to integrate or, alternatively, according to their attitude towards sovereignty. That there are differences in the will to integrate and in particular in the attitude towards sovereignty among the member states of the EC is obvious, can easily be explained historically and psychologically, and is perfectly 'normal' from a realistic political point of view. Thomas Oppermann appears to have been correct in referring to a 'silent' or 'factual' constitutional change on the occasion of the extension of the EC to states with such a high preference for sovereignty as Great Britain and Denmark.[102] Yet there are two processes of a different quality: either to accept that the decision-making process of the EC is influenced by a disparity in the will to integration among member states or, alternatively, to acknowledge this disparity through changes in primary Community law—which amounts to a constitutional recognition.

Both examples of development discussed above are unsettling. We have established that the basic structure of the EC is a federal one. The disparity of member states cannot be reconciled with this basic federal structure, for one of the fundamental principles of a federal state order is federal equality,[103] which refers to at least legal, if not to a certain extent actual, equality of the constituent parts of the federation. That federal equality is indeed a vital ingredient of a federal state order has recently been reaffirmed by the process of German reunification—see 'Neue Ungleichheit'[104]—and by the conflict about the inclusion of the new *Länder* in the system of the equalization of financial burdens.[105]

5. PROSPECTS FOR THE DEVELOPMENT OF EUROPEAN INTEGRATION AND THE EUROPEAN CONSTITUTION

5.1. On the Relation between the Development of Integration and of the Constitution

One possibility is for the development of a constitution to precede the development of integration; it can provide the driving force and the legal framework in the hope that a European constitution modelled on nation-state standards will facilitate the qualitative step towards a kind of federal structure in the evolution of a European state. Alternatively, the development of a constitution may be understood as mirroring the process of integration, securing it and reinforcing it; this would amount to a process of incremental development of the constitution, thereby abandoning the idea of a programmatic design.

Based on the first of these two points of view are the comprehensive recommendations for reform by the European Parliament which envisage the establishment of a European political union.[106] The same is true of the draft programme of the German group of the Bertelsmann foundation, entitled 'Wie Europa verfasst sein soll'.[107] The essence of both these sets of suggestions has been summarized by Günther F. Schäfer:[108]

The European Parliament becomes the central law-making body, given legitimacy through direct elections by European citizens. All other institutions (except for the Council of Union) derive their democratic legitimacy from its parliamentary control.

The Council of Ministers becomes the Council of Union, which represents the federative element. It is composed of representatives of member states and alongside the Parliament it has an equally important role in the making of law. This change puts an end to the dominance of the Council of Ministers as a lawmaking body, and it creates a two-chamber legislature in which the Parliament represents the popular component while the Council of Union, as the upper house, represents the member states.

The Commission becomes the Government of the Community. Its President, nominated by the European Council and elected by the European Parliament, becomes the head of government of the Community. Together with the other commissioners, he forms the cabinet of the government, which is directly responsible to Parliament. Each commissioner is responsible for a ministry, for which he is no longer nominated by member states but is appointed by the President, who together with the commissioners forms the government.

The European Council, composed of heads of government or of state of the member states, takes on the role of a collective presidency which formulates the general directives and goals of Community policy. It is then up to the Commission to translate these goals into a legislative programme, which is then put to the vote in the Council of Union and the European Parliament.

It has rightly been pointed out that the realization of these recommendations would mark a radical break with present procedure, as well as a radical change in the constitution of the Community.[109] This is not all. The recommendations are based on a misunderstanding of the purpose and function of constitutional development in international and supranational communities, which are still—at least as far as institutional development is concerned—dependent on the consent of member states. Herein lies its difference from the type of constitution of a nation-state. The European constitution is not only—to use Ipsen's description—a constitution of change, it is also necessarily a *mirror-image constitution*, reflecting the respective degree of integration and the will to integrate of the member states. In this sense, one can fully endorse Schäfer's view that the process of constitutional development can be regarded as one of successive adaptation:[110]

As attractive as it may seem intellectually to draft perfect blueprints and ideal systems of government for the Community, their realization cannot be expected in the foreseeable future. The present design of the European Community is the result of an integration process of almost fifty years of successes, failures, and disappointments. This process will continue. In the same measure as political and economic integration will develop, there will be institutional adaptation and successive revision of the treaties. It is highly unlikely that a revision of the Treaties—except perhaps for the formulation of grand goals—will precede the actual stage of integration.

This function of acting as a mirror-image is clearly prominent; it should not, however, lead to the misunderstanding that the constitution of a supranational community like the EC is necessarily lagging behind and is therefore merely a constitution of adaptation. I think that the constitution of the EC should have three functions:

It has to reflect the achieved stage of integration of the Community, and the will to integrate of the member states. In this sense there is a congruity or parallelism of integrational and constitutional development. This can be termed the *mirror-image function* of the European constitution.

On the other hand, it has to secure the achieved stage of integration by providing institutions and procedures which are well suited to organizing the integration process on a certain level and with a certain intensity. Integration has to be put into effect and organized by the constitution. In this sense we can talk of the *organizational function* of the constitution.

Additionally, it has to keep the options of the integration process open for the future. This can be done not only by including programmatic definitions of goals in the constitutional text but also, for example, by anticipating a change of decision-making procedures in stages such as the smooth transition from unanimity to majority rule. This can be termed the *function of prolongation* of the constitution.

If these considerations are correct, we will thereby obtain, automatically as it were, the criteria which a European constitution has to fulfil at a given stage of integration of the Community. Deficits which so far have been criticizable only from the point of view of democratic theory can now be identified in their concrete form; in particular, it can now be asked whether the design, the order, and the functions of the institutions of the Community are in accordance with its development. However, the development of the constitution and the discussion of constitutional policy is thus always dependent on the integration process and also on political reality. The following section deals with this aspect.

5.2. On the Two Pillars of European Union

As has been shown in the description of the stages of the European integration process, ever since the Single European Act the European Union has rested on the two—in Oppermann's view 'uneven'[111]—pillars of the European Communities and European political co-operation (EPC). These two pillars are not only different in strength and weight; they are also elements of construction which are not easily reconcilable with each other, given the difference in their functional logic. While the design of EPC is directed towards classic intergovernmental co-ordination, reciprocal information, and co-operation, the EC, as an economic and legal community,[112] is aimed at integration of *one* European market and of *one* European order of Community law,[113] which goes far beyond an alignment of particular interests of member states. For the different functional logic of these elements of a comprehensive European Union, there are also different institutional requirements which have to be fulfilled by the constitution of Europe. Three requirements can be distinguished:

There must be institutions and procedures which allow for and maintain European political co-operation. Since this political co-operation takes the form of classic co-ordination of nation-state policies and interests, the organizational structure of such 'institutions of co-operation' or 'institutions of compromise' is one in which the member states are equally represented (Model of Council), while the question of whether heads of governments, foreign ministers, or 'merely' secretaries of state should form the Council of Co-operation is more one of organizational design. The institutional set-up of EPC currently follows this model.

There must be institutions and procedures which maintain and extend the process of integration within the European Communities. Since—as argued above—the growing intensity of integration requires an institutional dependency on nation-states, further development in this area will be procedural rather than institutional, in the sense of what Meng has described as the intensification of the degree of integration through procedural regulations[114] (transition from the principle of unanimity to that of majority decision-making). Whether this trend will persist will be of decisive importance to the development of integration.

There must be institutions and procedures which connect and amalgamate the two pillars. The importance of such an amalgamated institutional and procedural structure for the practical functioning of the European Union can hardly be overestimated. It is significant that the institutional changes with which the Maastricht Treaty continued the process started by the Single European Act concern this very amalgamation of the Communities and of—what is no longer called—the EPC.[115] This too provides further evidence for our thesis that European constitutional development is less concerned with a radical, momentous institutional change, but refers rather to a successive, cautious transformation of institutional arrangements.

In general, it can be said that the institutions of the European Union can only be explained from the point of view of an incremental development of the integration process, and that their order and amalgamation roughly mirror the state of integration of the EC: at least partly, these processes resemble the successive extension of a building, in the course of which a bay or little tower is added here and a new passage or spiral staircase there. Such incremental development of institutions quite naturally shows deficits and pathologies, and it furthermore has to be prepared for future developments. The concluding section will deal with this problem.

5.3. Institutional Deficits and Future Challenges

The incremental policy of the development of the European institutional system described above almost inevitably leads to an opaque, rather inscrutable, strongly interconnected and therefore also cumbersome system of institutions and decision-making. This has often been criticized,[116] and such criticism should not be taken lightly, given widespread popular unease about the Brussels bureaucracy.[117]

It is in particular the involvement of the Council and the Commission in the direct application of EC law and the system of committees—commonly termed 'comitology'—which are inscrutable and whose functioning is obvious only to insiders. There is some justification for Schäfer's comments on the so-called 'implementation deficit', when he speaks of a kind of European policy network, and of European nepotism among highly qualified European officials who know their way around the intricate decision-making process.[118] As important as such forms of policy networks are to the practical business of integration, and as 'natural' as it appears for them to develop and grow, the danger should not be ignored that the European Union itself may thereby create the image of being uncontrollable and inscrutable—a trend which provoked the negative reactions to the Maastricht Treaty in the referenda.

This, however, is only one point of view. In essence it will be important whether institutional procedures of the EC will prove capable of meeting the challenges of the single market. Experts expect the successive realization of the single market to promote centralism,[119] and the Commission's President, Jacques Delors, even anticipated that, by the year 2000, 80 per cent of macro-economic decisions in the Community would no longer be taken at the level of member states but by the Community.[120] It is not difficult to forecast that the Community in its present institutional constitution will hardly be in a position to cope efficiently and effectively with this increase in power,[121] and that the persistent question of democratic legitimacy will reappear in a stronger form.

Given these developments, and given the basic view of a successive development of the European institutional system advanced here, Schäfer's recommendations for institutional development appear to me to be particularly plausible; some extracts appear below.[122]

The Council of Ministers has to arrange its decision-making process more efficiently and effectively, for example by elevating its working parties to the status of permanent committees of leading officials of a member state with real policy competences, as well as by transforming the committee of permanent representatives into a management committee. Majority decision-making should be extended, and unanimity should be reserved for constitutional or institutional questions only.

An improvement of the management capacity of the Commission and its officials, and the development of new forms of implementation, perhaps in cross-boundary committees in which officials of the member states successively improve the co-operation in implementation, is necessary.

The role of the President of the Commission has to be strengthened with the aim of its becoming that of head of government of the Community, and becoming the inward and outward centre of European political competency. It is imperative to make the President directly responsible to Parliament and the Council.

There is a need further to develop the parties in the European Parliament, combined with a strengthening of its role in the decision-making process, as well as for new forms of co-operation between the European and the national parliaments.

Even if only some of these reform recommendations were to become reality, Europe would be one important step further in its evolution as a state.

Notes

1. Treaty of Rome, 25 Mar. 1957 (*Bundesgesetzblatt*, 2 (1957), 766), in the Treaty on European Union, 7 Feb. 1992 (*Bundesgesetzblatt*, 2 (1992), 1253–6).
2. Single European Act, 28 Feb. 1986, *Bundesgesetzblatt*, 2 (1986), 1102; *Amtsblatt der Europäischen Gemeinschaften*, L 169/1 (1987); in the Treaty on European Union, 7 Feb. 1992, *Bundesgesetzblatt*, 2 (1992), 1253–95; *Amtsblatt der Europäischen Gemeinschaften*, C 191 (1992).
3. R. Voigt (ed.), *Abschied vom Staat—Rückkehr zum Staat?* (Baden-Baden, 1993), 159.
4. Thomas Oppermann speaks of single pre-federal characteristics in *Europarecht* (Munich, 1991), 297; see also Ulrich Everling, 'Zur föderalen Struktur der Europäischen Gemeinschaft', in K. Heilbronner, G. Ress, and T. Stein (eds.), *Staat und Völkerrechtsordnung* (Berlin, 1989), 179.
5. See R. Mayntz, 'Föderalismus und die Gesellschaft der Gegenwart', *Archiv des öffentlichen Rechts* (*AöR*), 115 (1990), 232.
6. See also G. F. Schuppert, 'Die Neue Ungleichheit—der deutsche Föderalismus vor neuen Herausforderungen', in Josef Becker (ed.), *Wiedervereinigung in Mitteleuropa* (Munich, 1992), 219.

7. On 'federal state balance' see P. Badura, 'Die Kunst der föderalen Form—der Bundesstaat in Europa und die europäische Föderation', in P. Badura and R. Scholz (eds.), *Wege und Verfahren des Verfassungslebens* (Munich, 1993), 369; on federalism as a changing structural principle of the Basic Law, see also M. Brenner, 'Der unitarische Bundesstaat in der Europäischen Union', *Die öffentliche Verwaltung (DöV)* (1992), 903.

8. See Ulrich Scheuner, *Struktur und Aufgaben des Bundestaats in der Gegenwart*, *DöV* (1962), 641; a pioneering discussion of this point is found in Arthur Benz, *Föderalismus als dynamisches System. Zentralisierung und Dezentralisierung im föderativen Staat* (Opladen, 1985).

9. Cf. Hans-Peter Schneider, 'Kooperation, Konkurrenz oder Konfrontation? Entwicklungstendenzen des Föderalismus in der Bundesrepublik', in Arno Klönne *et al.*, *Lebendige Verfassung—das Grundgesetz in Perspektive* (Neuwied, 1981), 91; see also Joachim Jens Hesse and Wolfgang Renzsch, 'Zehn Thesen zur Entwicklung und Lage des deutschen Föderalismus', *Staatswissenschaften und Staatspraxis* (1990), 562.

10. On this point, see K. D. Henke and G. F. Schuppert, *Verfassungrechtliche und finanzwissenschaftliche Probleme der Neuordnung der Finanzbeziehungen von Bund und Ländern im vereinten Deutschland* (Baden-Baden, 1993).

11. *Kommission für die Finanzreform*, 2nd edn. (Kohlhammer, 1966), TZ. 73.

12. See Jürgen Schwarze, 'Verfassungsentwicklung in der Europäischen Gemeinschaft', in Jürgen Schwarze and Roland Bieber (eds.), *Eine Verfassung für Europa* (Baden-Baden, 1984), 15; see also Pierre Pescatore, 'Die Gemeinschaftsverträge als Verfassungrecht—ein Kapitel Verfassungsgeschichte in der Perspektive des europäischen Gerichtshofs, systematisch geordnet', in Wilhelm G. Grewe, Hans Rupp, and Hans Schneider (eds.), *Europäische Gerichtsbarkeit und nationale Verfassungsgerichtsbarkeit* (Baden-Baden, 1982), 319.

13. This phrase has been coined by Hans Peter Ipsen, 'Die Verfassungsrolle des Europäischen Gerichtshofs für die Integration', in Jürgen Schwarze (ed.), *Der Europäische Gerichtshof als Verfassungsgericht und Rechtsschutzinstanz* (Baden-Baden, 1983), 29.

14. On this see G. F. Schuppert, 'Rigidität und Flexibilität von Verfassungsrecht. Überlegungen zur Steuerungsfunktion von Verfassungsrecht in normalen wie in "schwierigen Zeiten"', *AöR* 1 (1993).

15. See Dieter Grimm, 'Verfassungsfunktion und Grundgesetzreform', *AöR* 97 (1972), 489.
16. Though going far beyond a mere chronology, there is abundant chronological material to be found in Roland Bieber, 'Verfassungsentwicklung in der Europäischen Gemeinschaft, Formen und Verfahren', in Schwarze and Bieber, *Eine Verfassung für Europa.*
17. Press conference by de Gaulle on 5 Sept. 1960, cited in Oppermann, *Europarecht*, 14.
18. Ibid. 15.
19. Cited in Michael Schweitzer and Waldemar Hummer, *Textbuch zum Europarecht*, 5th edn. (Munich, 1991), No. 10.
20. Rudolf Streinz, *Europarecht* (Heidelberg, 1992), 67.
21. See also R. Lahr, 'Die Legende vom "Luxemburger Kompromiss" ', *Europa-Archiv (EA)* (1983), 223; M. Schweitzer, 'Die Stellung der Luxemburger Vereinbarung im europäischen Gemeinschaftsrecht', in Franz Burkei and Dirk Meints Poter (eds.), *Rechtsfragen im Spektrum des Öffentlichen Rechts: Festschrift für Hubert Armbruster* (Berlin, 1976), 75; and M. Vasey, 'Decision-Making in the Agriculture Council and the "Luxembourg Compromise" ', *Common Market Law Review (CML Rev.)* (1988), 725.
22. See Fritz W. Scharpf, 'Decision Rules, Decision Styles and Policy Choices', Max-Planck-Institut für Gesellschaftsforschung, Discussion Paper 3 (Cologne, 1988).
23. 'Die Politikverflechtungs-Falle: Europäische Integration und deutscher Föderalismus im Vergleich', *Politische Vierteljahresschrift (PVS)*, 26 (1985), 323–56.
24. G. F. Schuppert, 'Institutional Choice im öffentlichen Sektor', in Dieter Grimm (ed.), *Staatsaufgaben* (Baden-Baden, 1993).
25. Werner Meng, *Das Recht der Internationalen Organisationen—eine Entwicklungsstufe des Völkerrechts. Zugleich eine Untersuchung zur Rechtsnatur des Rechts der Europäischen Gemeinschaften* (Baden-Baden, 1979), 103.
26. Ibid. 207.
27. Streinz, *Europarecht*, 10.
28. This is rightly emphasized by Oppermann, *Europarecht*, 112.
29. W. Hill, *Aus Politik und Zeitgeschichte*, 51–2 (1983), 3.
30. Oppermann, *Europarecht*, 18.
31. *Bundesgesetzblatt*, 2 (1986), 1104; *Amtsblatt der Europäischen Gemeinschaften*, L 169/1 (1987).
32. Comprehensively dealt with in Siegfried Magiera, 'Die Einheitliche Europäische Akte und die Fortentwicklung der Europäischen Gemeinschaft zur Europäischen Union', in W. Fiedler and S. Ress (eds.), *Verfassungsrecht und Völkerrecht* (Cologne, 1989), 507.
33. Streinz, *Europarecht*, 11.

34. Oppermann, *Europarecht*, 112.
35. Streinz, *Europarecht*, 13.
36. See Christoph Vedder, *Vertrag zur Gründung der Europäischen Gemeinschaft vom 25: März 1957: Das Neue Europarecht* (1992), 41 ff.
37. See also Albert Bleckmann, 'Der Vertrag über die Europäische Union. Eine Einführung', *Deutsches Verwaltungsblatt (DVB 1)* (1992), 335; Ludwig Graf Stauffenberg and Christiane Langenfeld, 'Maastricht— Ein Fortschritt für Europa?', *Zeitschrift für Rechtspolitik (ZRP)* (1992), 252; and Martin Seidel, 'Zur Verfassung der Europäischen Gemeinschaft nach Maastricht', *Europarecht (EuR)* (1992), 125.
38. Peter M. Huber, 'Maastricht—ein Staatsstreich?', *Jenaer Schriften zum Recht*, 1 (1993).
39. Stauffenberg and Langenfeld, 'Maastricht', 253.
40. See the summary in Bleckmann, 'Der Vertrag über die Europäische Union', n. 45.
41. Streinz, *Europarecht*, 15.
42. See G. F. Schuppert, 'Institutional Choice im öffentlichen Sektor', in Grimm, *Staatsaufgaben*.
43. 'Budgetary Strategies of Administrative Agencies' (1964), repr. in part in Raymond E. Wolfinger (ed.), *Readings in American Political Behavior* (Englewood Cliffs, NJ, 1966).
44. See the basic ruling of the European Court of 15 July 1964 in the case of Costa/ENEL (RS/64).
45. See Karl Matthias Meessen, 'Zur Theorie allgemeiner Rechtsgrundsätze des internationalen Rechts. Der Nachweis allgemeiner Rechtsgrundsätze des Europäischen Gemeinschaftsrechts', *Jahrbuch für Internationales Recht*, 17 (1974), 283.
46. See Peter Häberle, *Gemeineuropäisches Verfassungsrecht*, *Europäische Grundrechte-Zeitschrift* (1991), 261.
47. See Jürgen Schwarze (ed.), *Der Europäische Gerichtshof als Verfassungsgericht und Rechtsschutzinstanz* (Baden-Baden, 1983).
48. Streinz, *Europarecht*, 15.
49. In particular in para. 5: Institutions, p. 89.
50. Oppermann, *Europarecht*, 13.
51. Ibid. 118.
52. Vertrag zur Einsetzung eines gemeinsamen Rates und einer gemeinsamen Kommission der Europäischen Gemeinschaften vom 8. April 1965, *Bundesgesetzblatt*, 2 (1965), 1454; *Amtsblatt der Europäischen Gemeinschaften*, 152 (1967); Art. 10 was repealed by Art. P, Vertrag über die Europäische Union vom 7. Februar 1992, *Bundesgesetzblatt*, 2 (1992), 1253; *Amtsblatt der Europäischen Gemeinschaften*, C 191 (1992).
53. Oppermann, *Europarecht*, 110.

54. For a description of this dual function see Streinz, *Europarecht*, 70.
55. Oppermann, *Europarecht*, 110.
56. Ibid. 117.
57. Ibid.
58. 'Voraussetzungen einer Europäischen Verfassung', in Schwarze and Bieber, *Eine Verfassung für Europa*, 91.
59. 'Mit einer Aufwertung des Europa-Parlaments ist es nicht getan: das Demokratiedefizit der EG hat strukturelle Ursachen', in Thomas Ellwein *et al.* (eds.), *Jahrbuch zur Staats- und Verwaltungswissenschaft*, 6 (1993/4), 13.
60. Grimm, 'Verfassungsfunktion', 16.
61. Taken from Streinz, *Europarecht*, 128–9.
62. Oppermann, *Europarecht*, 107–8.
63. Meng, *Das Recht der Internationalen Organisationen*, 105.
64. Ibid. 106.
65. See also Oppermann, *Europarecht*, 129; and Christoph Sasse, *Regierungen, Parlamente, Ministerrat, Entscheidungsprozesse in der Europäischen Gemeinschaft* (Bonn, 1975).
66. On the problem of legitimacy in general see Ernst Wolfgang Böckenförde, 'Demokratie als Verfassungsprinzip', in J. Isensee and P. Kirchhof (eds.), *Handbuch des Staatsrechts*, 1 (1987), 887.
67. See Lackhoff and Rich (eds.), *Private Government* (Carbondale, Ill., 1973).
68. See Helmut K. Anheier and Wolfgang Seibel (eds.), *The Third Sector: Comparative Studies of Nonprofit Organizations* (Berlin, 1990).
69. Christopher Hood and Gunnar Folke Schuppert (eds.), *Delivering Public Services in Western Europe: Sharing Western European Experience of Para-government Organizations* (London, 1988).
70. G. F. Schuppert, 'Quangos als Trabanten des Verwaltungssystems', *DöV* (1981), 153.
71. See G. F. Schuppert, 'Verselbständigte Verwaltungseinheiten und Parafiski—Elemente zur Theorie der Parafiskalität', in Klaus Tiepelmann and Gregor van der Beek (eds.), *Theorie der Parafiski* (Berlin, 1992), 137.
72. Birger P. Priddat, 'Para- und Nonfiski—zur ökonomischen Theorie "intermediärer Organisationen"', in Tiepelmann and van der Beek, *Theorie der Parafiski*, 163.
73. See G. F. Schuppert, *Die Erfüllung öffentlicher Aufgaben durch verselbständigte Verwaltungeinheiten* (Göttingen, 1981); and Horst Dreier, *Hierarchische Verwaltung im demokratischen Staat* (Tübingen, 1991).
74. Similar problems appear with regard to qualifications of administrative work orientated towards legal protection; on this point see Eberhard Schmidt-Assmann, 'Die Lehren von den Rechtsformen des

Verwaltungshandels. Ihre Bedeutung im System des Verwaltungsrechts und für das verwaltungsrechtliche Denken der Gegenwart', *DVB* 1 (1989), 535.

75. On the state of the discussion see Peter M. Huber, 'Die Rolle des Demokratieprinzips im europäischen Integrationsprozeß', *Staatswissenschaften und Staatspraxis* (1992), 349.
76. No. 11 (15 Mar. 1993), 143.
77. J. Frowein, 'Die rechtliche Bedeutung des Verfassungsprinzips der parlamentarischen Demokratie für den europäischen Integrationsprozeß', *EuR* (1983), 301, 309.
78. P. Badura, 'Bewahrung und Veränderung demokratischer und föderativer Verfassungsprinzipien der in Europa verbundenen Staaten', *Zeitschrift für Schweizerisches Recht*, Neue Fassung, 109 (1990), 115.
79. See Schuppert, 'Institutional Choice im öffentlichen Sektor'.
80. Badura, 'Bewahrung und Veränderung', 132.
81. Ibid. 120.
82. BVerfGE 22, 296.
83. A prime example is the legal decisions concerning the legal qualification of regional planning; see I. Richter and G. F. Schuppert, *Casebook Verwaltungsrecht* (Munich, 1991), 269.
84. Oppermann, *Europarecht*, 297.
85. Streinz, *Europarecht*, 31.
86. Oppermann, *Europarecht*, 305.
87. Streinz, *Europarecht*, 33.
88. Meng, *Das Recht der Internationalen Organisationen*.
89. Voigt, *Abschied vom Staat*.
90. Contribution to the discussion, *Veröffentlichungen der Vereinigung der Deutschen Staatsrechtslehrer*, 50 (1991), 171.
91. Contribution to the discussion, ibid. 152–3.
92. *Europäisches Gemeinschaftsrecht* (Tübingen, 1972).
93. Ibid. 197–8.
94. Badura, 'Bewahrung und Veränderung'.
95. 'Representation and the Future Euro-Polity', *Staatswissenschaften und Staatspraxis* (1992), 379.
96. Ibid. 389.
97. Ibid. 391.
98. *Nationalstaat, Solidarstaat, Effizienzstaat. Neue Staatsgrenzen für neue Staatstypen* (Darmstadt, 1992).
99. Ibid. 54–5.
100. See Eberhard Grabitz, *Abgestufte Integration* (1984).
101. 'Protokoll über die Konvergenzkriterien nach Art. 109 j des Vertrages zur Gründung der Europäischen Gemeinschaft, Schlußakte zum Vertrag über die Europäische Union (Maastricht-Vertrag) vom 7.

Februar 1992', *Bundesgesetzblatt*, 2 (1992), 1253; *Amtsblatt der Europäischen Gemeinschaften*, C 191 (1992).

102. Oppermann, *Europarecht*.

103. Hans-Peter Schneider, 'Die bundesstaatliche Ordnung im vereinigten Deutschland', *Neue Juristische Wochenschrift* (1991), 2448.

104. This term is found in Fritz W. Scharpf, 'Föderalismus an der Wegscheide: Eine Replik'; Joachim Jens Hesse and Wolfgang Renzsch, in 'Zehn Thesen zur Entwicklung und Lage des deutschen Föderalismus', speak of the 'development of new disparities', both in *Staatswissenschaften und Staatspraxis* (1990), 562, 579.

105. See a number of relevant contributions in vol. 1 (1993) of *Staatswissenschaften und Staatspraxis*.

106. On this see Schwarze and Bieber, *Eine Verfassung für Europa*.

107. Gütersloh, 1990.

108. 'Die institutionelle Weiterentwicklung der Europäischen Gemeinschaft. Überlegungen zu neuen Strukturen der EG-Institutionen', *DöV* (1991), 261.

109. Ibid. 267.

110. Ibid. 268.

111. Oppermann, *Europarecht*, 111.

112. See Carl Otto Lenz, 'Gemeinsame Grundlagen und Grundwerte des Rechts der Europäischen Gemeinschaften', *ZRP* (1988), 449; also Michael Stolleis, 'Die verfassungsgeschichtlichen Fundamente des europäischen Hauses' (forthcoming).

113. Compare Coing, Europäisierung der Rechtswissenschaft, NJW 1990, S. 937 ff; zur Europäisierung der Staatsrechtslehre Häberle, Diskussionsbeitrag, in: VVDStRL 50, 1991, S. 157; see most recently 'Zur Europäisierung des allgemeinen Verwaltungsrechts', E. Schmidt-Assmann, Festschrift Lerche, 1993, 513 ff.

114. op. cit. 102 ff.

115. Evidence in Streinz, op. cit. 151.

116. Oppermann, op. cit. 103 ff.

117. The *Spiegel* article already cited speaks of a 'Brussels administration dictatorship'.

118. op. cit. 264.

119. Compare the report in the FAZ, 24 4 1993, entitled 'Strengthening National Parliaments against Centralization by Brussels'.

120. Quoted from Schäfer, 261.

121. Schäfer also to the point, 262.

122. op. cit. 270.

PART VII
CONCLUSION

15

The Agenda of Constitutional Change in Europe: Adaptation, Transformation, and Internationalization

JOACHIM JENS HESSE AND NEVIL JOHNSON

It is no exaggeration to suggest that constitutional arrangements throughout Europe are exposed to a powerful 'wind of change'. But this wind blows with differing degrees of intensity, and perhaps in different directions, according to where we look on the continent. In its Eastern parts the collapse of the Soviet Union has imposed the need for a radical transformation of political life and institutions. At the same time the countries affected by this political upheaval are anxious to reconstruct their economies and to connect up with global economic structures and relationships which impose their own pressures and, not least, demand a capacity to compete in world markets. All this means that the challenge is one of trans-formation—social, economic, and political. As several of the contri-butions to this book indicate, constitutional frameworks are required which will help accommodate such comprehensive pro-cesses of change.

In other parts of Europe, that is to say in the West, the challenge is different and, on the surface at least, less dramatic and compre-hensive. There are in many countries well-established constitutional procedures which have stood the test of time for most or all of the post-war era. Nevertheless, social values evolve and change, the tasks of government have expanded, and yet in some respects this expansion has failed to satisfy expectations, and there is the com-mon factor of exposure to the demanding pressures of an open and competitive world economy, and of adapting to the post-Cold War geo-political situation. To these multiple demands there seem to have been two main responses. One is the familiar process of adapting political and constitutional methods pragmatically to new demands and situations. This is indeed what is to be observed in many countries, and this too is a process with which some of the contributors here deal. The other response is to seek a broader structural context within which to solve a wide range of problems—economic, social, technological, and political. It is this response—already well established for a considerable time—which has led to the process of internationalization of political and constitutional relationships in Western Europe, embodied most fully and decisively in the development of European economic and political integration. But such a process may also prompt critical reactions: there are anxieties about what will happen to both the nation-states and the subdivisions within them. Some of these worries find expression too in contributions to this volume.

In what follows we try to summarize some features of these different experiences of the constitutional challenges facing Europe, as they are presented first in Western Europe and then in Central and Eastern Europe. Finally we move to the level at which integration has occurred and is continuing. This is, of course, a process of integration which so far has chiefly affected Western Europe. But it should not be forgotten that the European Union is to be enlarged soon through the accession of new Western European members, and that this process of enlargement may within the foreseeable future embrace at least some of the states of central Europe too. So the internationalization of constitutional links is certainly on the wider European agenda.

1. WESTERN EUROPE

In the aftermath of the Second World War, the constitutional reconstruction which took place in many parts of Western Europe was strongly influenced by the desire to prevent repetition of the recent past. Priorities included guarantees of democratic government and respect for human rights, and above all political arrangements which would promote stability and offer safeguards against the excesses of the totalitarian past. In some countries, mainly the smaller ones with well-established constitutional traditions, reconstruction consisted chiefly in the restoration of what had been generally stable forms of government disrupted by war; in others, notably France and Italy, new constitutions had to be drawn up; whilst in the western part of Germany a new state took shape in 1949 with the drafting of the Basic Law.

In respect of the form of government, constitutional reconstruction after 1945 was marked by a renewed commitment to parliamentary methods and structures, usually operating under multi-party conditions. In one major instance, France, parliamentary government of the traditional type worked indifferently, with the result that executive instability became a serious handicap. Elsewhere, parliamentary government, whether 'stabilized' in the West German manner, or corresponding to the straightforward liberal model in which the executive depends directly on retaining support in an elected chamber, has endured successfully for the past four decades and longer. This has been attributable in many cases to the willingness of political parties to collaborate effectively in the maintenance of coalition relationships for the purposes of government, a collaboration which also encouraged the steady increase in economic prosperity and individual social security occurring throughout Western Europe since the early 1950s. It is reasonably clear that the achievement of constitutional stability was greatly assisted over a long period by the maintenance of a favourable social and economic environment.

Radical reappraisals of constitutional arrangements have subsequently been rare. In France in 1958, one such radical reshaping of the constitutional order did take place, and resulted in the establishment of a mixed presidential and parliamentary regime, with the parliamentary elements considerably modified to make way for a stronger executive authority. But this example has had little influence elsewhere; and when, after 1975, Spain received a new constitutional structure, it embodied the parliamentary form of government under a constitutional monarch. Similarly, at the present time there is relatively little pressure in Italy, despite the collapse of the familiar party structures, for the introduction of something like the French constitutional model.

Basic political and civil rights have been widely acknowledged and, for the most part, reasonably well protected in post-war Western Europe. A sharpened focus on human rights as the principal guarantee of individual freedom and autonomy is a relatively recent development, and points towards more meticulous constitutional checks on governments and lawmakers than were generally regarded as necessary in the years of post-war reconstruction. This trend has had an impact at the level of the integrative European institutions too, most notably through the European Convention on Human Rights and the Court of Justice of the European Communities (now bearing in addition the designation of European Union). Federal solutions remain relevant here, not least because of the evolution of the European Community after the creation of the single market.

Overall the constitutional reconstruction after 1945, along with later exercises in constitutional renewal and reappraisal in Western Europe, present a series of remarkable achievements.[1] Superficially at least, the extent of the success can be seen in the way in which in many countries constitutional conflict was diminished or vanished altogether. Broadly speaking, by the early 1980s the whole of Western Europe was fully committed to democratic government, the protection of basic human rights, and the pursuit by the political authorities of a high level of economic well-being and social security. There were disputes between parties about how best to pursue these economic and social objectives, some arguing for more reliance on market relationships and conditions, others pressing for more emphasis to be placed on social protection in a market economy through a measure of public-service provision and regulation. But these are for the most part differences in degree and not of principle. This has been confirmed by the strong revival of market-oriented policies in many countries during the 1980s. Far from stimulating a reinforcement of policies of a collectivist or socialist nature, this phase has accelerated the decline of genuinely socialist arguments and proposals. The social framework for Western European constitutionalism thus remains, with variations of emphasis, managed capitalism and a socially conscious market.

Under these conditions most countries of Western Europe have not faced pressing demands to engage in a radical reappraisal of their prevailing constitutional forms and methods. Support for a democratic political order, which is strictly committed to achieving consensus and sensitive to the individualist emphasis on the sanctity of private rights and claims, is strong and seems likely to persist. Even the recent breakdown of the old party political order in Italy does not yet seem to indicate a desire to abandon familiar constitutional principles. Nevertheless, during the past ten to fifteen years a number of issues have begun to have a substantial impact on constitutional development in most Western European countries. The most important of these are calls for decentralization and deregulation, growing pressures for a more meticulous attention to human rights, and the need to adapt to the continuing erosion of the rights of the traditional nation-states within the framework of the European Union.

First, as regards decentralization and deregulation, there is no single or decisive source of the differing demands for such measures. In some cases, arguments in favour of decentralization are put forward by national minorities distinguished in varying degrees by language, culture, or religion from the majority of the population. In others, it seems to be more a reaction against the alleged remoteness of governing institutions and a call for more opportunities for citizen participation. Examples of the first kind are to be found in Great Britain, Spain, or Italy. In Belgium, too, such problems are prevalent. The circumstances here are unusual, in that they involve a division of the whole population into two main communities distinguished from one another by language. Constitutional amendments in fulfilment of earlier constitutional commitments have, therefore, been made in this country. Similarly, the new Spanish Constitution provided for a process of far-reaching political devolution, whilst in France measures of administrative decentralization were put into effect without constitutional change after 1981. Even in Britain, the 1970s saw attempts to confer a degree of political devolution on Scotland and Wales, though these were ultimately unsuccessful and did not come into operation after adverse popular votes had been recorded in 1979. Whether constitutional concessions can accommodate the demands of minorities depends, however, on the extent to which such demands are negotiable. In some instances, for example in the case of Basque separatism and Republicanism in Northern Ireland, the nature of the demands rules out a negotiated solution in the form of an agreement on acceptable constitutional amendments. This is due to the fact that the minorities in question reject entirely the state of which they are part: their objective is unilateral independence.

The movement in favour of privatization and deregulation testifies to changes in the prevailing view of the responsibilities of government and, therefore, of the boundaries of the state that

might eventually be of considerable importance to the future constitutional debate in Europe. Whereas the development of the welfare
state during the first decades after the end of the Second World War
saw a constant rise in public-authority activities, the world-wide
checks to economic growth since the late 1970s have forced governments to cut back on expenditure and to redefine their roles and
strategies, including policies to redress the boundaries of the state,
to re-evaluate welfare state programmes, and to rethink the relationships between the state, the economy, and the society. Efforts
at privatization assumed a major role amongst the policies
prompted by this shift. Fostered by the rise of Conservative governments inspired by neo-liberal thinking—and here the programmes
put forward by Margaret Thatcher after her election to the British
premiership were particularly influential—privatization policies
turned into a tidal wave, being considered an adequate response to
the seemingly outdated welfare state model pursued in so many
developed countries. Originally intended as a transfer of entire
agencies, a variety of forms of privatization became apparent. Some
countries did not quite follow the radical departure of Britain and
restricted their policies to contracting-out, giving up effective direct
state control; others cut staff or particular programmes and called
that 'privatization'. But whatever the approach or policy, privatization certainly became an answer to the widespread disillusionment
with the performance of the public sector and to the growing
scarcity of resources. It was, furthermore, hoped that it would
relieve governments of detailed management and possibly contentious subsidies by enabling the new owners to offer their products
at market rates, to streamline operations, and to rid themselves of
publicly protected 'feather-bedding'.

Other attempts to change state–society relationships and to reduce public tasks, or to re-establish them within a different context,
can be summarized under the label of 'deregulation', too. The
intention here was not just to promote further public–private part-
nerships, or to abolish or severely curtail public services on the
assumption that private provision would fill the gap, but to free
previously heavily regulated tasks from the public grip. There was
a managerial element attached to that too, since management was
expected to be freer in exercising authority over resources and
personnel when set free from detailed state supervision. Deregulation of this kind can be observed in a number of forms and in

almost all Western European countries. With regard to the empirical evidence it is interesting to note, however, that the pendulum seems now to be swinging back somewhat. This is even true for former champions of the underlying anti-state approach, such as the UK. At the autumn 1993 conference of the Conservative Party, for example, Douglas Hurd, the Foreign Secretary, warned of further attempts to reduce the role of the state. Criticizing supporters of a 'permanent revolution', he stressed the Government's commitment to respect as well as to reform the public sector. Those remarks echo similar considerations in a number of countries, signalling that the debate might have passed its apogee. It is, furthermore, worth noting that the willingness and ability to privatize and to deregulate has in any case been distributed unevenly amongst the countries of the West. If one compares, for example, the relevant figures for the UK, Germany, France, and other West European countries, one can detect in some cases structural conditions that allow for only a modest departure from previous policies. It does not come as a surprise, therefore, that these issues have not really reached the level of constitutional change, and that obvious cross-pressures in public management mean that there are variations of pace and movement in the discussions of centralization/decentralization, co-ordination/deregulation, and control/delegation. The policies then adopted very much depend on national characteristics and pressures.

Second, in all Western societies, sensitivity in respect of human rights has over the years become greater. This trend has to some extent been accelerated by the consolidation of institutions at the European level, notably the European Community and its body of law, and the European Court and Commission of Human Rights, which operate within the framework provided by the Council of Europe and the European Convention. As a result of these developments it has become possible for citizens and organizations to challenge their domestic jurisdictions in various ways, by demanding that those jurisdictions apply the highest standard embodied in provisions to which their own states have acceded. Slowly and in a piecemeal way, something like a European jurisprudence relating to the rights of individuals and private corporate bodies is taking shape. The response to these trends varies according to individual countries. In France there has since 1974 been some strengthening of the Constitutional Council's powers to rule on the compatibility

of proposed legislation with the Constitution. A *médiateur* has been
appointed who functions as a kind of Ombudsman, to whom
individuals can appeal for redress of grievances. In Germany, in
contrast, it has not been deemed necessary to extend further the
protection already afforded by the procedures of individual constitutional appeal, though in the face of modern data-storage action
has been taken to strengthen the protection of individual privacy.
The country most seriously affected by pressures for an extensive
and meticulous interpretation of rights is Britain. One reason for
this is to be found not so much in the abuse of powers in Britain, or
in real limitations affecting the range of individual rights, as in the
tensions produced by the impact of formalized principles and procedures on a constitutional tradition which is unwritten and informal, which relies extensively on judicial case law, and which has
embodied the principle of parliamentary sovereignty. It has so far
proved hard to reconcile these contrasting approaches to rights
protection—on the one hand specific, flexible, and discretionary, on
the other general, abstract, and often inflexible. No enactment of
the European Convention into domestic law has so far occurred in
Britain, despite the demand for such action which has been generated by the relatively large number of decisions reached during the
1980s by the European Commission confirming breaches of the
Convention on Human Rights.

Third, there is undoubtedly the need to adapt the West European
nation-state to ever closer integration within the European Union,
even though this occurs at a time when the deepening and widening
of this association seems to take place almost simultaneously. So far
it has been possible to achieve a large measure of economic integration without a serious clash between the Union and one or more
of its member states, and without changes making it obvious to
citizens that they are no longer subject to the exclusive jurisdiction
of the domestic political authorities. But this is something of a
constitutional illusion, and cannot really be sustained much longer.
The Treaty of Maastricht has to be viewed as a significant step
towards a European constitution, carrying with it significant implications for the member states and their sovereignty. Constitutional
adaptation might, therefore, have to go much further than originally envisaged. The common provisions of the Treaty define the
European Union and, while they avoid setting a federal goal, they

re-emphasize the 'ever closer union of the peoples of Europe' (Article A). The introduction of a citizenship of the Union, although presented as a means to protect the rights and interests of nationals of member states, actually involves for the first time the creation of a direct relationship between the union and its citizens as individuals. It has, furthermore, to be noted that seventeen protocols and thirty-three declarations are attached to the Treaty. They cover matters ranging from the British opt-out and opt-in clauses on economic and monetary union and social policy to special provisions giving the Danes privileged access to second homes in parts of rural Denmark and reservations in respect of Irish anti-abortion law.

While these opt-outs and special provisions are designed to safeguard the special interests of particular nation-states, they cannot halt the general drive forward. Assuming the continuation of current trends, the powers of the European Union can be expected to reduce significantly the legislative and judicial autonomy of nation-states. In the face of this encroachment, the adoption of subsidiarity as a general principle may not by itself eliminate the need to adapt the constitutions of the member states. In this context, it can only be a temporary solution for the German Constitutional Court to rule European Union law to be applicable only if it does not violate the principles enshrined in the Basic Law. Indeed, the principle of subsidiarity seems to restrict the power of central governments in Europe, and to bolster those of the constituent parts. Whilst the German *Länder* already aim to redefine the jurisdictional boundaries *vis-à-vis* the federal government, regional authorities in France and Spain can be expected to voice similar demands. Perhaps the most radical adaptation of a national constitution implied by the principle of subsidiarity may yet take place in Britain. Opponents of the curbing of local authority competences as well as proponents of nationalist aspirations in Scotland and Wales have gained powerful arguments against central government control. But the need to adapt national constitutions to the new environment of the European Union, whilst being obvious, is only one side of the bargain which needs to be struck: simultaneously there are calls for the European Union itself to develop further its constitutional arrangements. The issues raised here will be discussed further below.

2. CENTRAL AND EASTERN EUROPE

In contrast to Western Europe, where adaptation predominates, Central and Eastern European countries have experienced a much more rapid and fundamental process of constitutional change since the collapse of communist/socialist rule towards the end of the 1980s. The states, as well as their constitutions, which were usually ignored, have themselves been discredited, along with the old ruling élites. What was then sought was a complete negation of the legacy of communist/socialist rule. Such feelings have, at least initially, provided the chief impetus for constitutional change. The agenda, therefore, derived from the rejection of basic features of the previous administrations. These included extreme centralization, with pervasive hierarchical controls over the lower levels of administration, implying, for example, the absence of an independent sphere of local government. Centralization was coupled with concentration of powers, which meant the fusion of executive and legislative functions in the highest organs of the state, which in turn were controlled by the ruling party. The latter's influence extended over all levels and branches of state administration, and its apparatus was closely intertwined with that of the state. The will of the party was superior to the rule of law; consequently the principle of legality played only a secondary role in state activities which were not subjected to effective external controls. A further feature of the legacy of communist/socialist rule lay in its perceived failure to manage an economy based in theory on public ownership.

In the attempt to negate the features of the communist/socialist experience, the agenda of constitutional change, therefore, included three main tasks: first, economic reform through a programme of privatization, deregulation, and the restoration of private property; secondly, a redefinition of the role of the state as well as a reorganization of its institutions; thirdly, the protection of individual rights from state interference. The process of constitutional change in Central and Eastern Europe since the upheavals of the late 1980s with respect to these three main areas will now be looked at briefly.

With regard to economic reform, it appears that most of the constitutional provisions necessary for the programme of privatization have been put in place. Not least because of the need to attract inward investment, an evolutionary approach to the introduction of a market economy was rejected, despite the fact that, even under communist rule, the economies had displayed some very limited elements of a market system. Most governments embarked, therefore, on a radical economic reform programme emphasizing stabilization, liberalization, the creation of market institutions, and privatization. With some modifications, these programmes still provide the basis for ongoing reform policies. However, whilst it is comparatively easy to ascertain what reform measures have been formally adopted and legislated for, the stage of implementation reached is difficult to judge. Furthermore, there is a temptation to overestimate the real economic change which has already taken place. With increasing frequency it has been suggested that economic transformation might take much longer than many had initially expected.

By far the most difficult and contentious element in constitutional change lay in the definition of the functions of the state and in the organization of its institutions. The overriding importance of this item on the agenda for constitutional change lies in the fact that it is closely linked with both the success of economic reform and the protection of individual rights. The success of privatization programmes, and in particular of the drive to attract foreign investment, will depend on a clear and stable definition and organization of the state, so as to prevent the latter from interfering with the economic rights of individuals and of private corporate bodies.

There are, of course, two dimensions to the task of defining and organizing the state. First, the experience of one-party domination of the organs of the state requires a redistribution of power within the basic structure of government. In this respect, the process of constitutional reform has taken different courses in the countries concerned. While republican constitutions came into force in Slovakia and the Czech Republic in October 1992 and January 1993 respectively, a final settlement has thus far proved elusive in the case of Poland and Hungary. Instead, there have been numerous amendments to the constitutions inherited from the communist/socialist regimes, which have fundamentally altered constitutional law and created a legal framework for pluralist, democratic governments and market-based economies. The failure to agree on new constitutions was, however, the result of fundamental disagreements among the main political forces. In Poland it was only with President Wałęsa's signing of the 'Little Constitution' (Constitutional Act on the Relation between Legislative and Executive Branches of the Republic of Poland and on Local Self-Government) on 17 November 1992 that the relations between the president, government, and parliament were redefined. This agreement temporarily ended (but by no means concluded) months of bitter constitutional conflict which had repeatedly resulted in institutional deadlock. In Hungary, too, the process of constitutional reform has taken a different course from the one originally envisaged. The present Hungarian Constitution is the result of compromises reached in the course of 1989, when the then ruling Hungarian Socialist Workers' Party and the opposition forces agreed on amending the previous constitution. It was commonly accepted that the revised constitutional order would have a merely transitory character, and that a completely new constitution should then be adopted after the first free parliamentary elections. Whilst a number of additional amendments have been passed since October 1989, the aim of a new constitution has proved increasingly elusive and the constitutional debate has become notably less intense. There appears no reason to expect the reformed socialist party which was returned to power in May 1994 to revive this debate. In both Poland and Hungary, therefore, the amendment of existing constitutions rather than the drafting of completely new ones has meant that there is no longer a decisive impetus for further constitutional reform. In short, the main political actors have learned to live with the amended constitutions, and the adoption of a new document, should this occur in some cases, is more likely to resemble a 'tidying-up' exercise than to amount to a radical departure from what are by now the established constitutional conventions and practices.

The most striking characteristic common to the reorganization of state authority in Central and Eastern European countries is—apart from the somewhat unexpected rather limited adjustments at the centre of government—the uncertainty about the future of the intermediate level of government and of intergovernmental arrangements in general. Whilst the previous district offices were abolished almost everywhere, the future of the regional level remains unsettled. Frequently, the number of regional authorities has been altered, their boundaries redrawn, and their competences redefined. In Hungary, the resulting administrative confusion has even gone as far as depriving the central institutions of adequate implementation organs. New layers of public administration have been implemented—such as specialized, deconcentrated administrations and co-ordinating 'Commissioners of the Republic' in Hungary—or proposed—such as the re-introduction of a general district level in Poland. In the Czech and Slovak Republics too, special administrative units have developed at the district level following the abolition of the regions. Taken together, there is a great deal of instability and confusion concerning the appropriate arrangements for the intermediate level of government in the Central and Eastern European countries. Old intermediate authorities have been discredited and, as a result, decisively weakened; the new arrangements have led to the proliferation of specialized, deconcentrated units of state administration. However, the multitude of institutions with partly overlapping competences has led to serious problems of co-ordination and control. The present intergovernmental relations at the intermediate level have, therefore, become a serious bottleneck for the continuing process of reform.

Turning to the attempts at reconstructing local government in Central and Eastern Europe, it is important to distinguish between the changes in the normative legal framework on the one hand and the actual practice of local government on the other. As a reaction to excessive socialist centralism, reform legislation in Central and Eastern Europe was meant to ensure that local authorities no longer acted as representatives of central government, and that they ceased to be subordinated to central directives and control. Instead, constitutional legislation aimed at creating a dual system in which state and local government were to act within their own spheres of influence. This approach promised to fulfil the twin goals of limiting the power of central government and increasing public participation at the local level. In view of the very short time that has elapsed since the 1990/1 reforms and the still unstable environments in which they have to be implemented, it is not surprising that the reality of local government falls short of the normative ideal. Nevertheless, in both legal and political terms these constitutional changes represent the most far-reaching departure from the communist past to date. In Poland, this break with the tradition of uniform, centralized state power was not achieved primarily through a decentralization of tasks to the local level; rather, the present system is distinguished by the degree of autonomy and discretion which local governments now enjoy in performing their public functions. The twofold subordination of local government under the Communist Party bureaucracy and the directives of central governments has thereby been broken. In other Central and Eastern European countries, local authorities have not only acquired independent legal status but have also gained substantial powers from the former regions and districts; they are now also free from central government control in matters other than the legality of their activities. However, serious bottlenecks continue to affect the performance of the localities. Their capacity to deal with increased tasks was partly overestimated, given their inexperience in respect of the fundamentally altered political, legal, and financial framework. Conversely, there has been a significant underestimation of the need for central steering and control, which is magnified by the extreme deconcentration and fragmentation of governmental and administrative resources at the local level. Inevitably, the reaffirmation of the overemphasized principle of local autonomy has led to significant problems in achieving intergovernmental co-ordination and co-operation, not least of all due to the absence of effective institutions at the intermediate level of government.

In sum, therefore, the attempts to redefine and reorganize state authority in Central and Eastern Europe have so far achieved only limited success.[2] While the distribution of power among the principal organs of the state, presidency, government, and parliament, has been—if, in some cases, temporarily—settled, the measures taken to decentralize state authority are not as yet working effectively. It is hoped that continued constitutional reform will seek to adopt a more pragmatic approach towards these issues, and will recognize the importance of intergovernmental co-ordination and co-operation. So far, decentralization has been driven far too much by the desire to negate central authority, rather than being concerned with building a structure in which all levels of government can work alongside and with one another without resorting to direct interference from the centre.

If constitutional reform in economic matters was a reaction to the planned economy, and if decentralization was intended to eliminate excessive central control, a third reaction to the experience of socialist/communist rule in Central and Eastern European nations was the desire to protect the individual from arbitrary state interference. First and foremost, this refers to the issue of human rights, which was of particular importance given the instability of the social, economic, political, and in some cases ethnic environments. Here again, the experience of constitutional change since 1989 has varied. Human rights, including social and economic rights, are covered to varying degrees by all of the new constitutions. However, it has been pointed out that 'the protection of rights is undermined by the fact that the relevant constitutional clauses are often circumscribed by clauses that render their import somewhat uncertain'.[3] Even where the latter kind of clause does not exist, the varying degrees of ambiguity in the formulation of human rights may seriously limit their applicability in practice. In any case, even where constitutional human rights are meant to protect the individual from interference by the state, the experience of the exceptionally repressive political climate under communist/socialist rule strongly suggests the need for guarantees that the state will not simply choose to ignore the constitutional provisions. This does, of course, raise the issue of judicial review. Here again, the process of constitutional change since 1989 has produced varying results. While all the countries concerned practise *ex ante* and *ex post* reviews of legislation by constitutional courts, the power of the latter varies considerably, ranging from perhaps the weakest provisions in Bulgaria to what has been described as 'the most powerful constitutional court in the world' in the case of Hungary.

In sum, therefore, it appears that, while most of the core constitutional principles are now in place in Central and Eastern European countries, constitutional practice continues to lag behind the normative provisions. Further constitutional reform is likely to place emphasis on the successive adaptation of these existing provisions as a reaction to the experience gained from their application and performance. The impetus to engage in the formulation of 'grand designs' has clearly vanished along with the common spirit of opposition to a hostile regime.

3. THE EUROPEAN UNION

The possibility of constitutional change has also received growing attention at the level of the European Community. Following the

Single European Act of 1986, which committed the member states to the creation of a single market, the constitutional debate has recently culminated in the discussions accompanying and following the negotiations of the Treaty of Maastricht in 1992, which created the new 'European Union' (EU). Despite the change of its name for some purposes the Community/Union is still seen mainly as a level at which traditional nation-states work together so as to increase the effectiveness of their co-operation. Given the continuing dominance of the Council of Ministers over decision-making within the Union, no one can seriously argue that the path towards 'ever closer union among the peoples of Europe' has reached its final destination. The process leading up to this goal, as well as the goal itself, are being called into question amongst the national governments concerned, and increasingly also in public debate within most states. Naturally, the issue of constitutional change cannot be debated in a disinterested fashion, since the question whether there is, or ever should be, a European constitution is itself a bone of contention.

Whilst some see the Maastricht Treaty as an important but imperfect step towards a federal constitution, others regard it merely as a practical and useful improvement in the legitimacy, efficiency, and effectiveness of the Union relative to the provisions originally contained in the Treaty of Rome and the Single European Act. Yet another, if heterogeneous, group view the Maastricht Treaty as a step too early and too far, allowing the Brussels authorities to become over-centralized and over-bureaucratized, thereby encroaching on the nation-state as the natural unit of political organization and administration. Not surprisingly, this group advocates a redistribution of competences back to the nation-state through the strict application of the principle of subsidiarity, aiming at a much 'leaner' European organization. For some, the ideal structure may well be indistinguishable from what would be no more than a free-trade area. A further, and certainly the most critical, view of the Maastricht Treaty advocates the dissolution of the EU altogether. Here it is argued that the removal of the external threat has made the process of integration of Western Europe, as originally conceived, obsolete. Supra-nationalism in general, and the Maastricht Treaty in particular, are seen as outdated policies which depended on the rationale provided by the circumstances of the Cold War confrontation.

Given this wide variety of views held on the Maastricht Treaty, ranging from the most enthusiastic advocates of constitutional change in Europe to the most critical opponents of the enterprise in its entirety, there is a need for a closer look at the actual provisions of the Treaty so as to ascertain some of its constitutional implications.

One of the Maastricht Treaty provisions with constitutional implications is the proposed Economic and Monetary Union (EMU), which is seen by some as a logical development following the European Monetary System and its Exchange Rate Mechanism which had been established in 1979. Although the recent crisis in the ERM casts some doubt on the proposed timetable and the preconditions for implementing EMU, a number of the EU member states remain committed to the full transition by 1999 at the latest. By this time it is assumed that European Monetary System parities will have been fixed, and that a European Central Bank will have been established which will issue and control the common European Currency Unit, the ECU. The planned introduction of a single European currency will undoubtedly have important constitutional implications, inasmuch as it will remove one of the central functions of the nation-state: the right to issue and to control the supply of money.

However, further and potentially greater constitutional consequences are inherent in the clauses of the Maastricht Treaty which seek to establish a political union. A number of measures have been taken which include new areas of Community responsibility in relation to the environment, industrial policy, education, health, cultural policy, and research and development. On some of these issues, as well as on part of the existing single-market legislation, the Council has been authorized to decide by majority rule rather than unanimity voting procedures. Additional powers have also been granted to the European Parliament which have extended the latter's right to draft amendments and to require a second reading of proposed EU legislation, as well as giving parliamentarians a right to veto single-market legislation. Further provisions of the Maastricht Treaty aiming at the creation of political union hold out the promise of a common foreign and security policy administered through the Western European Union, and of increased co-operation in the areas of justice and home affairs. And finally, the Treaty has established a European citizenship and granted to EU nationals the right to vote in the local elections of any member state they choose to reside in.

This brief outline of some of the main provisions of the Maastricht Treaty has pointed to its character as a constitution, albeit an incomplete one. Whilst increased Community responsibilities, additional powers for the European Parliament, and European citizenship and voting rights are all changes which have an immediate constitutional impact, a common foreign and security policy and increased co-operation on justice and home affairs can both be expected to continue to function predominantly through intergovernmental co-operation for some time to come. The constitutional importance of these latter changes, and of the planned EMU, is not to be found in their present impact but rather in their potential for replacing central functions of nation-states. Future prospects may include a single European currency, a European army, common diplomatic representation in multilateral organizations, and a European police force.

In sum, therefore, this brief outline of some features of the Treaty suggests that, irrespective of which of the above views is held on its desirability, the EU does now contain some elements of a constitutional structure as well as exhibiting potential for far-reaching further constitutional development. However, the Treaty does not yet form the basis for a complete constitution. That other important constitutional elements are still lacking can be seen in the fact that the European Court of Justice has not been given jurisdiction over the 'Common Provisions' contained in the Treaty, and that no legally binding definition of human rights has been included. On the other hand, it is well known that the process of constitutional change in Europe has so far been incremental, and that it is very likely that further consideration will be given to these issues at some stage. The recent controversy surrounding the change in voting procedures of the Council after enlargement has already demonstrated the continuance of the constitutional argument. The Intergovernmental Conference planned for 1996, which is meant to review progress made towards EMU and institutional reform, will prove no exception in this regard. This is mainly due to the fact that despite their well-known differences over the speed with which to achieve—and, indeed, the desirability of political union and EMU, the political élites of all member states remain committed to the EU itself. Enormous differences of opinion are, however, still to be found with regard to goals and methods, and this fact alone will necessarily stimulate constitutional debate.

However, there are two important obstacles which need to be overcome before further constitutional change can take place. The first of these refers to the relationship between the EU and its member states. There are many signs of a growing reluctance on the part of most national governments and parliaments to relinquish any further powers to the Union, thus bringing the issue of sovereignty to the forefront of the debate. The second obstacle to further constitutional change lies in the growing disillusionment of the public, which not only fears a loss of sovereignty but is also opposed to what is seen as petty interference by distant Brussels bureaucrats, threatening to level out all distinctive national characteristics. It is not surprising that these two obstacles reinforce each other. Whilst on the one hand some politicians have heightened public fears with apocalyptic visions of a centralized superstate run by politically unaccountable bureaucrats, public disillusionment in turn has provided the electoral basis for the emergence of new, if so far small, anti-European parties in most member states. The danger of being outflanked by the latter has led most mainstream European parties to place greater emphasis on the risks involved in any further surrender of sovereignty.

The response of the pro-European political élites in the member states has been twofold. The first strategy seeks to quicken the pace of institutional reform at the European level, in an attempt to alleviate what is often referred to as the 'democratic deficit' characterizing the work of the EU. The increase of powers of the European Parliament has been one step in this direction. More far-reaching proposals envisage the creation of a complete state structure at the European level. Developing the European Parliament into a full legislative authority, transforming the Council of Ministers into a second chamber, and elevating the European Commission to the status of a European government elected by, and accountable to, the European Parliament, are all elements favoured by the most enthusiastic proponents of this strategy. However, there are obvious limits to this approach as a means of overcoming the two obstacles referred to. Doubts have been cast, in particular, on the possibility of developing the European Parliament into a full legislative body, given the absence of a truly European identity and public opinion, Europe-wide parties, lobbying organizations, and pressure groups, as well as the absence of a European media system as an external, even if informal, check on the performance of the Parliament. In any case, it is not so much the lack of legitimacy of EU institutions which lies behind governmental criticism and public disillusionment; references to the 'democratic deficit' should more accurately be regarded as a means of rationalizing the underlying fear about the prospective disappearance of the nation-state as the principal form of political organization and forms of loyalties. It is not surprising, therefore, that there is currently no intention on the part of political élites to pursue this first strategy at all seriously. Instead, a second strategy is favoured which aims at a complete redefinition of the EU–nation-state relationship. The principle of subsidiarity which has been attached to the Maastricht Treaty is an attempt to federalize the structure of the EU. Its Article 3a reads:

In the areas which do not fall within its exclusive jurisdiction, the Commission shall take action, in accordance with the principle of subsidiarity, only in so far as the objectives of the proposed action cannot be sufficiently achieved by the Member States and can therefore, by reason of scale or effects of proposed action, be better achieved by the Community.

In short, subsidiarity is a principle intended to prevent excessive centralization of power, and expresses the basic notion that the Community should decide only in areas in which national governments could not regulate more effectively. In this sense, it is meant to serve as a guiding principle for allocating responsibilities between the two levels. By implication, it also holds that political decisions should be taken at the closest possible level to those actually affected by them. However, significant problems remain in the definition of the principle and in its application to European decision-making. This stems in part from the fact that subsidiarity is essentially a dynamic and fluid concept which does not imply a fixed allocation of responsibilities to any particular level of government. The criteria for the distribution of competences may well be found in a performance-related cost–benefit analysis as propounded by theories of fiscal federalism. Such realities may change over time, and give rise to serious problems of demarcation in practice. One such example can be found in the provisions for EMU. These envisage a common monetary policy on the one hand, but a continuing application of the subsidiarity principle to economic and fiscal policies. It is by no means clear that a cost–benefit analysis will reveal that economic and fiscal policies are indeed best formulated at the national level once a single currency is issued and controlled by a supranational European Central Bank.

Furthermore, problems of demarcation of responsibilities are not limited to the relationship of the Union with its member states. There is also the problem of a reallocation from the nation-state downwards to the sub-national level. Though the principle of subsidiarity only raises this issue by implication, sub-national governments and pressure groups have quickly seized on the argument it provides. Regional pressures in Germany, Spain, and Belgium in particular have led to the creation of the new European Committee of the Regions. Although this new body has so far no formal powers and fulfils only an advisory function, its potential is far-reaching, illustrated by proposals for the creation of a European Regional Chamber as the upper house to the European Parliament, which will undoubtedly be tabled at the 1996 intergovernmental conference. This creates problems in particular for the British government, whose aversion to decentralization at home is well known. The 1994 European elections have already seen the Scottish and Welsh Nationalist Parties campaigning on a shared platform, demanding independent representation for their nations in Brussels, a trend which can be expected to continue. Overall, therefore, it is unclear whether the attempt at constitutional change in the form of a federalization in Europe will be successful in overcoming the two obstacles. The dynamic nature of the principle of subsidiarity may well lead in practice to a constant tug-of-war over responsibilities between the supranational and the national level, as well as between the national and the sub-national level.

It is extremely difficult to predict the future course of constitutional change in Europe. It remains doubtful whether either institutional change at the European level or the attempt at federalizing Europe will be able to overcome the reluctance exhibited by national governments and the growing disillusionment with the Union. Hence it is not so much the difficulty of finding an appropriate constitutional structure for Europe as the problem of gaining the approval of subjects which inhibits the completion of a new constitution for Europe. In this context, advancement of the cause of constitutional change seems to call for stronger efforts to illuminate the issues at stake in public debate.

Perhaps the most positive measure would be to dispel some of the myths used in the public discussions. First, with regard to the 'democratic deficit' and to 'undue interference with national characteristics', more emphasis could be put on the fact that EU rules and regulations have all been approved by the Council, which can be regarded as the democratically elected representation of member states. Secondly, with regard to the charge of 'over-bureaucratization', which is often levelled against the European Commission, it may be helpful to draw attention to the fact that the number of its staff is exceeded by that of a medium-size European city. Thirdly, and perhaps most importantly, there is a need for a clearer definition of the term 'federalism'. Again, the British example can illustrate this point. In Britain the term now consistently evokes a negative image, and it is frequently used when referring to the concentration of power in Brussels. Even the most ardent supporters of the EU in the Liberal Democrat Party tend to avoid using the term. But a contrary view is that 'federalism is always and by definition a two-way process of the delegation and the reservation of power'.[4] Whilst 'myths' of this kind may not be the most important obstacles to constitutional change, an effort to dispel them may lead to a more balanced analysis of the issues involved, thereby assisting the process of constitutional development itself.

Notes

1. N. Johnson, 'Constitutionalism in Europe since 1945: Reconstruction and Reappraisal', in D. Greenberg *et al.* (eds.), *Constitutionalism and Democracy: Transitions in the Contemporary World* (Oxford: Oxford University Press, 1993).
2. J. J. Hesse (ed.), *Administrative Transformation in Central and Eastern Europe: Towards Public Sector Reform in Post-Communist Societies* (Oxford: Blackwell, 1993).
3. Jon G. Elster, 'Constitution-Making in Eastern Europe: Rebuilding the Boat in the Open Sea', in Hesse, *Transformation in Central and Eastern Europe*, 169–217.
4. J. J. Hesse and Klaus H. Goetz, *Federalizing Europe? The Costs, Benefits and Preconditions of Federal Political Systems* (London: Anglo-German Foundation for the Study of Industrial Society, 1992), 4.

Index